TOKYO GHOUL

SUI ISHIDA

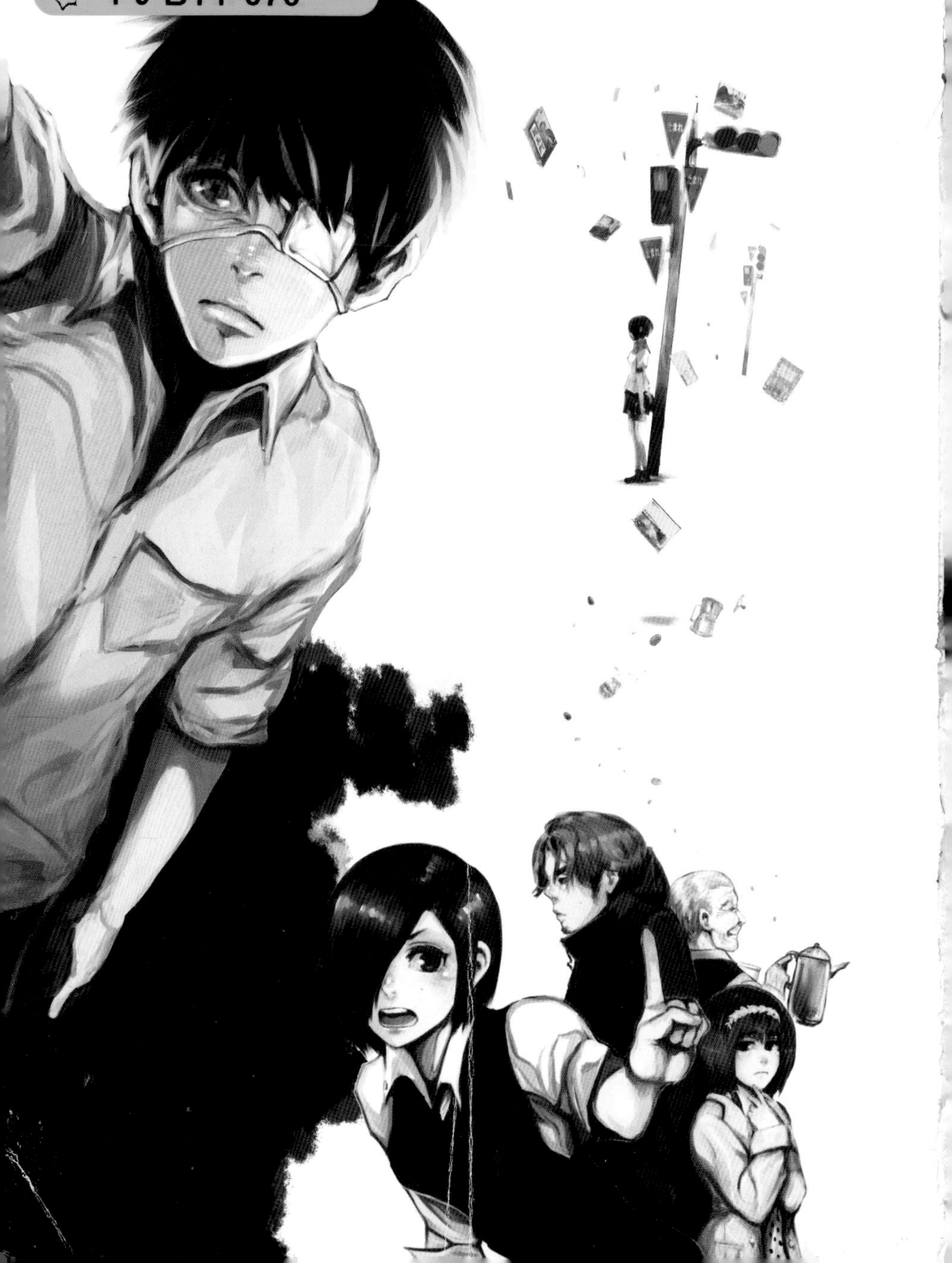

K E N
KANEKI

金　木　研（カ　ネ　キ　ケ　ン）

BORN December 20th   Sagittarius

Kamii University, 1st Year
Department of Literature, Japanese Literature

BLOOD-TYPE: A B

Size : 1 6 9 c m 5 5̃ kg   FEET 2̃ 5 . 5̃ CM

Likes : Reading, beautiful words, intelligent women,
hamburger steak

I   )(Ǝ   N   Ʌ   )(N   Ǝ   )(

SUI ISHIDA was born in Fukuoka, Japan.
He is the author of **Tokyo Ghoul** and
several **Tokyo Ghoul** one-shots, including
one that won him second place in the
Weekly Young Jump 113th Grand Prix award
in 2010. **Tokyo Ghoul** began serialization
in *Weekly Young Jump* in 2011 and was
adapted into an anime series in 2014.

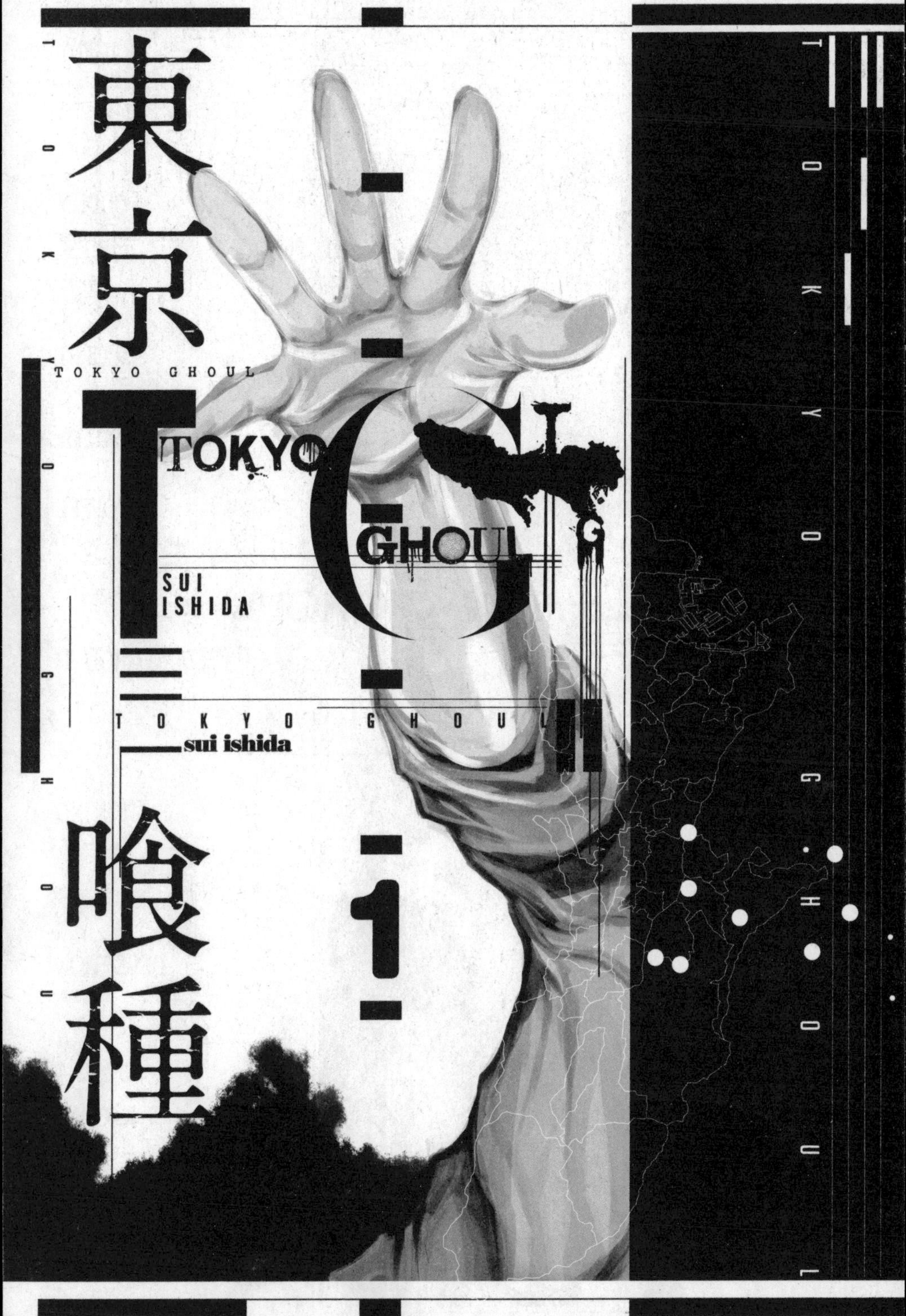
東京喰種
TOKYO GHOUL
TOKYO GHOUL
SUI ISHIDA
TOKYO GHOUL
sui ishida
1
TOKYO GHOUL
TOKYO GHOUL

東京喰種

TOKYO GHOUL

TOKYO GHOUL

SUI ISHIDA

1

CONTENTS

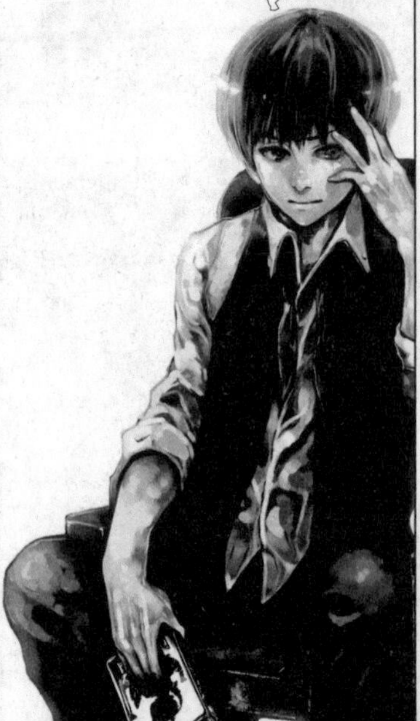

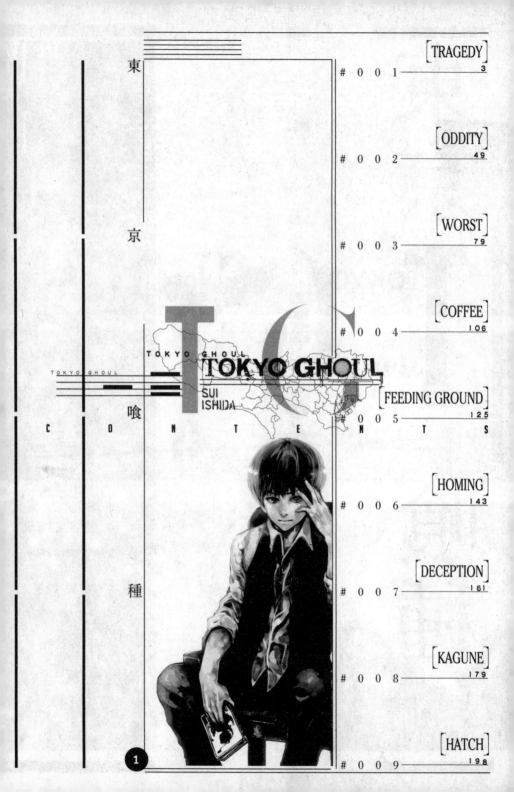

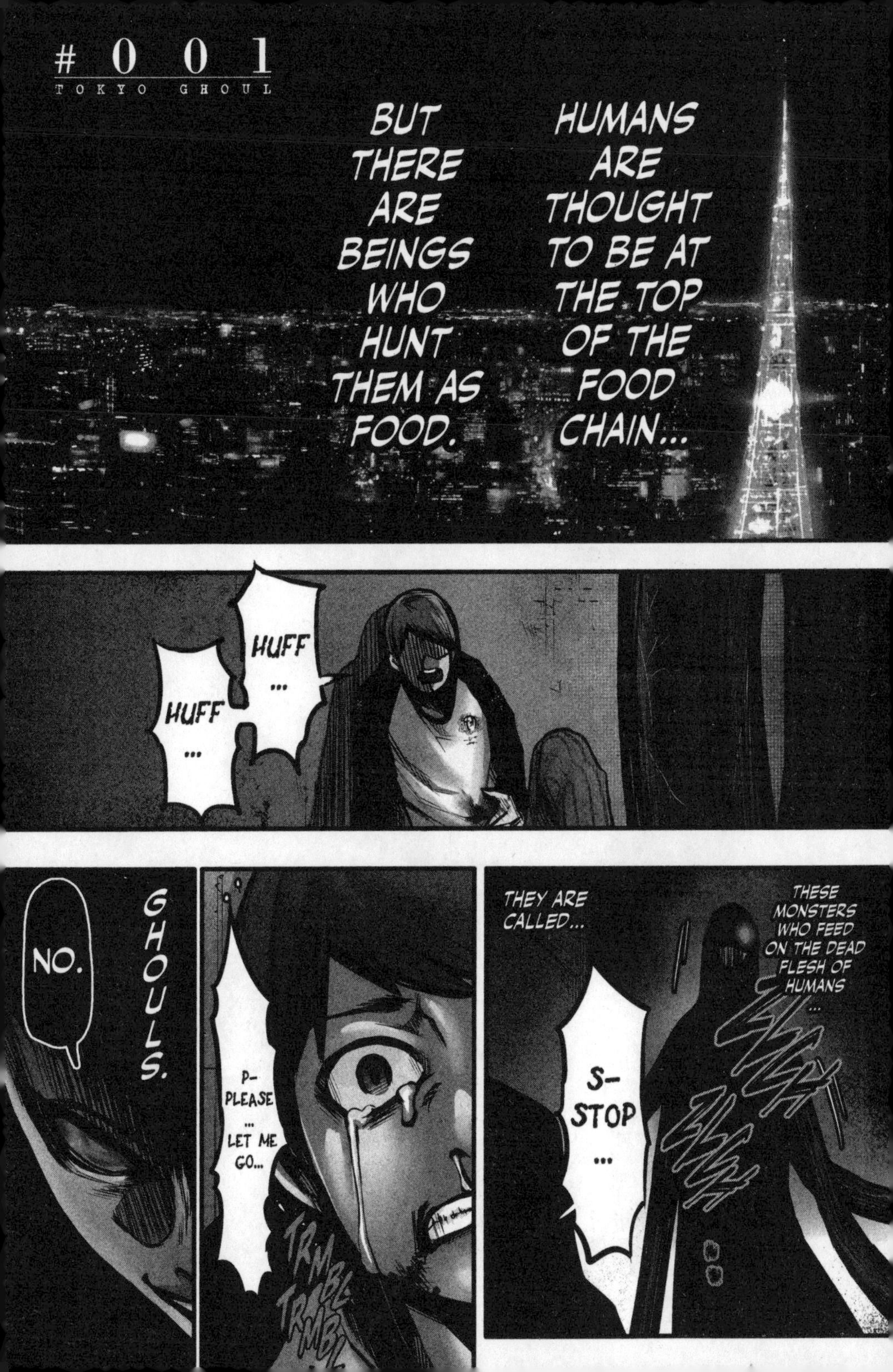

#001
TOKYO GHOUL
HUMANS ARE THOUGHT TO BE AT THE TOP OF THE FOOD CHAIN...
BUT THERE ARE BEINGS WHO HUNT THEM AS FOOD.
HUFF...
HUFF...
THESE MONSTERS WHO FEED ON THE DEAD FLESH OF HUMANS...
THEY ARE CALLED...
S-STOP...
P-PLEASE... LET ME GO...
TRMBL TRMBL
GHOULS.
NO.

#001 [TRAGEDY]

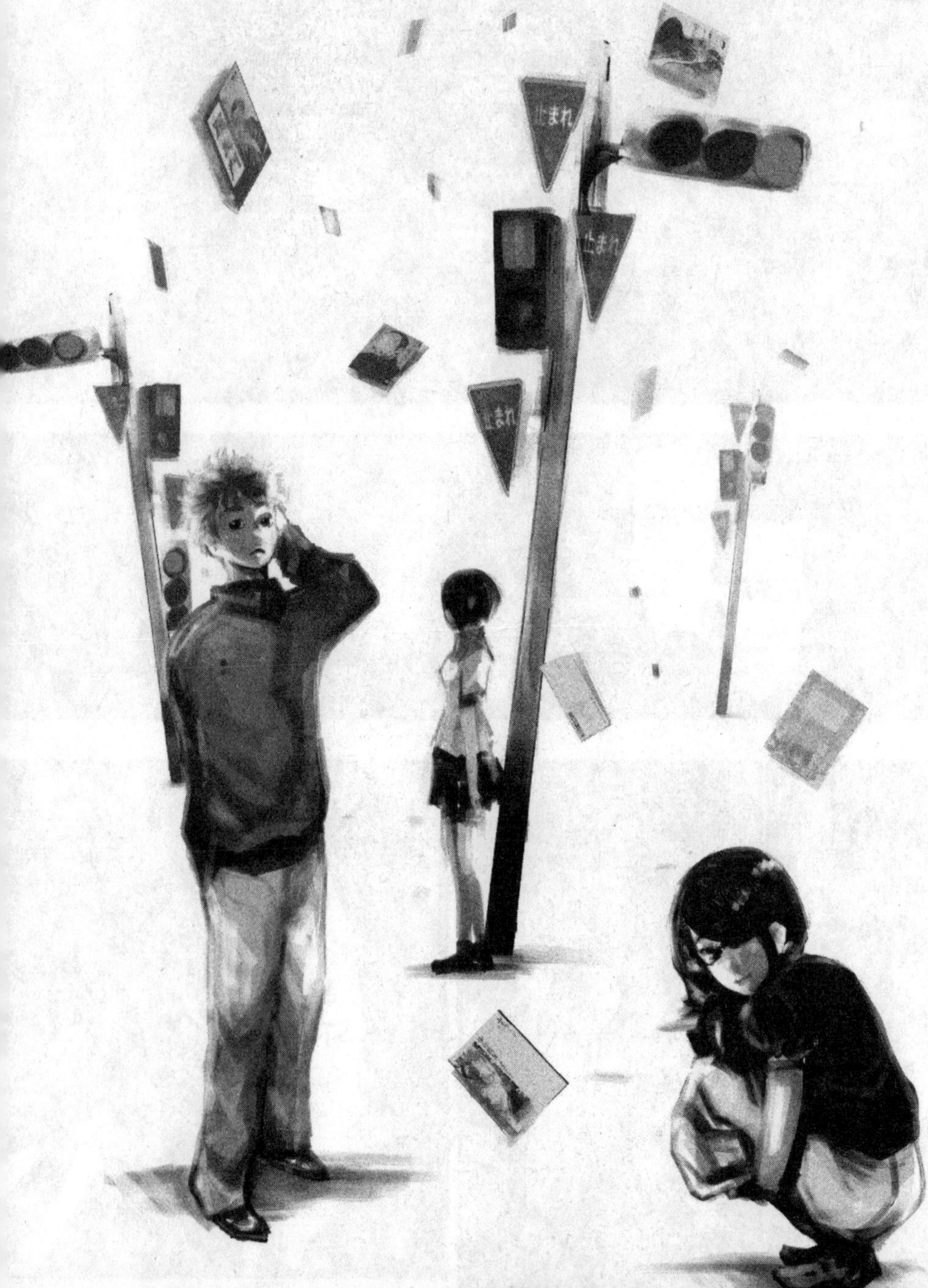

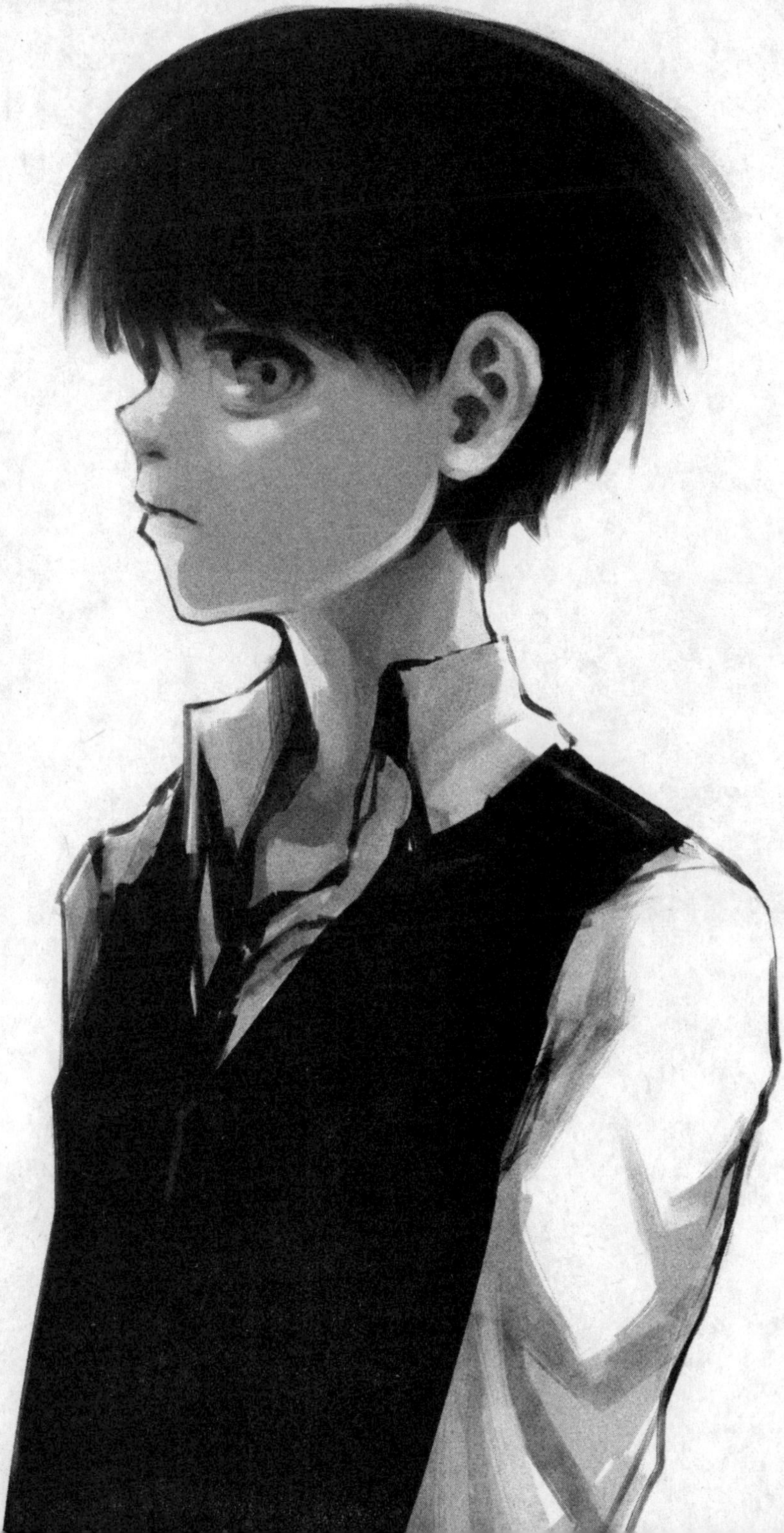

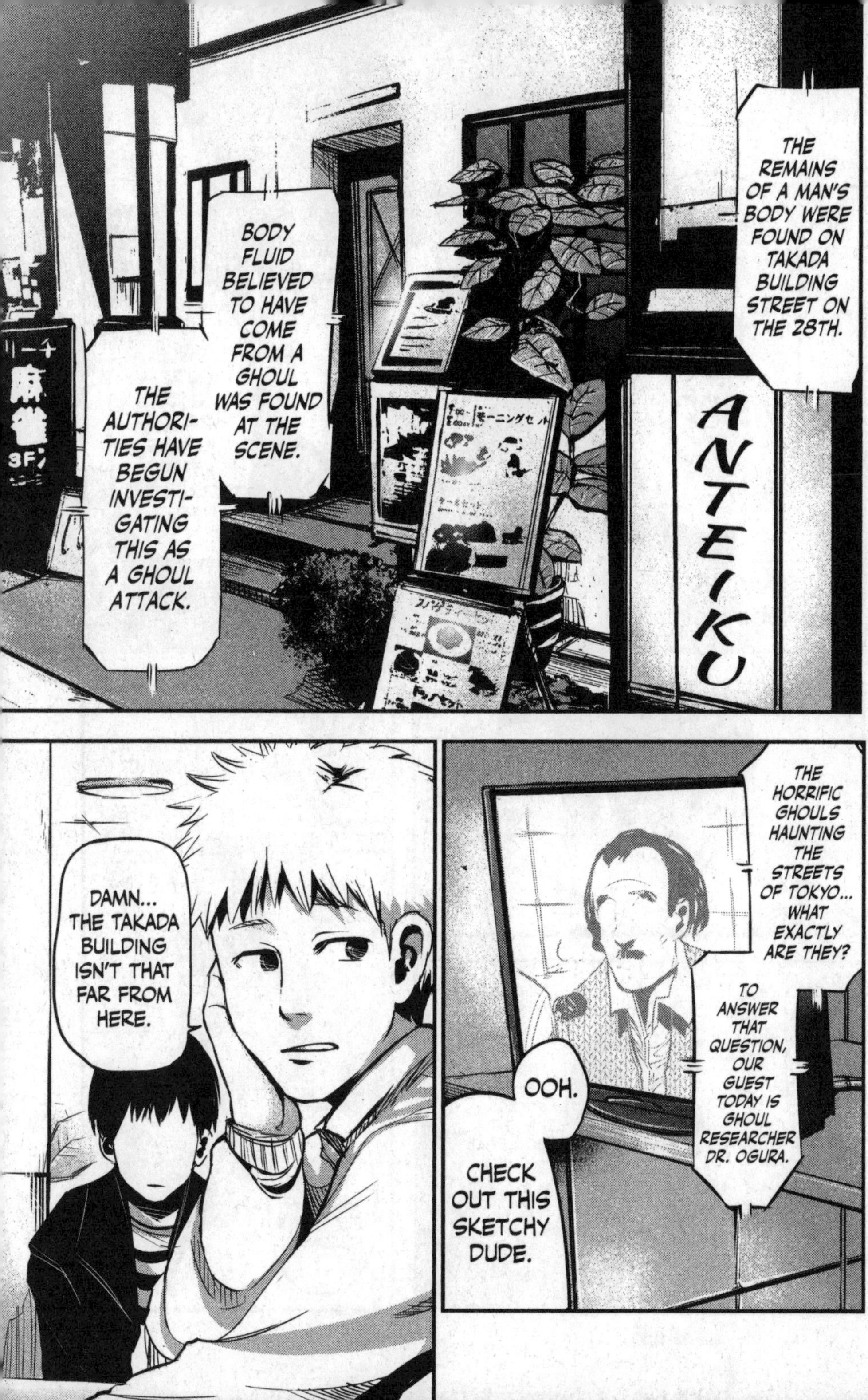
THE REMAINS OF A MAN'S BODY WERE FOUND ON TAKADA BUILDING STREET ON THE 28TH.
BODY FLUID BELIEVED TO HAVE COME FROM A GHOUL WAS FOUND AT THE SCENE.
THE AUTHORI-TIES HAVE BEGUN INVESTI-GATING THIS AS A GHOUL ATTACK.
ANTEIKU
THE HORRIFIC GHOULS HAUNTING THE STREETS OF TOKYO... WHAT EXACTLY ARE THEY?
TO ANSWER THAT QUESTION, OUR GUEST TODAY IS GHOUL RESEARCHER DR. OGURA.
OOH.
CHECK OUT THIS SKETCHY DUDE.
DAMN... THE TAKADA BUILDING ISN'T THAT FAR FROM HERE.

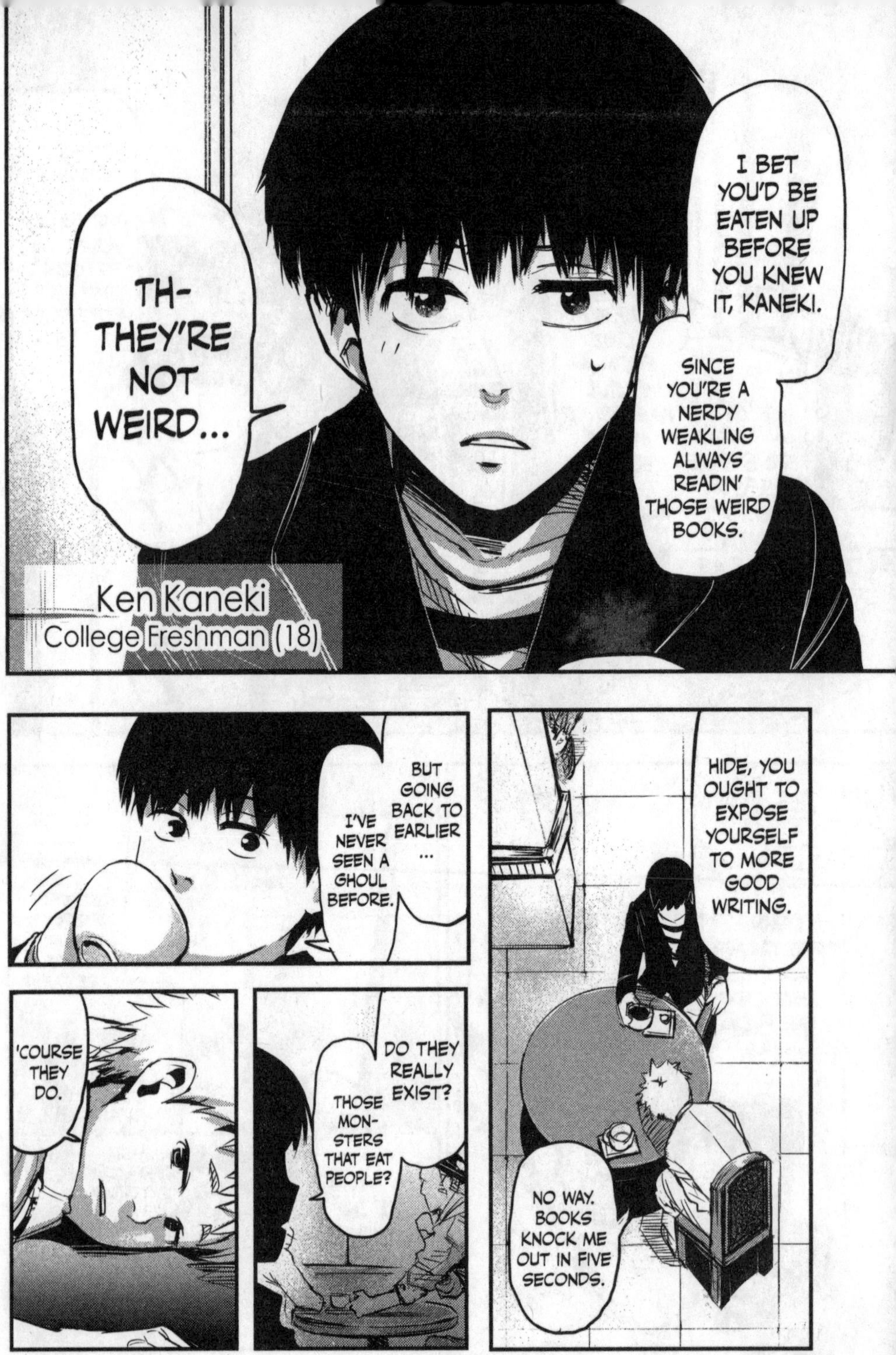
I BET YOU'D BE EATEN UP BEFORE YOU KNEW IT, KANEKI.
SINCE YOU'RE A NERDY WEAKLING ALWAYS READIN' THOSE WEIRD BOOKS.
TH-THEY'RE NOT WEIRD...
Ken Kaneki
College Freshman (18)
HIDE, YOU OUGHT TO EXPOSE YOURSELF TO MORE GOOD WRITING.
NO WAY. BOOKS KNOCK ME OUT IN FIVE SECONDS.
BUT GOING BACK TO EARLIER...
I'VE NEVER SEEN A GHOUL BEFORE.
DO THEY REALLY EXIST?
THOSE MON-STERS THAT EAT PEOPLE?
'COURSE THEY DO.

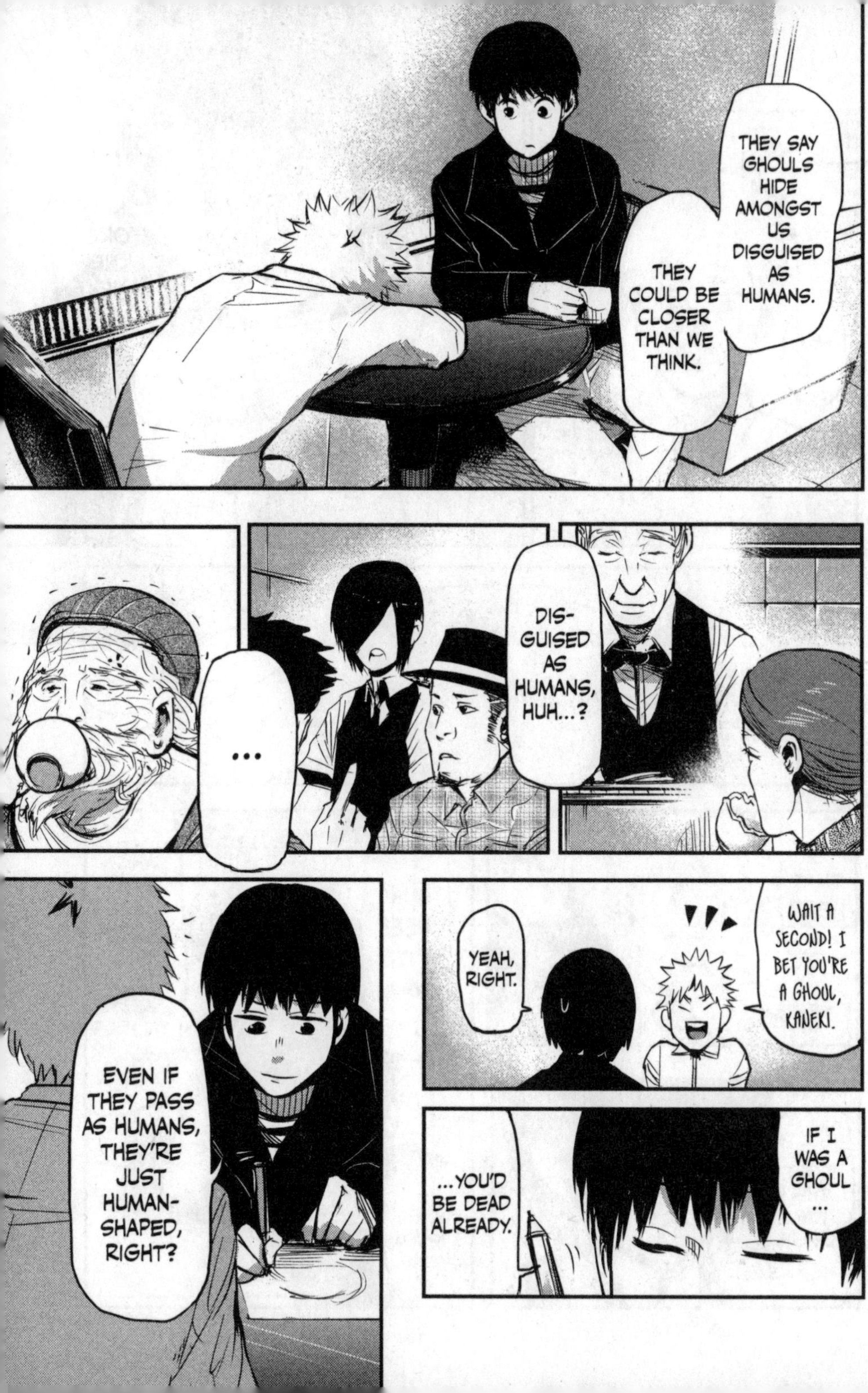
THEY SAY GHOULS HIDE AMONGST US DISGUISED AS HUMANS.
THEY COULD BE CLOSER THAN WE THINK.
DIS-GUISED AS HUMANS, HUH...?
...
WAIT A SECOND! I BET YOU'RE A GHOUL, KANEKI.
YEAH, RIGHT.
IF I WAS A GHOUL...
...YOU'D BE DEAD ALREADY.
EVEN IF THEY PASS AS HUMANS, THEY'RE JUST HUMAN-SHAPED, RIGHT?

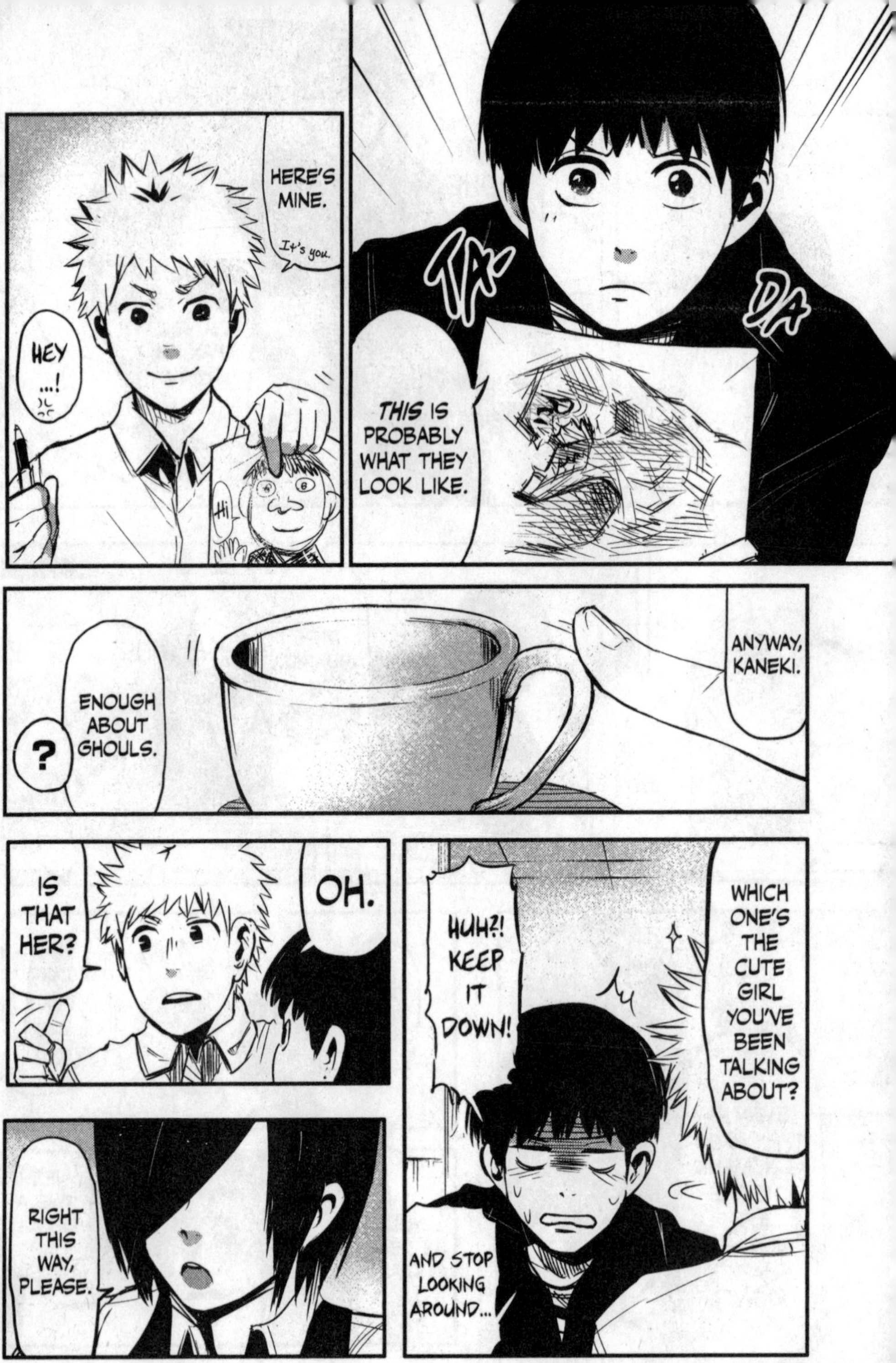
TA-
DA
THIS IS PROBABLY WHAT THEY LOOK LIKE.
HERE'S MINE.
It's you.
HEY ...!
Hi
ANYWAY, KANEKI.
ENOUGH ABOUT GHOULS.
?
WHICH ONE'S THE CUTE GIRL YOU'VE BEEN TALKING ABOUT?
HUH?! KEEP IT DOWN!
AND STOP LOOKING AROUND...
OH.
IS THAT HER?
RIGHT THIS WAY, PLEASE.

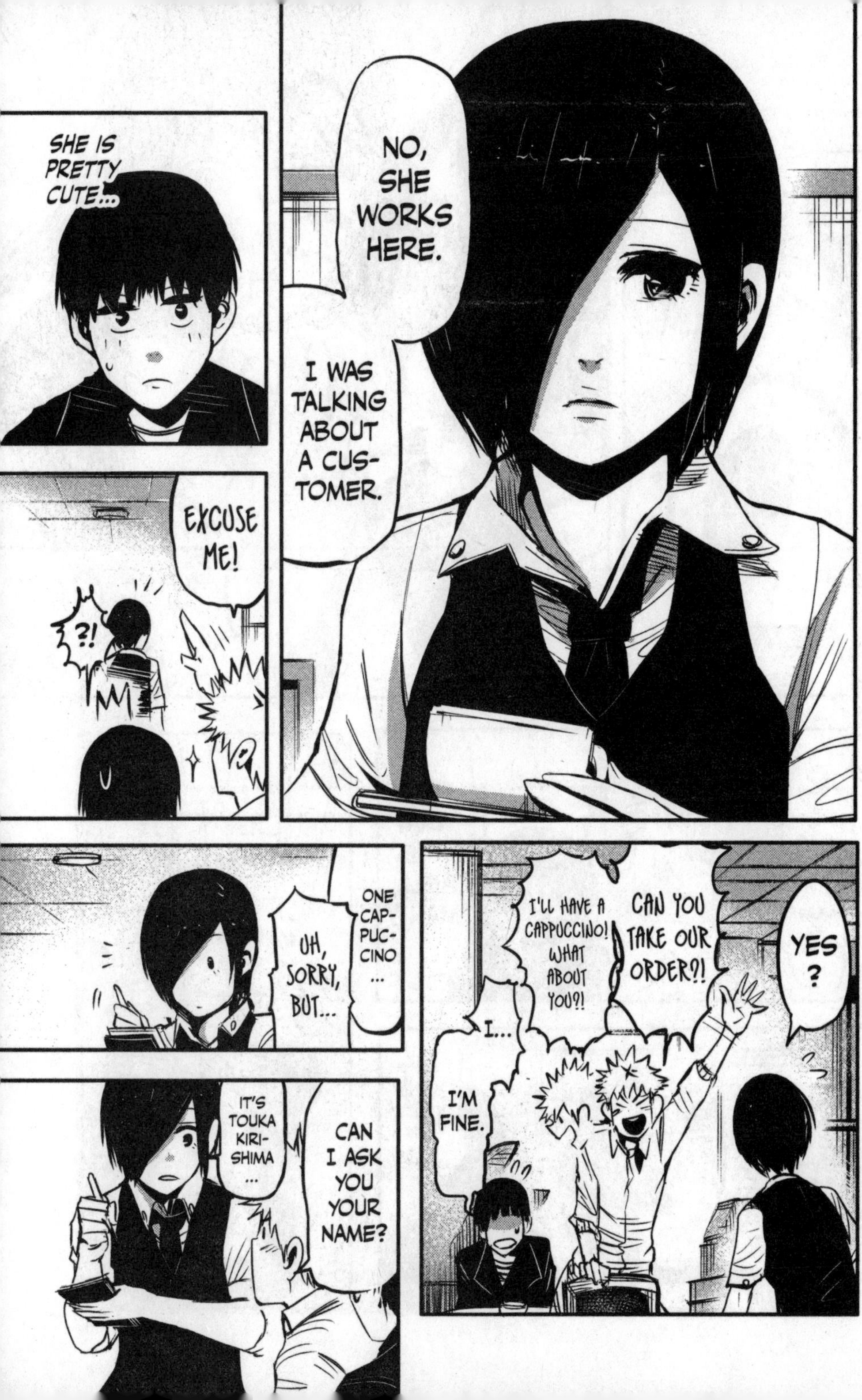
NO, SHE WORKS HERE.
I WAS TALKING ABOUT A CUS-TOMER.
SHE IS PRETTY CUTE...
EXCUSE ME!
?!
YES?
CAN YOU TAKE OUR ORDER?!
I'LL HAVE A CAPPUCCINO! WHAT ABOUT YOU?!
I...
I'M FINE.
ONE CAP-PUC-CINO...
UH, SORRY, BUT...
CAN I ASK YOU YOUR NAME?
IT'S TOUKA KIRI-SHIMA...

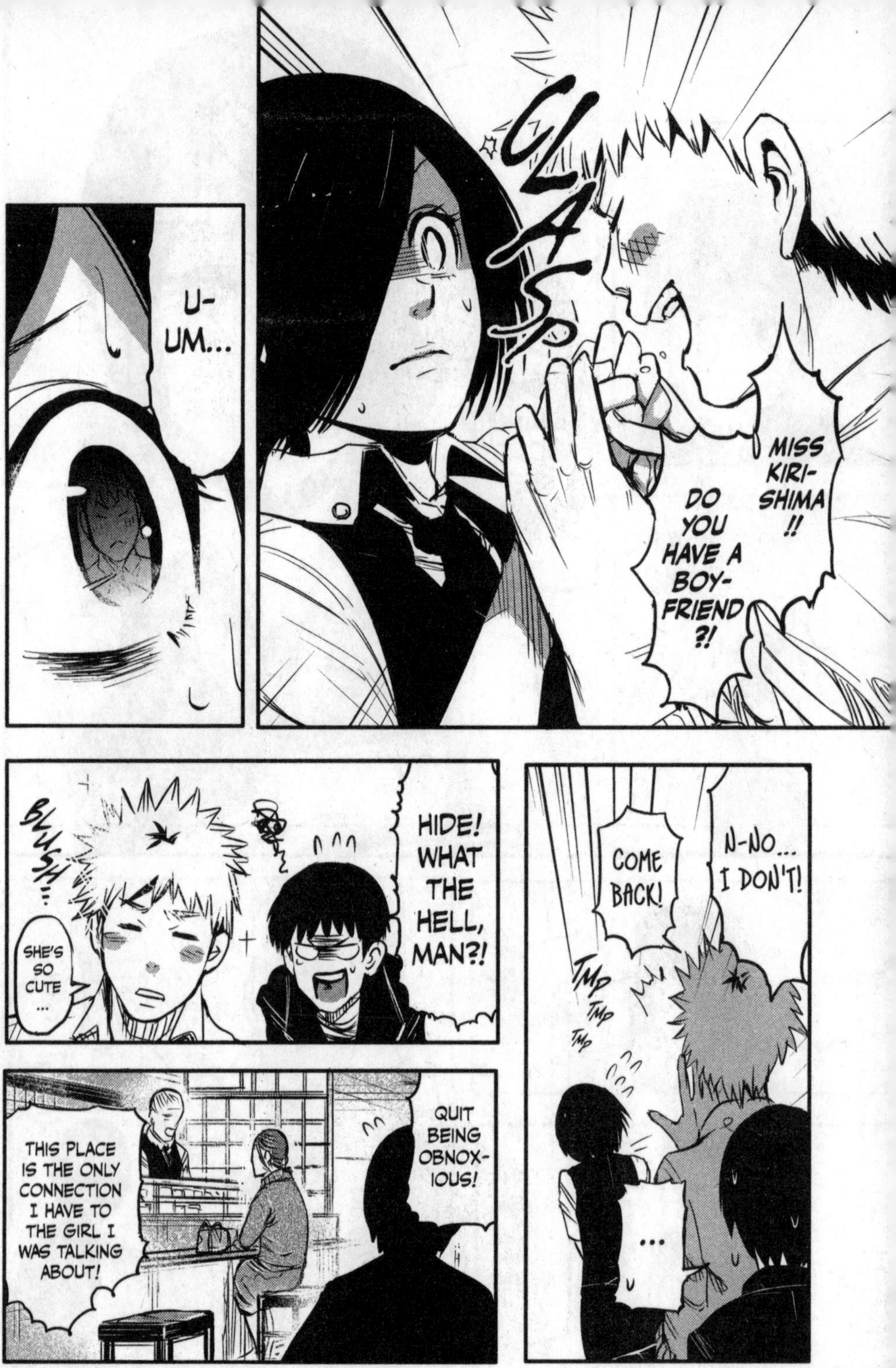
CLASP
MISS KIRI-SHIMA!!
DO YOU HAVE A BOY-FRIEND?!
U-UM...
N-NO... I DON'T!
COME BACK!
TMP TMP TMP
...
HIDE! WHAT THE HELL, MAN?!
BLUSH
SHE'S SO CUTE ...
QUIT BEING OBNOX-IOUS!
THIS PLACE IS THE ONLY CONNECTION I HAVE TO THE GIRL I WAS TALKING ABOUT!

JINGLE JINGLE

....!!!

WHAT IF THEY BAN US FROM--

OOPS, I'M SORRY!

....?

....!!

OVER THERE... THAT'S HER...

WHAT'S WRONG, DUDE?

SHE WAS SO CUTE I COULDN'T HELP MYSELF!

....?

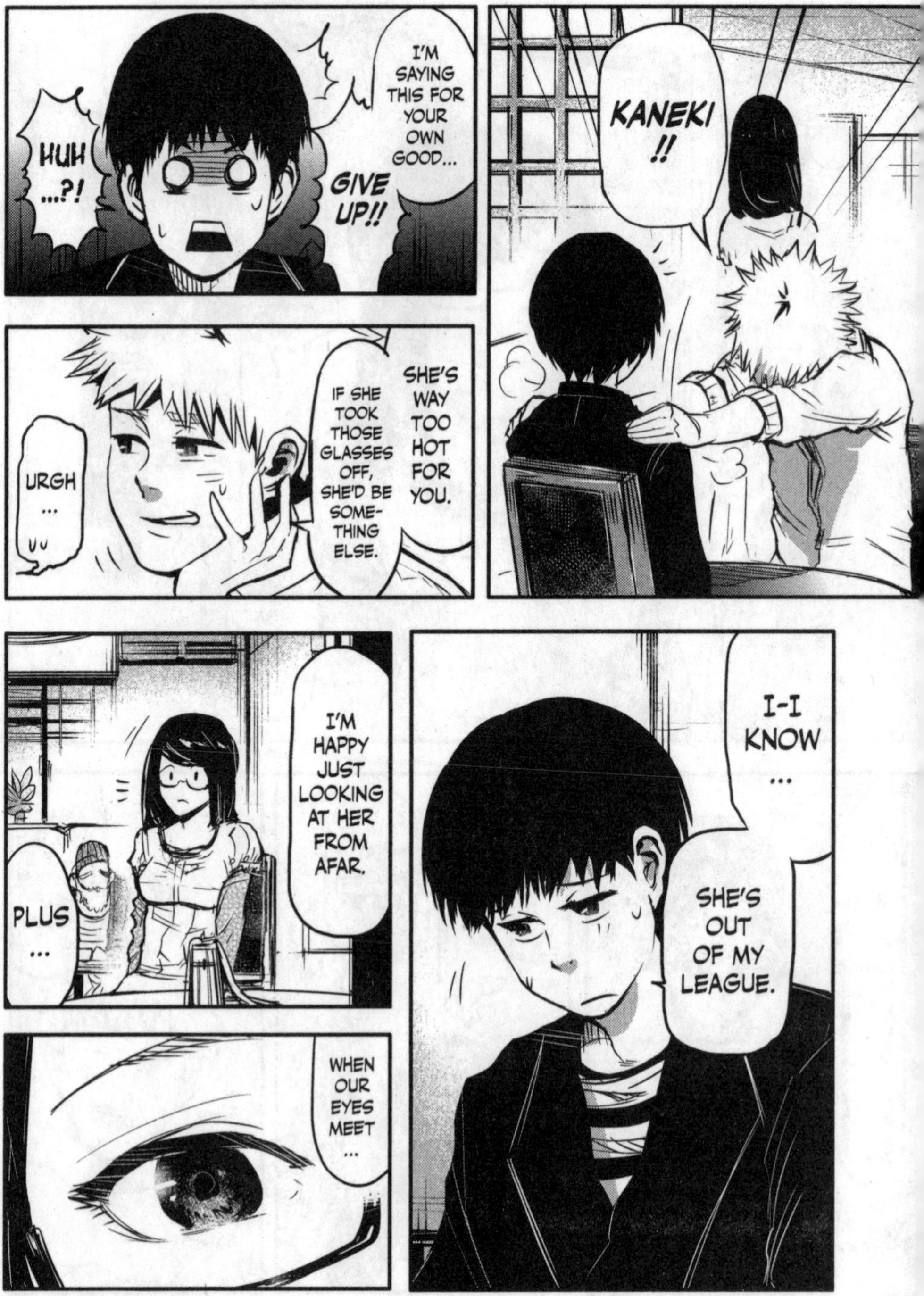
KANEKI!!
I'M SAYING THIS FOR YOUR OWN GOOD...
GIVE UP!!
HUH...?!
SHE'S WAY TOO HOT FOR YOU.
IF SHE TOOK THOSE GLASSES OFF, SHE'D BE SOME-THING ELSE.
URGH...
I-I KNOW...
SHE'S OUT OF MY LEAGUE.
I'M HAPPY JUST LOOKING AT HER FROM AFAR.
PLUS...
WHEN OUR EYES MEET...

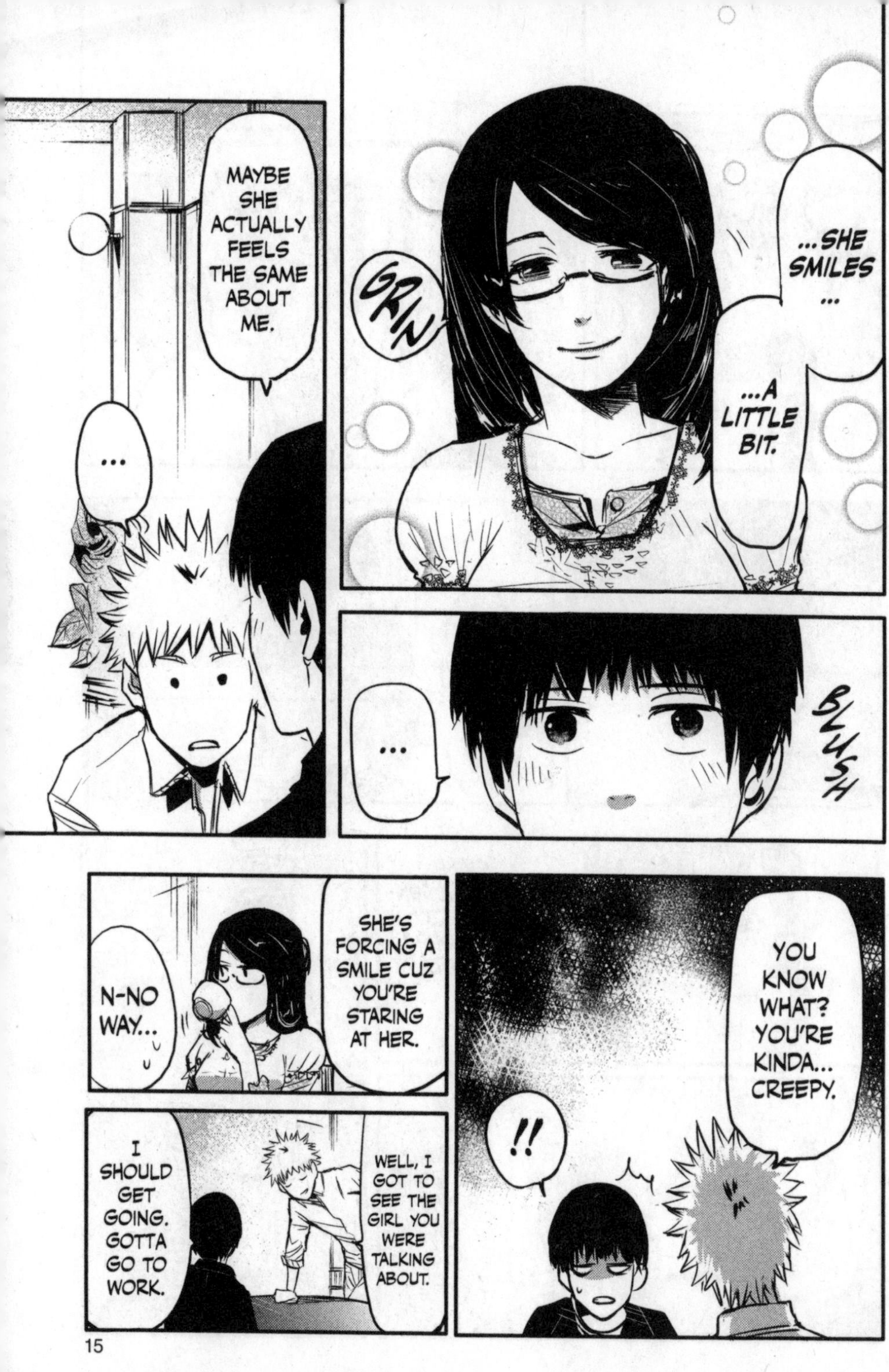
...SHE SMILES ...
GRIN
...A LITTLE BIT.
...
BLUSH
MAYBE SHE ACTUALLY FEELS THE SAME ABOUT ME.
...
YOU KNOW WHAT? YOU'RE KINDA... CREEPY.
!!
SHE'S FORCING A SMILE CUZ YOU'RE STARING AT HER.
N-NO WAY...
WELL, I GOT TO SEE THE GIRL YOU WERE TALKING ABOUT.
I SHOULD GET GOING. GOTTA GO TO WORK.

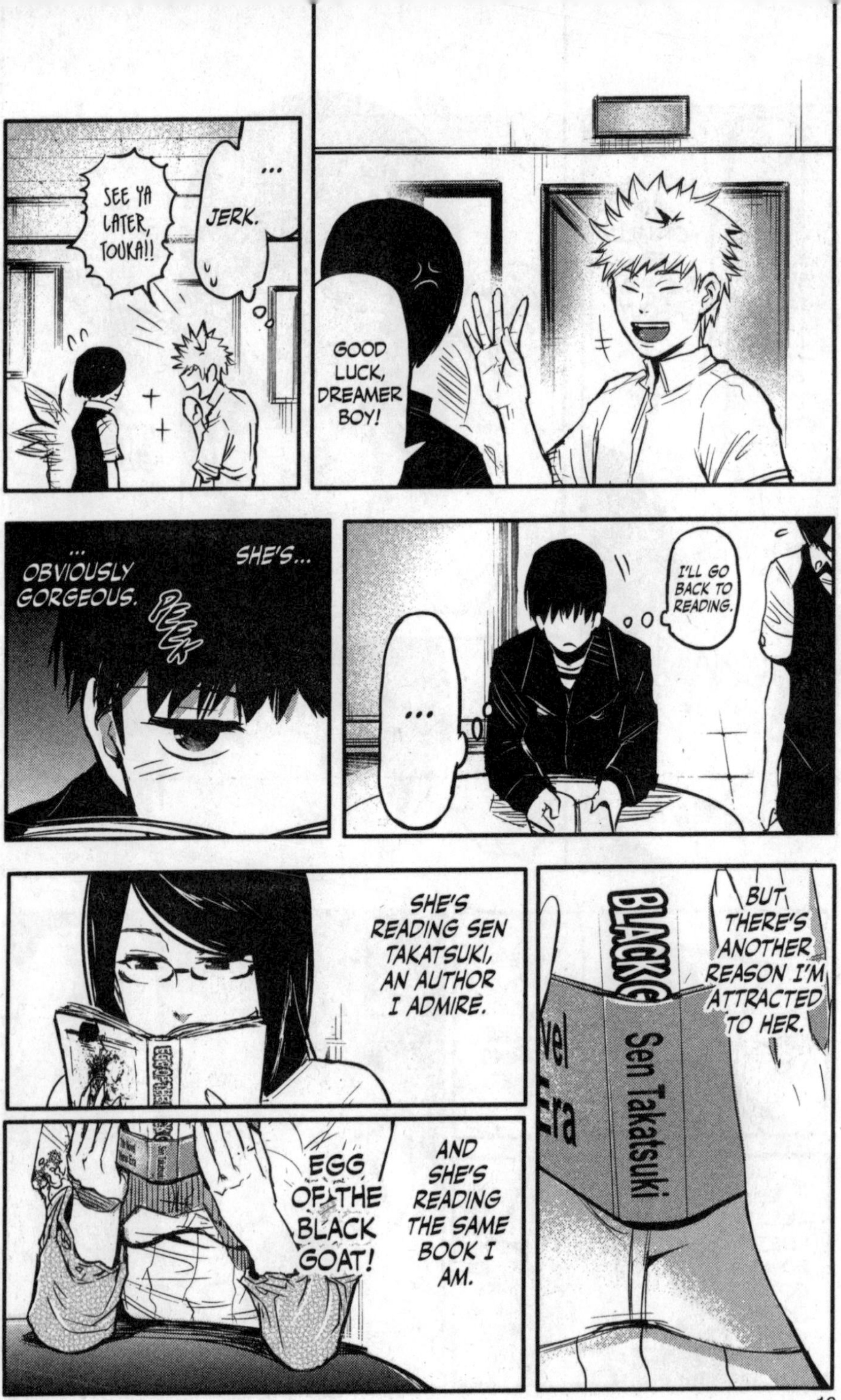
GOOD LUCK, DREAMER BOY!
... JERK.
SEE YA LATER, TOUKA!!
I'LL GO BACK TO READING.
...
SHE'S...
... OBVIOUSLY GORGEOUS.
PEEK
BUT THERE'S ANOTHER REASON I'M ATTRACTED TO HER.
Sen Takatsuki
SHE'S READING SEN TAKATSUKI, AN AUTHOR I ADMIRE.
AND SHE'S READING THE SAME BOOK I AM.
EGG OF THE BLACK GOAT!

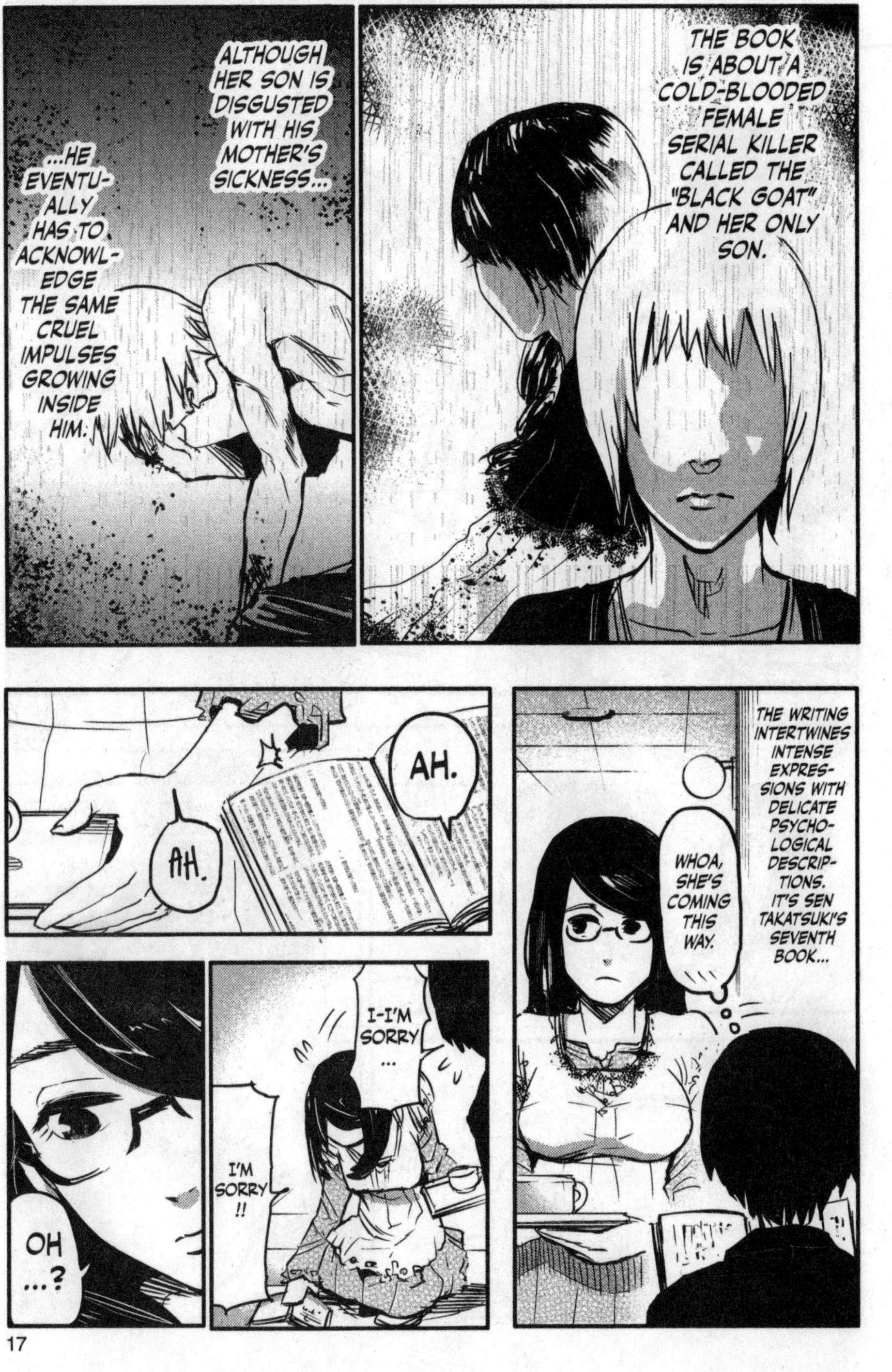
THE BOOK IS ABOUT A COLD-BLOODED FEMALE SERIAL KILLER CALLED THE "BLACK GOAT" AND HER ONLY SON.
ALTHOUGH HER SON IS DISGUSTED WITH HIS MOTHER'S SICKNESS...
...HE EVENTU-ALLY HAS TO ACKNOWL-EDGE THE SAME CRUEL IMPULSES GROWING INSIDE HIM.
THE WRITING INTERTWINES INTENSE EXPRES-SIONS WITH DELICATE PSYCHO-LOGICAL DESCRIP-TIONS. IT'S SEN TAKATSUKI'S SEVENTH BOOK...
WHOA, SHE'S COMING THIS WAY.
AH.
AH.
I-I'M SORRY ...
I'M SORRY !!
OH ...?

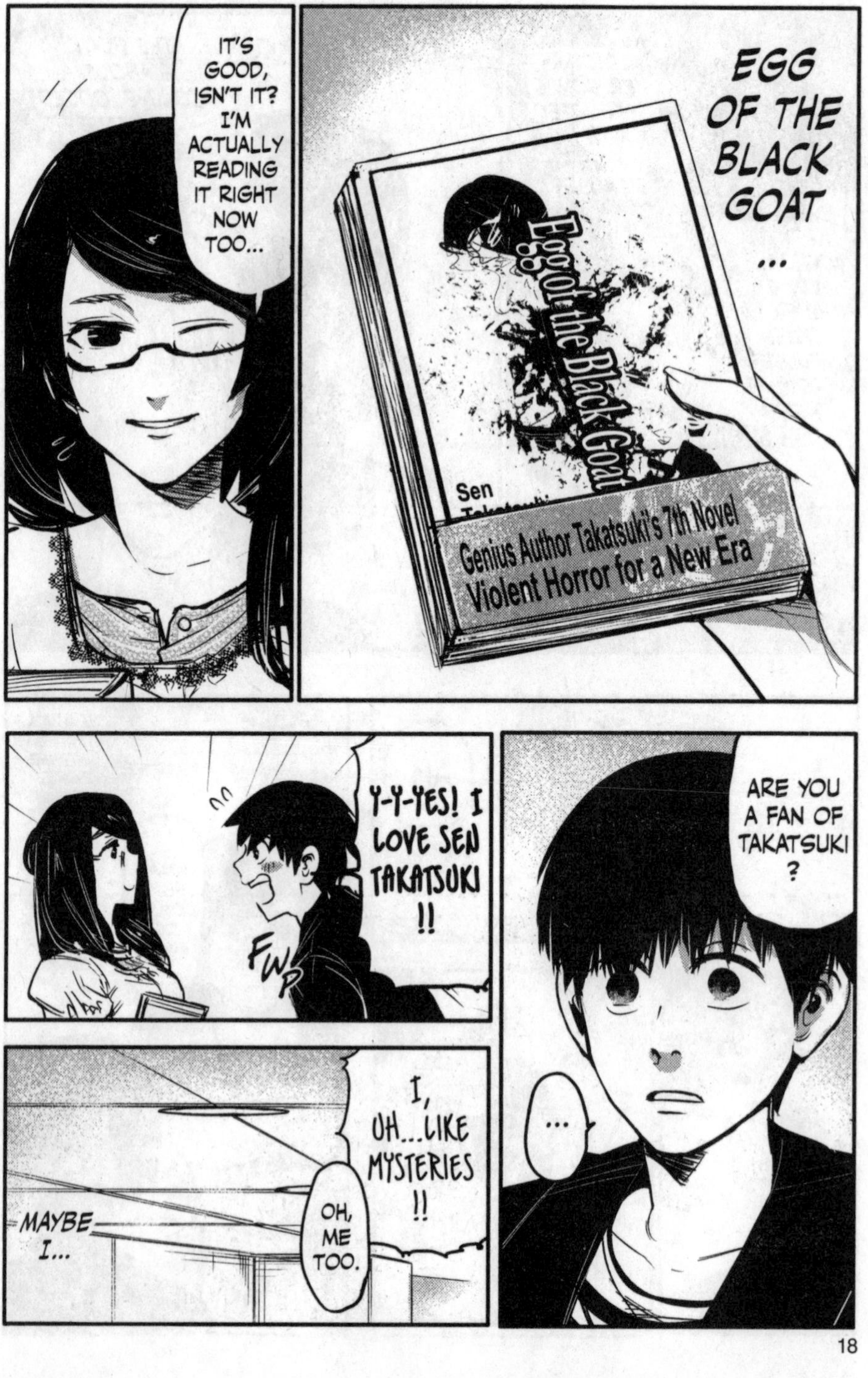
EGG OF THE BLACK GOAT ...
Egg of the Black Goat
Sen
Genius Author Takatsuki's 7th Novel
Violent Horror for a New Era
IT'S GOOD, ISN'T IT? I'M ACTUALLY READING IT RIGHT NOW TOO...
ARE YOU A FAN OF TAKATSUKI ?
...
Y-Y-YES! I LOVE SEN TAKATSUKI !!
FWP
I, OH...LIKE MYSTERIES !!
OH, ME TOO.
MAYBE I...

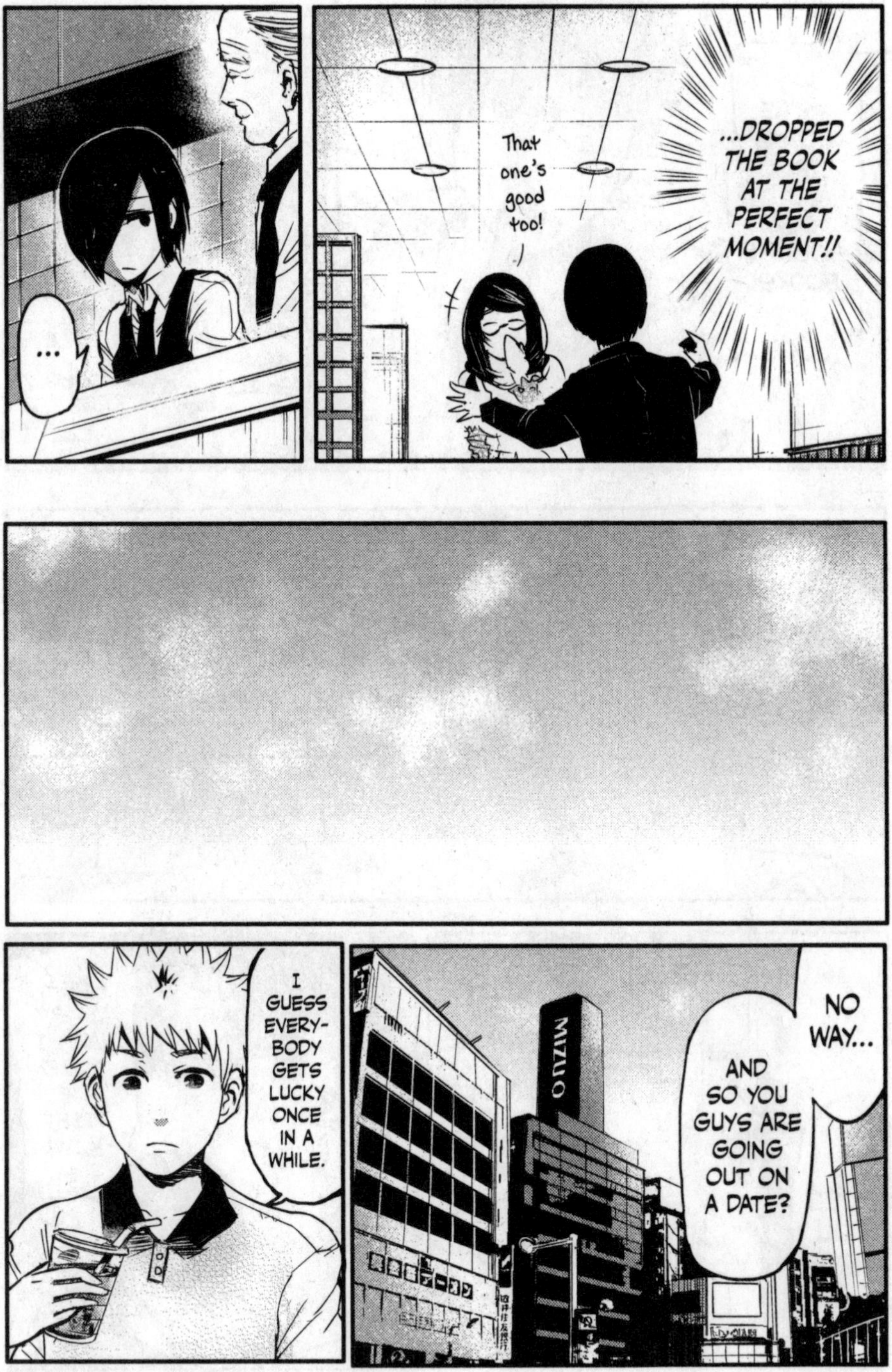
...DROPPED THE BOOK AT THE PERFECT MOMENT!!
That one's good too!
...
NO WAY...
AND SO YOU GUYS ARE GOING OUT ON A DATE?
MIZUO
I GUESS EVERY-BODY GETS LUCKY ONCE IN A WHILE.

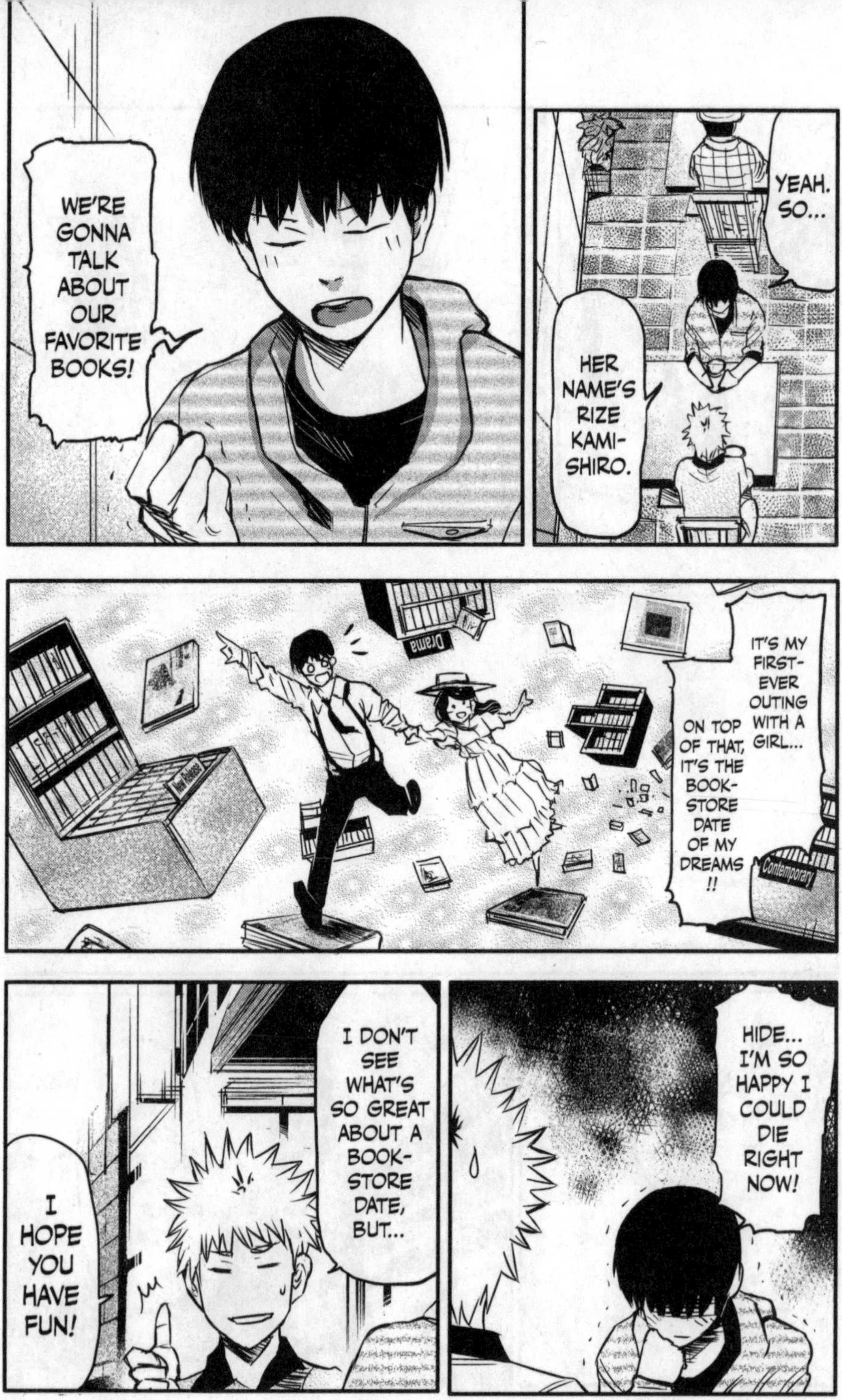
YEAH. SO...
HER NAME'S RIZE KAMI-SHIRO.
WE'RE GONNA TALK ABOUT OUR FAVORITE BOOKS!
IT'S MY FIRST-EVER OUTING WITH A GIRL...
ON TOP OF THAT, IT'S THE BOOK-STORE DATE OF MY DREAMS !!
Drama
Contemporary
HIDE... I'M SO HAPPY I COULD DIE RIGHT NOW!
I DON'T SEE WHAT'S SO GREAT ABOUT A BOOK-STORE DATE, BUT...
I HOPE YOU HAVE FUN!

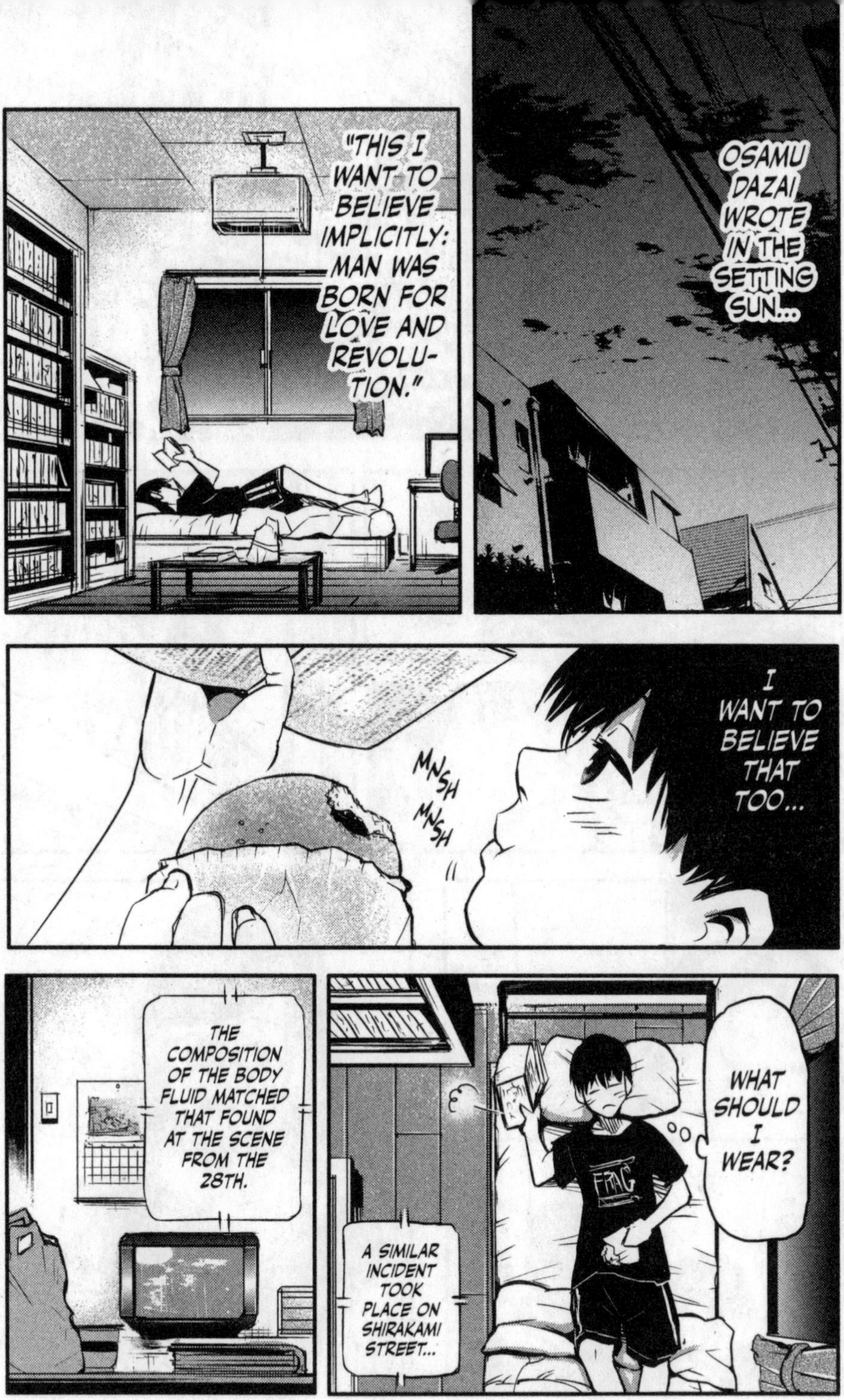
OSAMU DAZAI WROTE IN THE SETTING SUN...
"THIS I WANT TO BELIEVE IMPLICITLY: MAN WAS BORN FOR LOVE AND REVOLUTION."
I WANT TO BELIEVE THAT TOO...
MNSH MNSH
WHAT SHOULD I WEAR?
FRAG
A SIMILAR INCIDENT TOOK PLACE ON SHIRAKAMI STREET...
THE COMPOSITION OF THE BODY FLUID MATCHED THAT FOUND AT THE SCENE FROM THE 28TH.

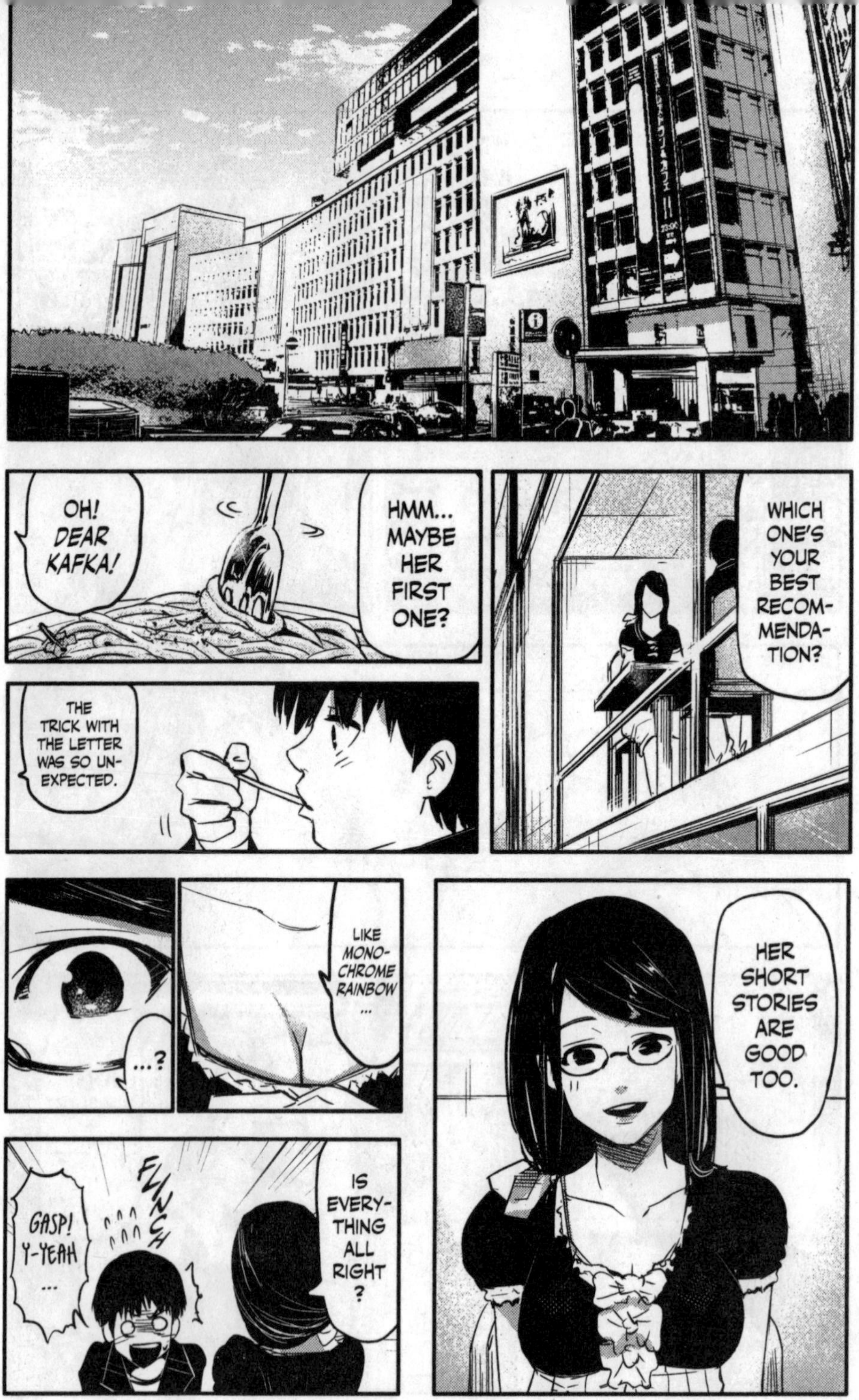
WHICH ONE'S YOUR BEST RECOMMENDATION?
HMM... MAYBE HER FIRST ONE?
OH! DEAR KAFKA!
THE TRICK WITH THE LETTER WAS SO UNEXPECTED.
HER SHORT STORIES ARE GOOD TOO.
LIKE MONOCHROME RAINBOW...
...?
FLINCH
IS EVERYTHING ALL RIGHT?
GASP! Y-YEAH...

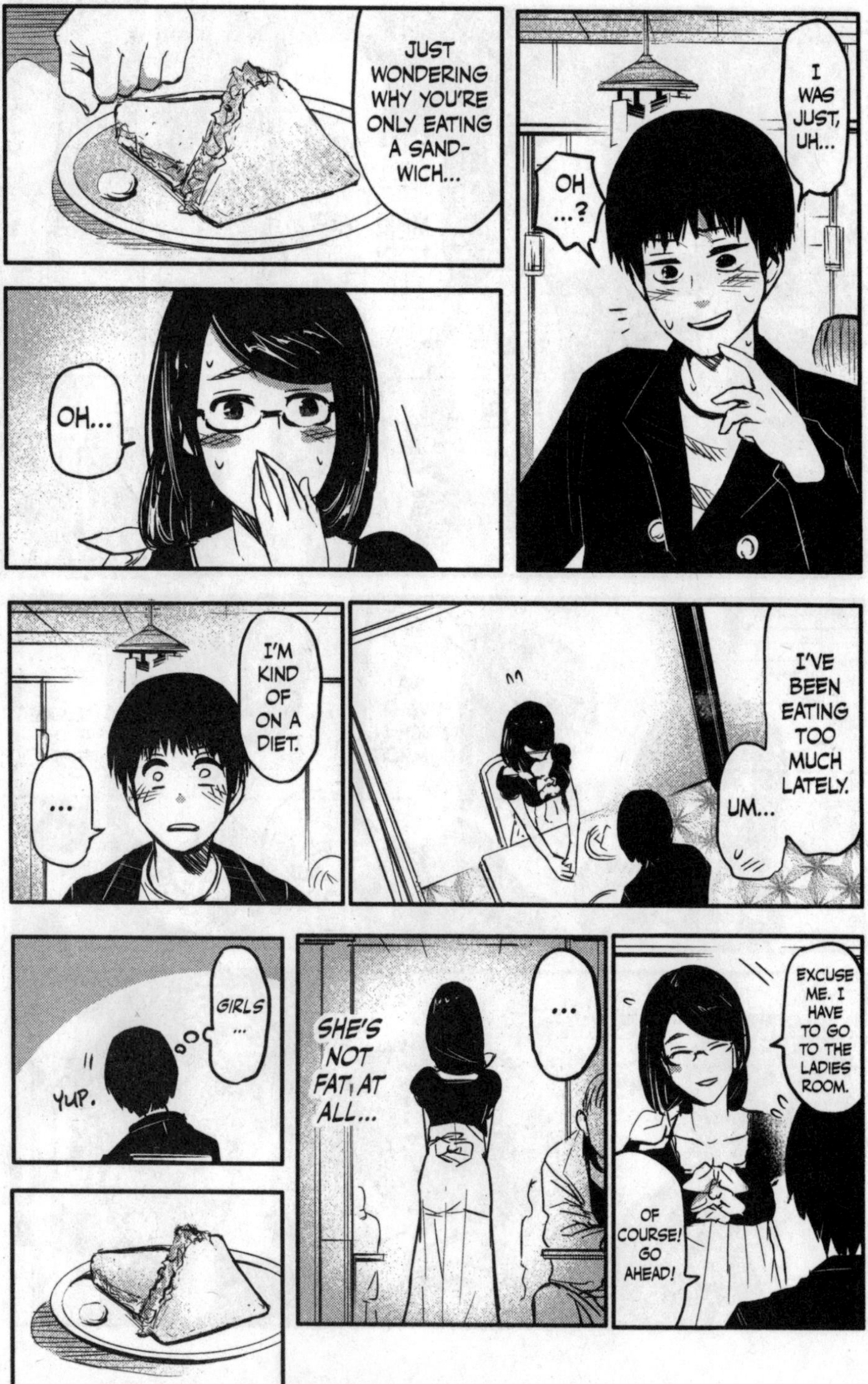
I WAS JUST, UH...
OH ...?
JUST WONDERING WHY YOU'RE ONLY EATING A SAND-WICH...
OH...
I'VE BEEN EATING TOO MUCH LATELY.
UM...
I'M KIND OF ON A DIET.
...
EXCUSE ME. I HAVE TO GO TO THE LADIES ROOM.
OF COURSE! GO AHEAD!
...
SHE'S NOT FAT AT ALL...
GIRLS ...
YUP.

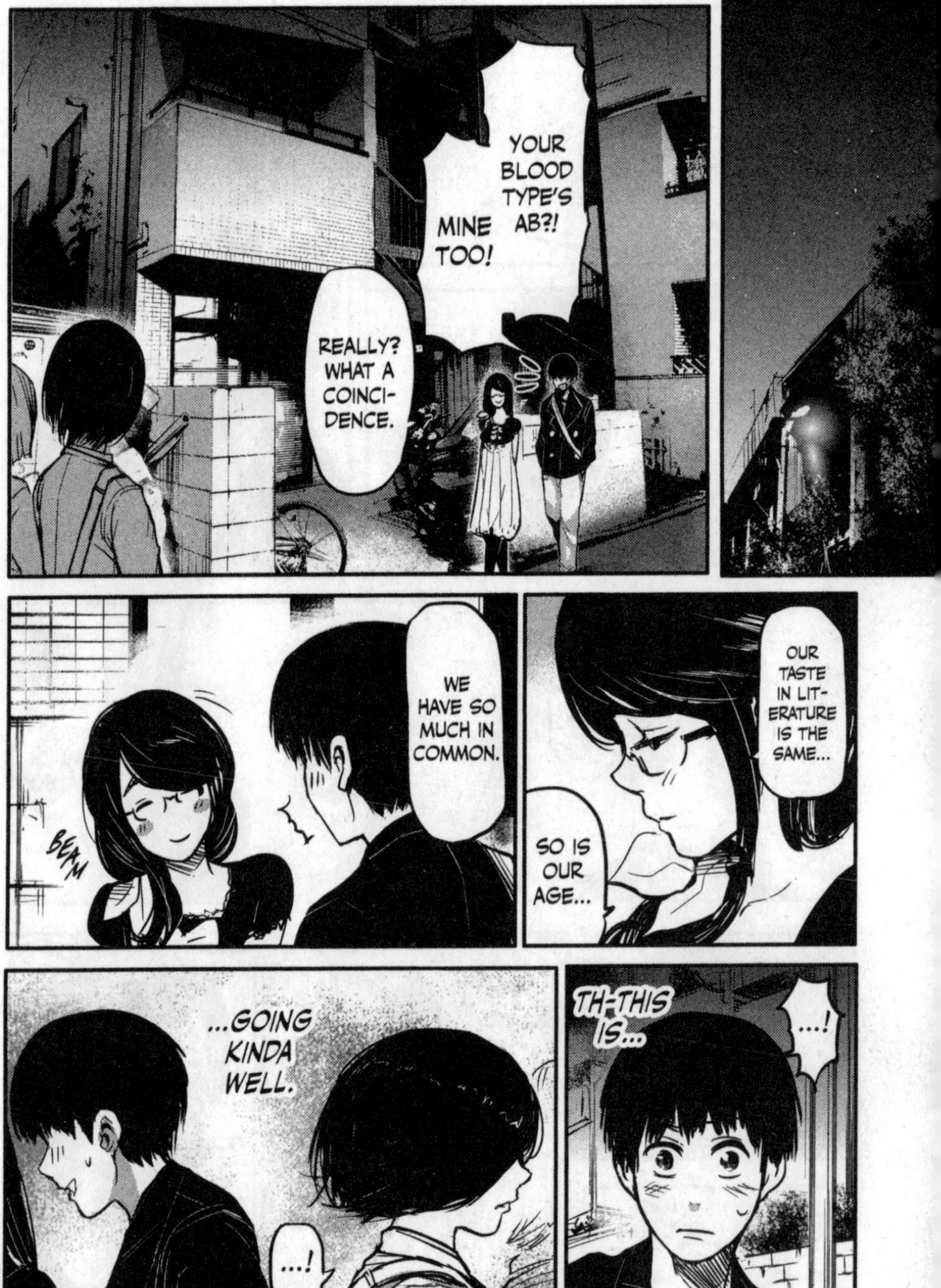
YOUR BLOOD TYPE'S AB?!
MINE TOO!
REALLY? WHAT A COINCIDENCE.
OUR TASTE IN LITERATURE IS THE SAME...
SO IS OUR AGE...
WE HAVE SO MUCH IN COMMON.
BEAM
...!
TH-THIS IS...
...GOING KINDA WELL.
...!

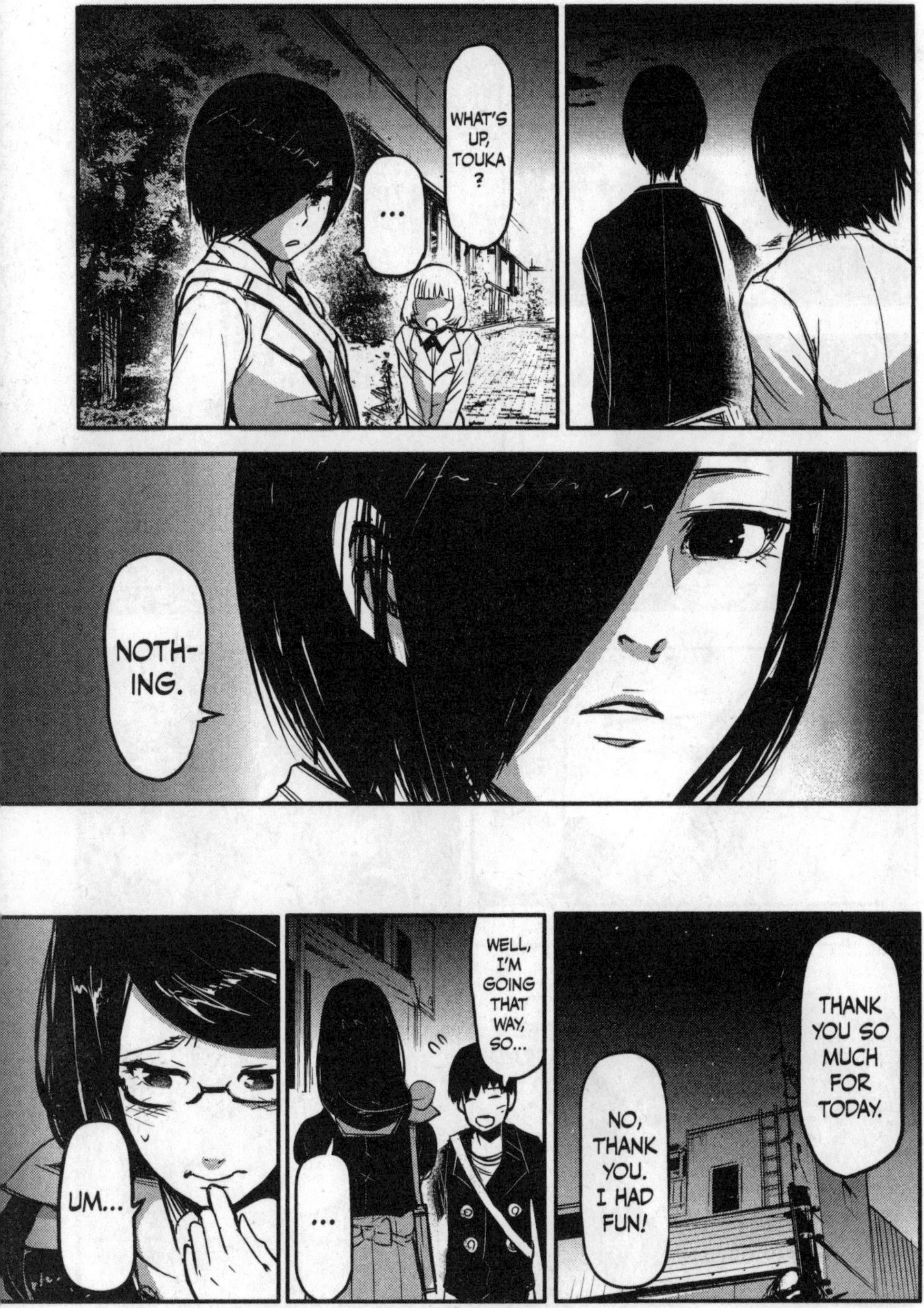
WHAT'S UP, TOUKA?
...
NOTH-ING.
THANK YOU SO MUCH FOR TODAY.
NO, THANK YOU. I HAD FUN!
WELL, I'M GOING THAT WAY, SO...
...
UM...

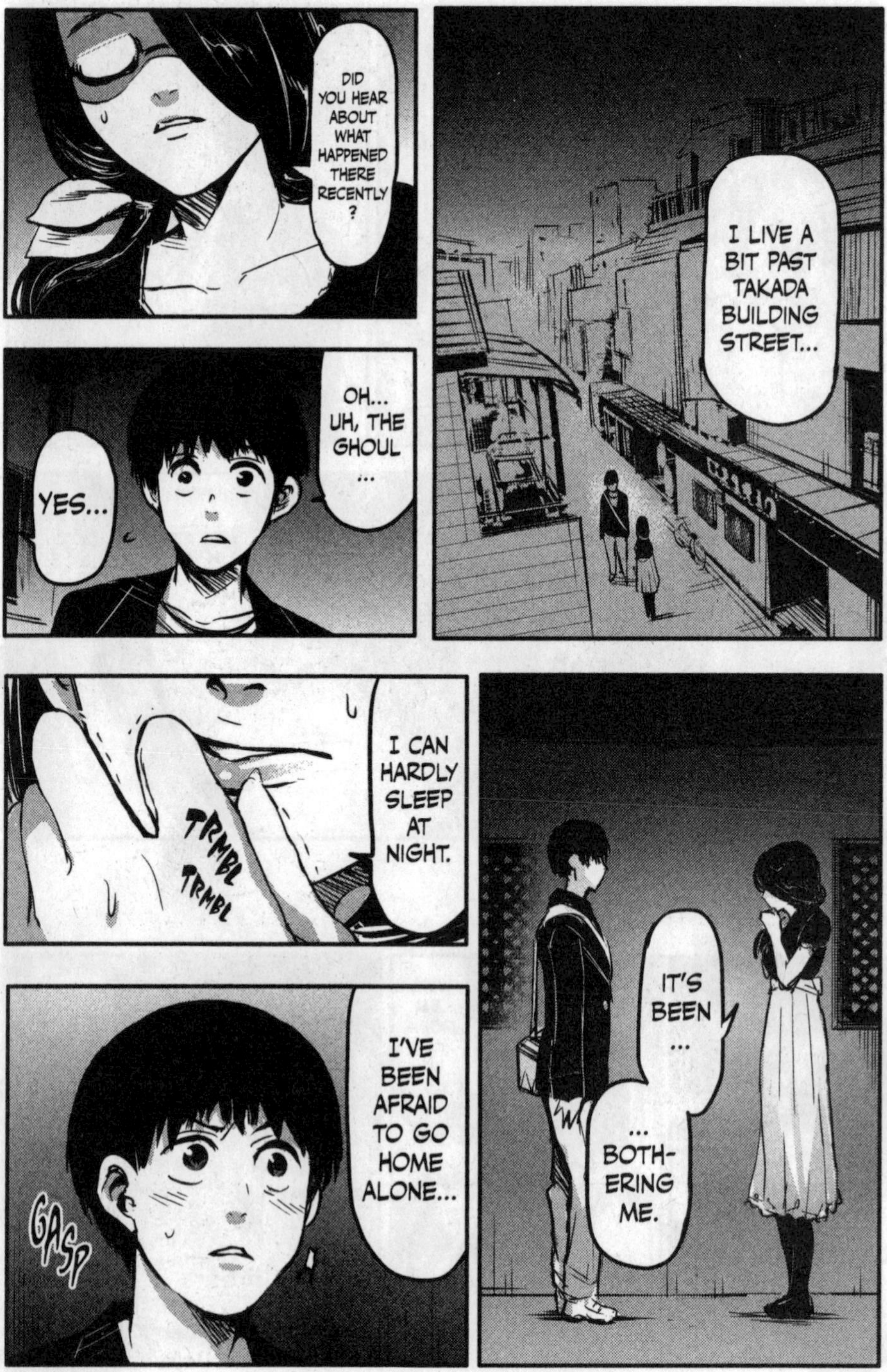
I LIVE A BIT PAST TAKADA BUILDING STREET...
DID YOU HEAR ABOUT WHAT HAPPENED THERE RECENTLY?
OH... UH, THE GHOUL...
YES...
IT'S BEEN...
...BOTHERING ME.
I CAN HARDLY SLEEP AT NIGHT.
TRMBL TRMBL
I'VE BEEN AFRAID TO GO HOME ALONE...
GASP

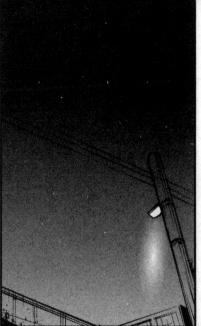

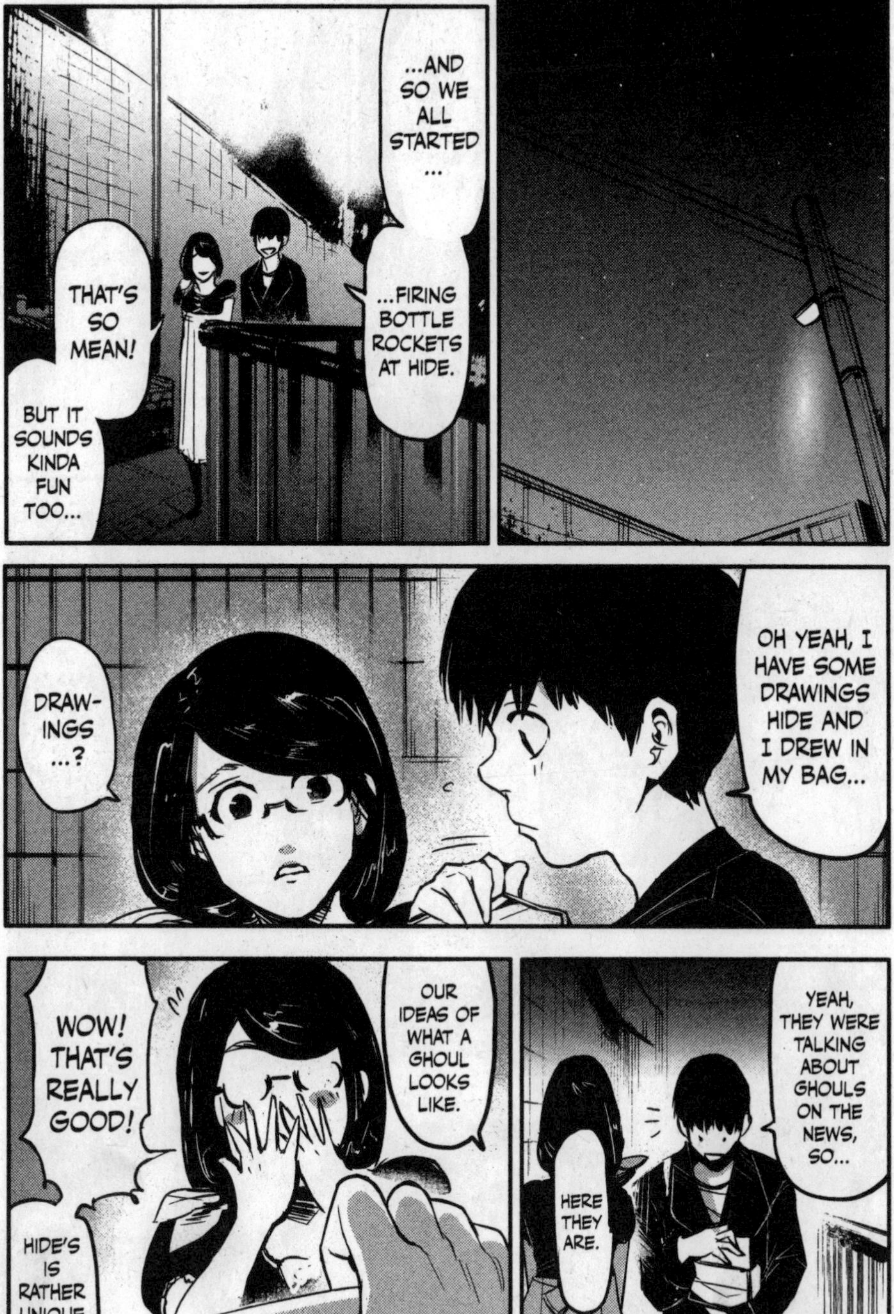
...AND SO WE ALL STARTED ...
...FIRING BOTTLE ROCKETS AT HIDE.
THAT'S SO MEAN!
BUT IT SOUNDS KINDA FUN TOO...
OH YEAH, I HAVE SOME DRAWINGS HIDE AND I DREW IN MY BAG...
DRAW-INGS ...?
YEAH, THEY WERE TALKING ABOUT GHOULS ON THE NEWS, SO...
HERE THEY ARE.
OUR IDEAS OF WHAT A GHOUL LOOKS LIKE.
WOW! THAT'S REALLY GOOD!
HIDE'S IS RATHER UNIQUE ...

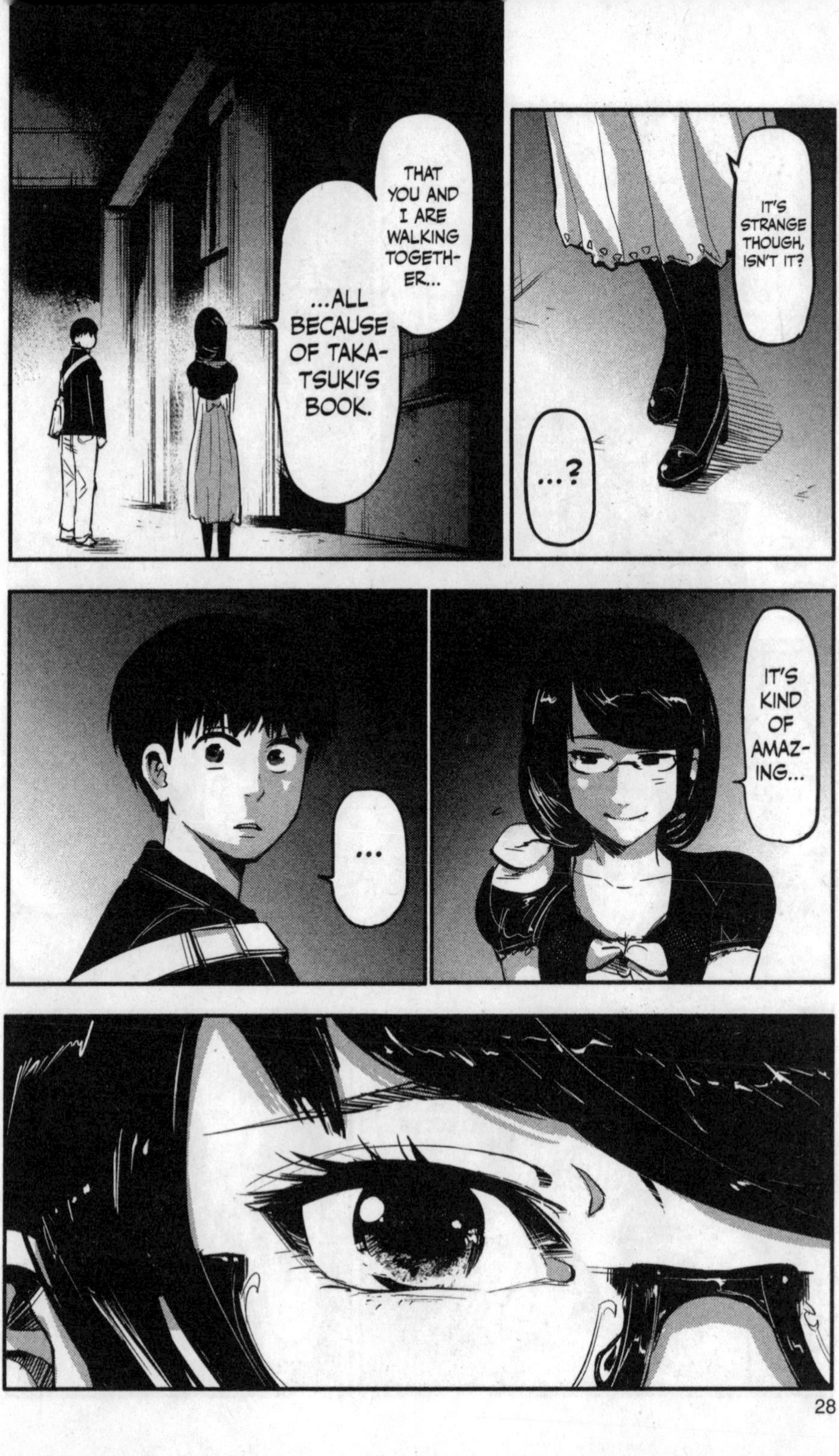
IT'S STRANGE THOUGH, ISN'T IT?
...?
THAT YOU AND I ARE WALKING TOGETH-ER...
...ALL BECAUSE OF TAKA-TSUKI'S BOOK.
IT'S KIND OF AMAZ-ING...
...

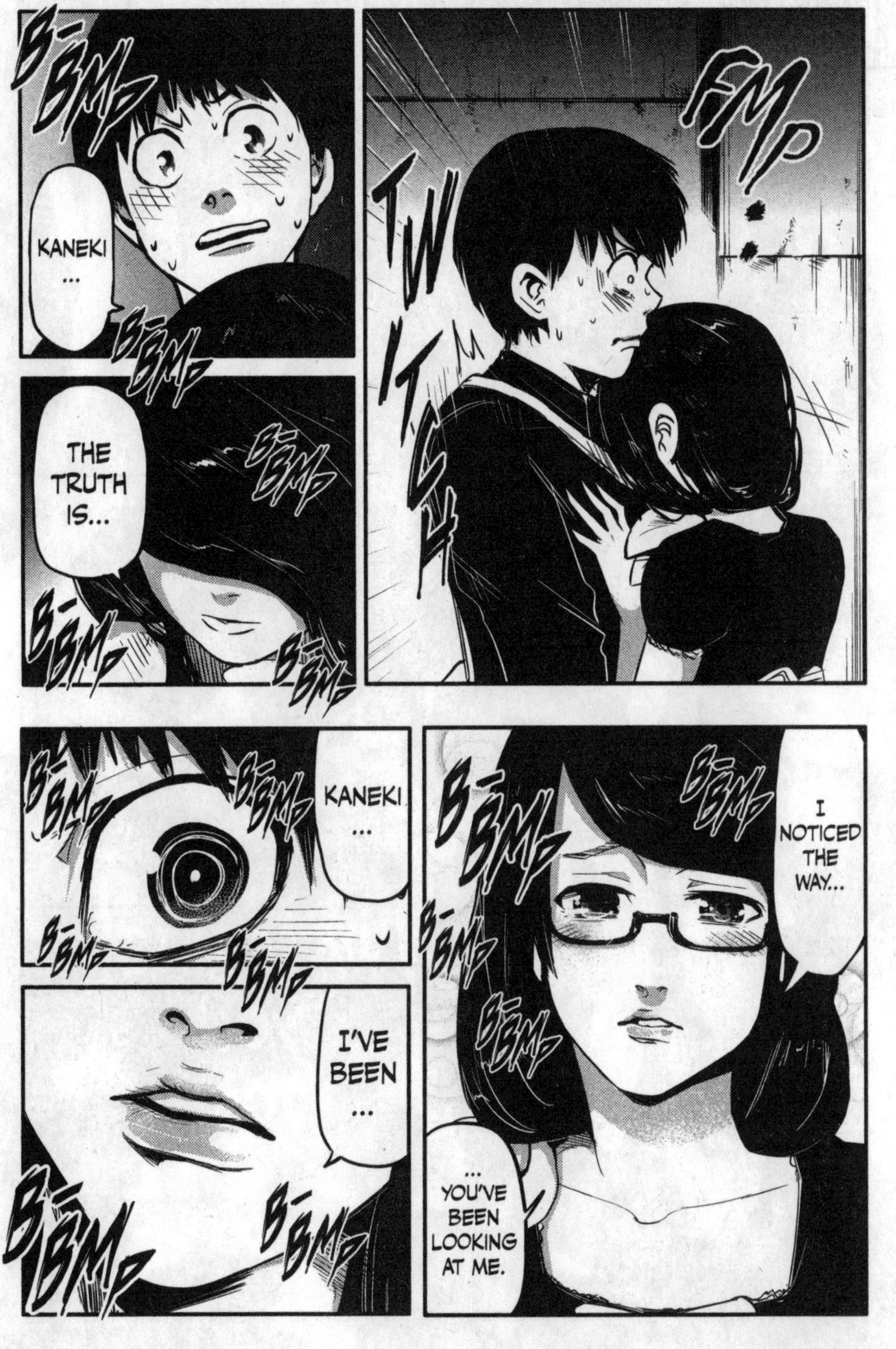
FMP
TWITCH
B-BMP
KANEKI ...
B-BMP
THE TRUTH IS...
B-BMP
B-BMP
B-BMP
B-BMP
I NOTICED THE WAY...
B-BMP
B-BMP
... YOU'VE BEEN LOOKING AT ME.
B-BMP
KANEKI ...
B-BMP
B-BMP
B-BMP
I'VE BEEN ...
B-BMP
B-BMP

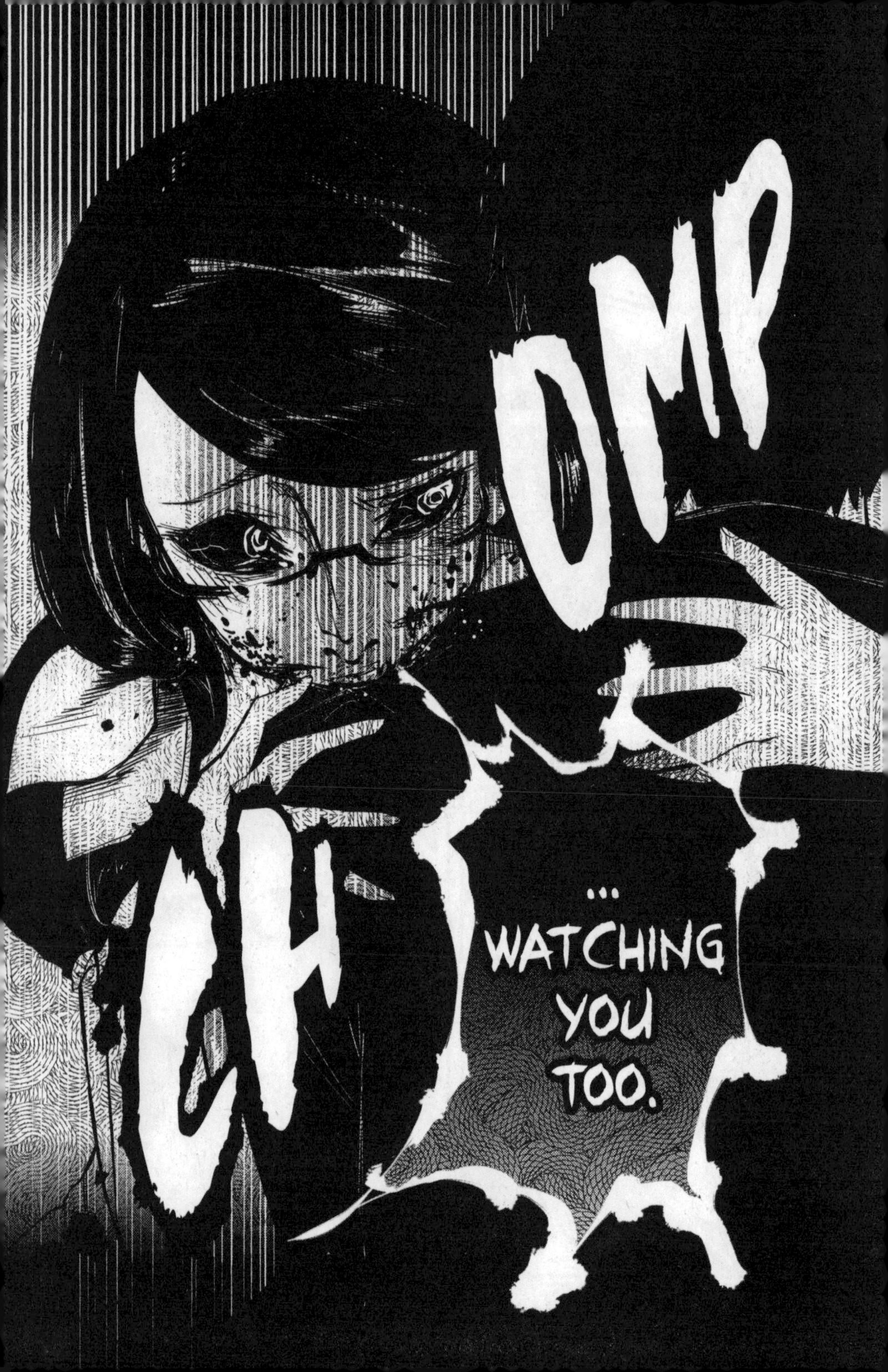
CHOMP
... WATCHING YOU TOO.

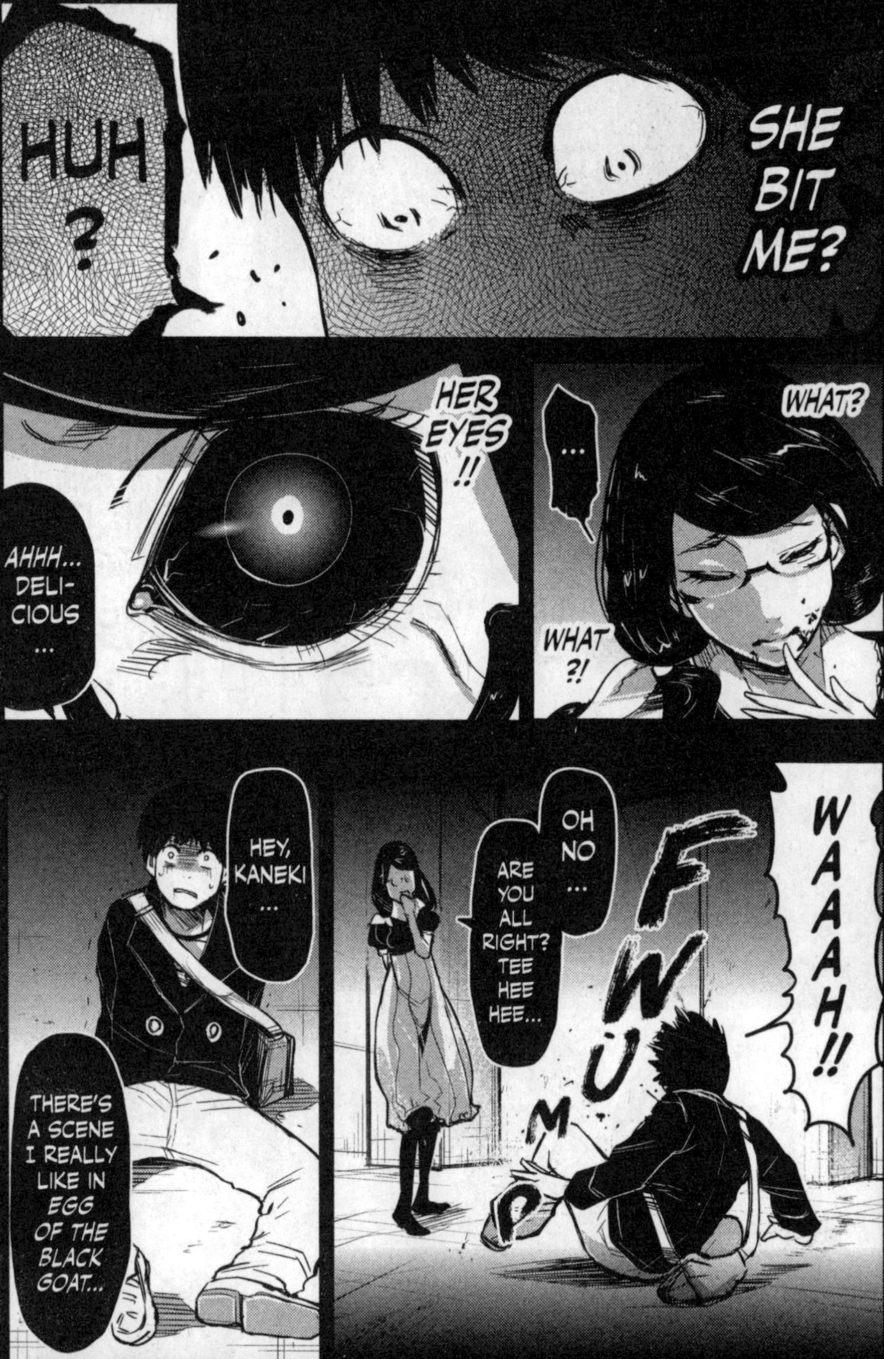
SHE BIT ME?
HUH?
WHAT?
...
WHAT?!
HER EYES!!
AHHH... DELICIOUS...
WAAAAH!!
FWUMP
OH NO...
ARE YOU ALL RIGHT? TEE HEE HEE...
HEY, KANEKI...
THERE'S A SCENE I REALLY LIKE IN EGG OF THE BLACK GOAT...

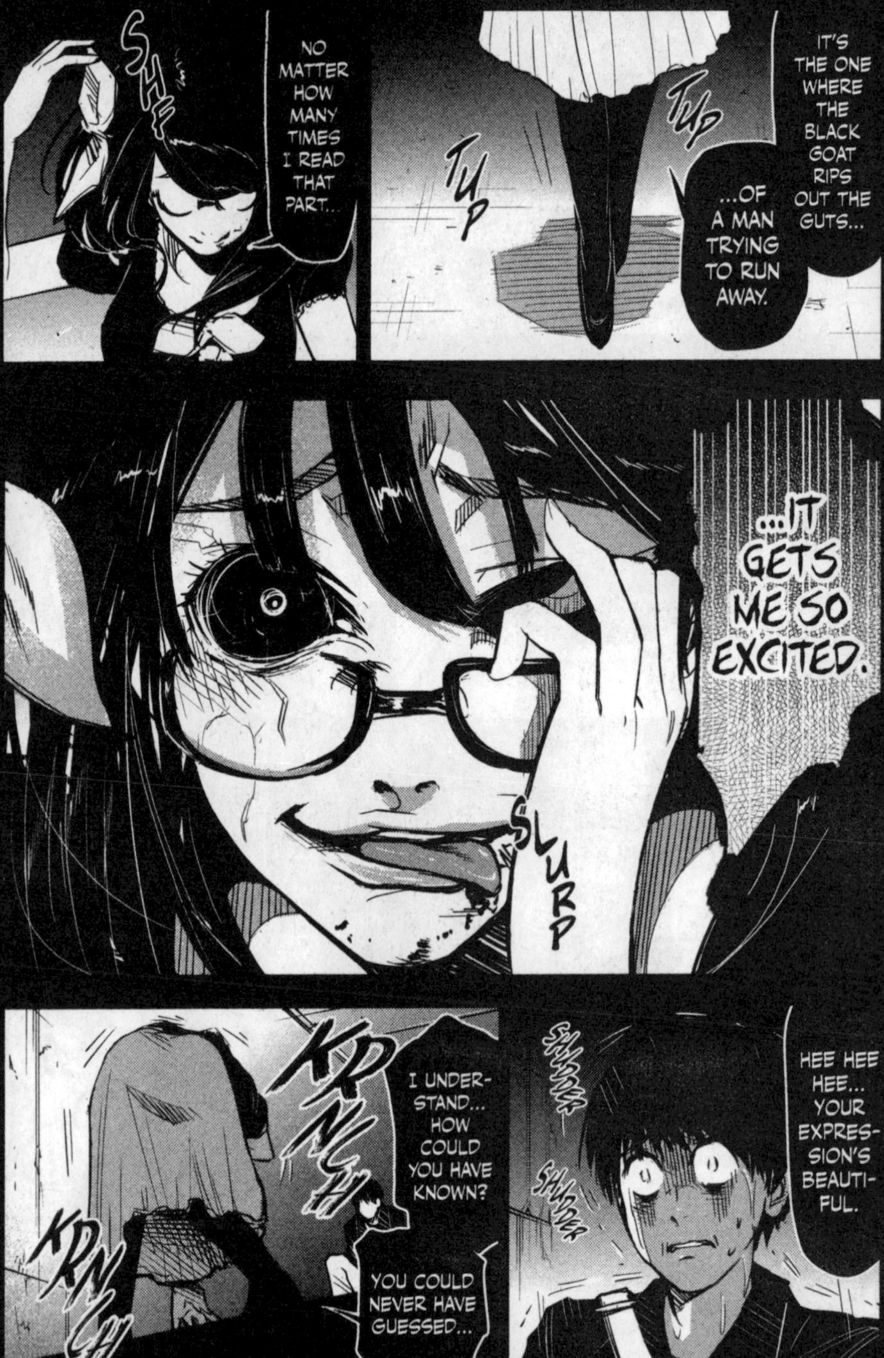
IT'S THE ONE WHERE THE BLACK GOAT RIPS OUT THE GUTS...
...OF A MAN TRYING TO RUN AWAY.
TUP
TUP
TUP
SHF
NO MATTER HOW MANY TIMES I READ THAT PART...
...IT GETS ME SO EXCITED.
SLURP
HEE HEE HEE... YOUR EXPRES-SION'S BEAUTI-FUL.
SHUDDER
SHUDDER
KRNCH
I UNDER-STAND... HOW COULD YOU HAVE KNOWN?
YOU COULD NEVER HAVE GUESSED...
KRNCH

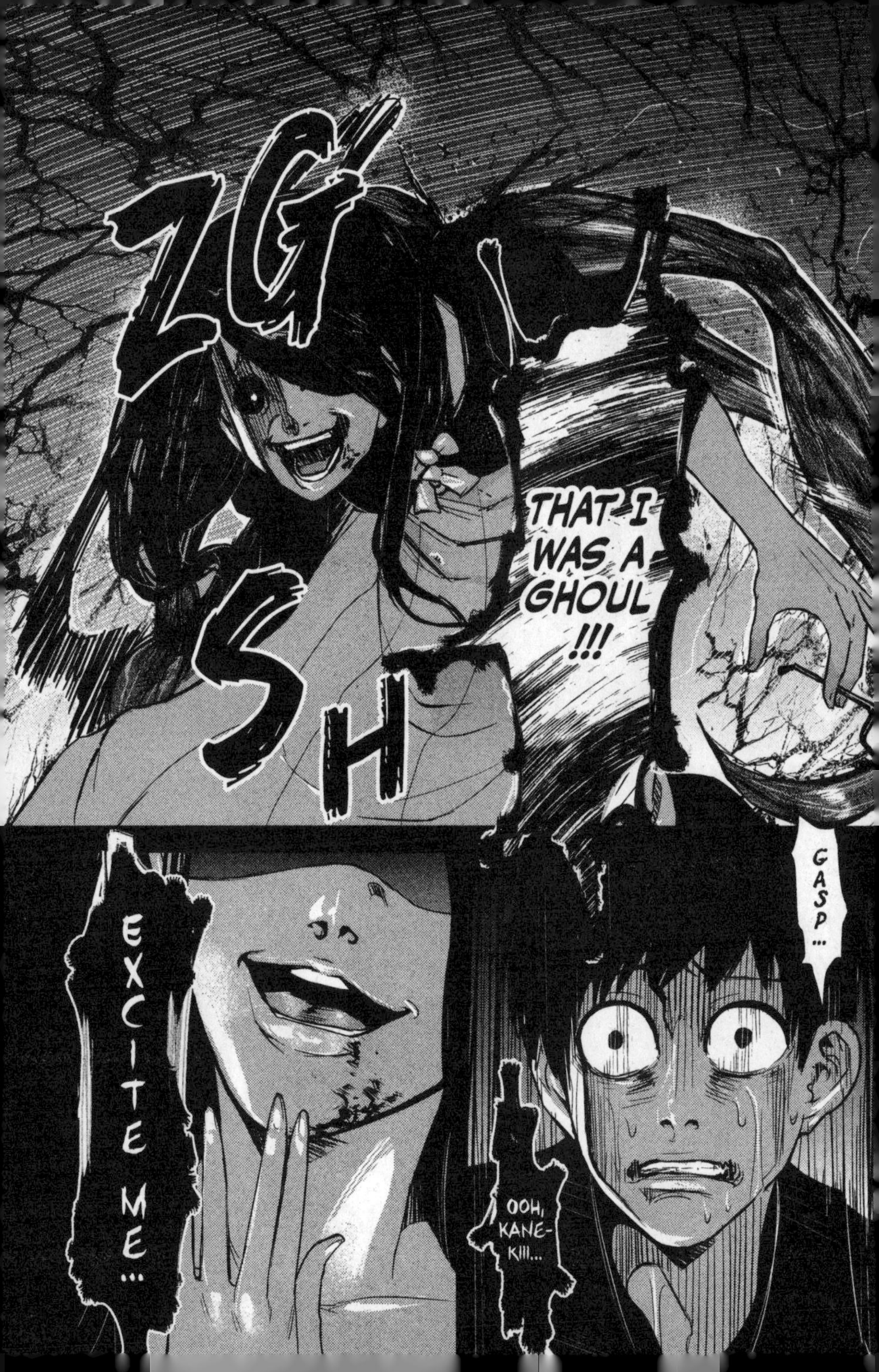
ZGSH
THAT I WAS A GHOUL !!!
GASP...
OOH, KANE-KIII...
EXCITE ME...

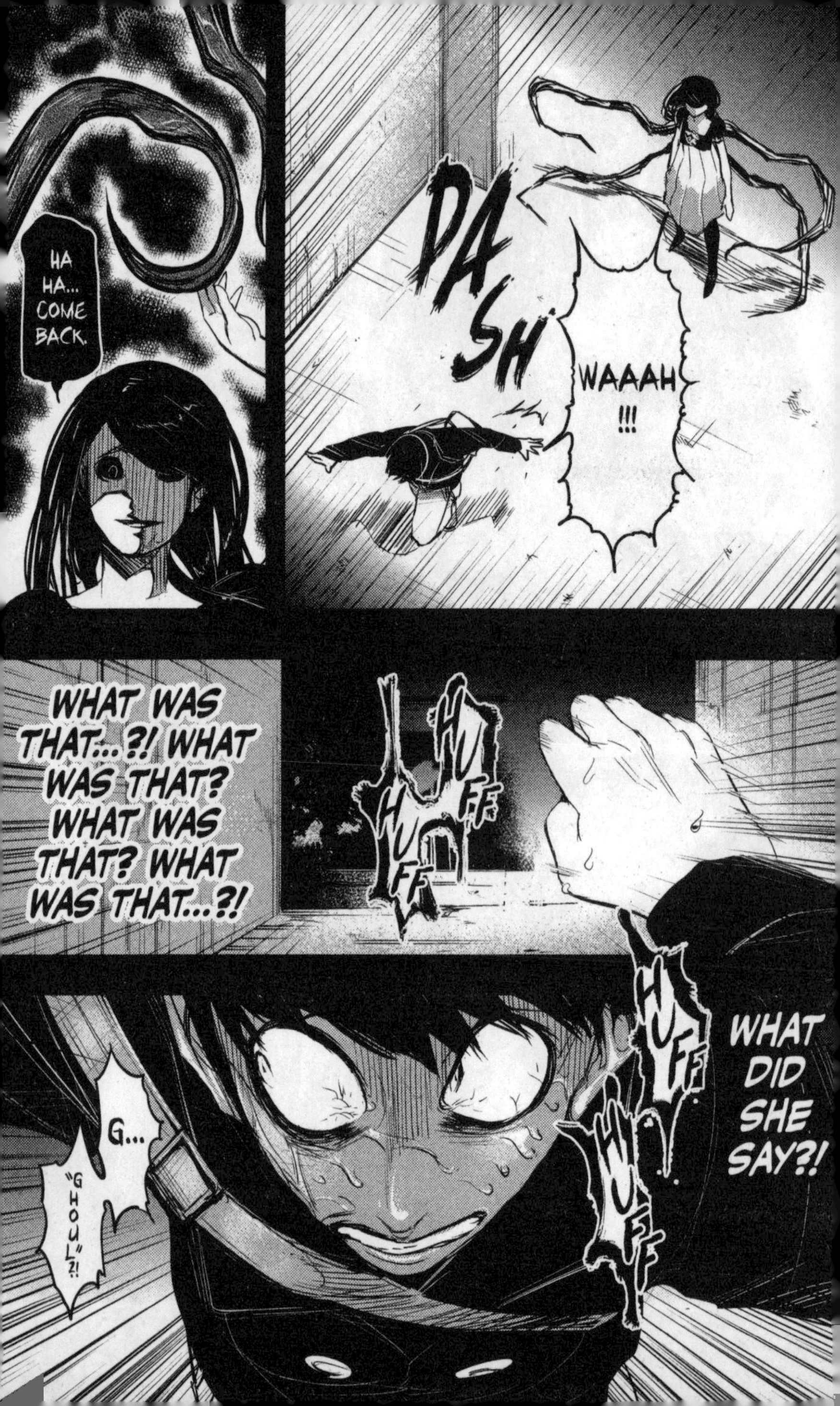
DASH
WAAAH!!!
HA HA... COME BACK.
HUFF HUFF
WHAT WAS THAT...?! WHAT WAS THAT? WHAT WAS THAT? WHAT WAS THAT...?!
WHAT DID SHE SAY?!
HUFF... HUFF...
G...
"GHOUL"?!

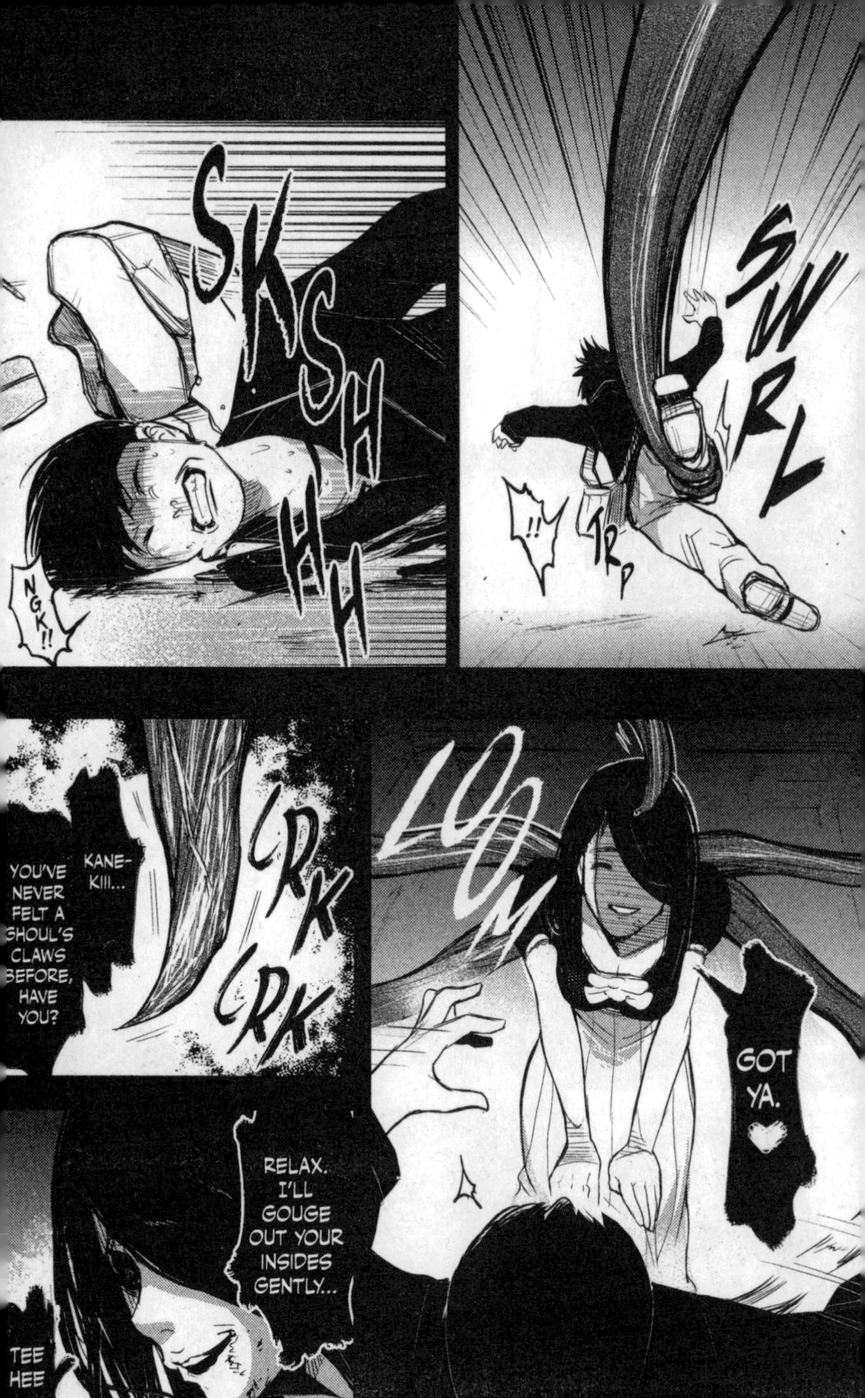
SWRV
!!
TRP
SKSHHHH
NGK!!
LOOM
GOT YA. ♥
CRK CRK
KANE-KIII...
YOU'VE NEVER FELT A GHOUL'S CLAWS BEFORE, HAVE YOU?
RELAX. I'LL GOUGE OUT YOUR INSIDES GENTLY...
TEE HEE...

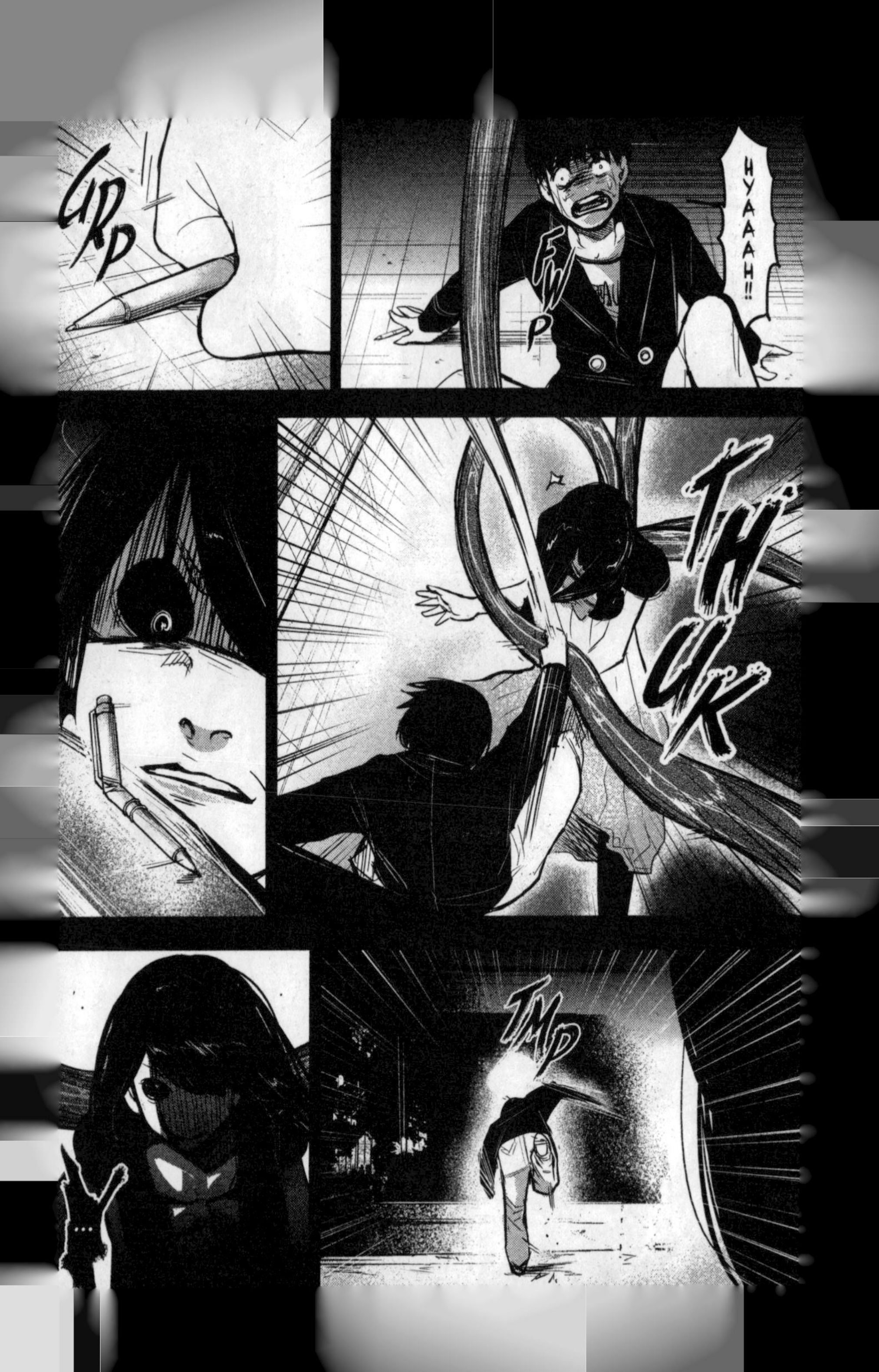
HYAAAH!!
FWP
URP
THUK
TMP
...

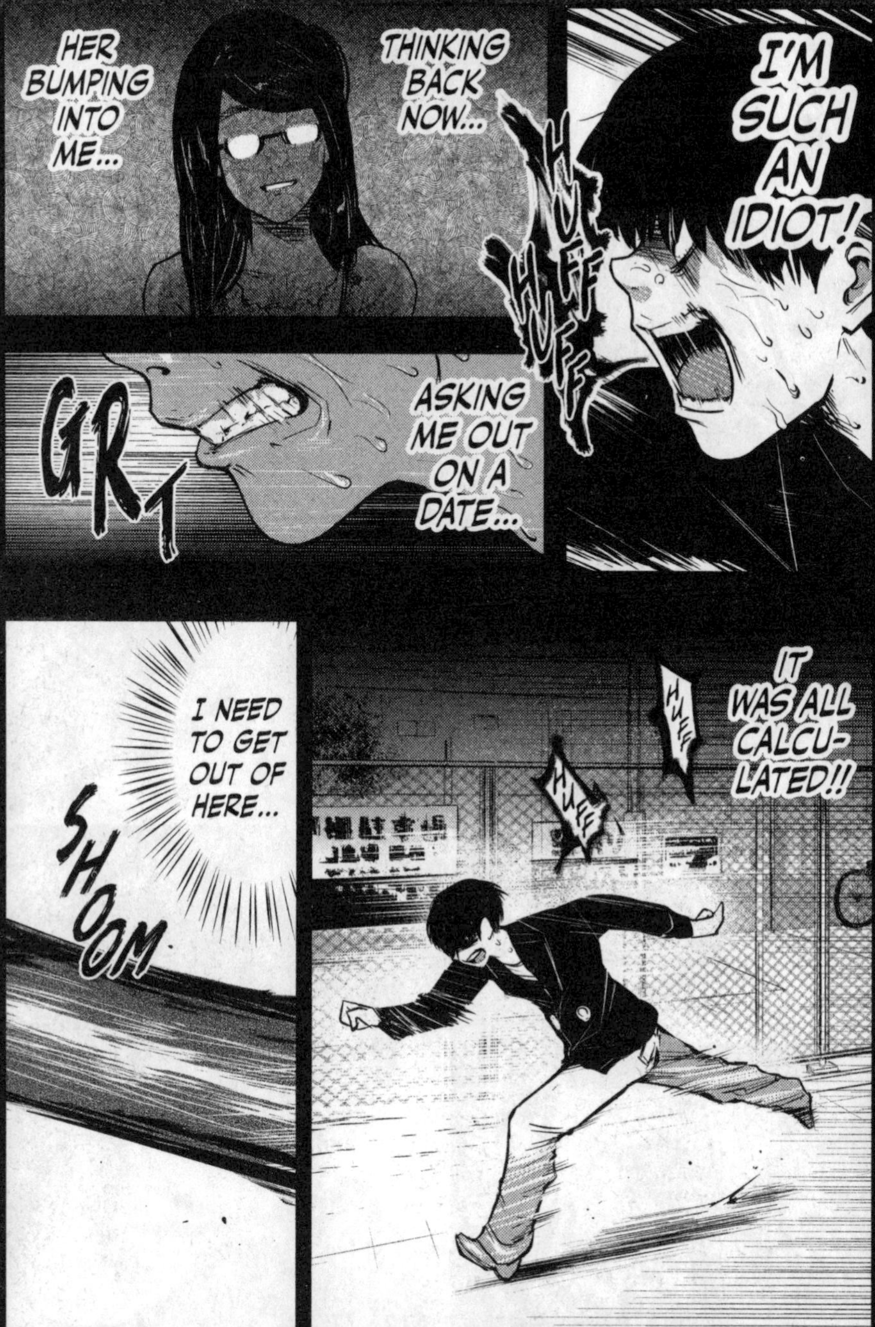
I'M SUCH AN IDIOT!
HUFF
HUFF
HUFF
THINKING BACK NOW...
HER BUMPING INTO ME...
ASKING ME OUT ON A DATE...
GRT
IT WAS ALL CALCU-LATED!!
HUFF
HUFF
I NEED TO GET OUT OF HERE...
SHOOM

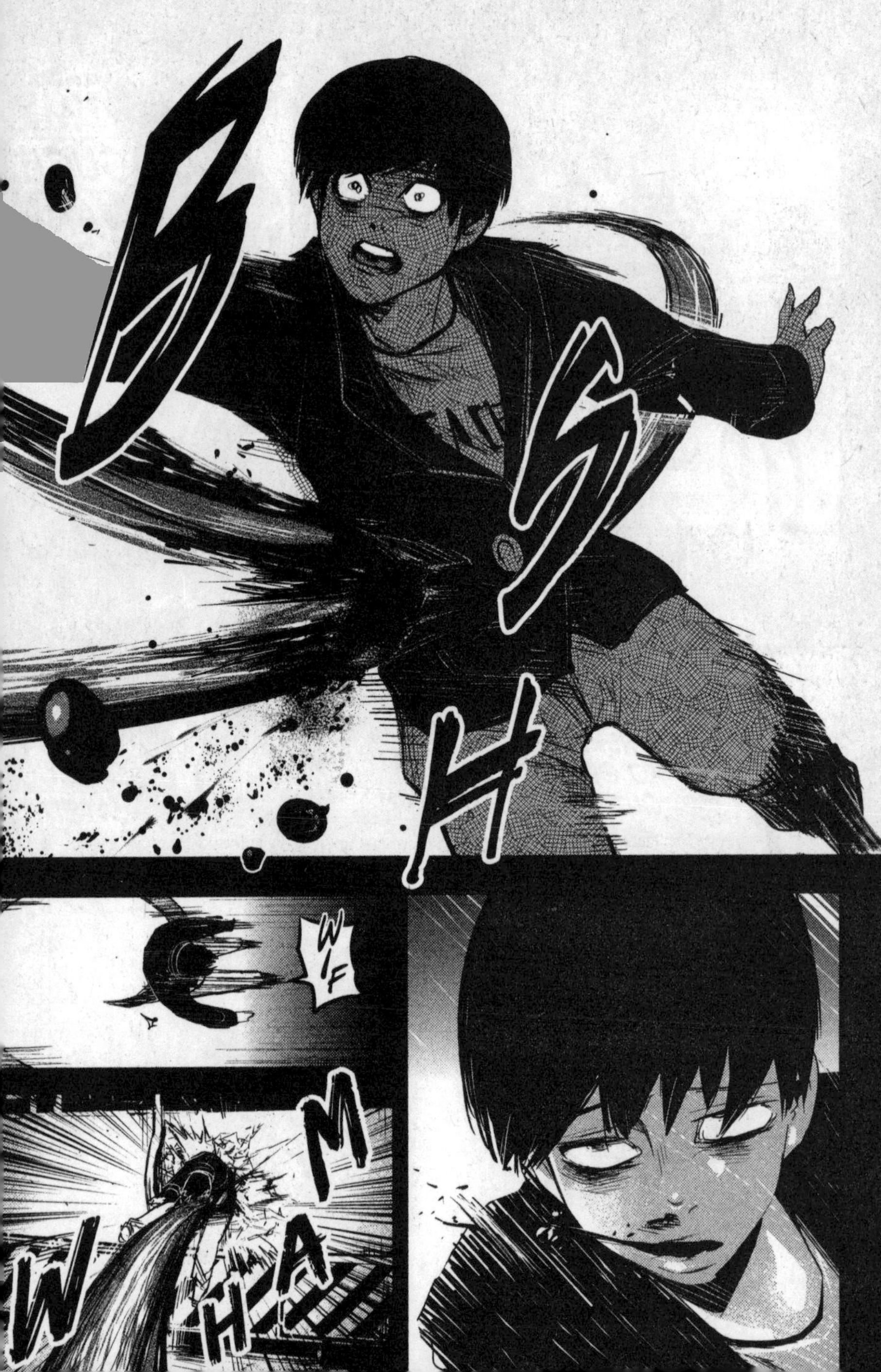
SSH
WIF
WHAM

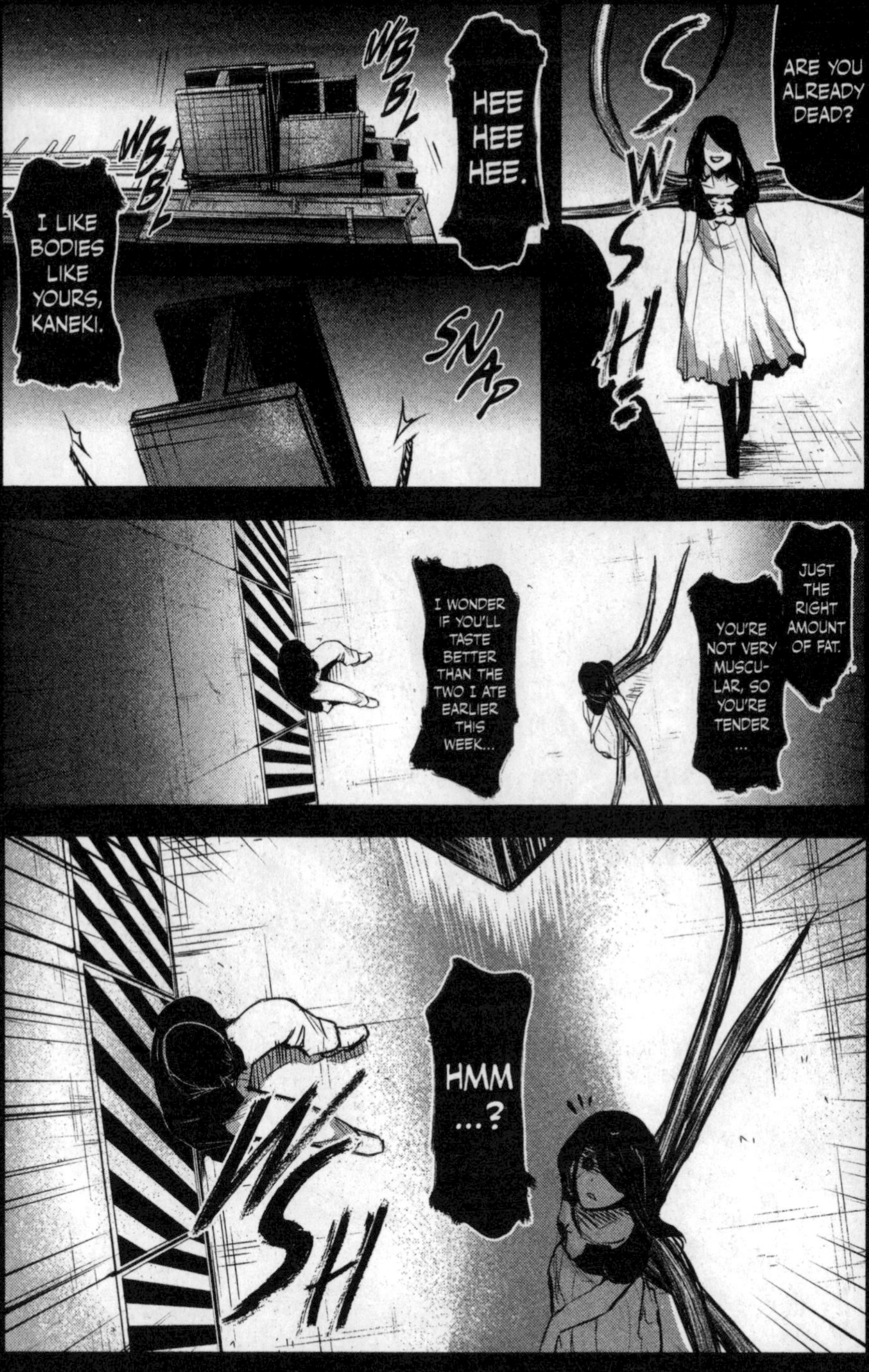
SWSSHH!
ARE YOU ALREADY DEAD?
HEE HEE HEE.
WBBL
WBBL
I LIKE BODIES LIKE YOURS, KANEKI.
SNAP
JUST THE RIGHT AMOUNT OF FAT.
YOU'RE NOT VERY MUSCU-LAR, SO YOU'RE TENDER ...
I WONDER IF YOU'LL TASTE BETTER THAN THE TWO I ATE EARLIER THIS WEEK...
HMM ...?
WSH

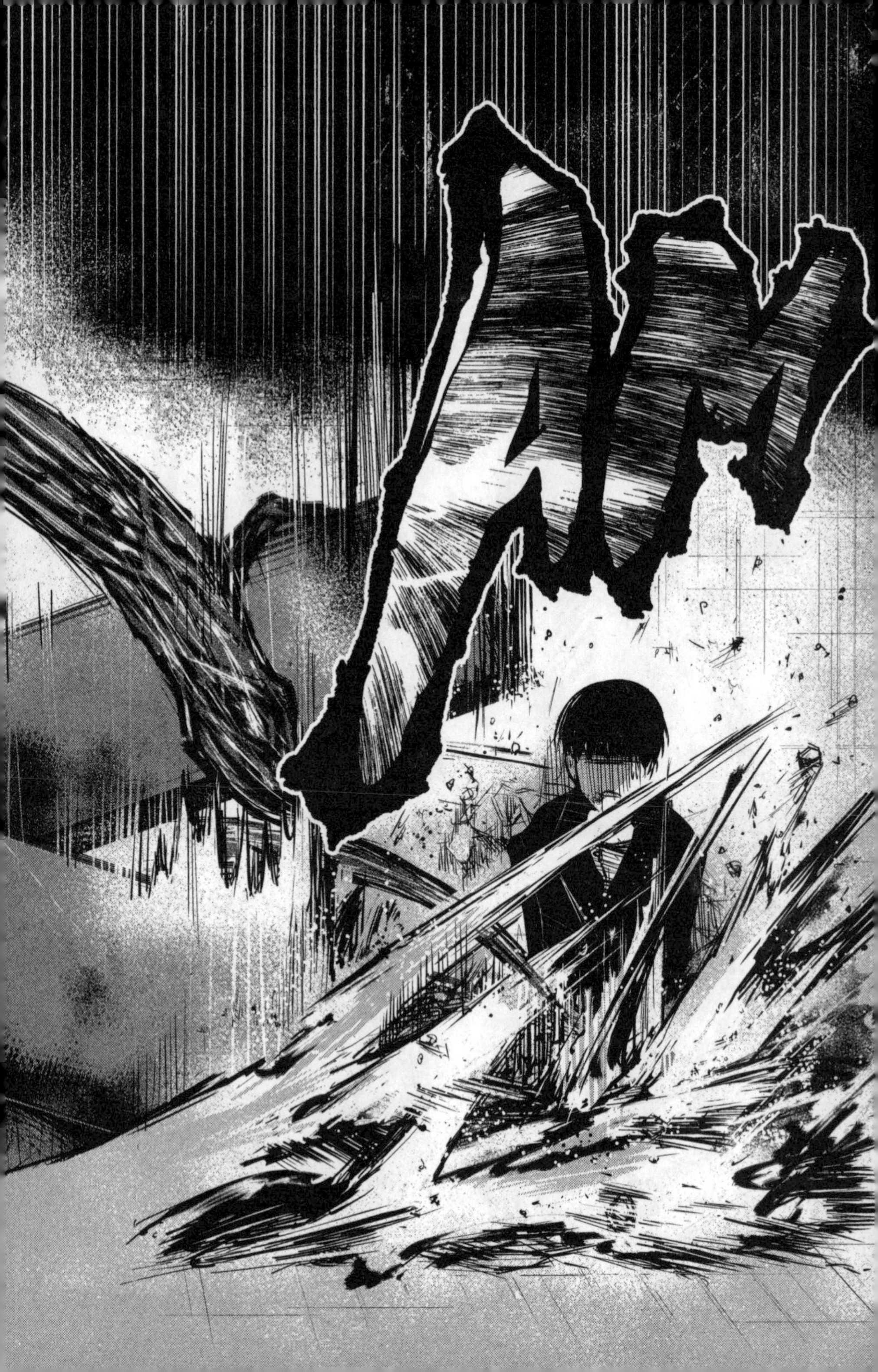

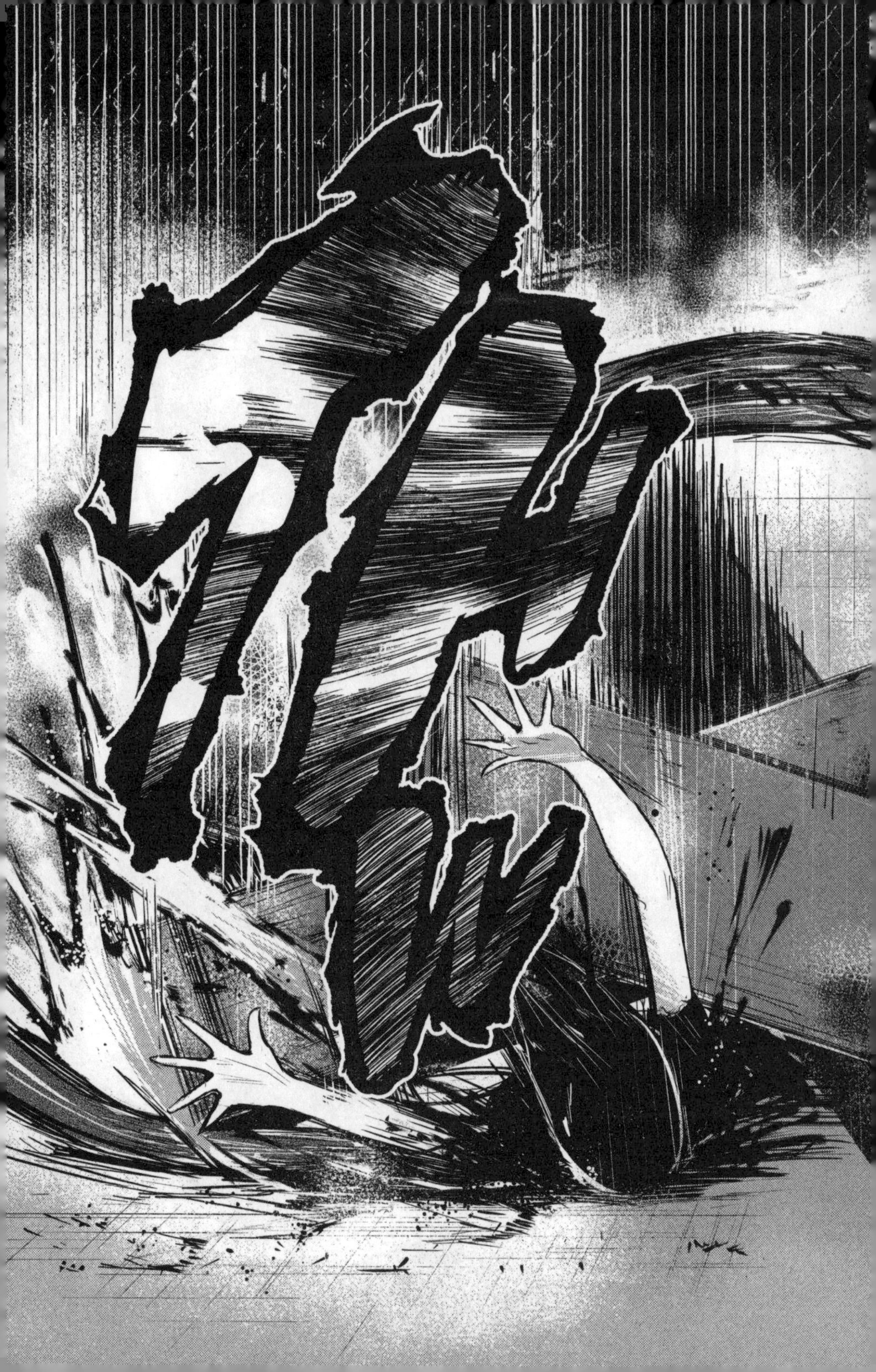

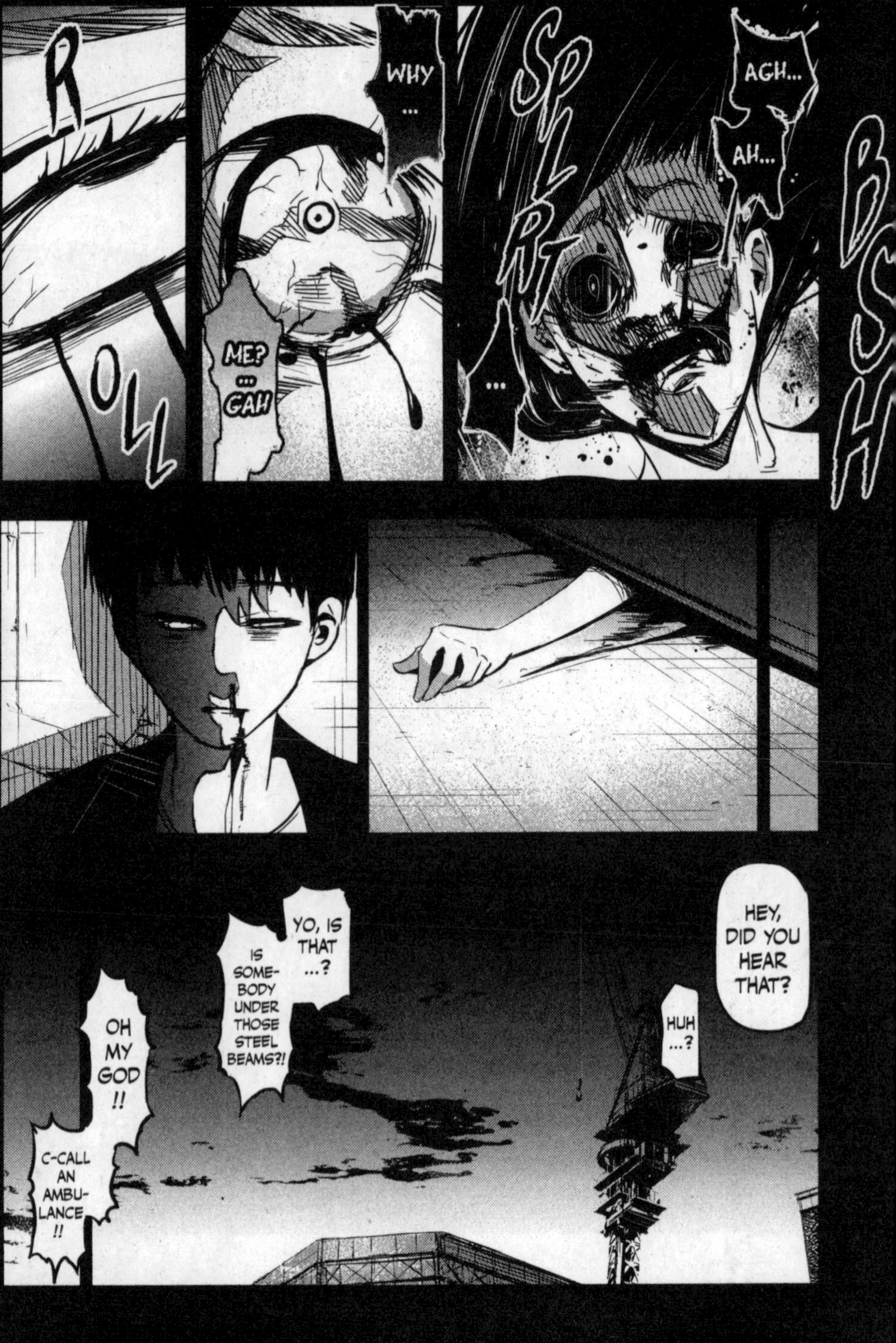
AGH...
AH...
BSH
SPLLRT
...
WHY ...
ME? ... GAH
ROLL
HEY, DID YOU HEAR THAT?
HUH ...?
YO, IS THAT ...?
IS SOMEBODY UNDER THOSE STEEL BEAMS?!
OH MY GOD !!
C-CALL AN AMBULANCE !!

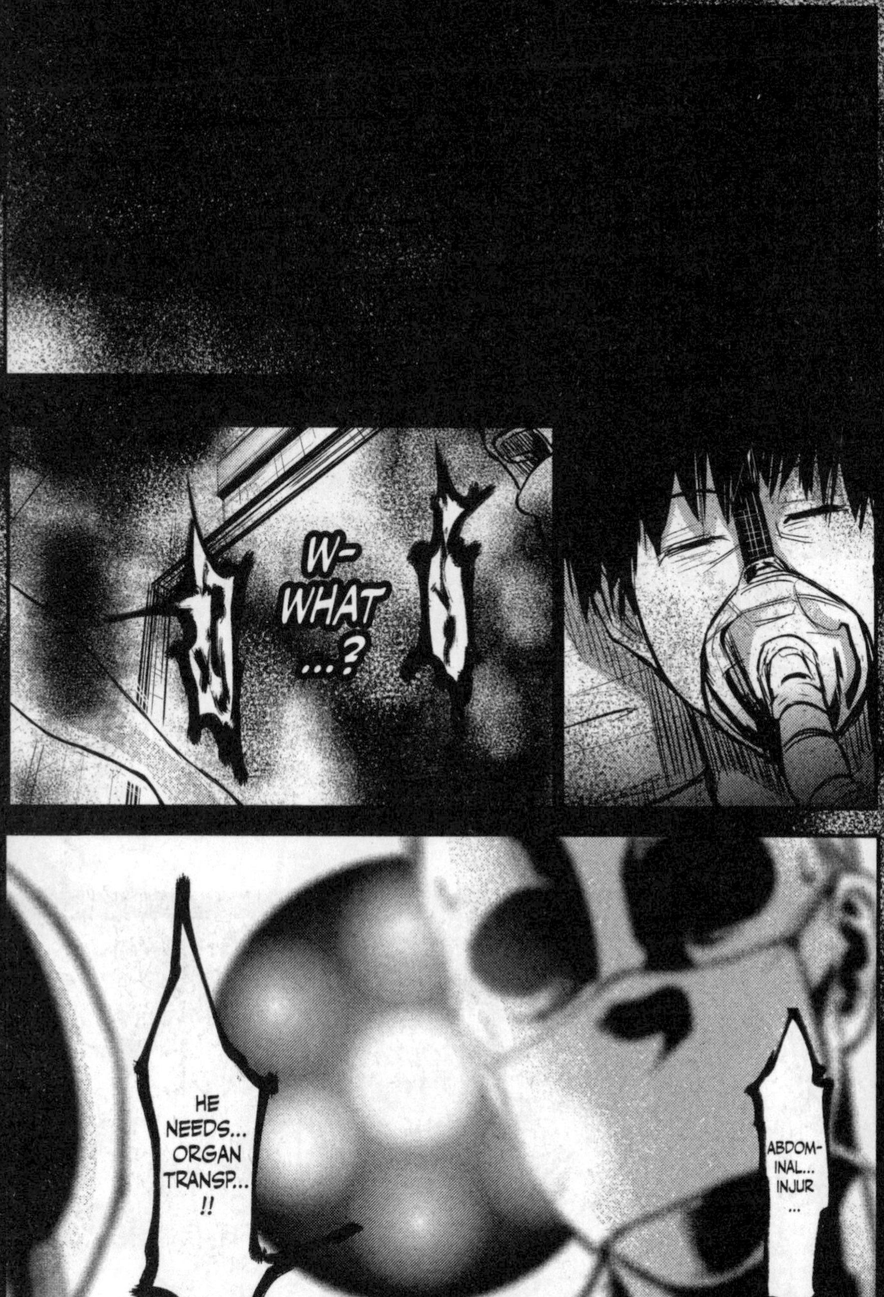
W-WHAT ...?
ABDOM-INAL... INJUR ...
HE NEEDS... ORGAN TRANSP... !!

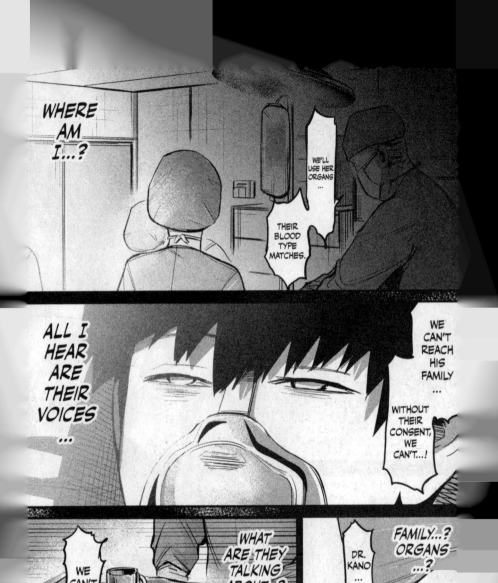

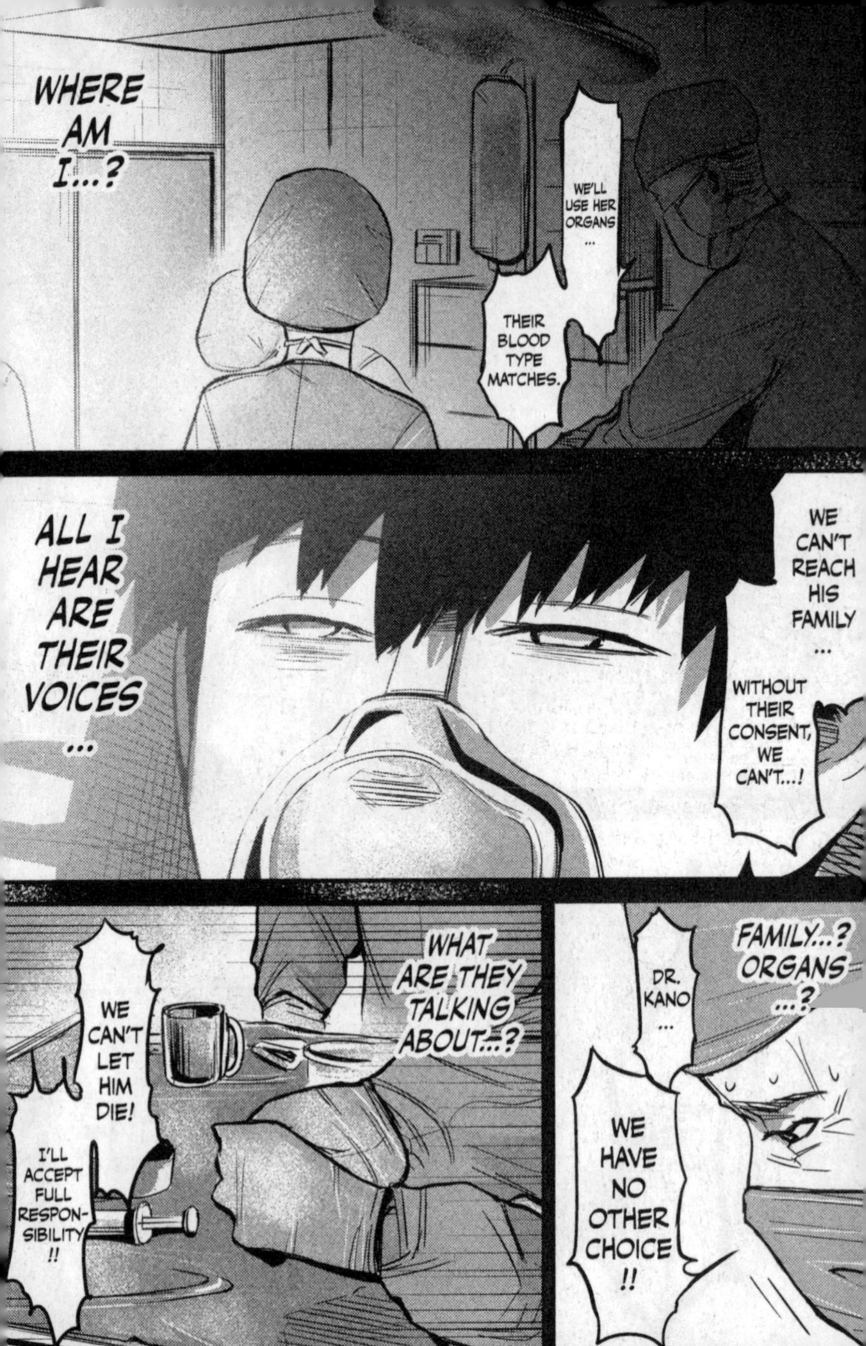
WE'LL USE HER ORGANS...
THEIR BLOOD TYPE MATCHES.
WHERE AM I...?
WE CAN'T REACH HIS FAMILY...
WITHOUT THEIR CONSENT, WE CAN'T...!
ALL I HEAR ARE THEIR VOICES...
FAMILY...? ORGANS...?
DR. KANO...
WE HAVE NO OTHER CHOICE!!
WHAT ARE THEY TALKING ABOUT...?
WE CAN'T LET HIM DIE!
I'LL ACCEPT FULL RESPONSIBILITY!!

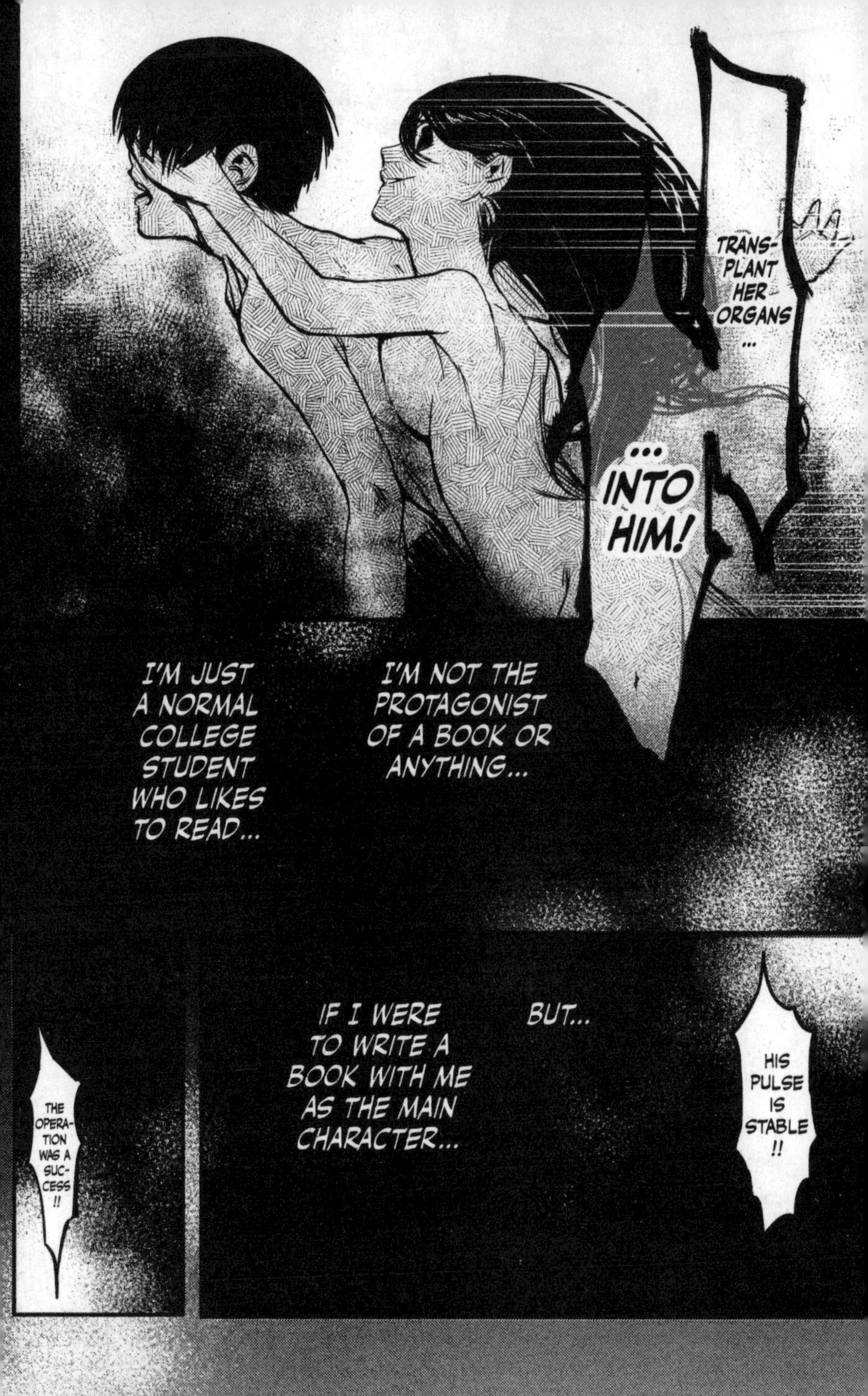
TRANS-PLANT HER ORGANS ...
... INTO HIM!
I'M NOT THE PROTAGONIST OF A BOOK OR ANYTHING...
I'M JUST A NORMAL COLLEGE STUDENT WHO LIKES TO READ...
HIS PULSE IS STABLE !!
BUT...
IF I WERE TO WRITE A BOOK WITH ME AS THE MAIN CHARACTER...
THE OPERA-TION WAS A SUC-CESS !!

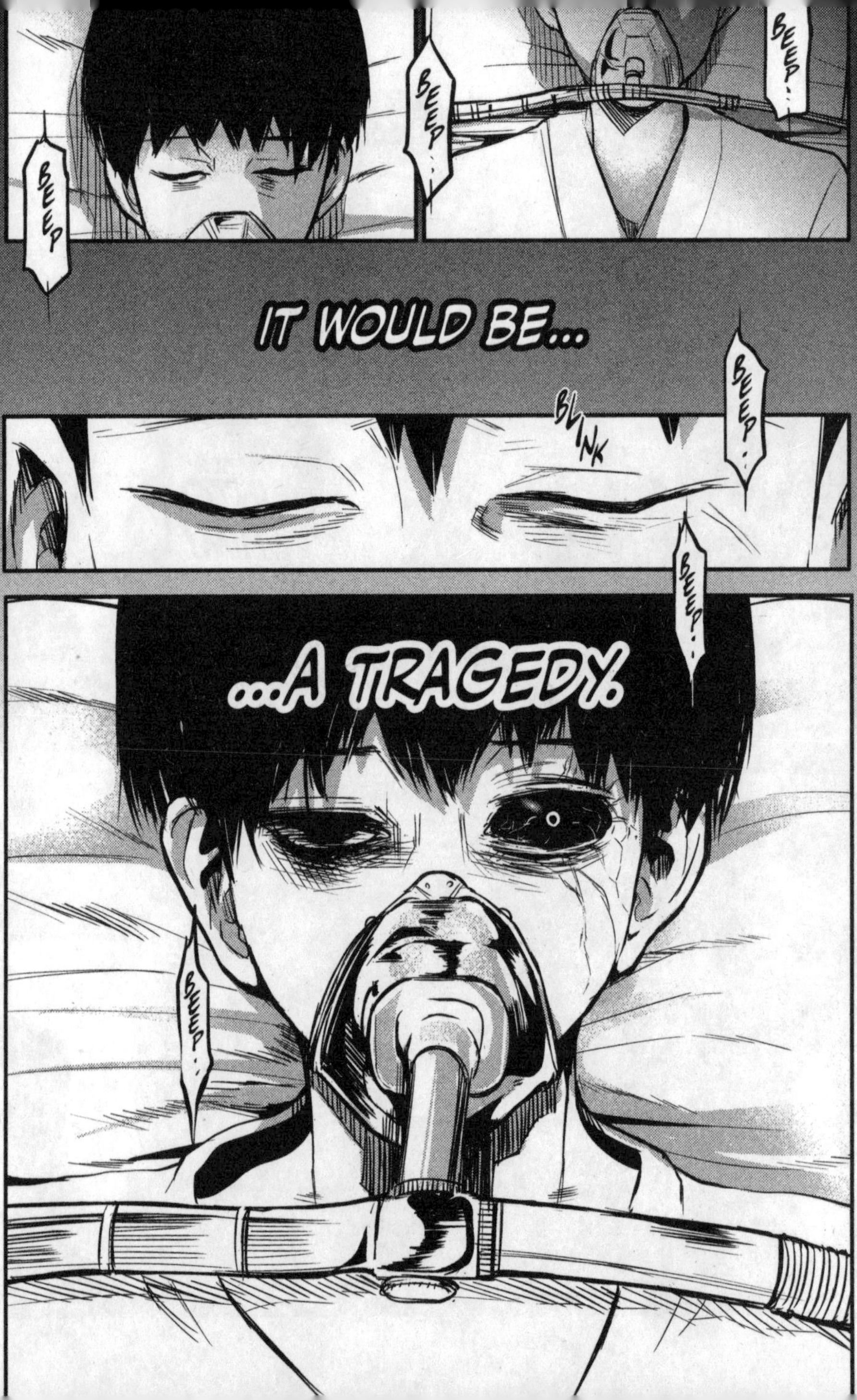
BEEP...
BEEP...
BEEP
BEEP...
IT WOULD BE...
BLINK
BEEP...
...A TRAGEDY.
BEEP...

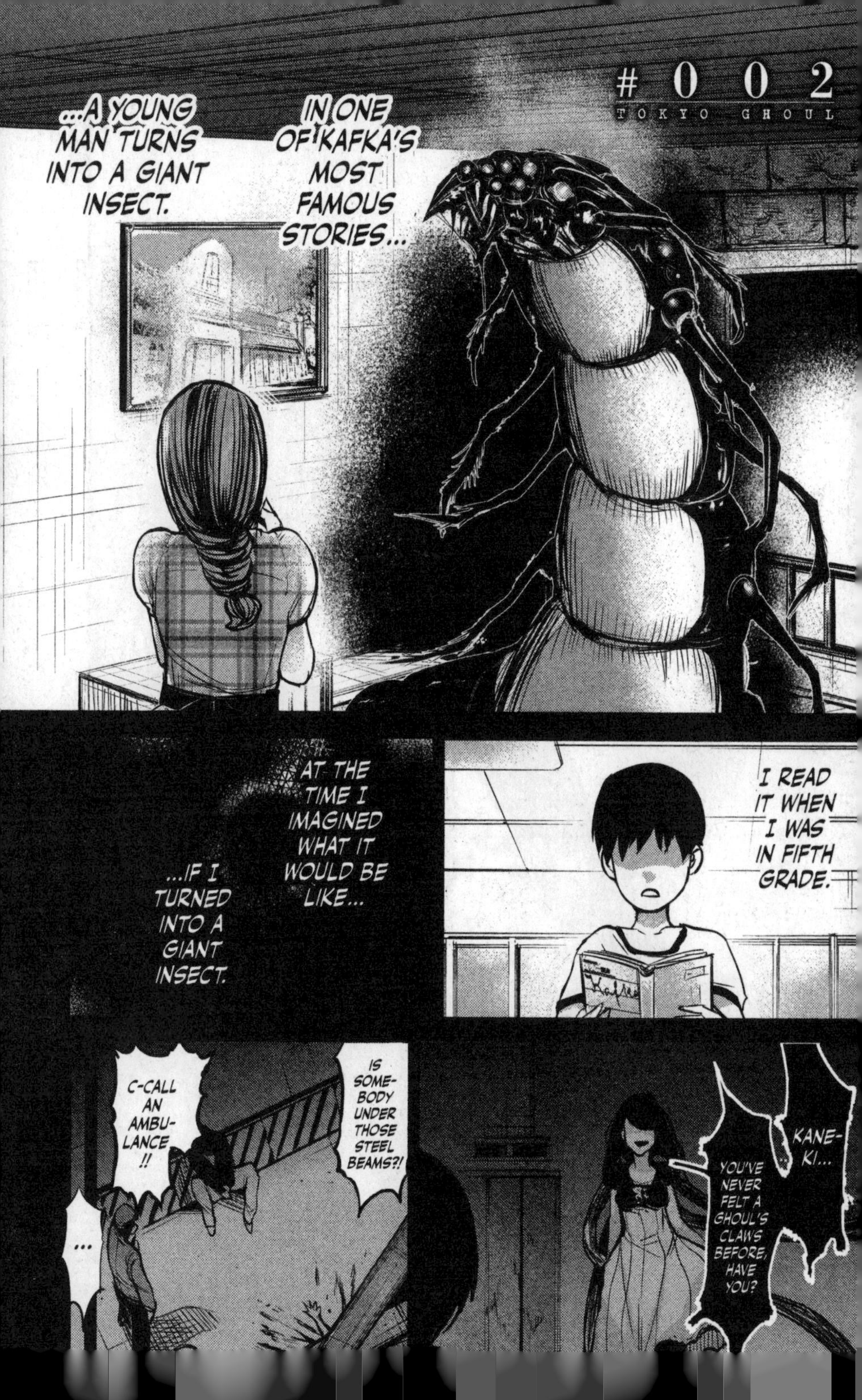
#002
TOKYO GHOUL
IN ONE OF KAFKA'S MOST FAMOUS STORIES...
...A YOUNG MAN TURNS INTO A GIANT INSECT.
I READ IT WHEN I WAS IN FIFTH GRADE.
AT THE TIME I IMAGINED WHAT IT WOULD BE LIKE...
...IF I TURNED INTO A GIANT INSECT.
KANE-KI...
YOU'VE NEVER FELT A GHOUL'S CLAWS BEFORE, HAVE YOU?
IS SOMEBODY UNDER THOSE STEEL BEAMS?!
C-CALL AN AMBULANCE!!
...

#002 [ODDITY]

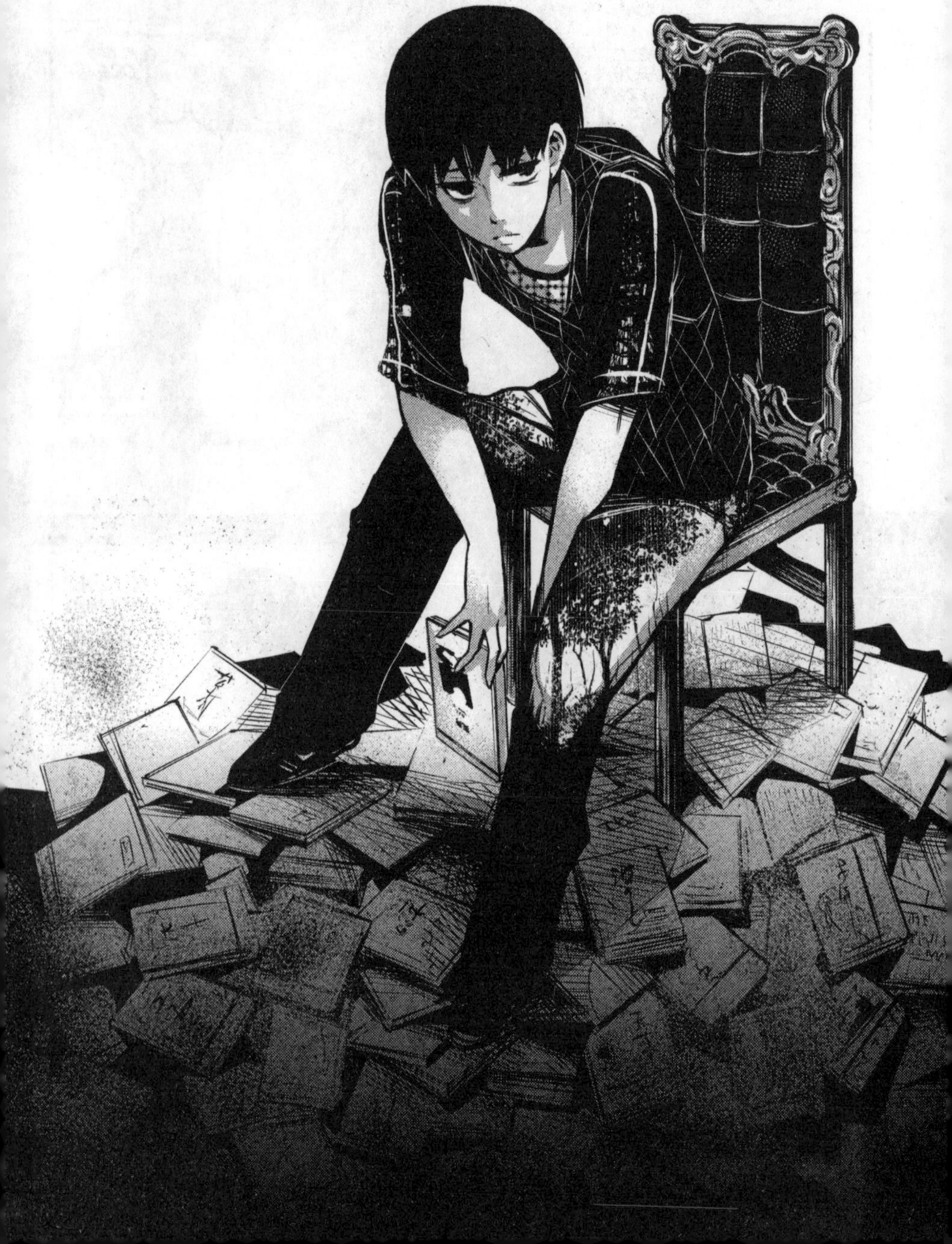

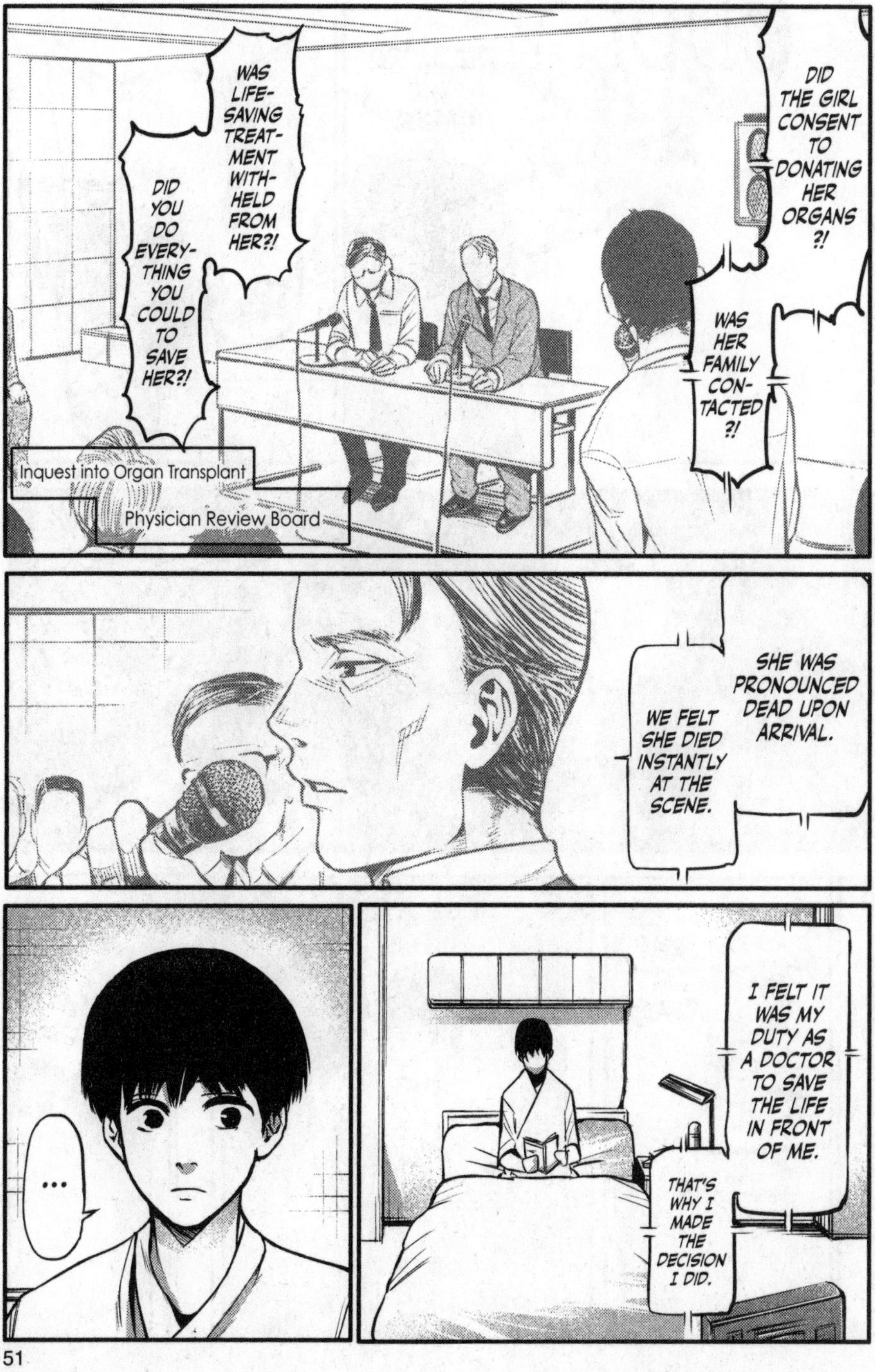
DID THE GIRL CONSENT TO DONATING HER ORGANS?!
WAS HER FAMILY CONTACTED?!
WAS LIFE-SAVING TREATMENT WITHHELD FROM HER?!
DID YOU DO EVERYTHING YOU COULD TO SAVE HER?!
Inquest into Organ Transplant
Physician Review Board
SHE WAS PRONOUNCED DEAD UPON ARRIVAL.
WE FELT SHE DIED INSTANTLY AT THE SCENE.
I FELT IT WAS MY DUTY AS A DOCTOR TO SAVE THE LIFE IN FRONT OF ME.
THAT'S WHY I MADE THE DECISION I DID.
...

THE MORE TIME PASSES...

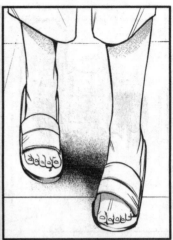

...SEEMS UNREAL.

...THE MORE THE INCIDENT THAT NIGHT...

SWf...

...THIS SCAR IS REAL.

BUT...

TOILET

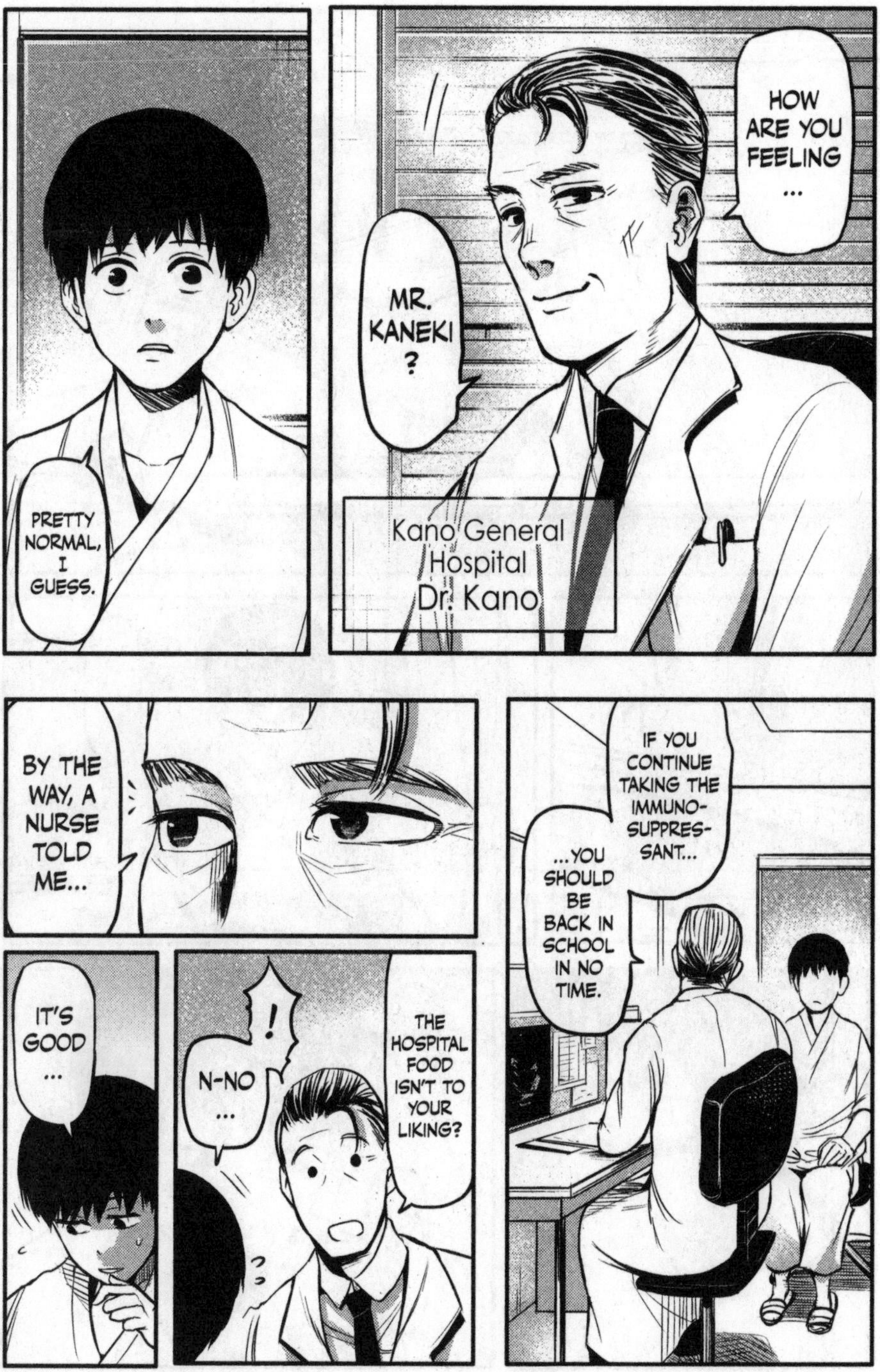
HOW ARE YOU FEELING ...
MR. KANEKI ?
Kano General Hospital
Dr. Kano
PRETTY NORMAL, I GUESS.
IF YOU CONTINUE TAKING THE IMMUNO-SUPPRES-SANT...
...YOU SHOULD BE BACK IN SCHOOL IN NO TIME.
BY THE WAY, A NURSE TOLD ME...
THE HOSPITAL FOOD ISN'T TO YOUR LIKING?
!
N-NO ...
IT'S GOOD ...

...
TK
MNCH

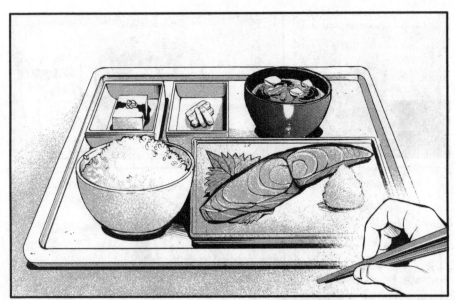

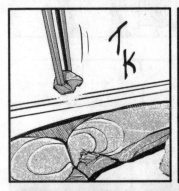

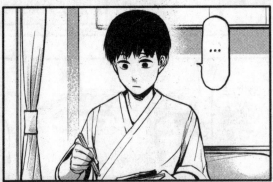

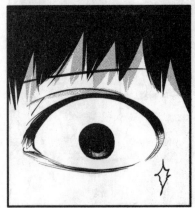

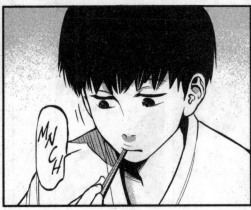

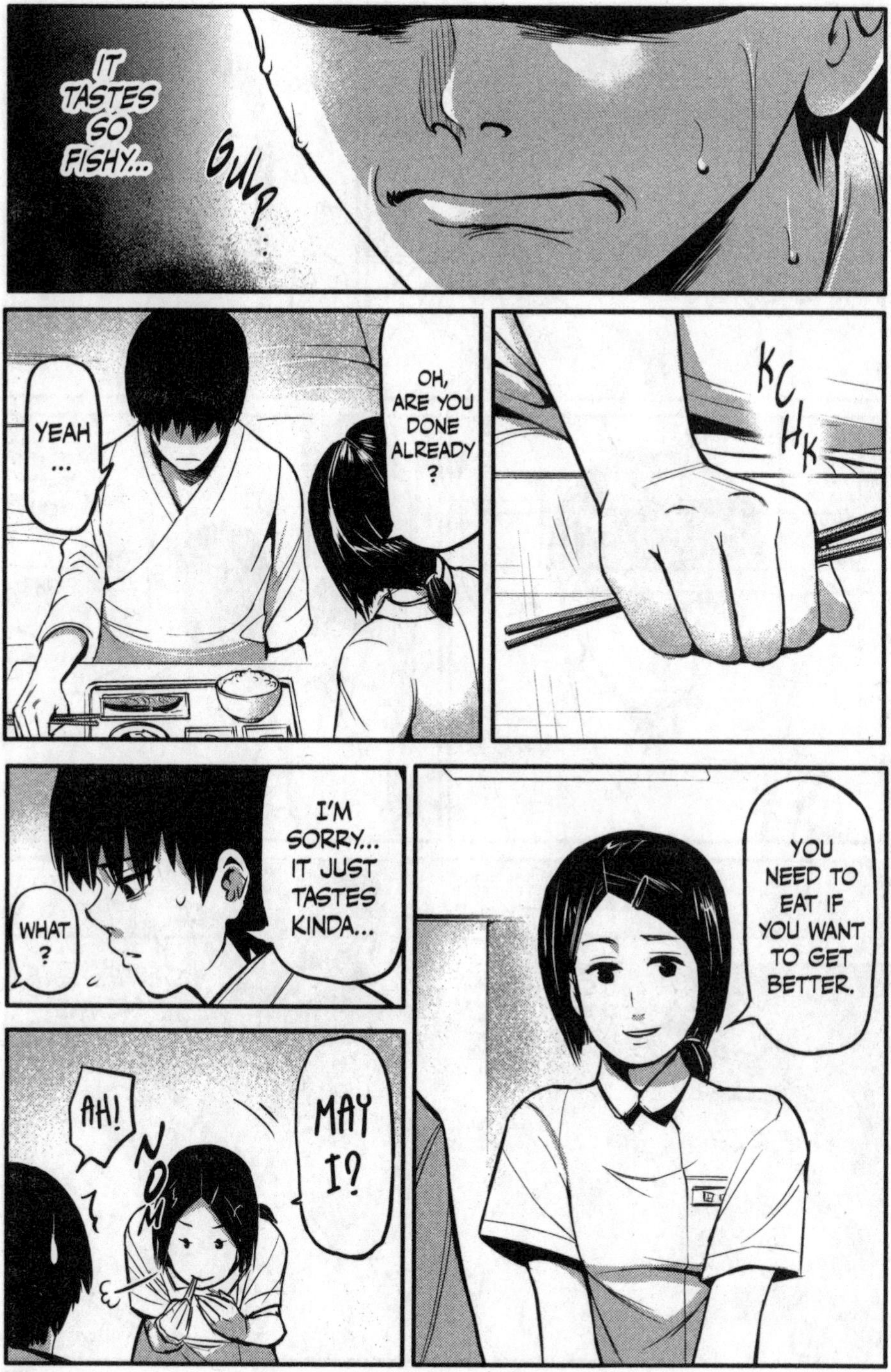
IT TASTES SO FISHY...
GULP...
KCHHK
OH, ARE YOU DONE ALREADY?
YEAH...
YOU NEED TO EAT IF YOU WANT TO GET BETTER.
I'M SORRY... IT JUST TASTES KINDA...
WHAT?
MAY I?
NOM
AH!

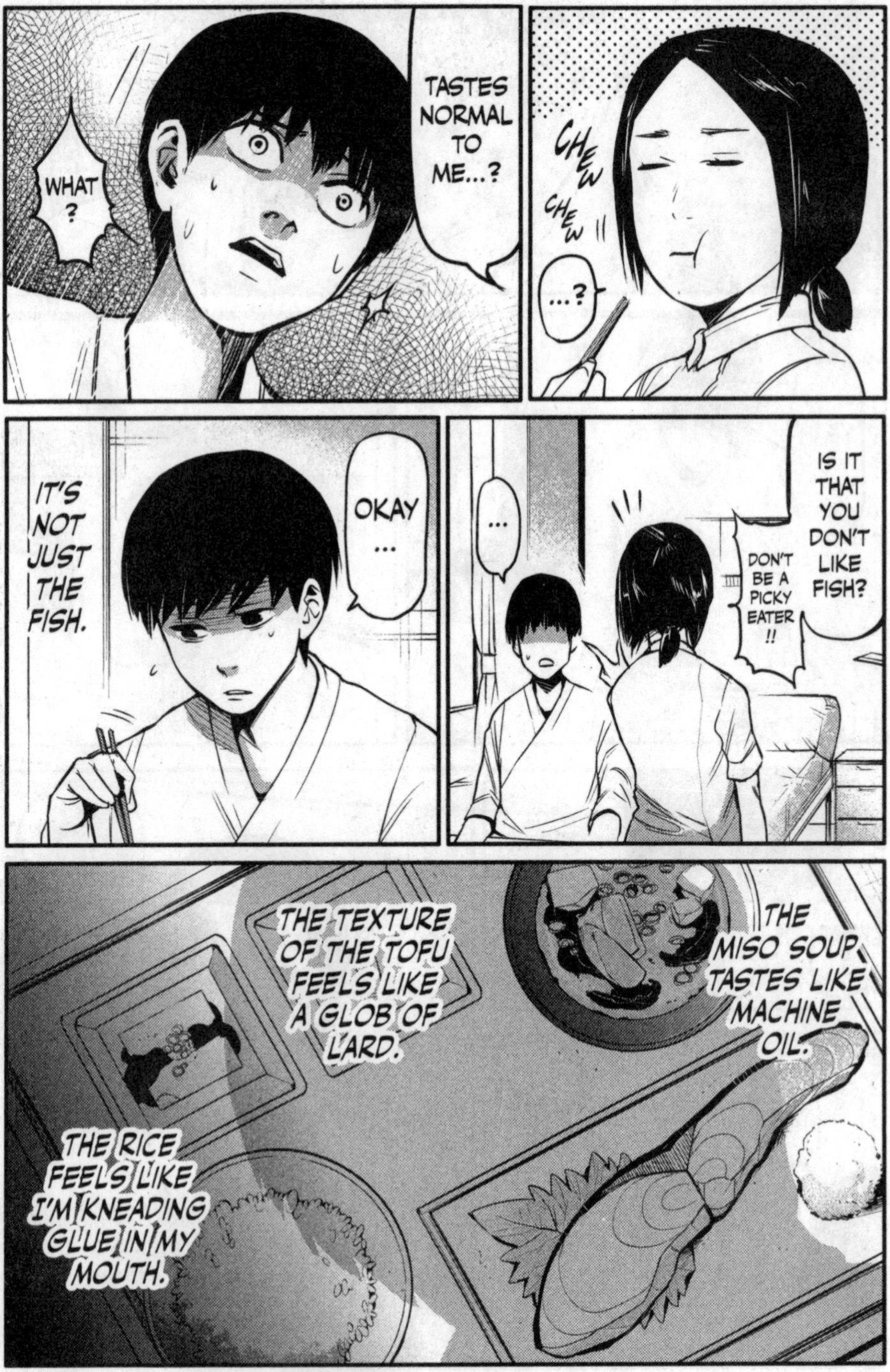
CHEW
CHEW
...?
TASTES NORMAL TO ME...?
WHAT?
IS IT THAT YOU DON'T LIKE FISH?
DON'T BE A PICKY EATER!!
...
OKAY...
IT'S NOT JUST THE FISH.
THE MISO SOUP TASTES LIKE MACHINE OIL.
THE TEXTURE OF THE TOFU FEELS LIKE A GLOB OF LARD.
THE RICE FEELS LIKE I'M KNEADING GLUE IN MY MOUTH.

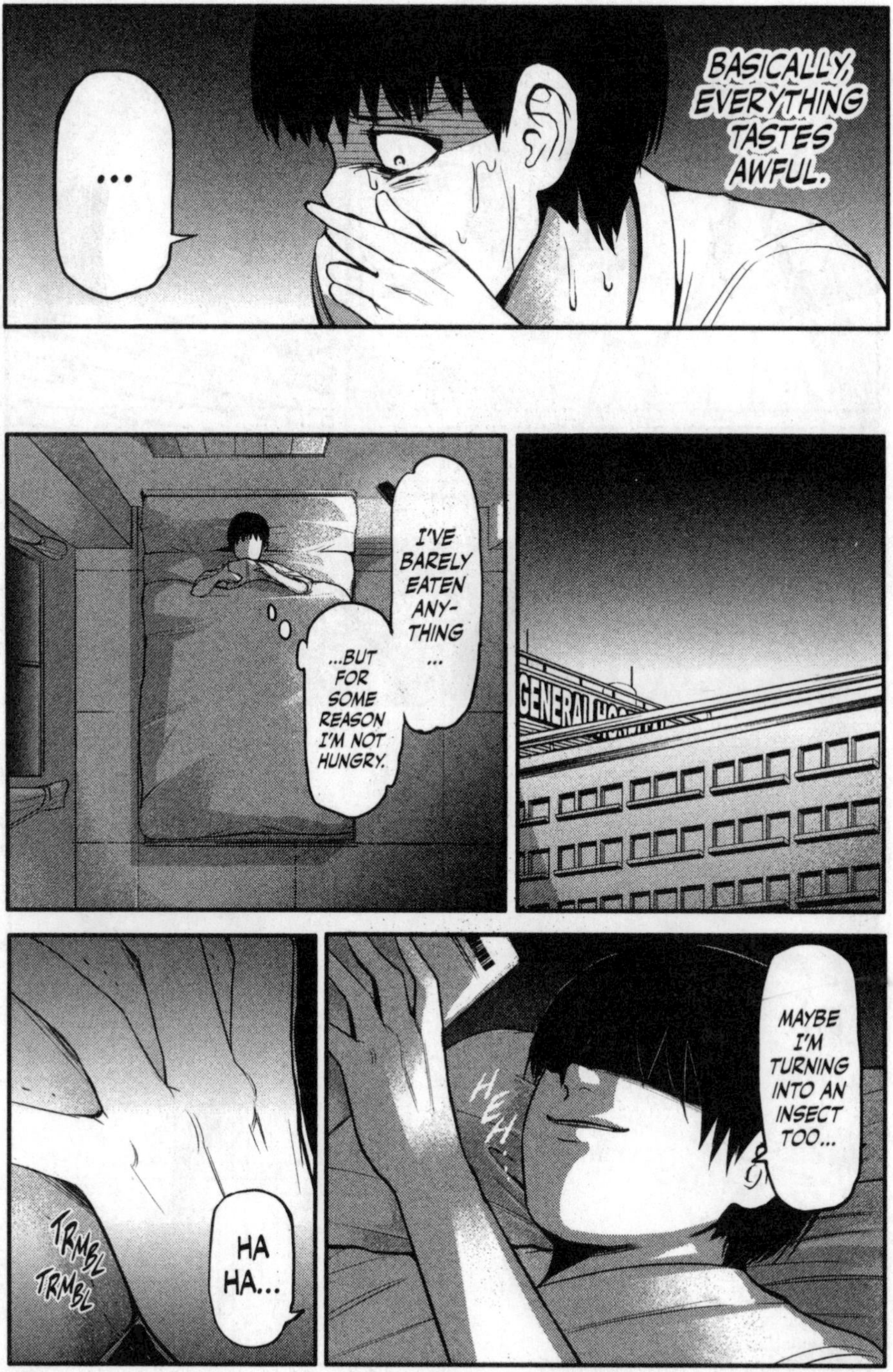
BASICALLY, EVERYTHING TASTES AWFUL.
...
I'VE BARELY EATEN ANYTHING...
...BUT FOR SOME REASON I'M NOT HUNGRY.
MAYBE I'M TURNING INTO AN INSECT TOO...
HEH
HA HA...
TRMBL TRMBL

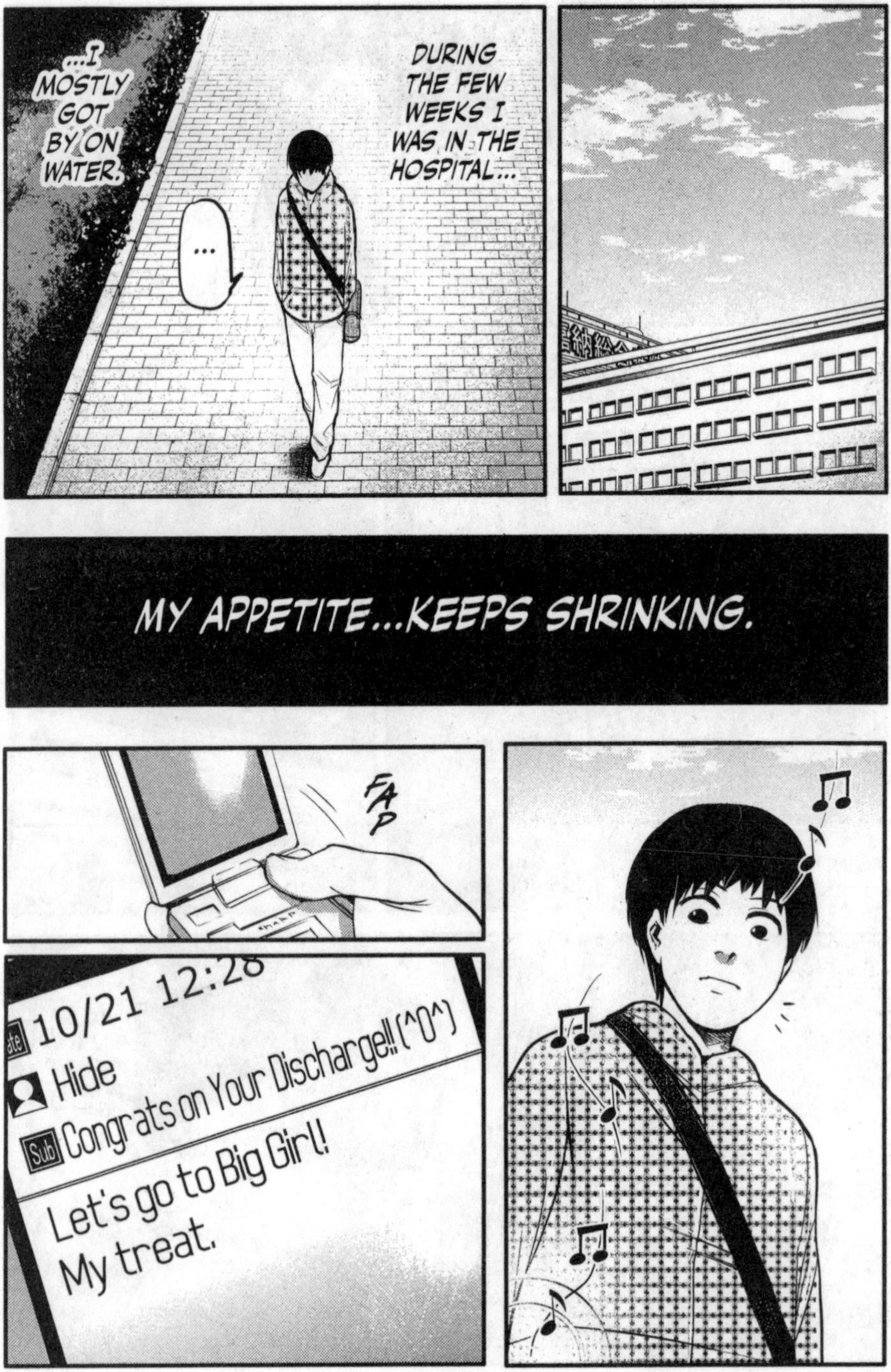
DURING THE FEW WEEKS I WAS IN THE HOSPITAL...
...I MOSTLY GOT BY ON WATER.
...
MY APPETITE...KEEPS SHRINKING.
FAP
10/21 12:28
Hide
Congrats on Your Discharge!! (^O^)
Sub
Let's go to Big Girl!
My treat.

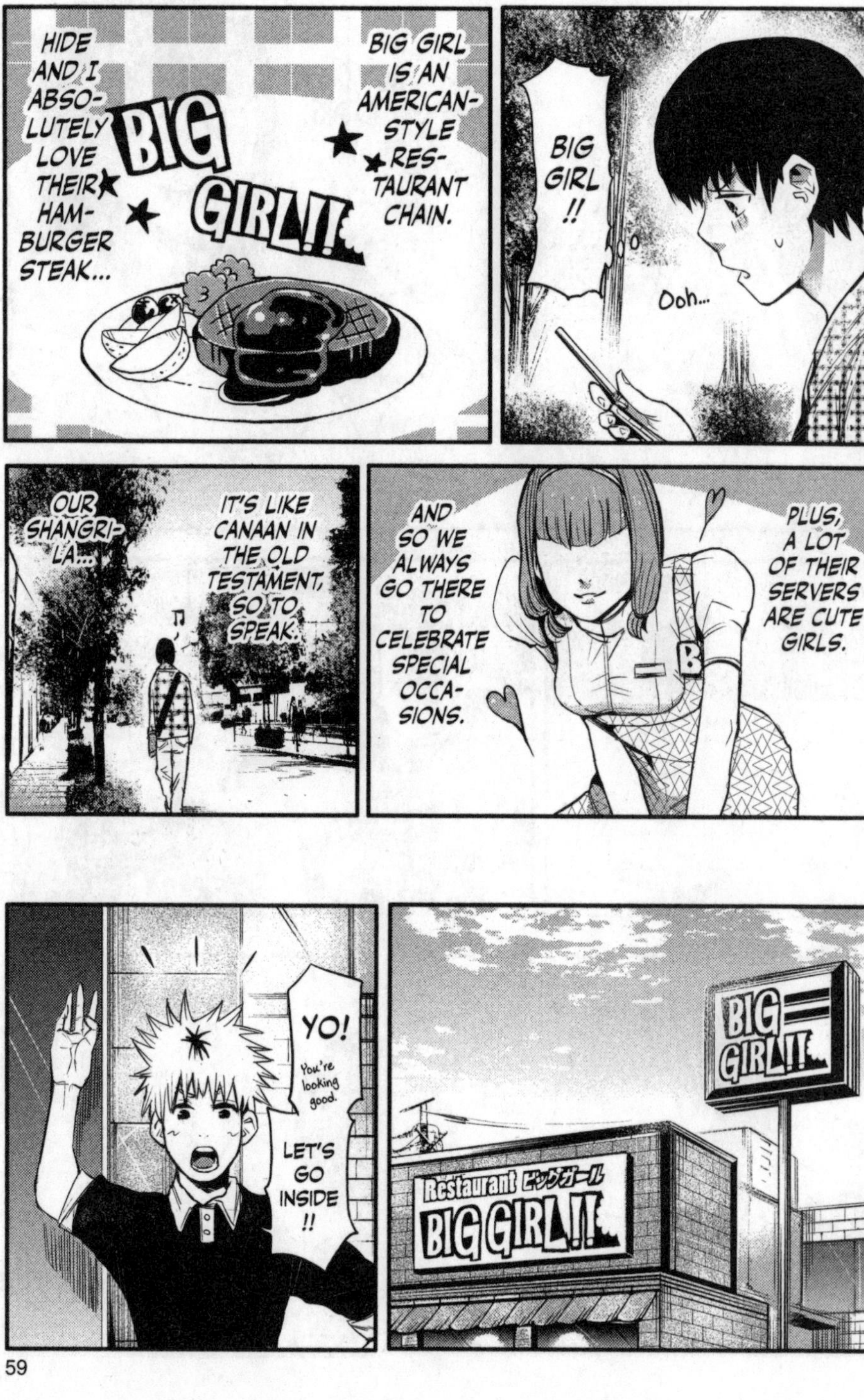

BIG GIRL !!
Ooh...
BIG GIRL IS AN AMERICAN-STYLE RESTAURANT CHAIN.
HIDE AND I ABSOLUTELY LOVE THEIR HAMBURGER STEAK...
BIG GIRL!!
PLUS, A LOT OF THEIR SERVERS ARE CUTE GIRLS.
AND SO WE ALWAYS GO THERE TO CELEBRATE SPECIAL OCCASIONS.
B
IT'S LIKE CANAAN IN THE OLD TESTAMENT, SO TO SPEAK.
OUR SHANGRI-LA...
BIG GIRL!!
Restaurant ビッグガール
BIG GIRL!!
YO!
You're looking good.
LET'S GO INSIDE !!

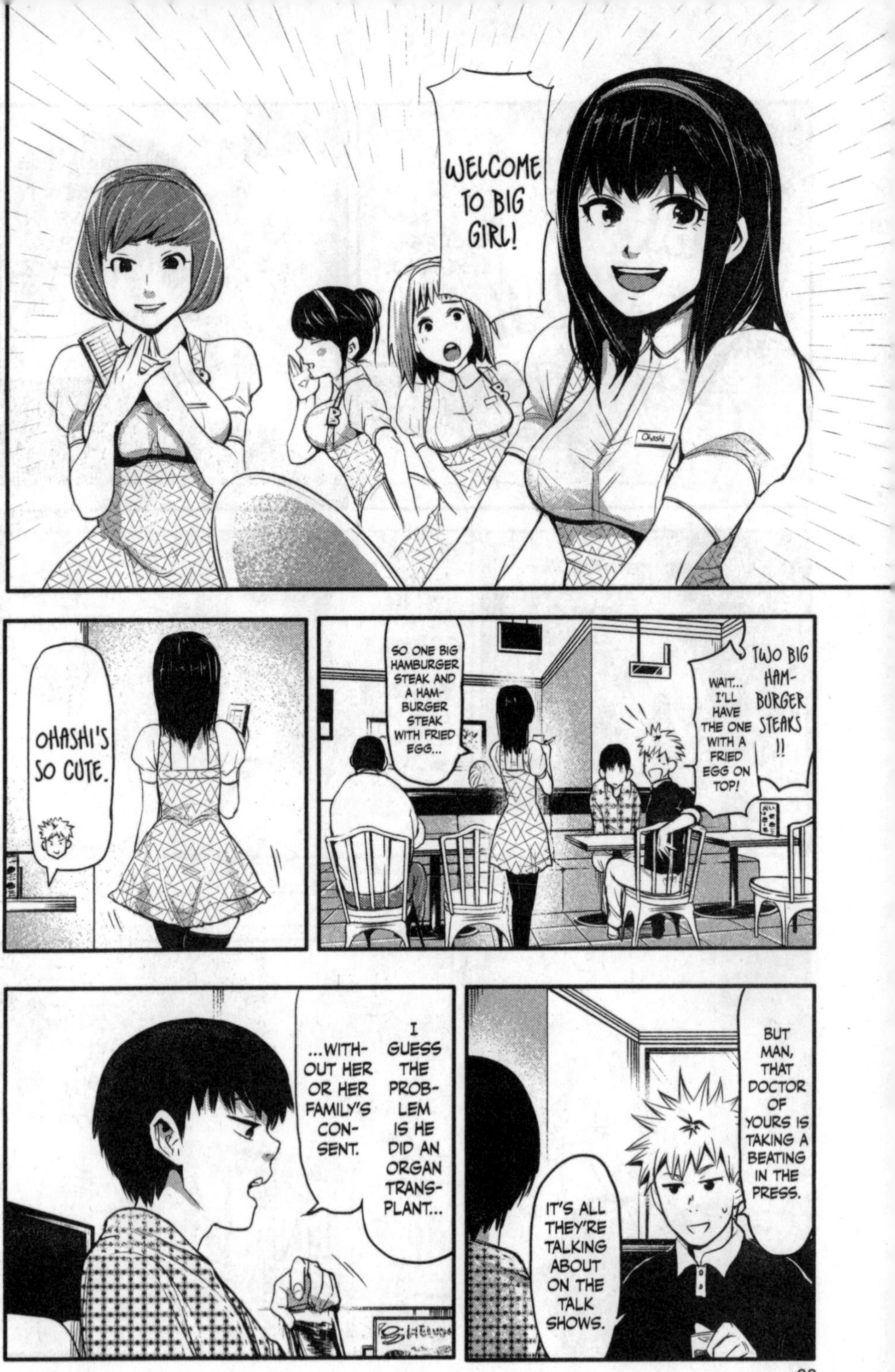
WELCOME TO BIG GIRL!
TWO BIG HAMBURGER STEAKS!!
WAIT... I'LL HAVE THE ONE WITH A FRIED EGG ON TOP!
SO ONE BIG HAMBURGER STEAK AND A HAMBURGER STEAK WITH FRIED EGG...
OHASHI'S SO CUTE.
BUT MAN, THAT DOCTOR OF YOURS IS TAKING A BEATING IN THE PRESS.
IT'S ALL THEY'RE TALKING ABOUT ON THE TALK SHOWS.
I GUESS THE PROBLEM IS HE DID AN ORGAN TRANSPLANT...
...WITHOUT HER OR HER FAMILY'S CONSENT.

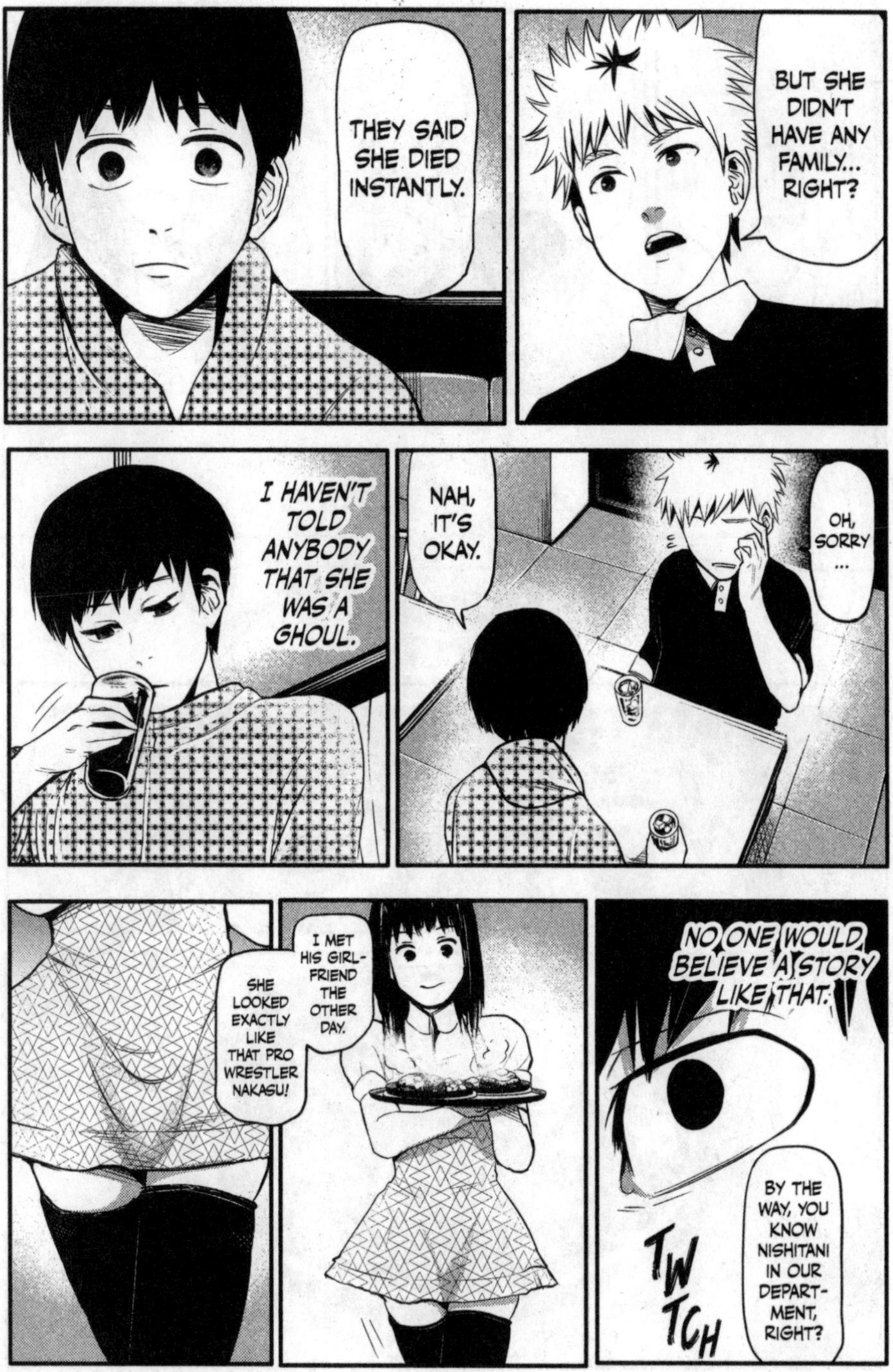
BUT SHE DIDN'T HAVE ANY FAMILY... RIGHT?
THEY SAID SHE DIED INSTANTLY.
OH, SORRY ...
NAH, IT'S OKAY.
I HAVEN'T TOLD ANYBODY THAT SHE WAS A GHOUL.
NO ONE WOULD BELIEVE A STORY LIKE THAT.
TWTCH
BY THE WAY, YOU KNOW NISHITANI IN OUR DEPARTMENT, RIGHT?
I MET HIS GIRLFRIEND THE OTHER DAY.
SHE LOOKED EXACTLY LIKE THAT PRO WRESTLER NAKASU!

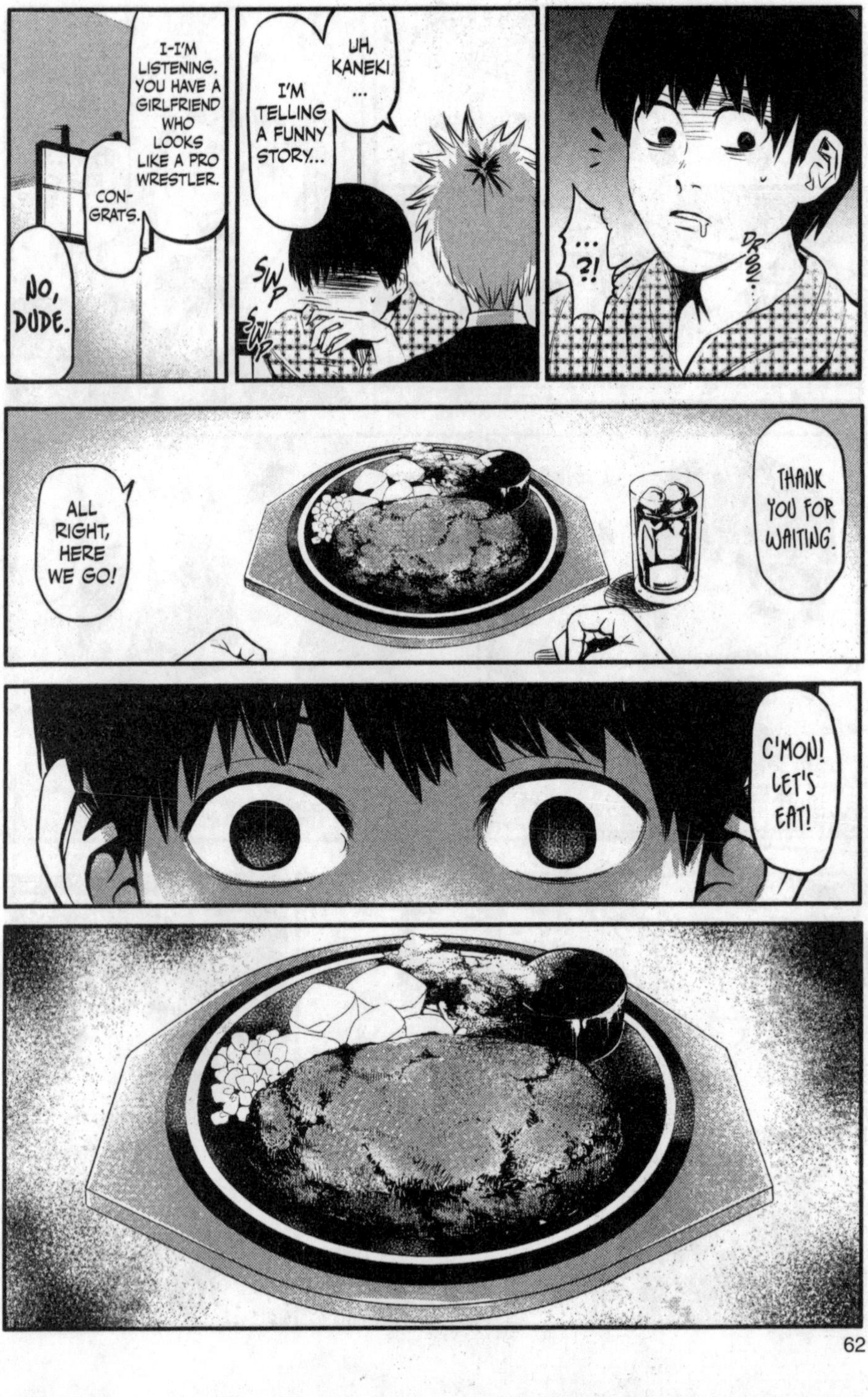
...?!
DROOL...
UH, KANEKI ...
I'M TELLING A FUNNY STORY...
SWP SWP
I-I'M LISTENING. YOU HAVE A GIRLFRIEND WHO LOOKS LIKE A PRO WRESTLER.
CON-GRATS.
NO, DUDE.
THANK YOU FOR WAITING.
ALL RIGHT, HERE WE GO!
C'MON! LET'S EAT!

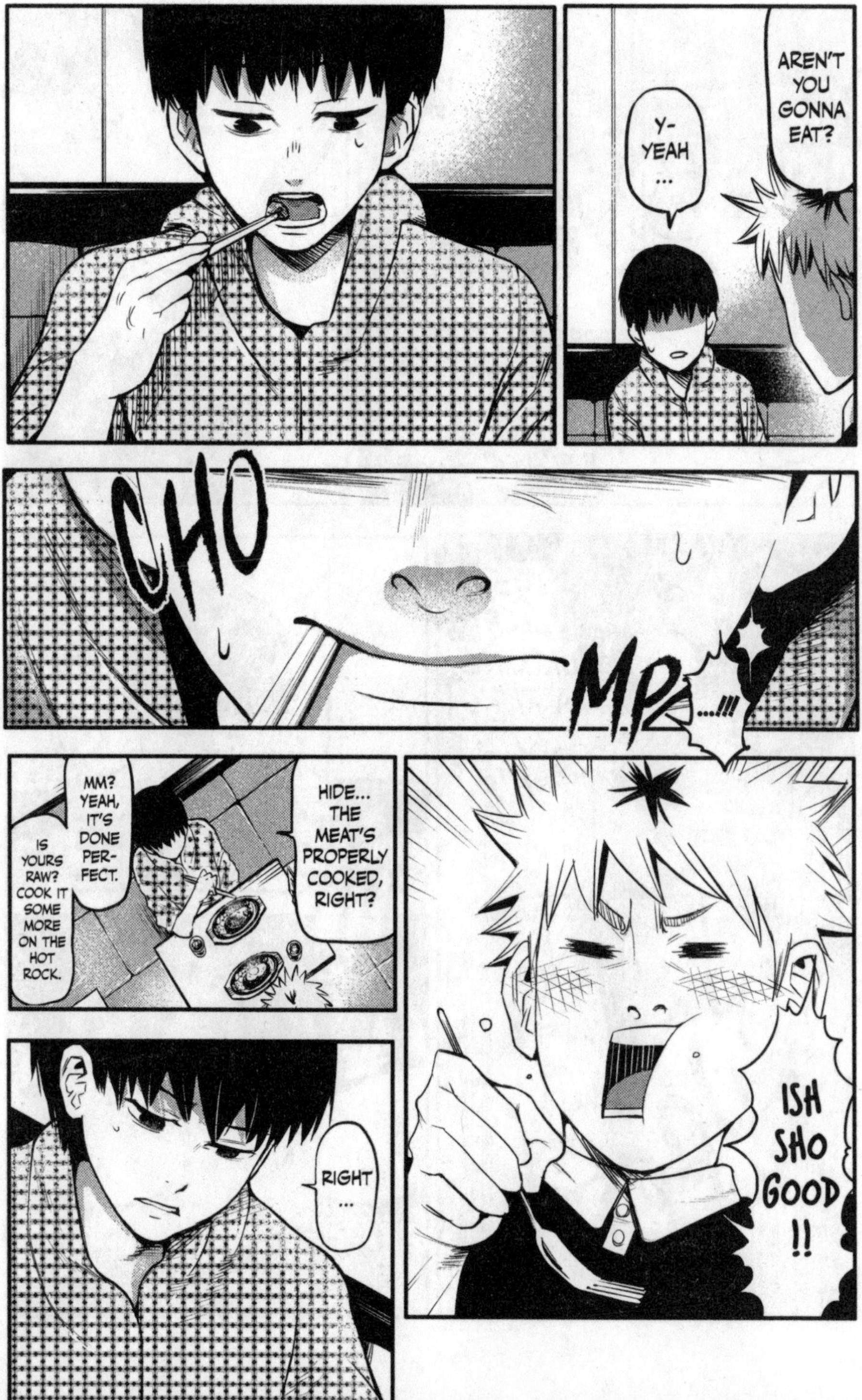

AREN'T YOU GONNA EAT?
Y-YEAH ...
CHOMP ...!!!
ISH SHO GOOD !!
HIDE... THE MEAT'S PROPERLY COOKED, RIGHT?
MM? YEAH, IT'S DONE PER-FECT.
IS YOURS RAW? COOK IT SOME MORE ON THE HOT ROCK.
RIGHT ...

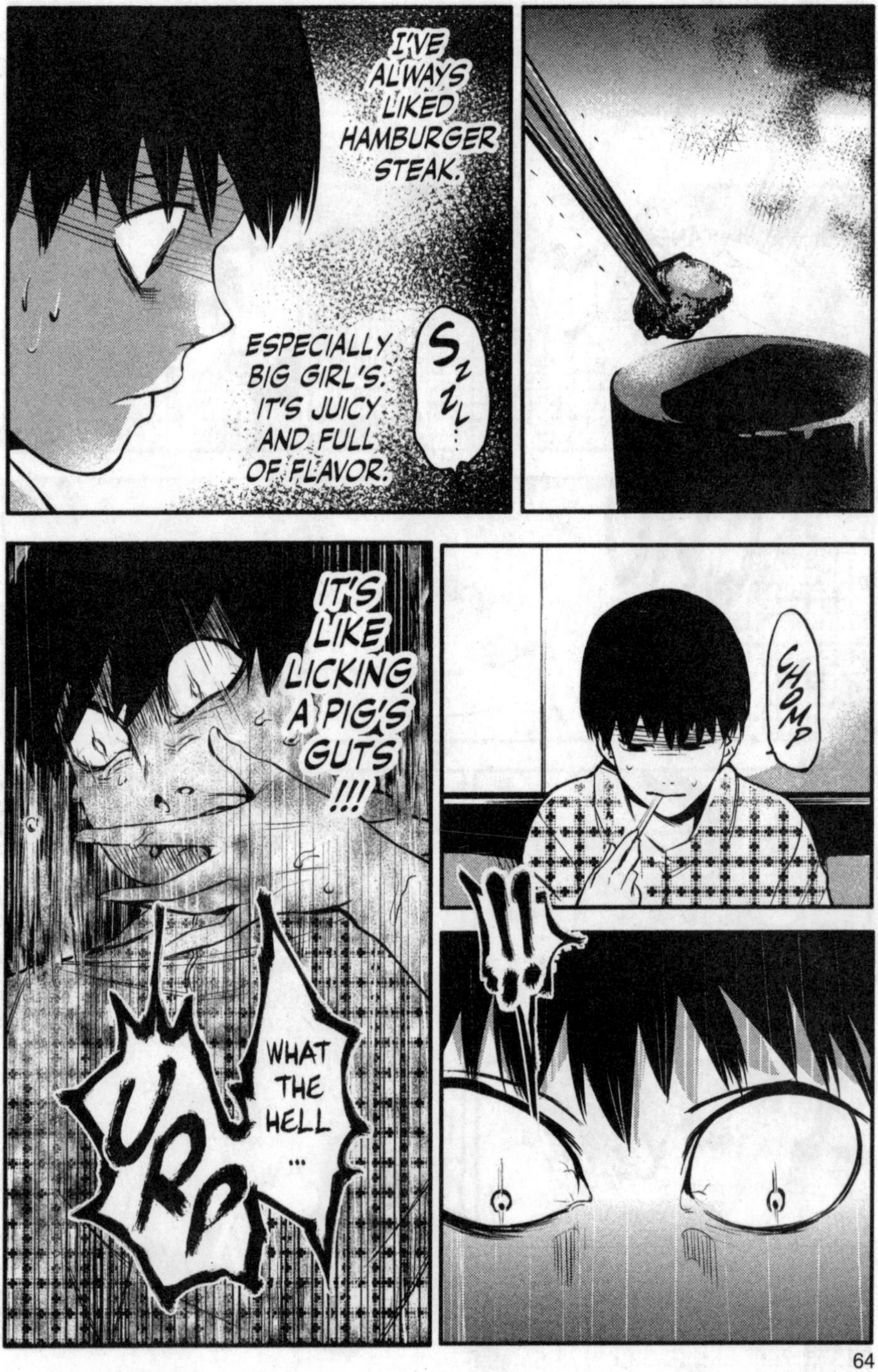
I'VE ALWAYS LIKED HAMBURGER STEAK.
ESPECIALLY BIG GIRL'S. IT'S JUICY AND FULL OF FLAVOR.
Szzl...
CHOMP
!!
IT'S LIKE LICKING A PIG'S GUTS!!!
WHAT THE HELL...
URP

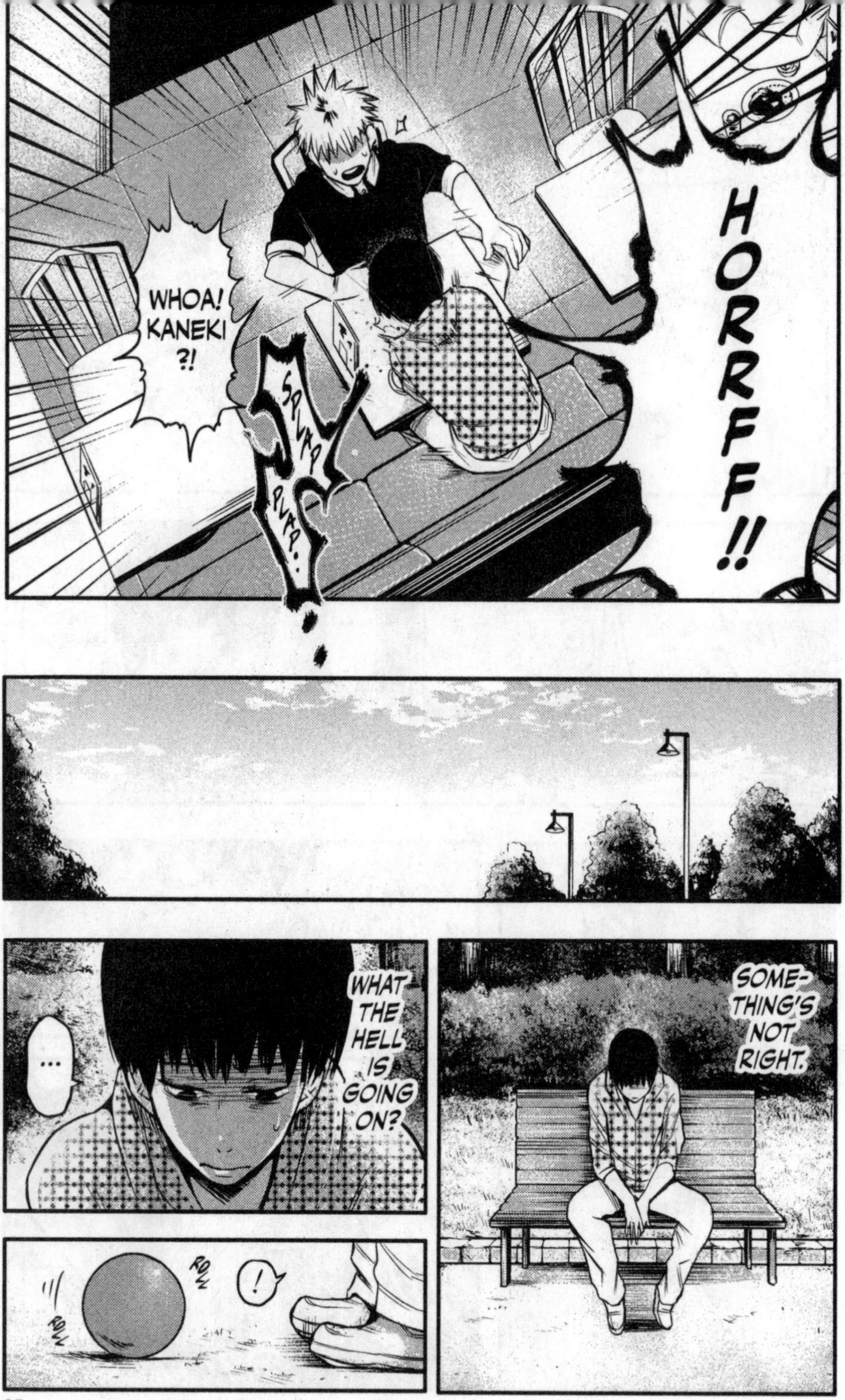
HORRFF!!
SPLAP PLAP...
WHOA! KANEKI ?!
SOME-THING'S NOT RIGHT.
WHAT THE HELL IS GOING ON?
...
!
ROLL
ROLL

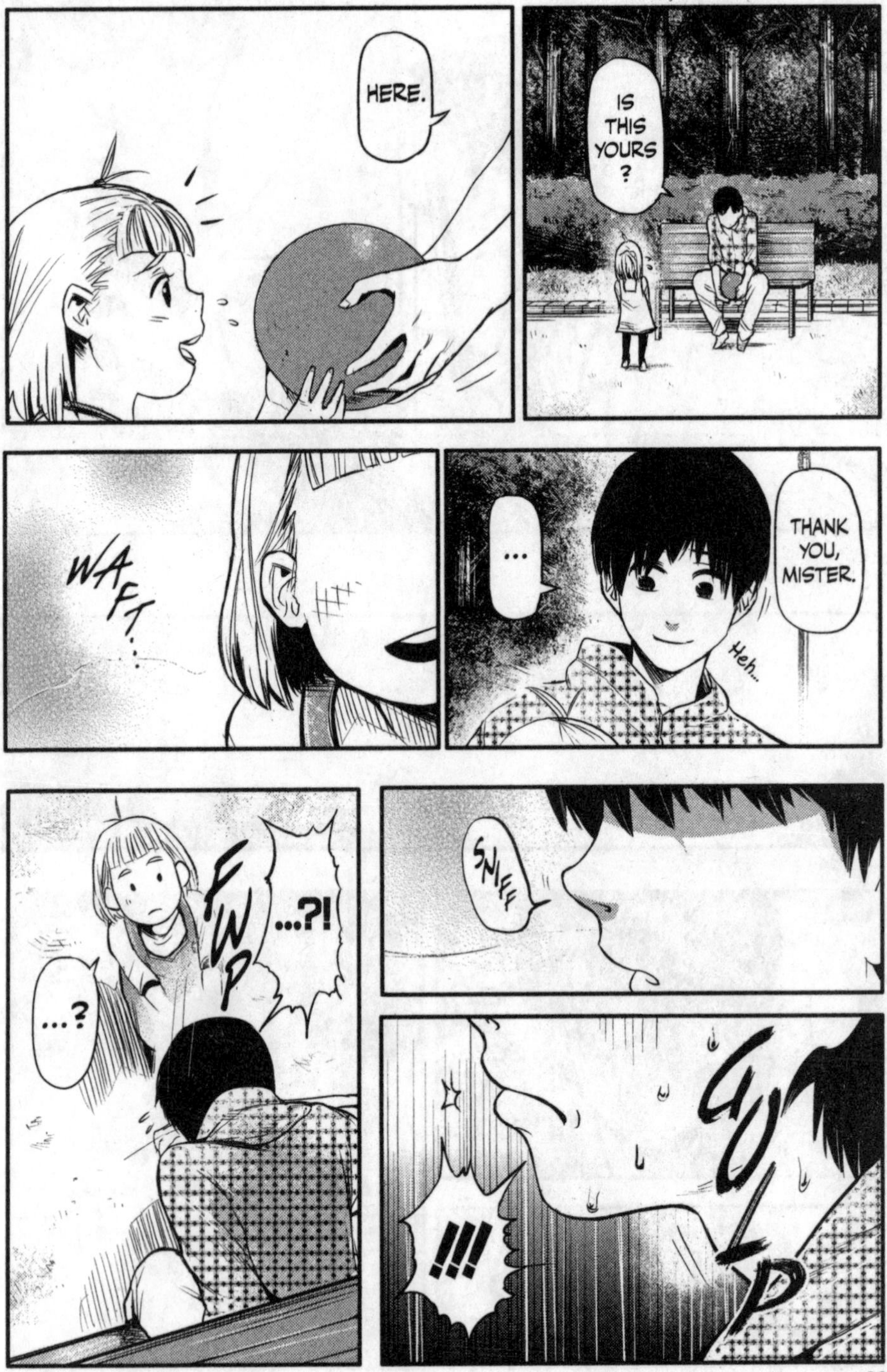
IS THIS YOURS ?
HERE.
THANK YOU, MISTER.
Heh...
...
WAFT...
SNIFF
GULP
!!!
FWP
...?!
...?

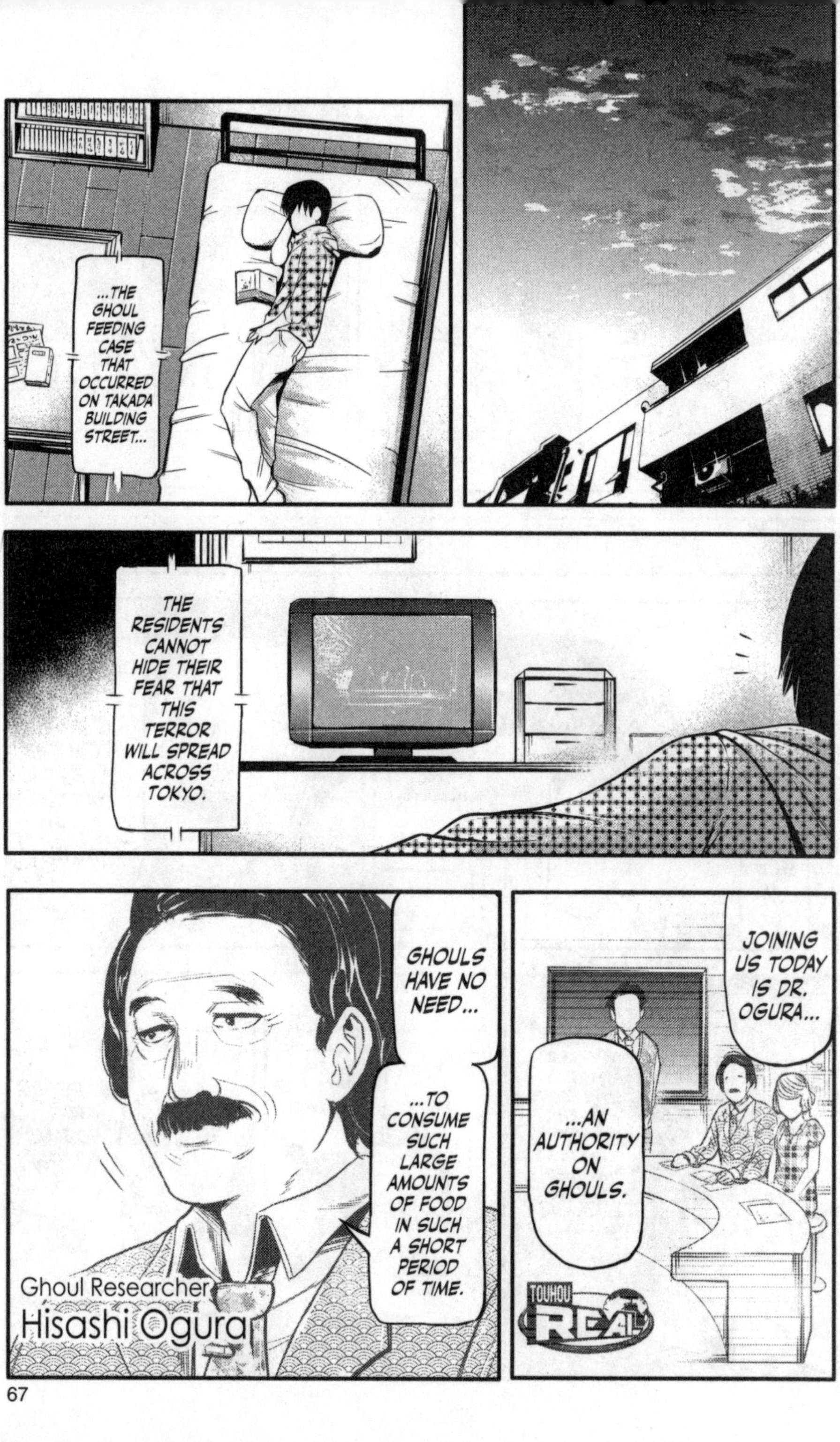
...THE GHOUL FEEDING CASE THAT OCCURRED ON TAKADA BUILDING STREET...
THE RESIDENTS CANNOT HIDE THEIR FEAR THAT THIS TERROR WILL SPREAD ACROSS TOKYO.
JOINING US TODAY IS DR. OGURA...
...AN AUTHORITY ON GHOULS.
TOUHOU REAL
GHOULS HAVE NO NEED...
...TO CONSUME SUCH LARGE AMOUNTS OF FOOD IN SUCH A SHORT PERIOD OF TIME.
Ghoul Researcher
Hisashi Ogura

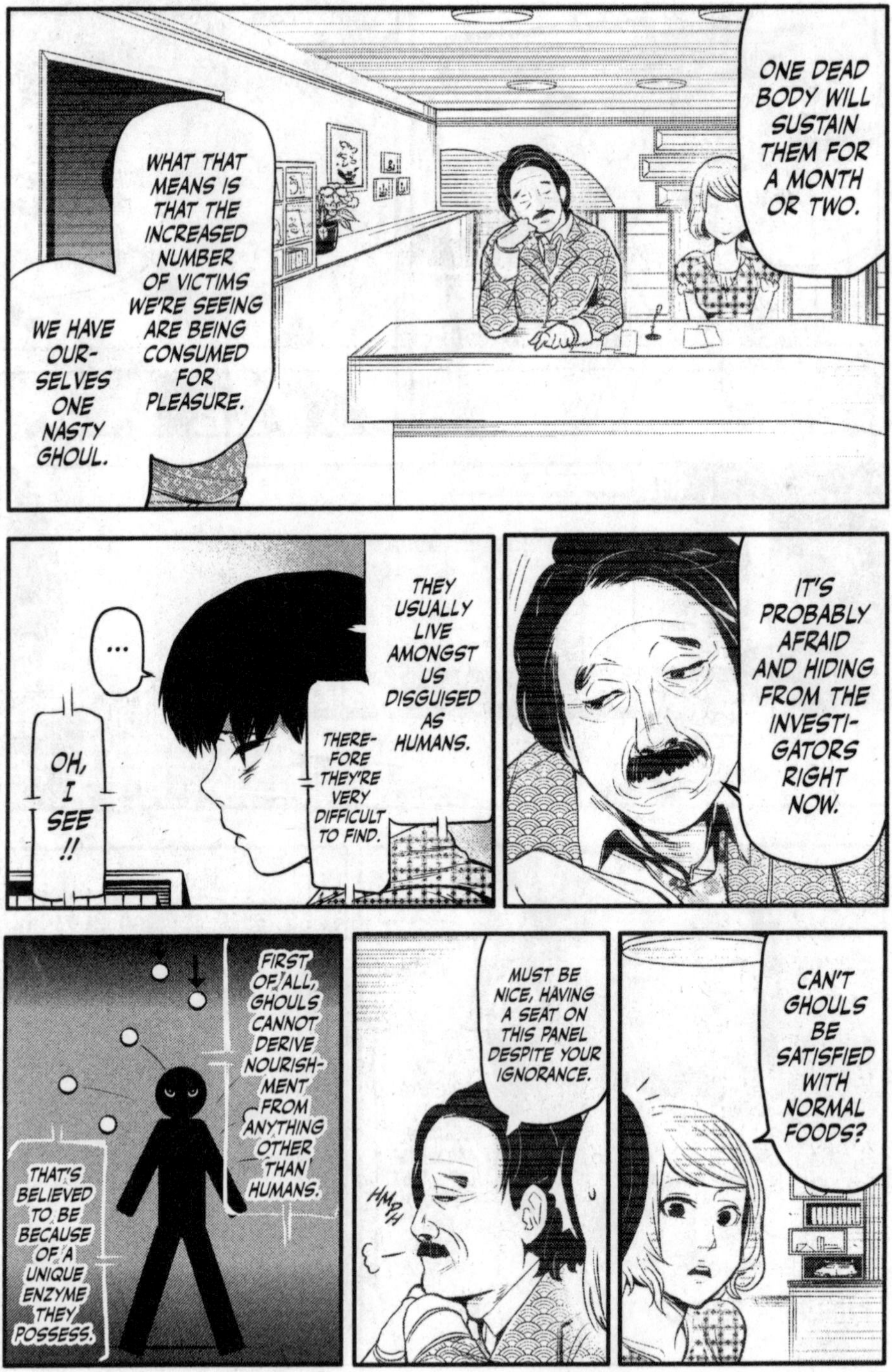
ONE DEAD BODY WILL SUSTAIN THEM FOR A MONTH OR TWO.
WHAT THAT MEANS IS THAT THE INCREASED NUMBER OF VICTIMS WE'RE SEEING ARE BEING CONSUMED FOR PLEASURE.
WE HAVE OURSELVES ONE NASTY GHOUL.
IT'S PROBABLY AFRAID AND HIDING FROM THE INVESTIGATORS RIGHT NOW.
THEY USUALLY LIVE AMONGST US DISGUISED AS HUMANS.
THEREFORE THEY'RE VERY DIFFICULT TO FIND.
...
OH, I SEE!!
CAN'T GHOULS BE SATISFIED WITH NORMAL FOODS?
MUST BE NICE, HAVING A SEAT ON THIS PANEL DESPITE YOUR IGNORANCE.
HMPH
FIRST OF ALL, GHOULS CANNOT DERIVE NOURISHMENT FROM ANYTHING OTHER THAN HUMANS.
THAT'S BELIEVED TO BE BECAUSE OF A UNIQUE ENZYME THEY POSSESS.

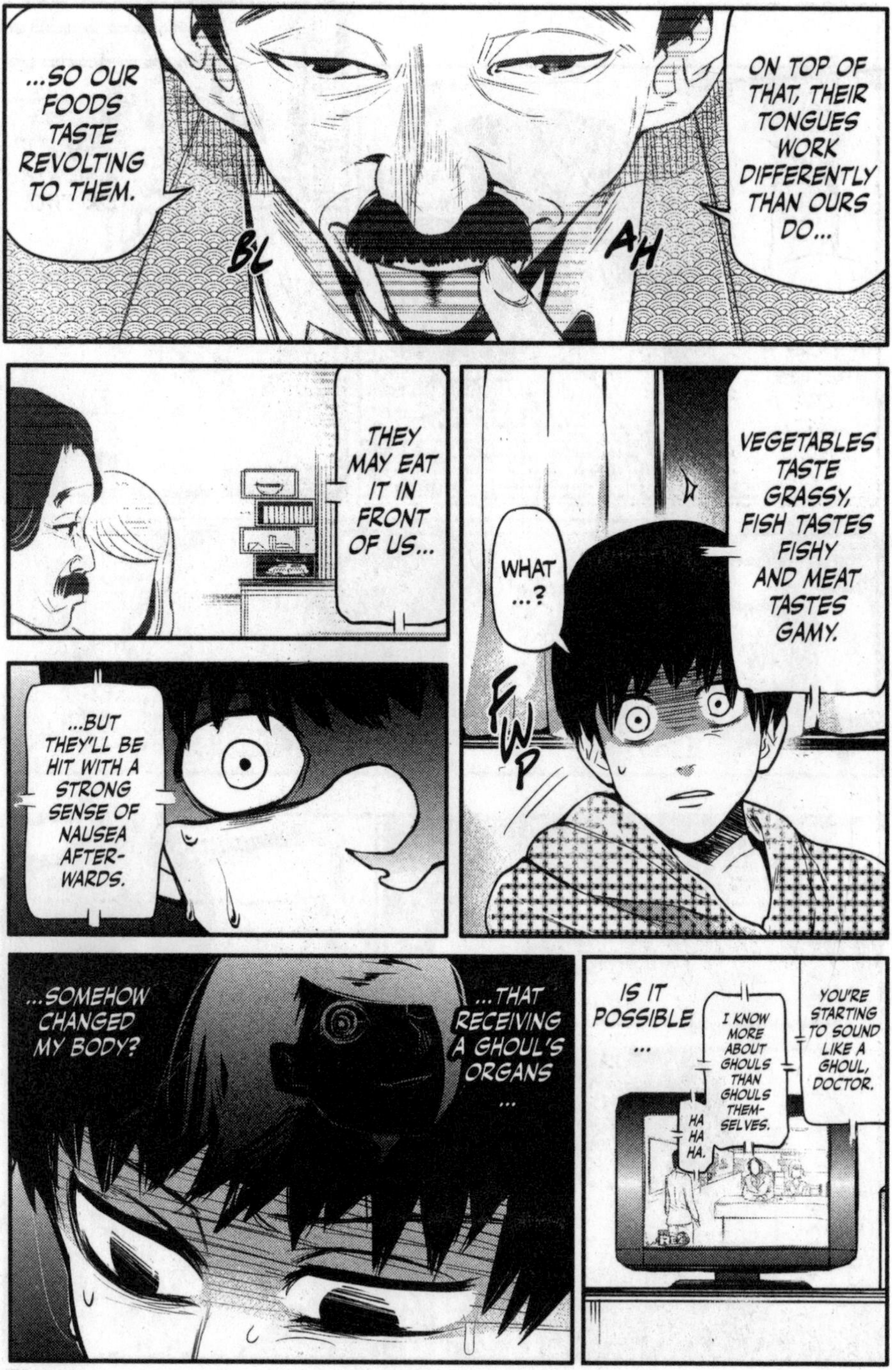

ON TOP OF THAT, THEIR TONGUES WORK DIFFERENTLY THAN OURS DO...
AH
BL
...SO OUR FOODS TASTE REVOLTING TO THEM.
VEGETABLES TASTE GRASSY, FISH TASTES FISHY AND MEAT TASTES GAMY.
WHAT ...?
FWP
THEY MAY EAT IT IN FRONT OF US...
...BUT THEY'LL BE HIT WITH A STRONG SENSE OF NAUSEA AFTER-WARDS.
YOU'RE STARTING TO SOUND LIKE A GHOUL, DOCTOR.
I KNOW MORE ABOUT GHOULS THAN GHOULS THEM-SELVES.
HA HA HA.
IS IT POSSIBLE ...
...THAT RECEIVING A GHOUL'S ORGANS ...
...SOMEHOW CHANGED MY BODY?

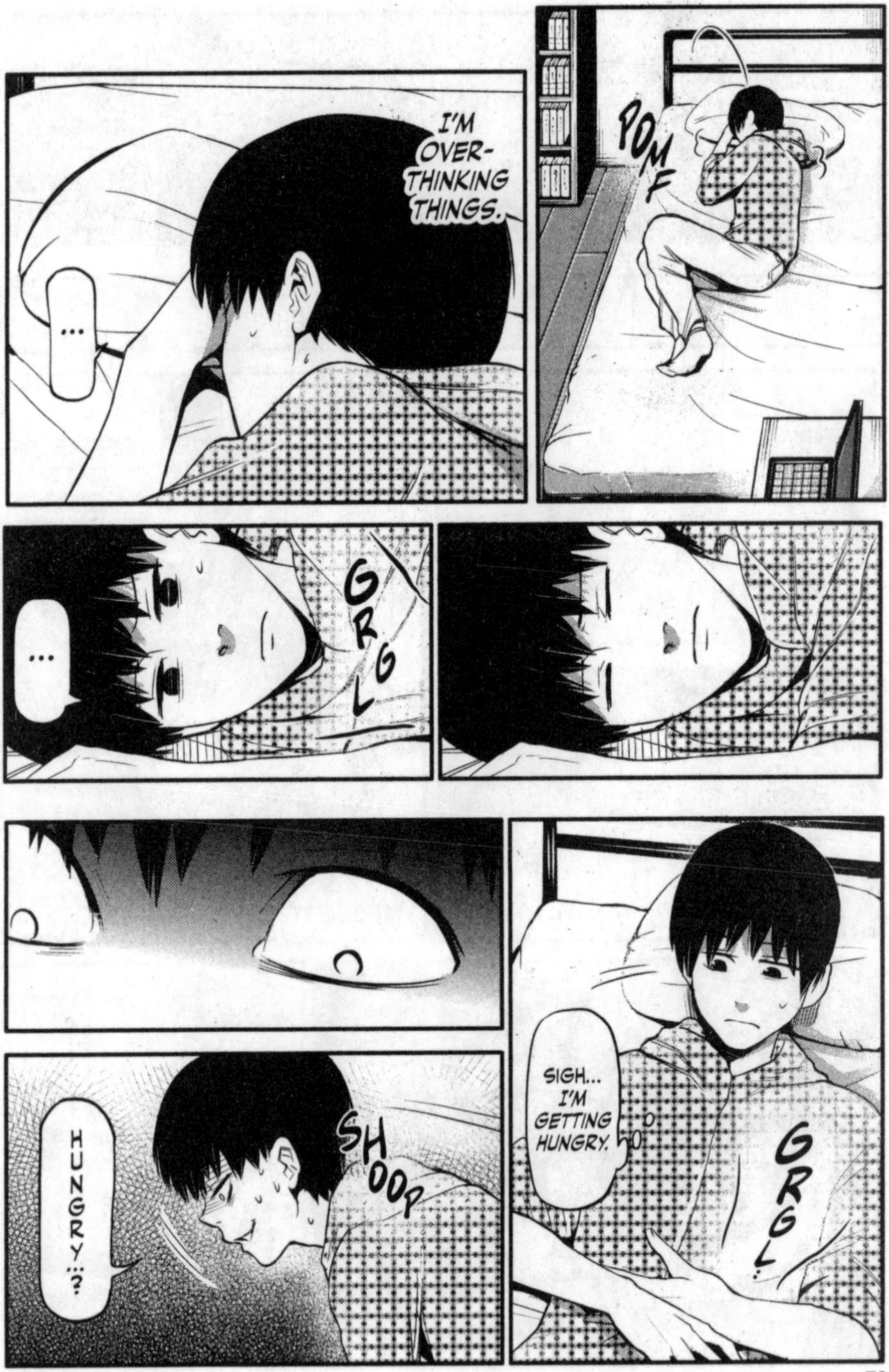
POMF
I'M OVER-THINKING THINGS.
...
GRGL
...
SIGH... I'M GETTING HUNGRY.
GRGL
SHOOP
HUNGRY..!?

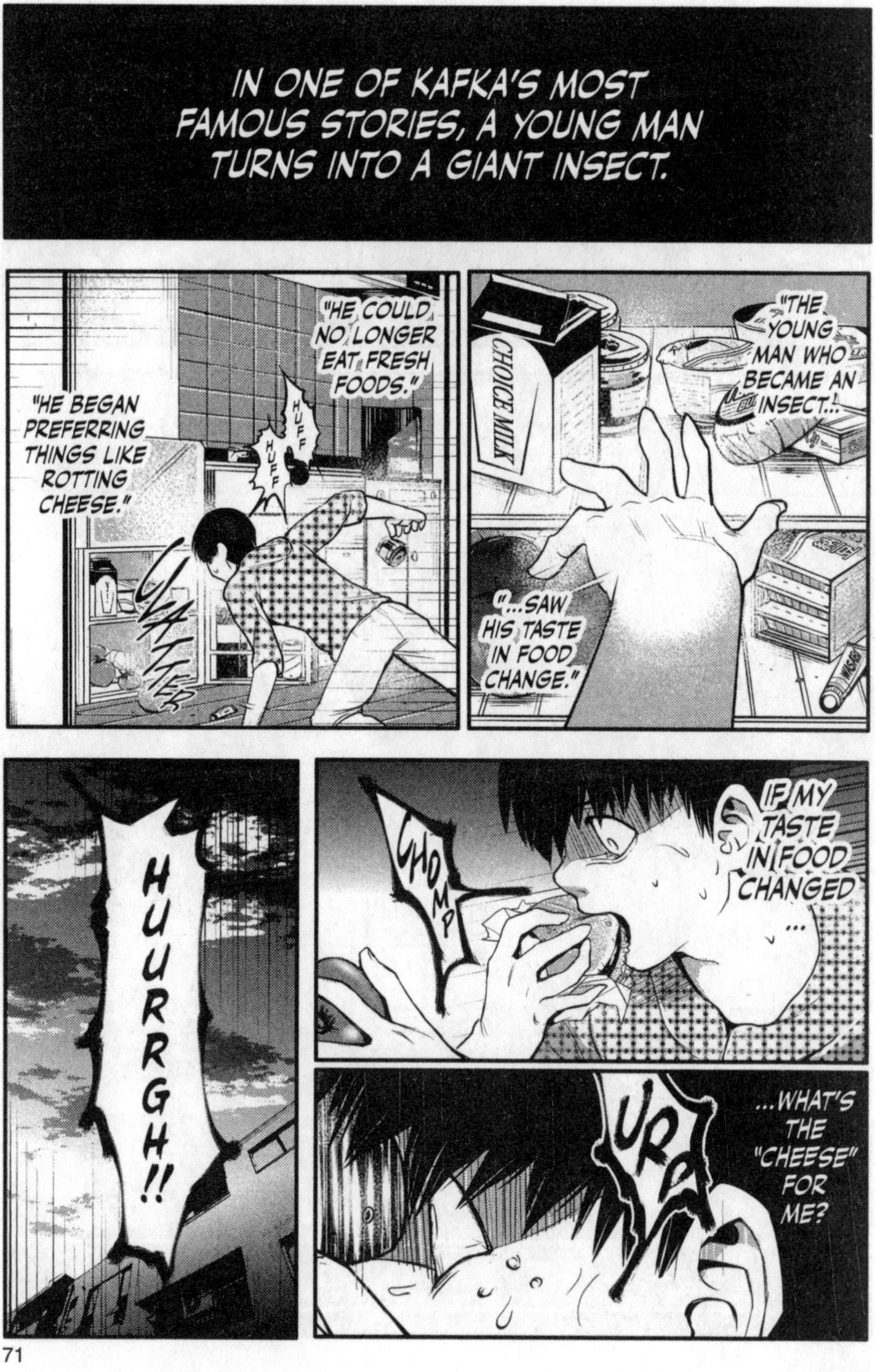
IN ONE OF KAFKA'S MOST FAMOUS STORIES, A YOUNG MAN TURNS INTO A GIANT INSECT.
"THE YOUNG MAN WHO BECAME AN INSECT...
CHOICE MILK
"...SAW HIS TASTE IN FOOD CHANGE."
"HE COULD NO LONGER EAT FRESH FOODS."
HUFF HUFF HUFF
"HE BEGAN PREFERRING THINGS LIKE ROTTING CHEESE."
IF MY TASTE IN FOOD CHANGED ...
CHOMP
...WHAT'S THE "CHEESE" FOR ME?
HUURRGH!!

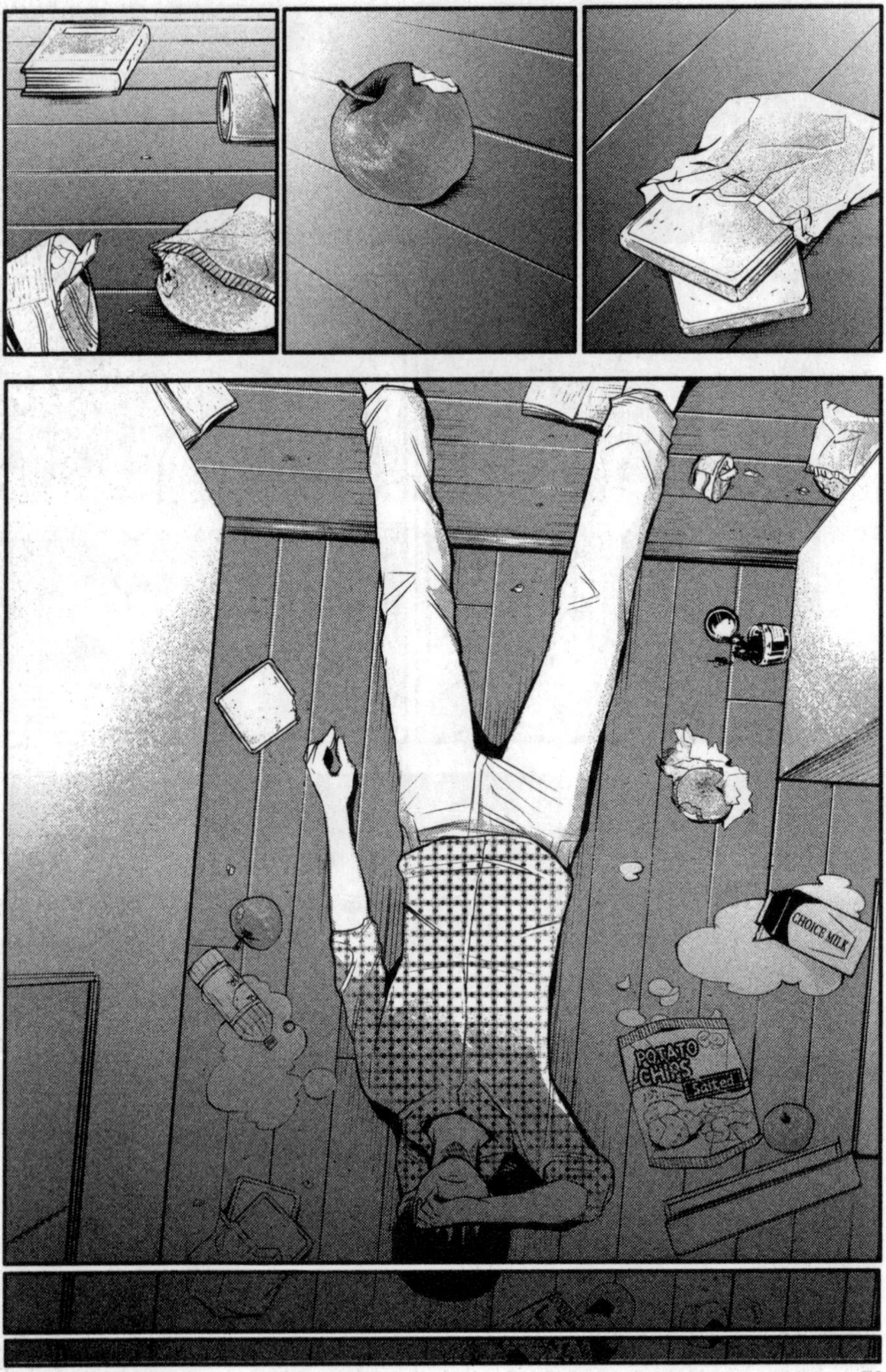
CHOICE MILK
POTATO CHIPS
Salted

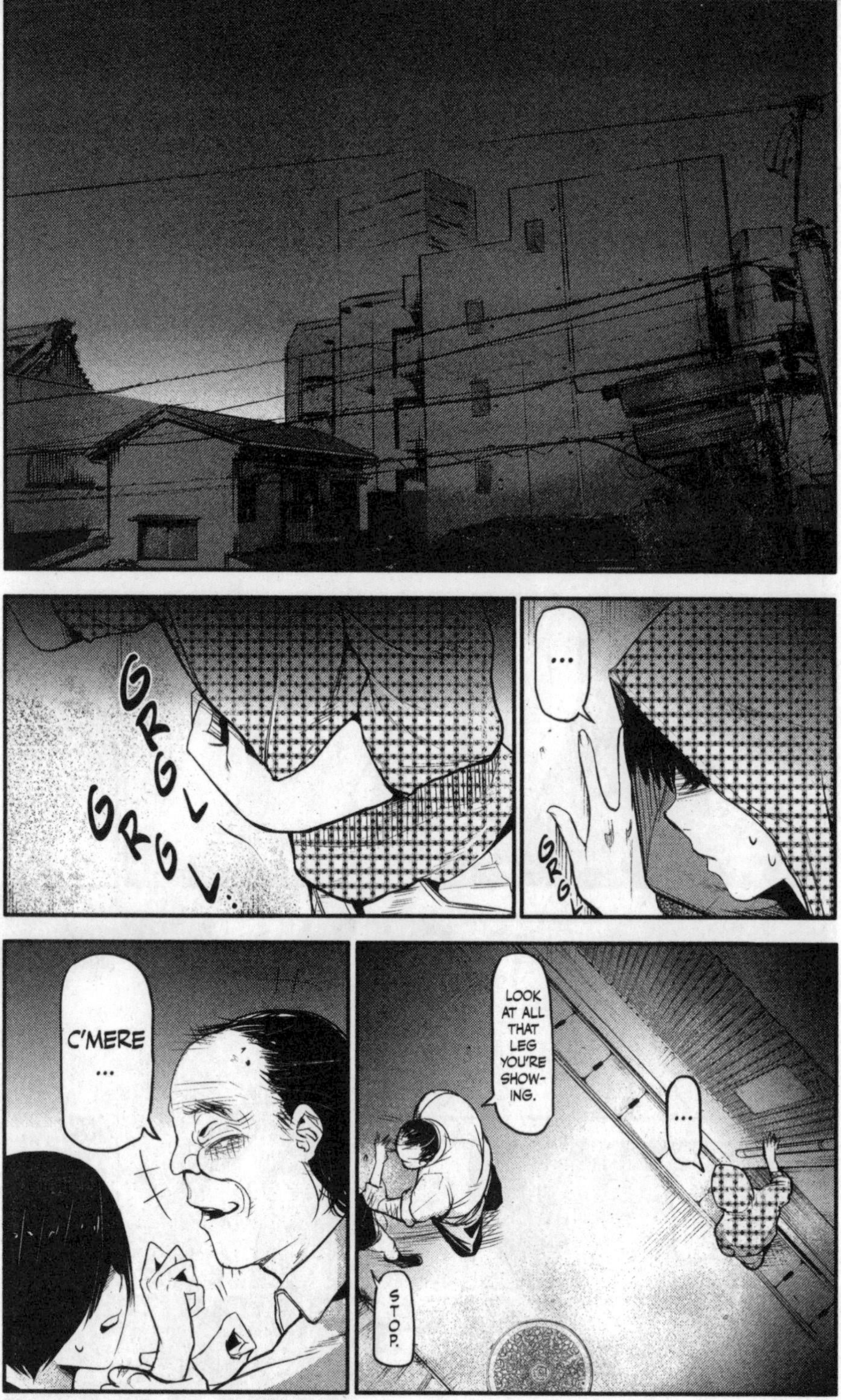
...
GRGL
GRGL GRGL...
LOOK AT ALL THAT LEG YOU'RE SHOWING.
...
STOP.
C'MERE ...

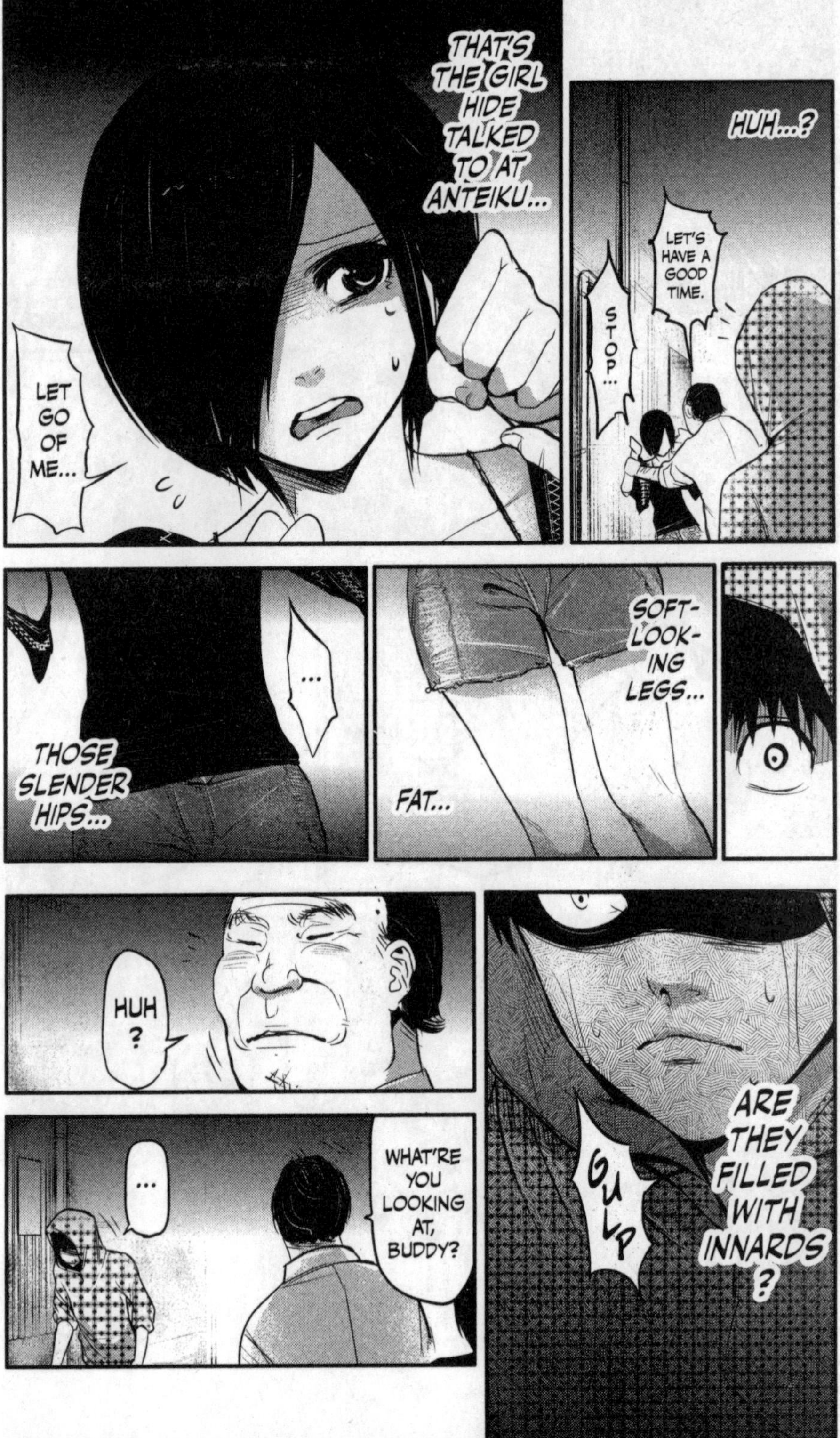
HUH...?
LET'S HAVE A GOOD TIME.
STOP...
THAT'S THE GIRL HIDE TALKED TO AT ANTEIKU...
LET GO OF ME...
SOFT-LOOKING LEGS...
FAT...
...
THOSE SLENDER HIPS...
ARE THEY FILLED WITH INNARDS?
GULP
HUH?
WHAT'RE YOU LOOKING AT, BUDDY?
...

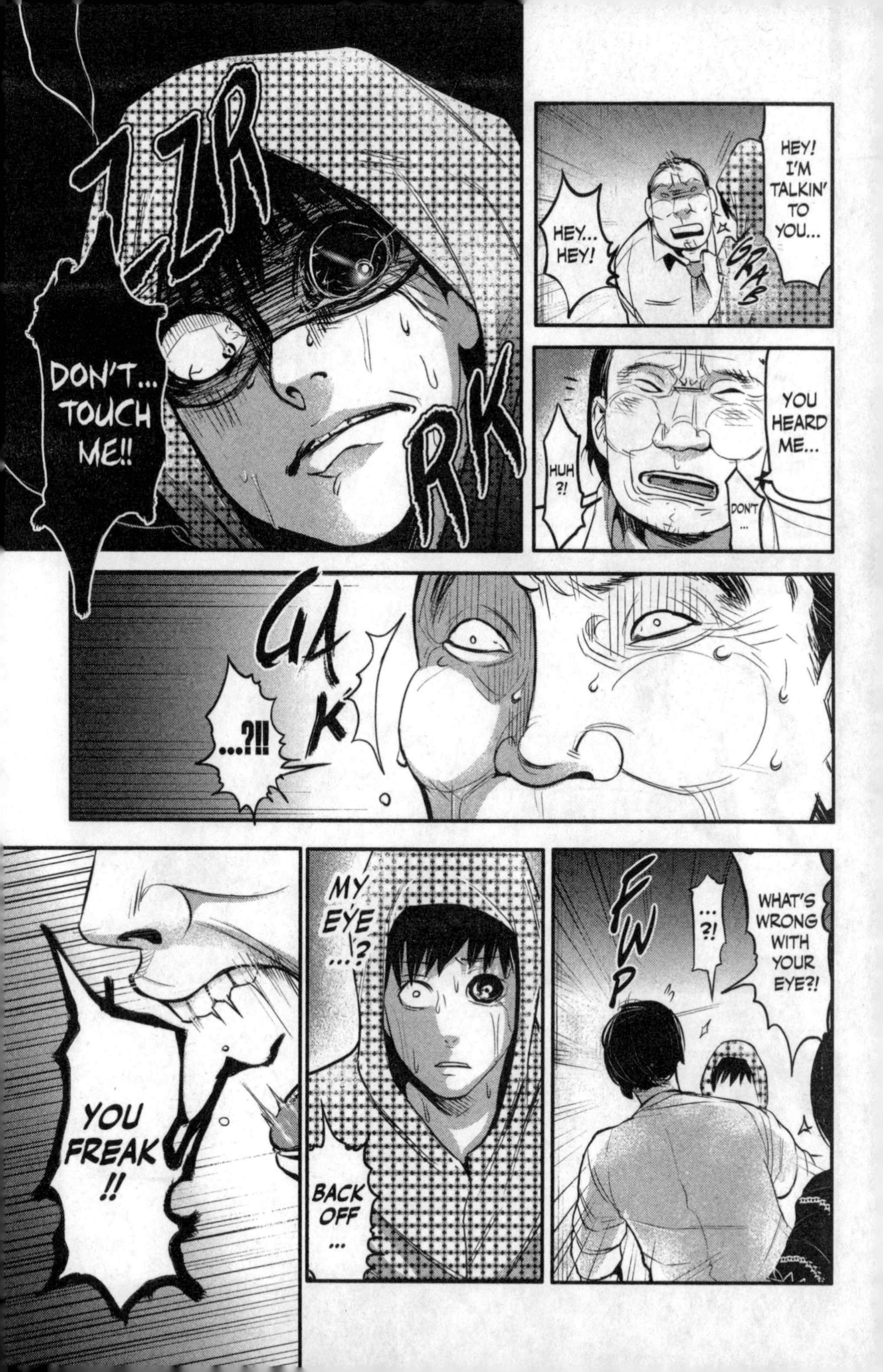
HEY! I'M TALKIN' TO YOU...
HEY... HEY!
GRAB
YOU HEARD ME...
DON'T ...
HUH ?!
ZZR
RK
DON'T... TOUCH ME!!
GAK
...?!!
WHAT'S WRONG WITH YOUR EYE?!
...?!
FWP
MY EYE ...!?
BACK OFF ...
YOU FREAK !!

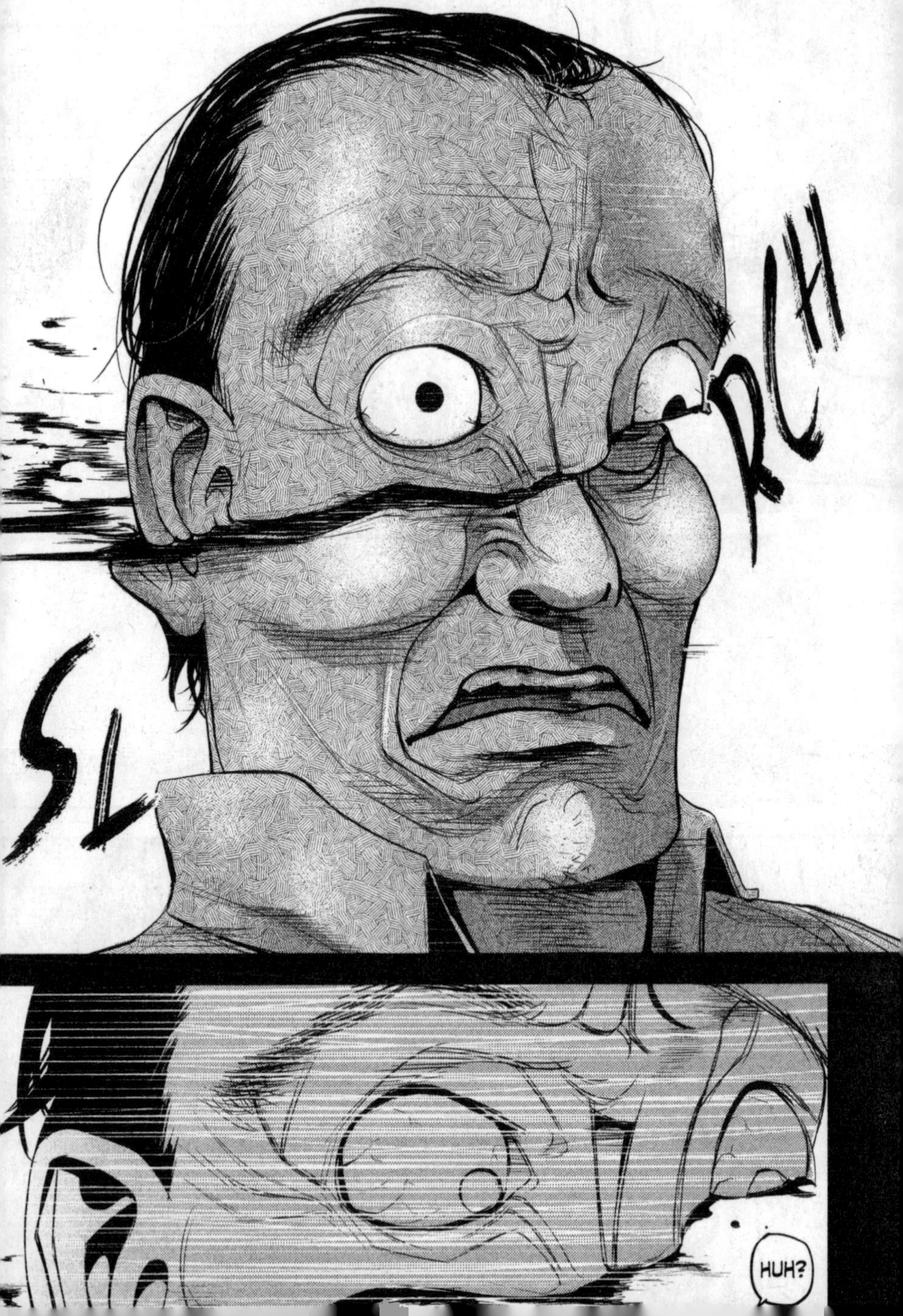
SLRCH
HUH?

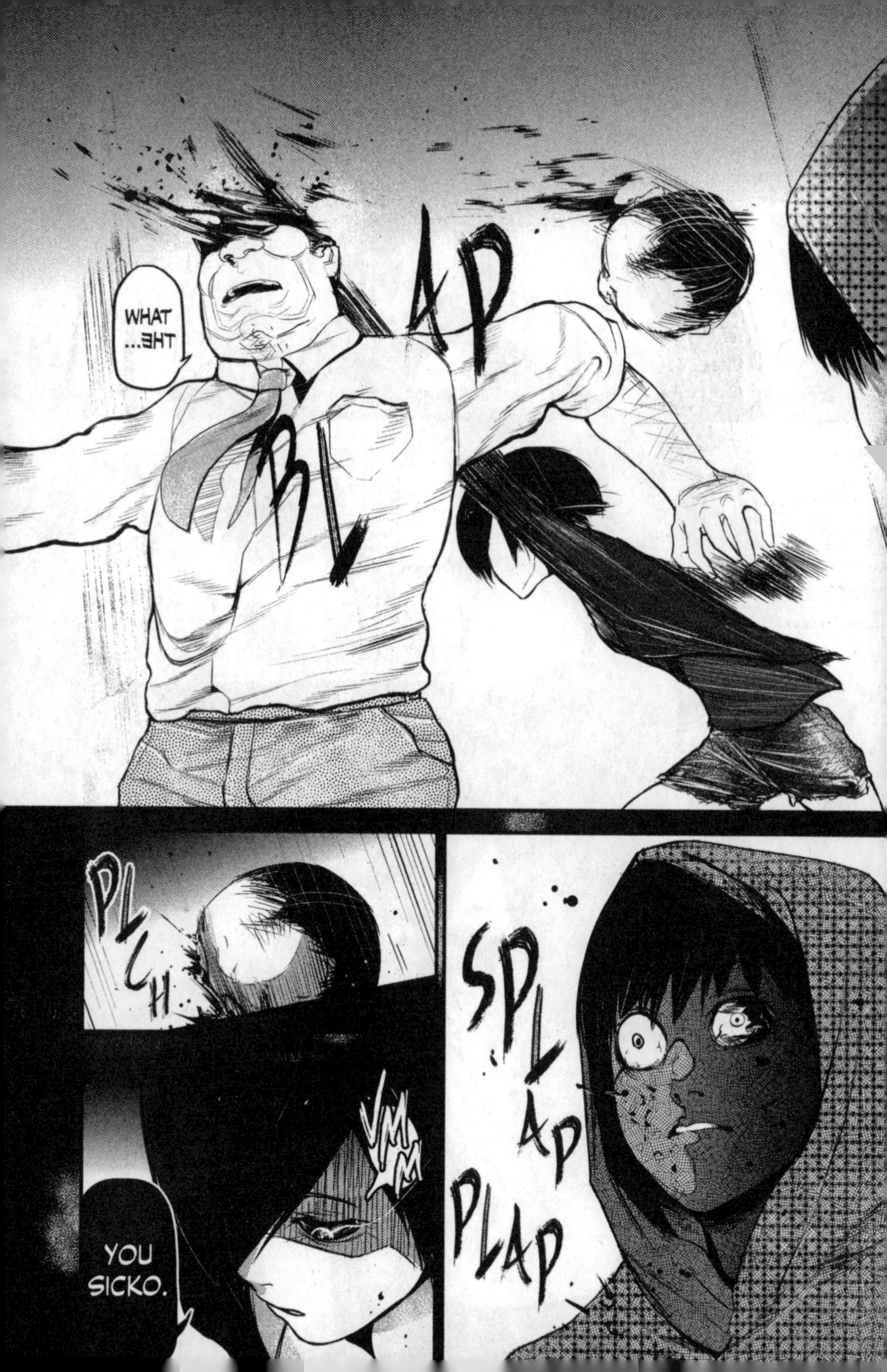
BLAP
WHAT THE...
SPLAP
PLAP
PLCH
VMM
YOU SICKO.

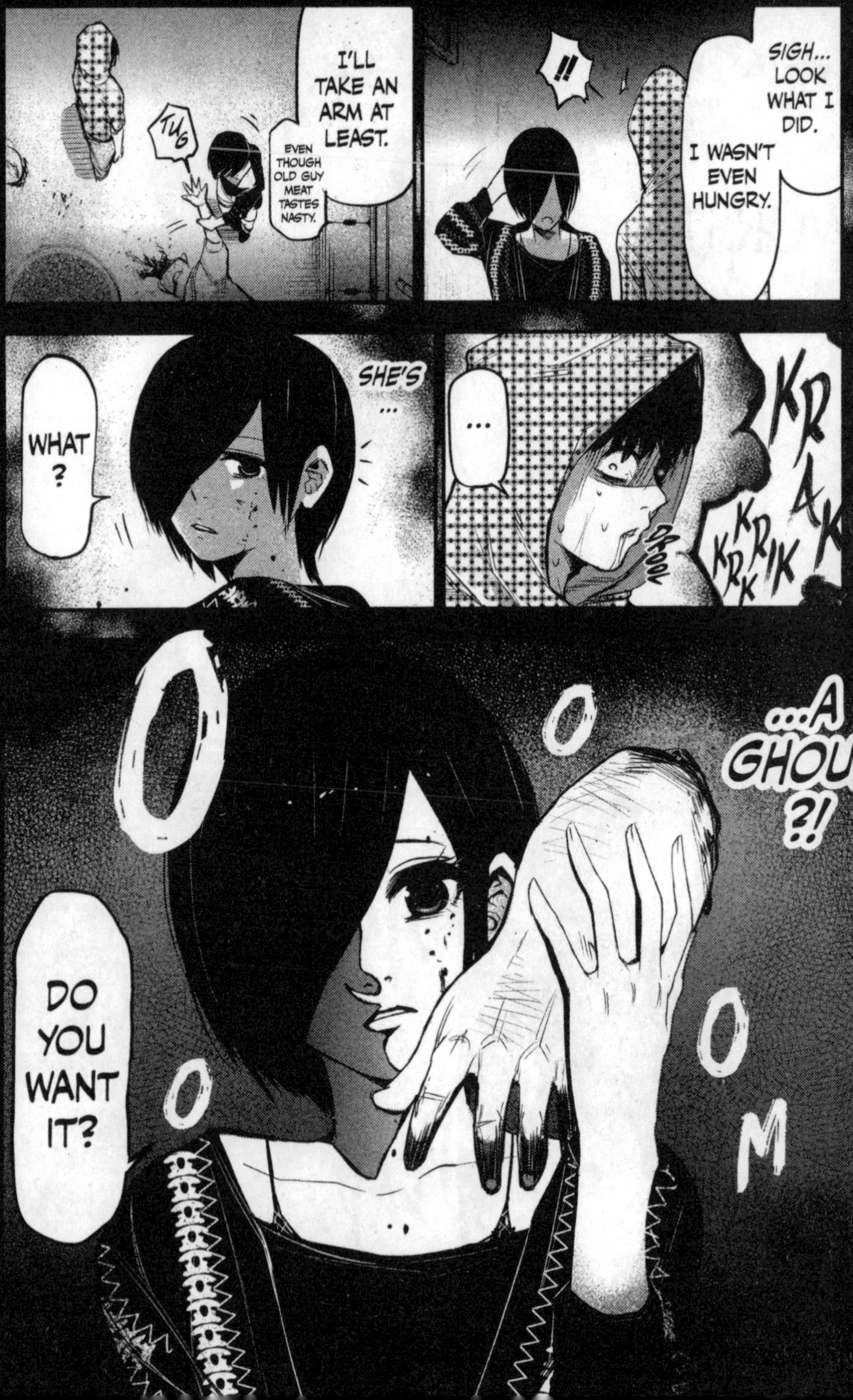
SIGH... LOOK WHAT I DID.
I WASN'T EVEN HUNGRY.
!!
I'LL TAKE AN ARM AT LEAST.
EVEN THOUGH OLD GUY MEAT TASTES NASTY.
TUG
KRAK
...
KRKRIK
DROOL
SHE'S...
WHAT?
...A GHOUL?!
DO YOU WANT IT?
OOOOM

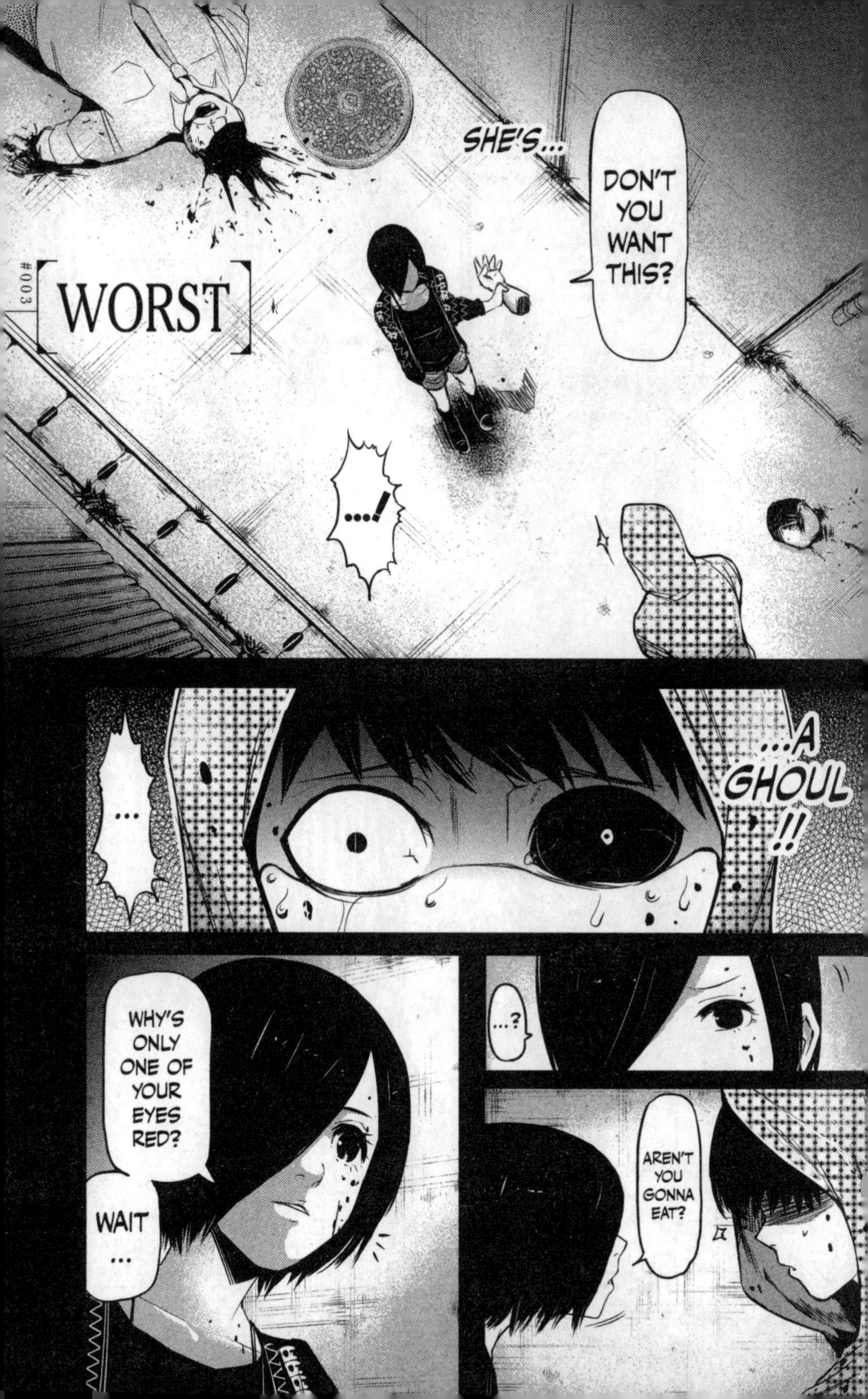
DON'T YOU WANT THIS?
SHE'S...
#003 [WORST]
...!
...A GHOUL!!
...
...?
AREN'T YOU GONNA EAT?
WHY'S ONLY ONE OF YOUR EYES RED?
WAIT ...

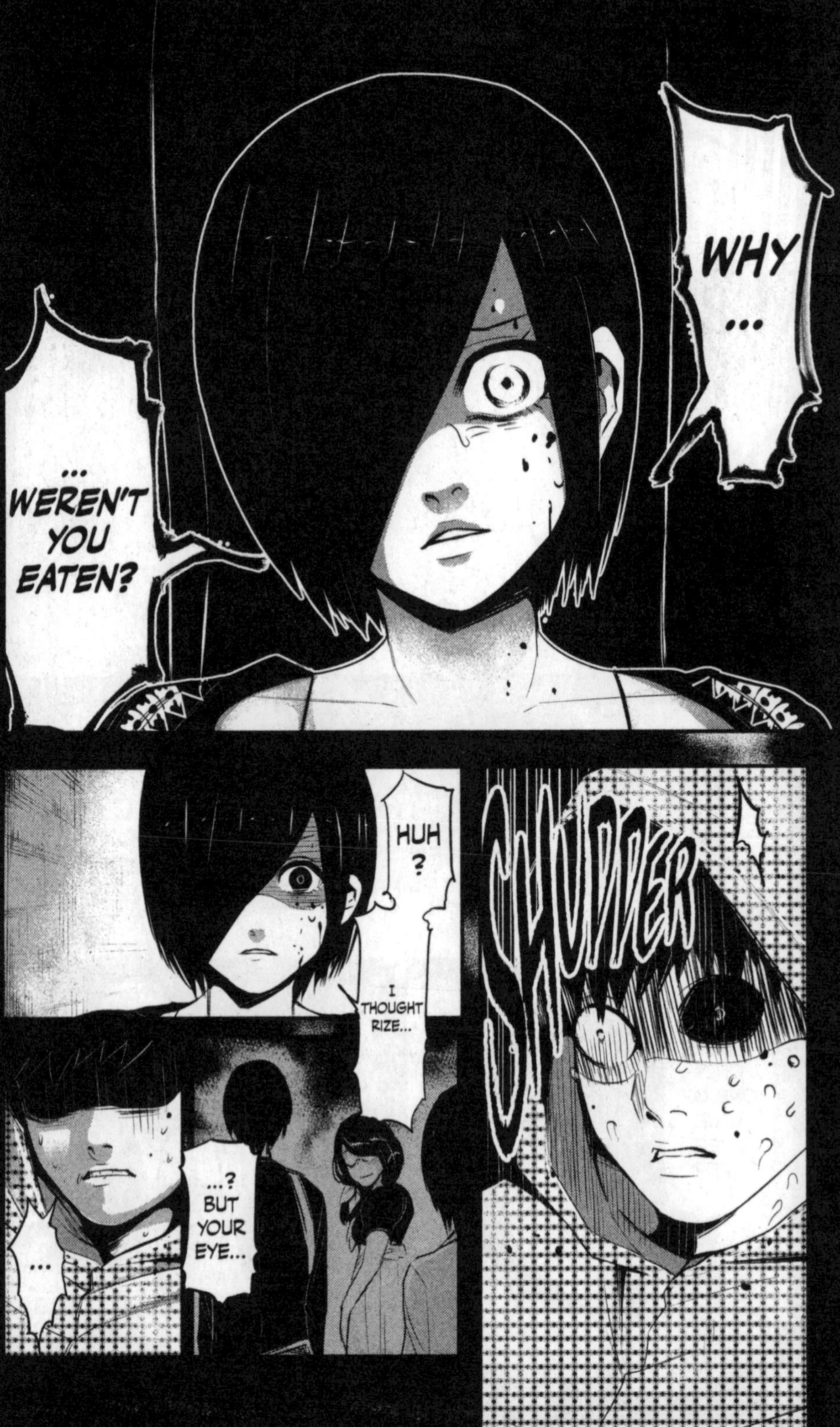
WHY...
...WEREN'T YOU EATEN?
SHUDDER
HUH?
I THOUGHT RIZE...
...? BUT YOUR EYE...
...

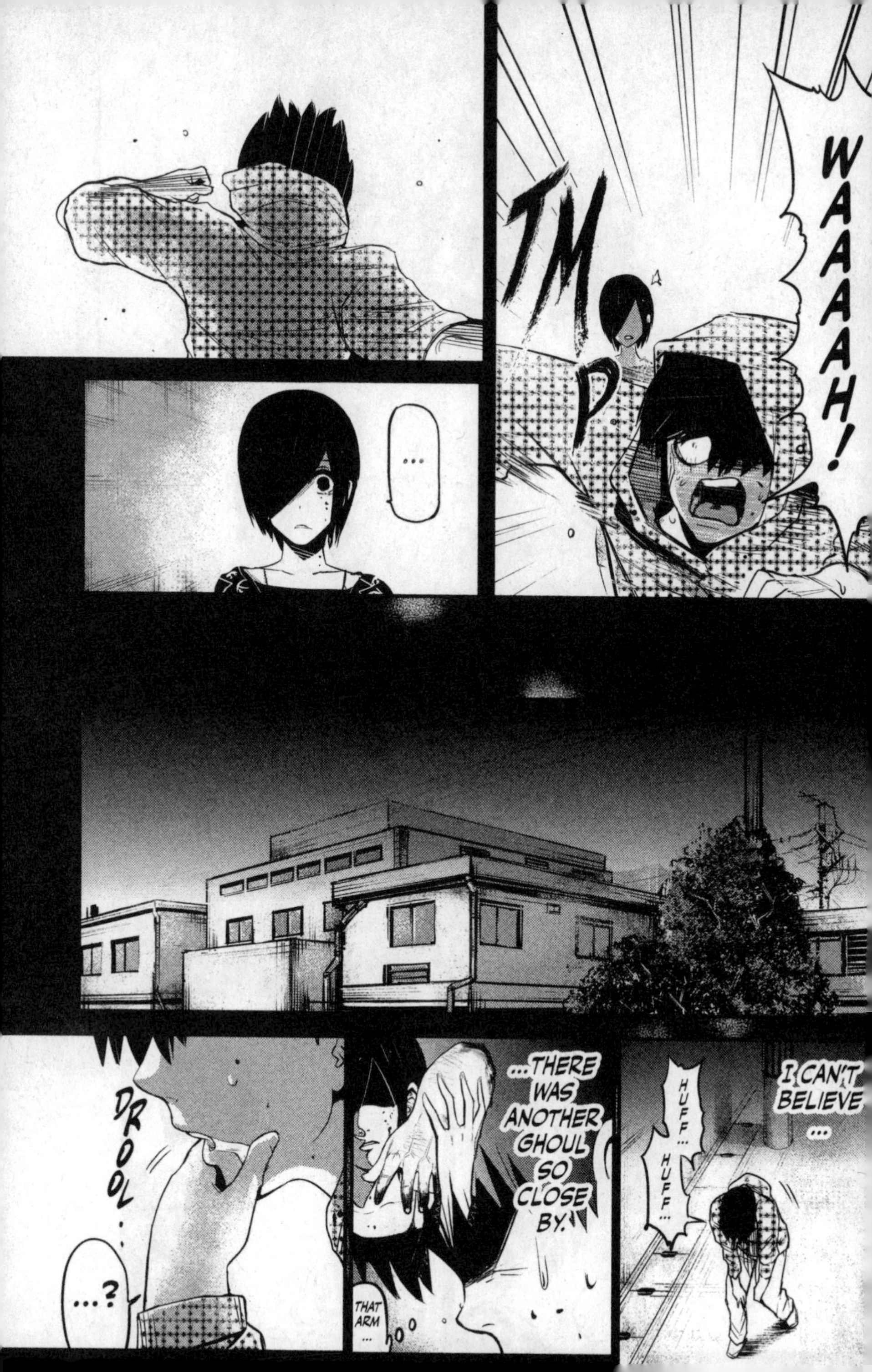
WAAAAAH!
TMP
...
I CAN'T BELIEVE...
HUFF... HUFF...
...THERE WAS ANOTHER GHOUL SO CLOSE BY.
THAT ARM...
DROOL...
...?

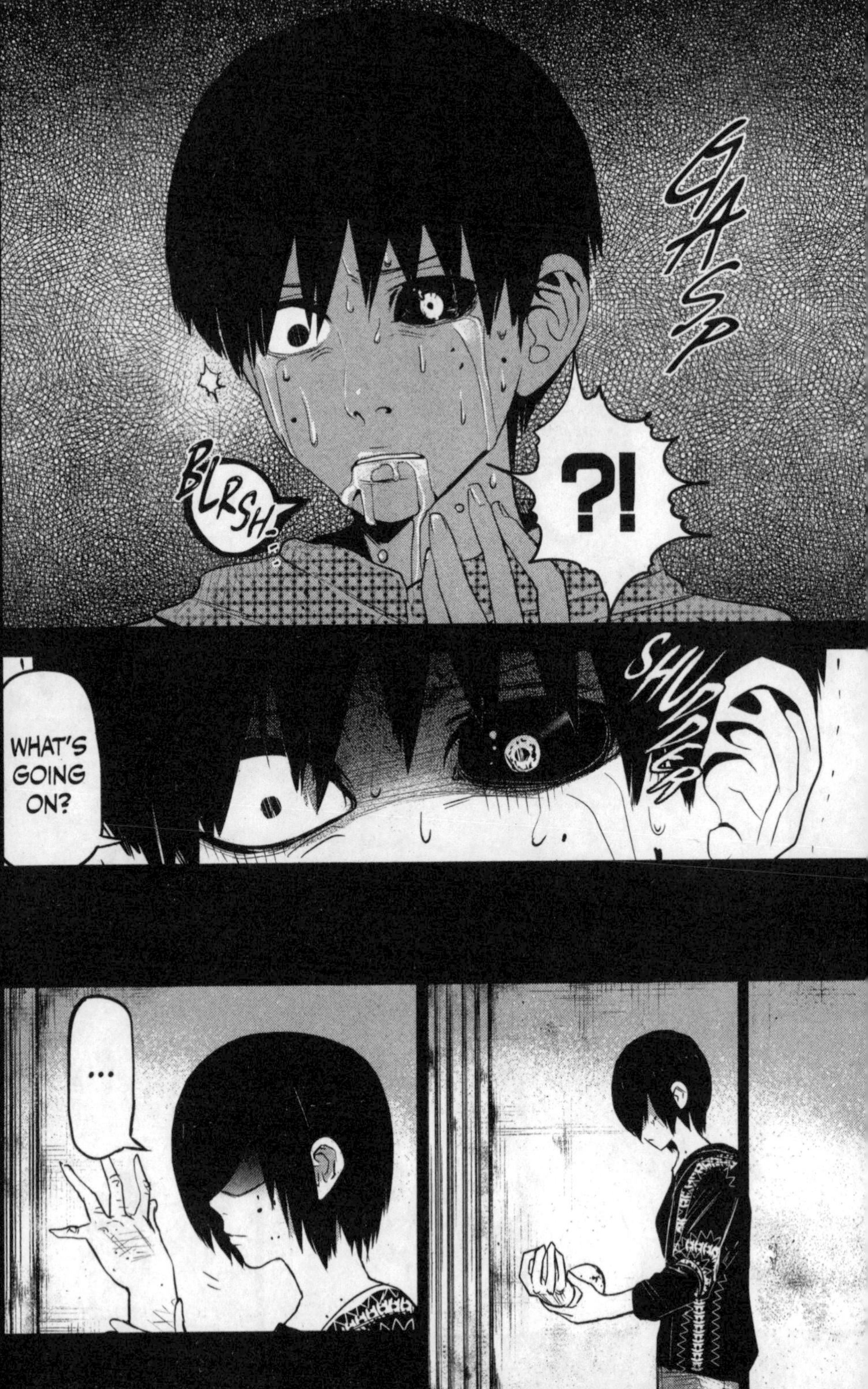
GASP
?!
BLRSH
SHUDDER
WHAT'S GOING ON?
...

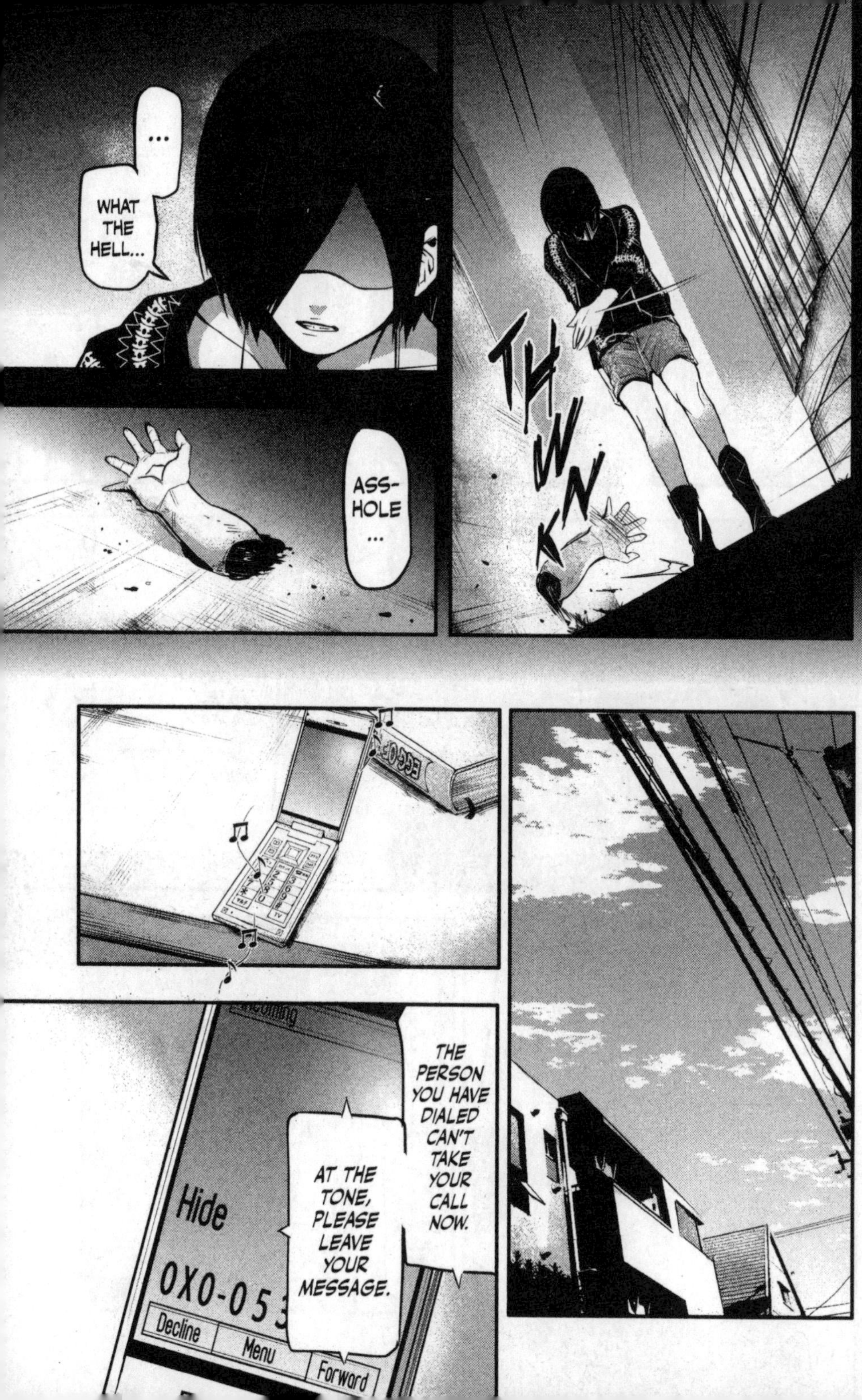
THWNK
...
WHAT THE HELL...
ASS-HOLE ...
Incoming
Hide
0X0-053
Decline
Menu
Forward
THE PERSON YOU HAVE DIALED CAN'T TAKE YOUR CALL NOW.
AT THE TONE, PLEASE LEAVE YOUR MESSAGE.

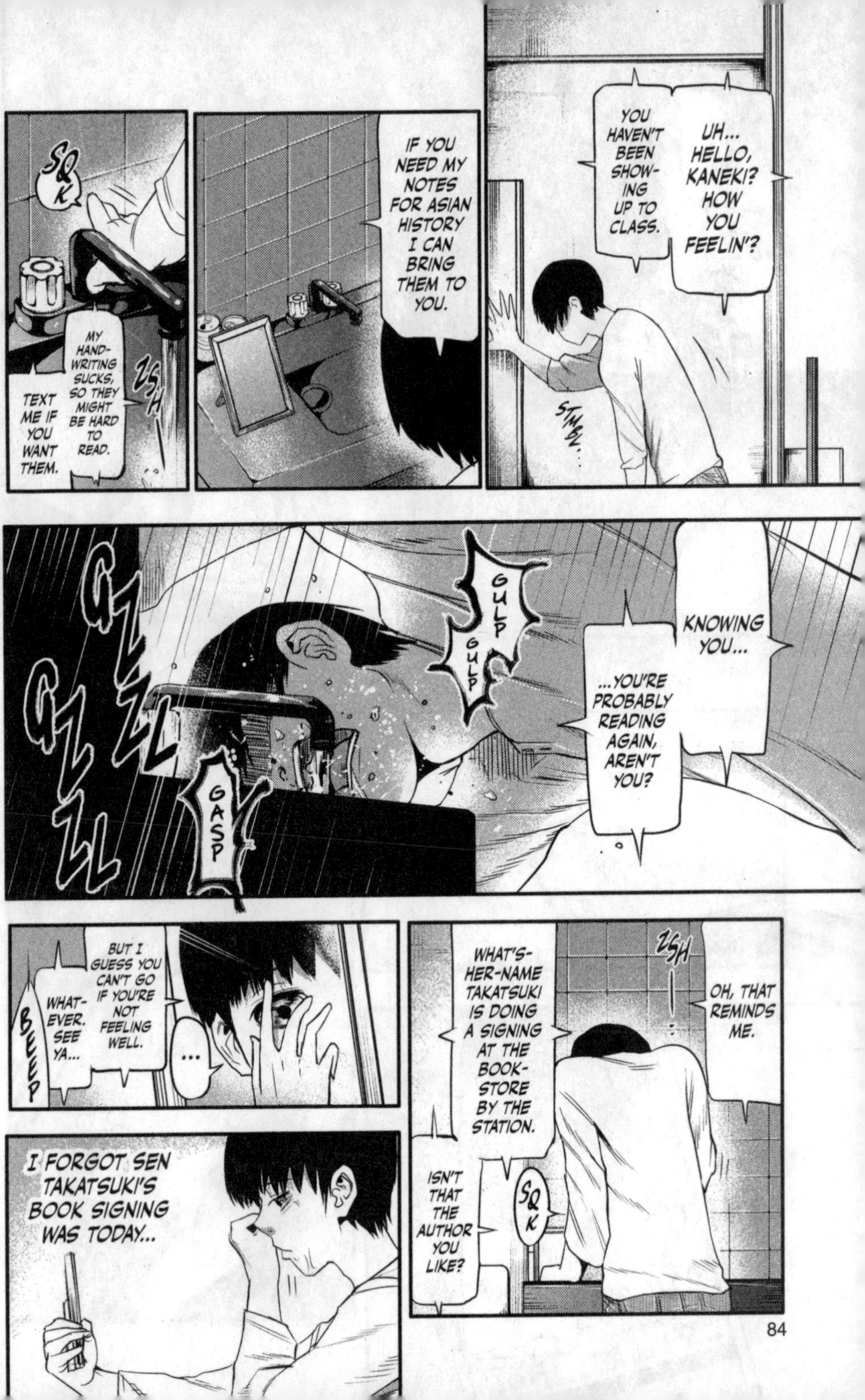
UH... HELLO, KANEKI? HOW YOU FEELIN'?
YOU HAVEN'T BEEN SHOW-ING UP TO CLASS.
STMBL...
IF YOU NEED MY NOTES FOR ASIAN HISTORY I CAN BRING THEM TO YOU.
SQK
MY HAND-WRITING SUCKS, SO THEY MIGHT BE HARD TO READ.
TEXT ME IF YOU WANT THEM.
ZSH
KNOWING YOU...
...YOU'RE PROBABLY READING AGAIN, AREN'T YOU?
GULP
GULP
GULP
GASP
GZZZLL
GZZZLL
OH, THAT REMINDS ME.
ZSH
WHAT'S-HER-NAME TAKATSUKI IS DOING A SIGNING AT THE BOOK-STORE BY THE STATION.
SQK
ISN'T THAT THE AUTHOR YOU LIKE?
BUT I GUESS YOU CAN'T GO IF YOU'RE NOT FEELING WELL.
WHAT-EVER. SEE YA...
BEEP
...
I FORGOT SEN TAKATSUKI'S BOOK SIGNING WAS TODAY...

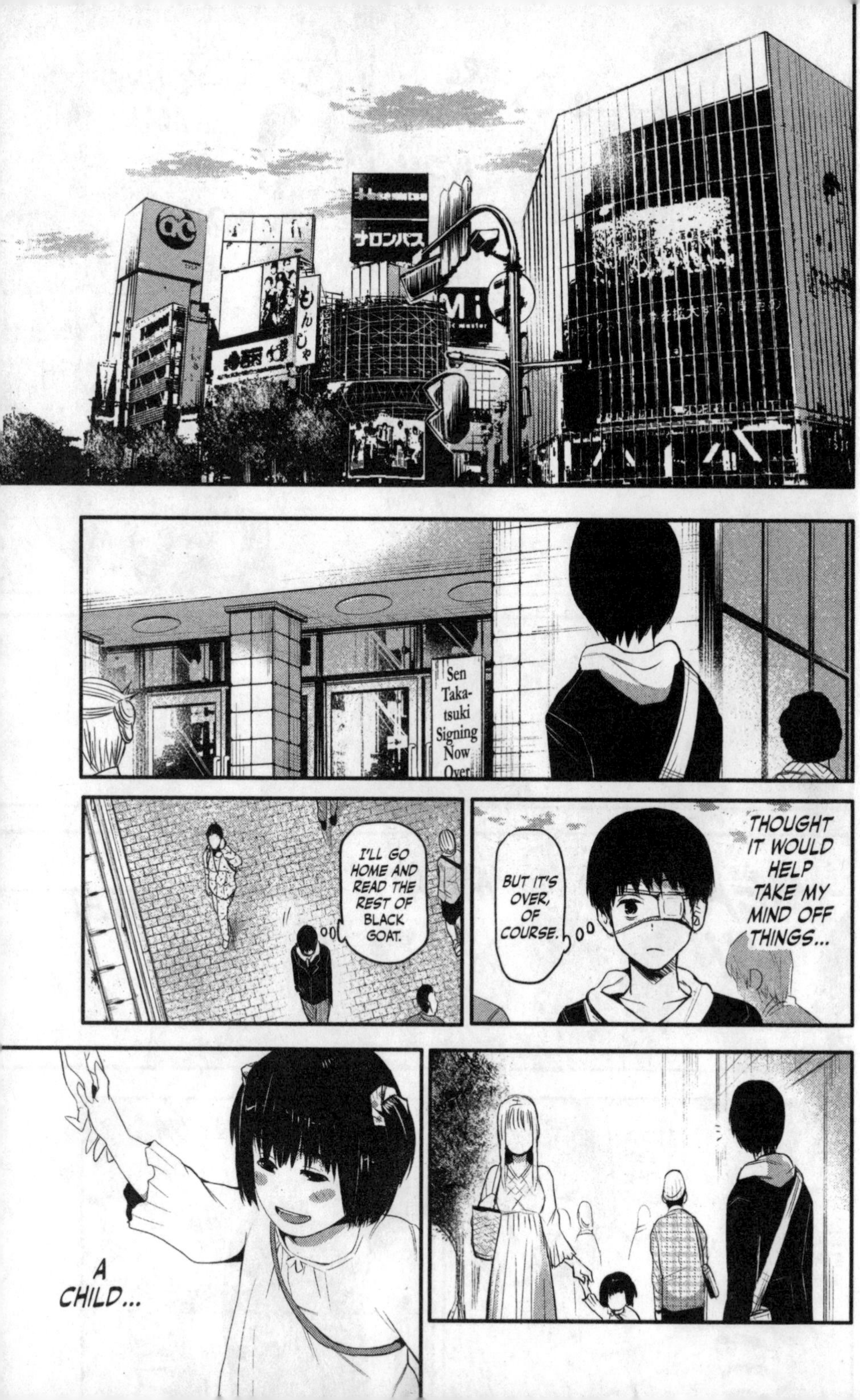
ナロンパス
もんじゃ
Sen Takatsuki Signing Now Over
THOUGHT IT WOULD HELP TAKE MY MIND OFF THINGS...
BUT IT'S OVER, OF COURSE.
I'LL GO HOME AND READ THE REST OF BLACK GOAT.
A CHILD...

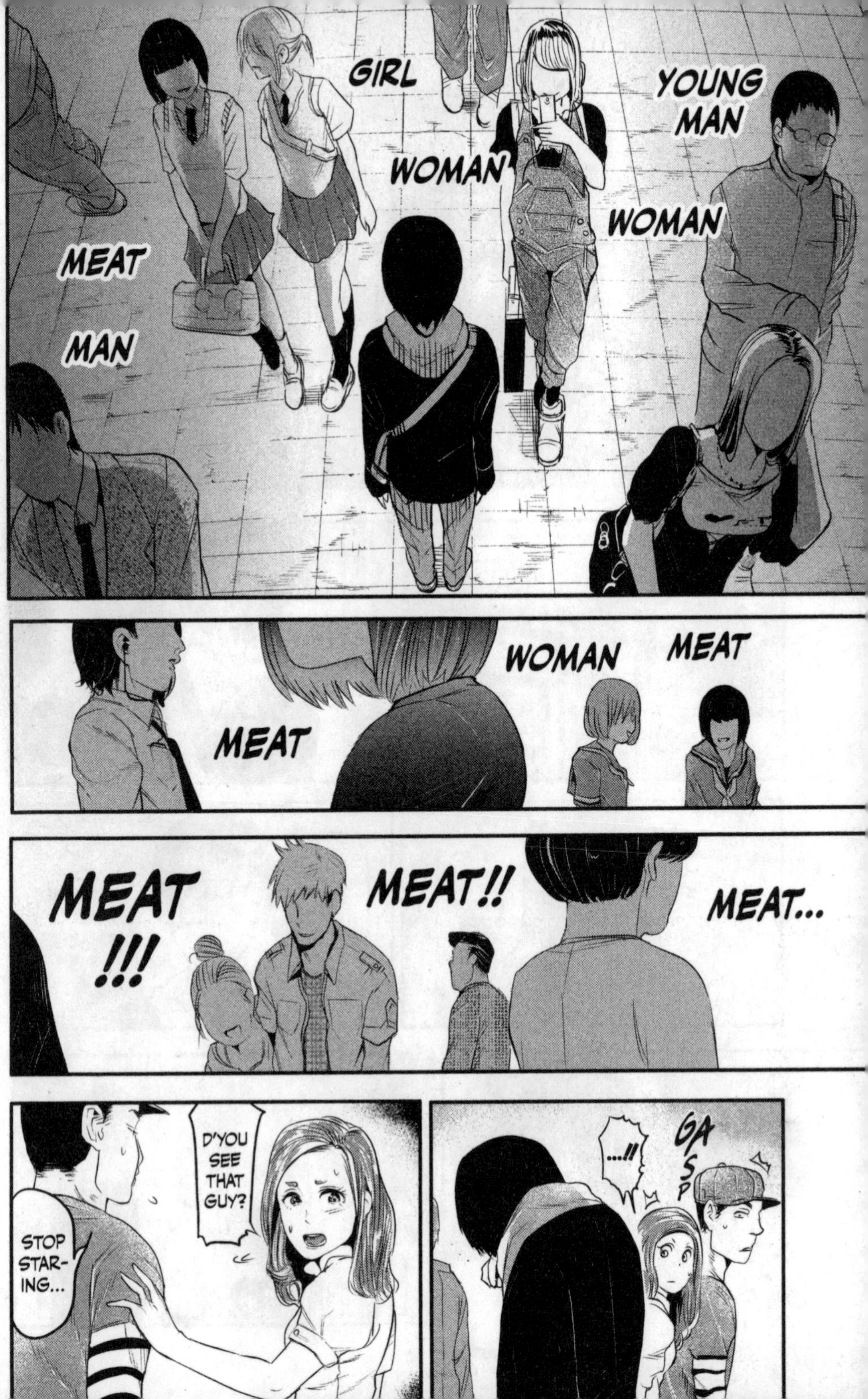
YOUNG MAN
WOMAN
GIRL
WOMAN
MEAT
MAN
MEAT
WOMAN
MEAT
MEAT...
MEAT!!
MEAT !!!
GASP
...!!
D'YOU SEE THAT GUY?
STOP STAR-ING...

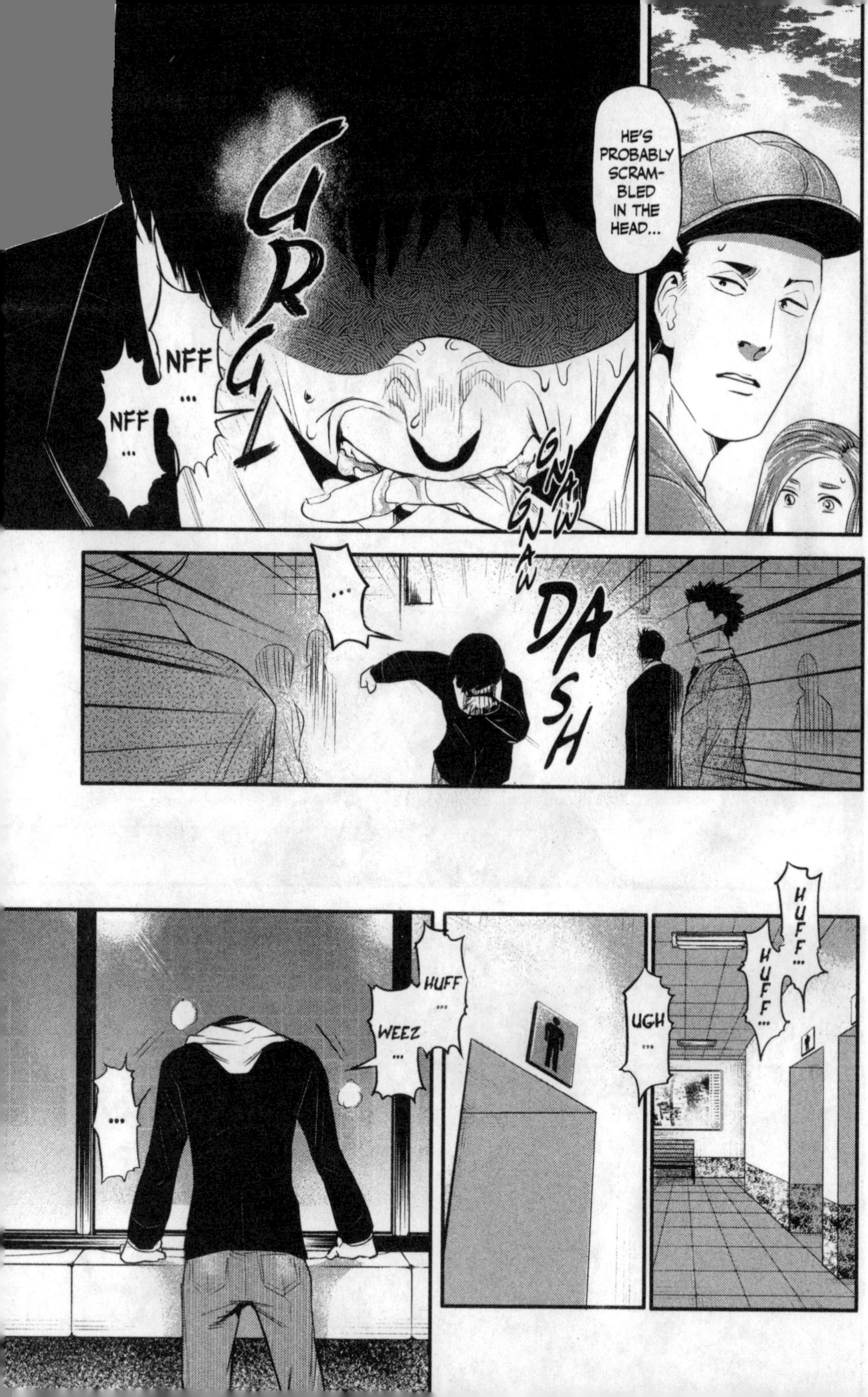
HE'S PROBABLY SCRAM-BLED IN THE HEAD...
URGL
GNAW GNAW GNAW
NFF... NFF...
DASH
...
HUFF... HUFF...
UGH...
HUFF... WEEZ...
...

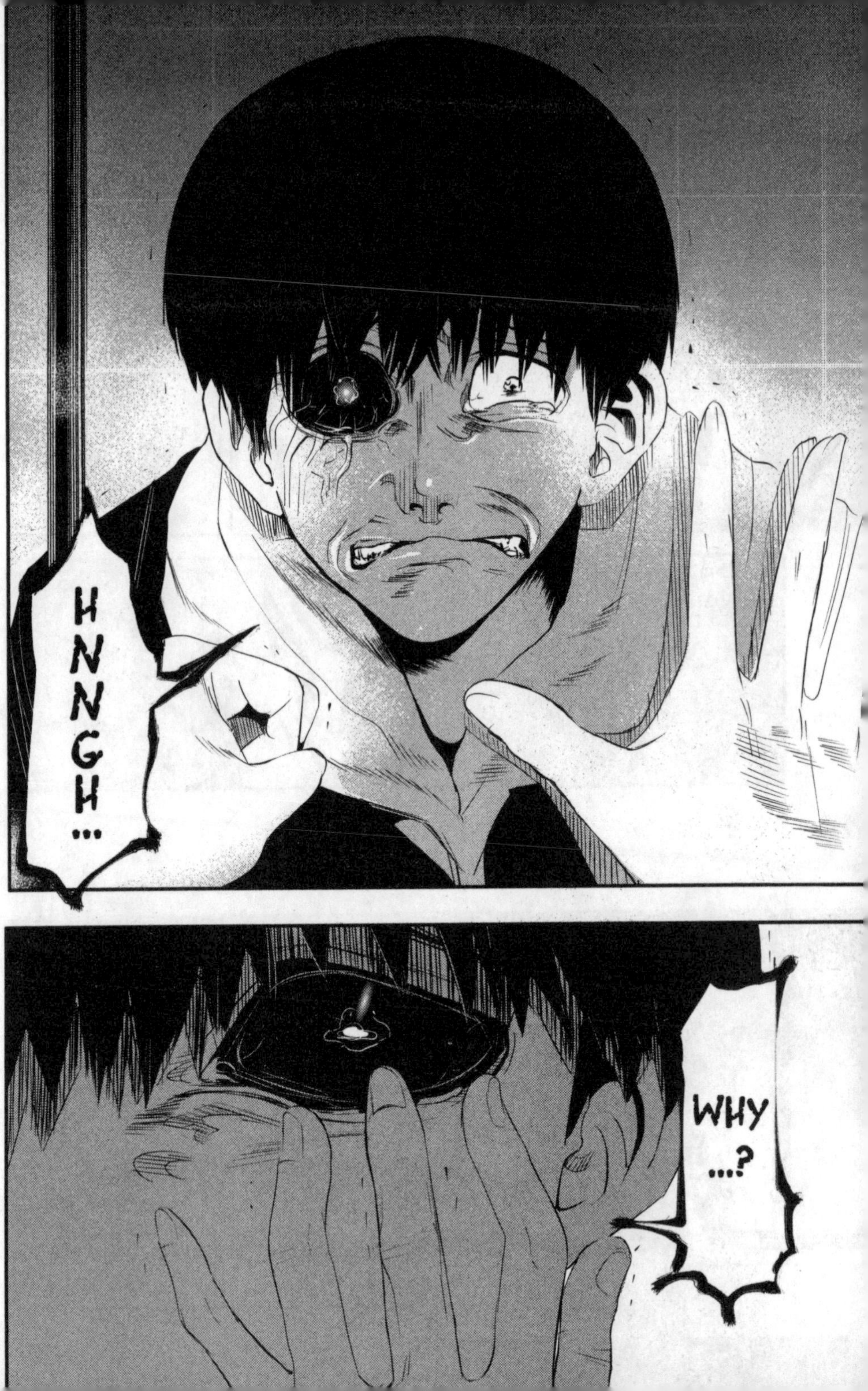
HNNGH...
WHY ...?

WHY ME?
WHY, GOD DAMN IT?!
KR SHAK
SLK
OW ...
!!
SHP ...
FWP
HUH ?!

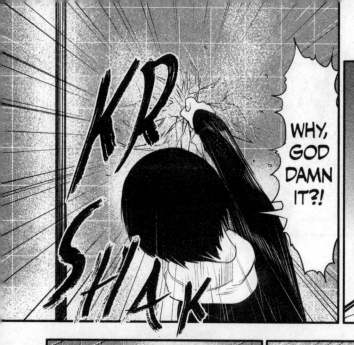

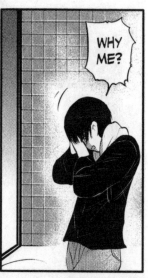

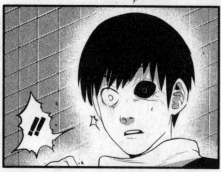

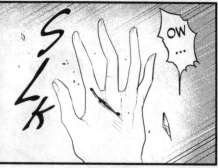

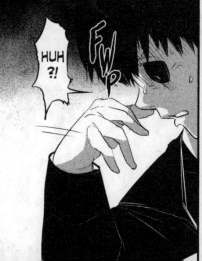

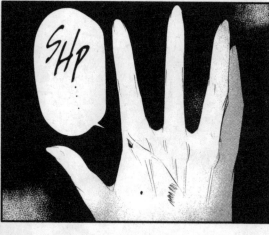

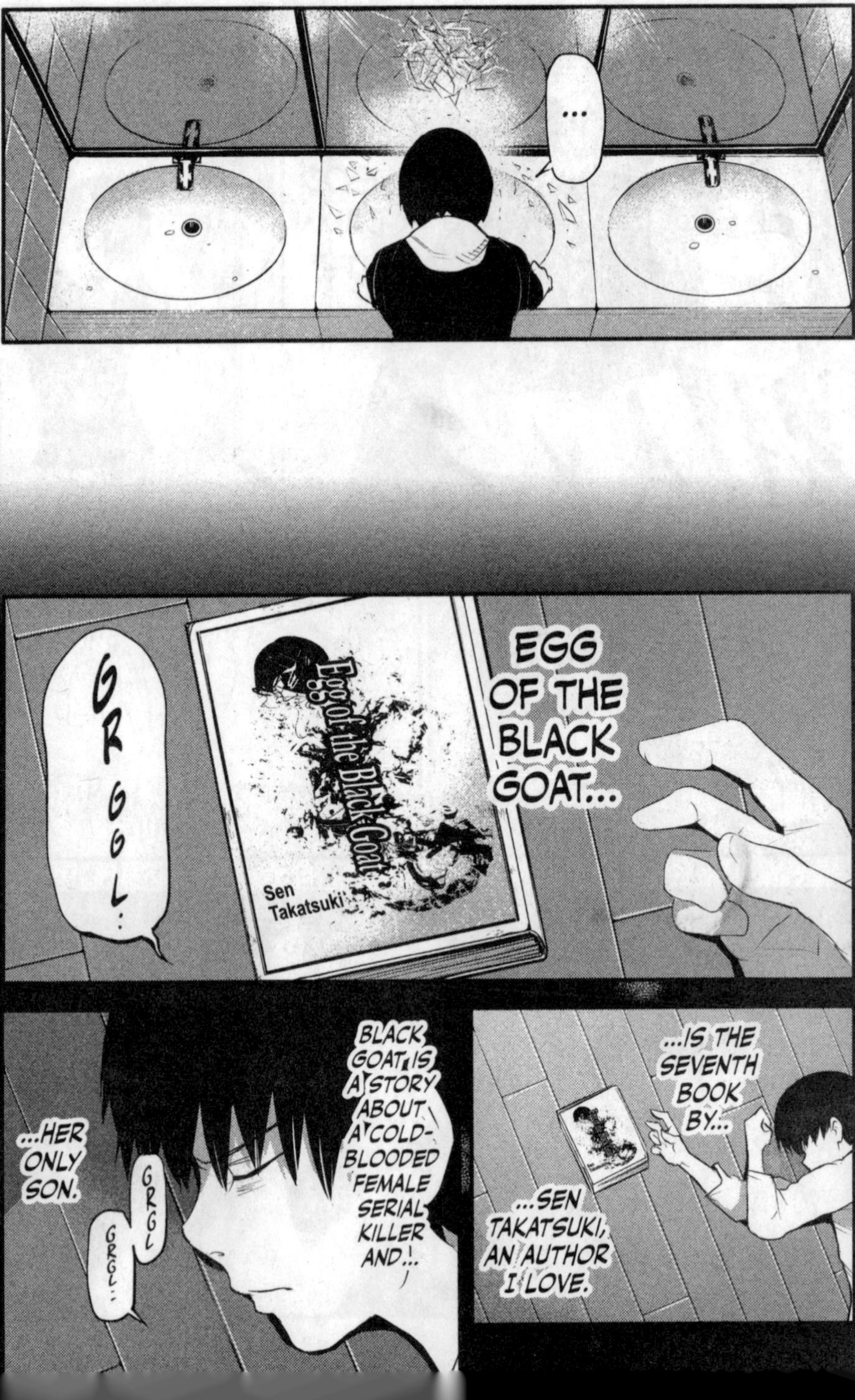
...
EGG OF THE BLACK GOAT...
Egg of the Black Goat
Sen Takatsuki
GRGGL..
...IS THE SEVENTH BOOK BY...
...SEN TAKATSUKI, AN AUTHOR I LOVE.
BLACK GOAT IS A STORY ABOUT A COLD-BLOODED FEMALE SERIAL KILLER AND...
...HER ONLY SON.
GRGL
GRGL..

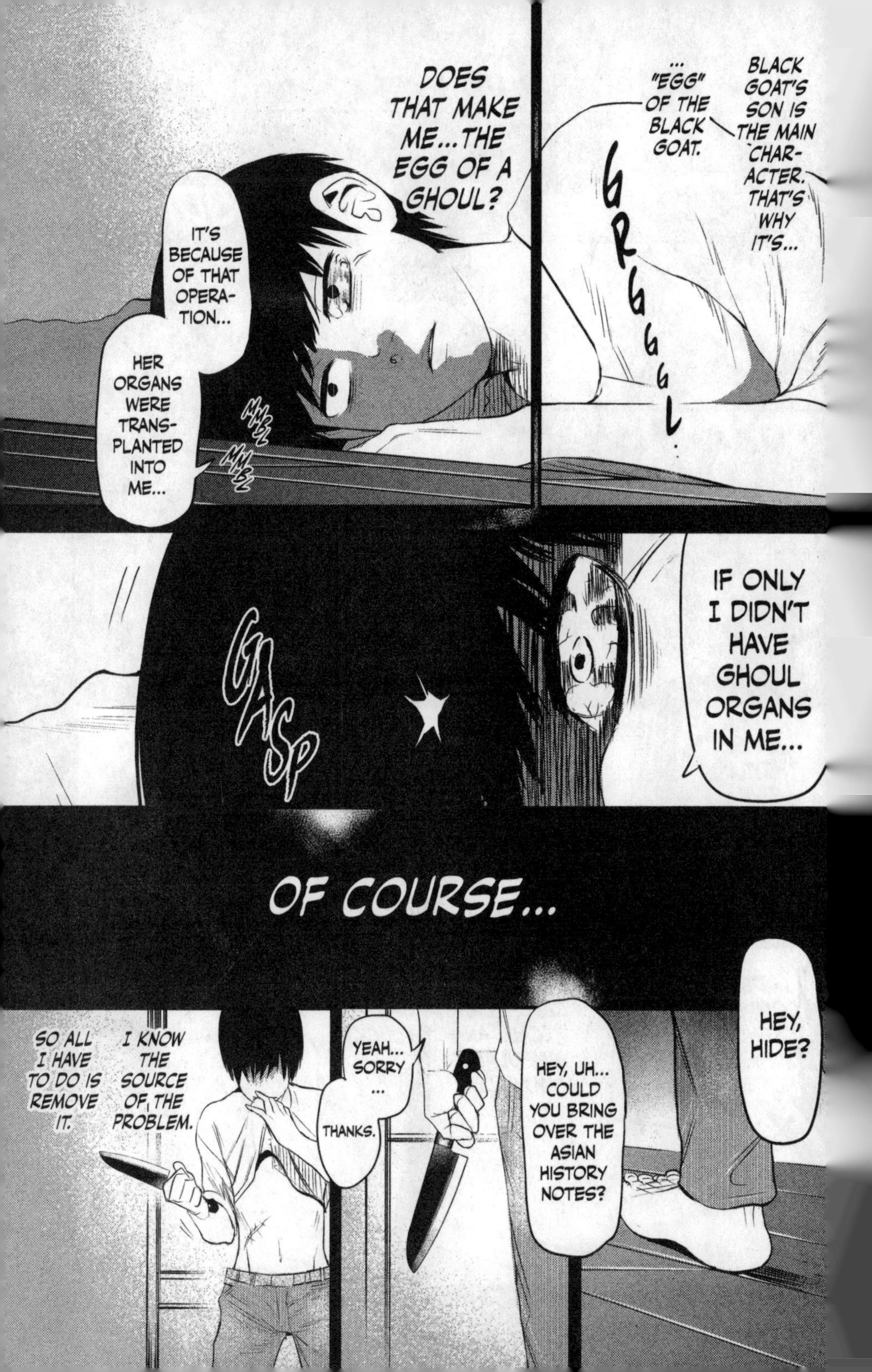
BLACK GOAT'S SON IS THE MAIN CHAR-ACTER. THAT'S WHY IT'S...
... "EGG" OF THE BLACK GOAT.
GRGGGL
DOES THAT MAKE ME...THE EGG OF A GHOUL?
IT'S BECAUSE OF THAT OPERA-TION...
HER ORGANS WERE TRANS-PLANTED INTO ME...
MMBL MMBL
IF ONLY I DIDN'T HAVE GHOUL ORGANS IN ME...
GASP
OF COURSE...
HEY, HIDE?
HEY, UH... COULD YOU BRING OVER THE ASIAN HISTORY NOTES?
YEAH... SORRY ...
THANKS.
I KNOW THE SOURCE OF THE PROBLEM.
SO ALL I HAVE TO DO IS REMOVE IT.

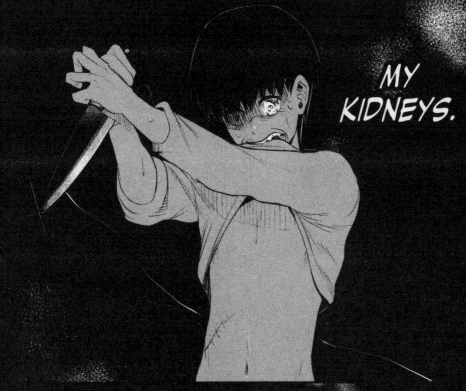

MY KIDNEYS.
IF I CAN DAMAGE MY KIDNEYS, AND IF I'M LUCKY...
...MAYBE THEY'LL GIVE ME NEW ONES.
THAT'S IF I GET LUCKY...
...
JUST IN CASE I CAN'T CALL AN AMBULANCE MYSELF...
...HIDE'S COMING TO SHOW ME HIS NOTES.

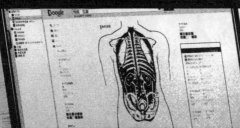

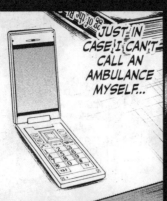

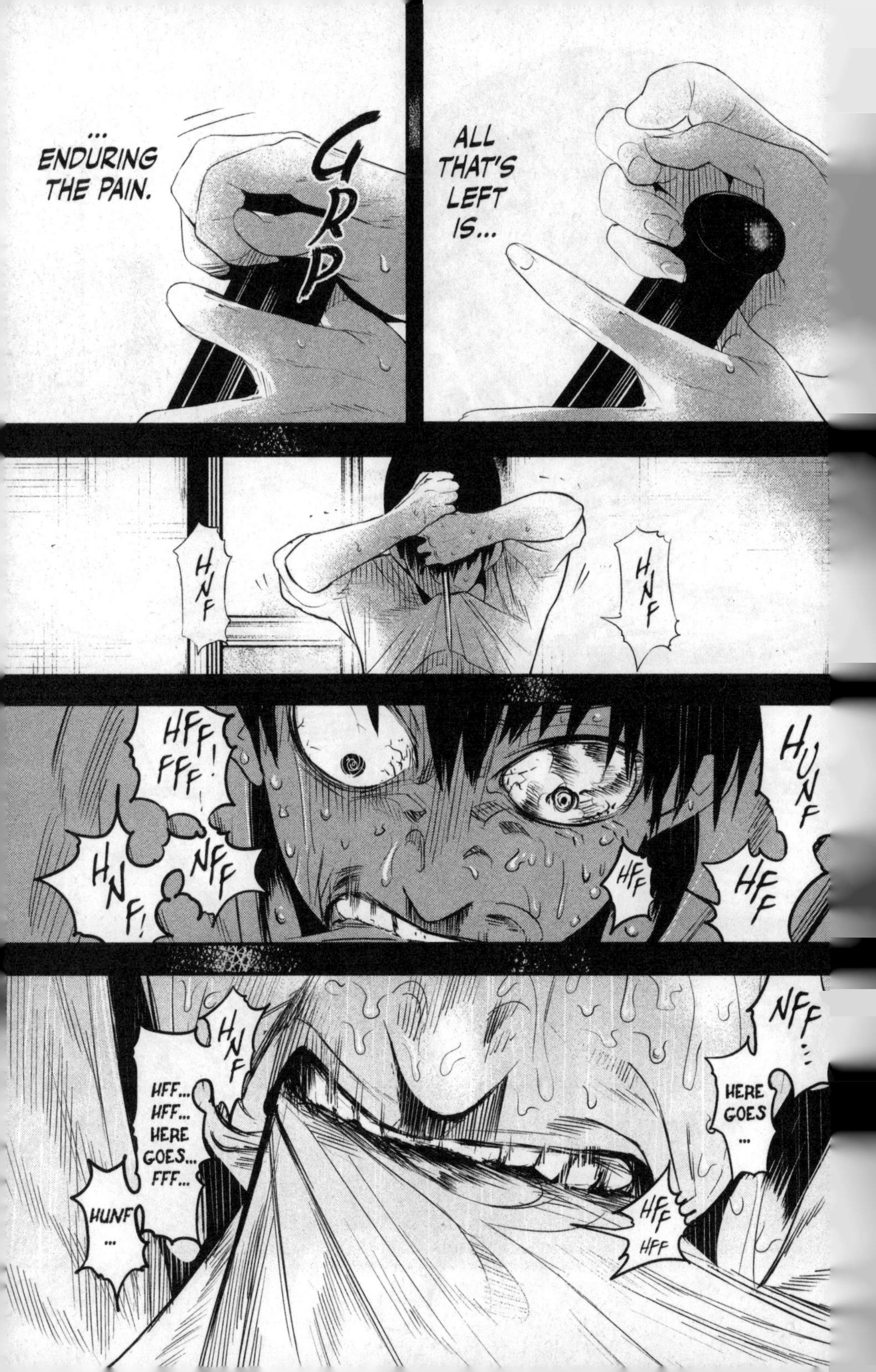
ALL THAT'S LEFT IS...
... ENDURING THE PAIN.
GRP
HNF
HNF
HUNF
HFF
HFF
HFF! FFF!
NFF
HNF!
NFF...
HERE GOES ...
HFF HFF
HNF
HFF... HFF... HERE GOES... FFF...
HUNF ...

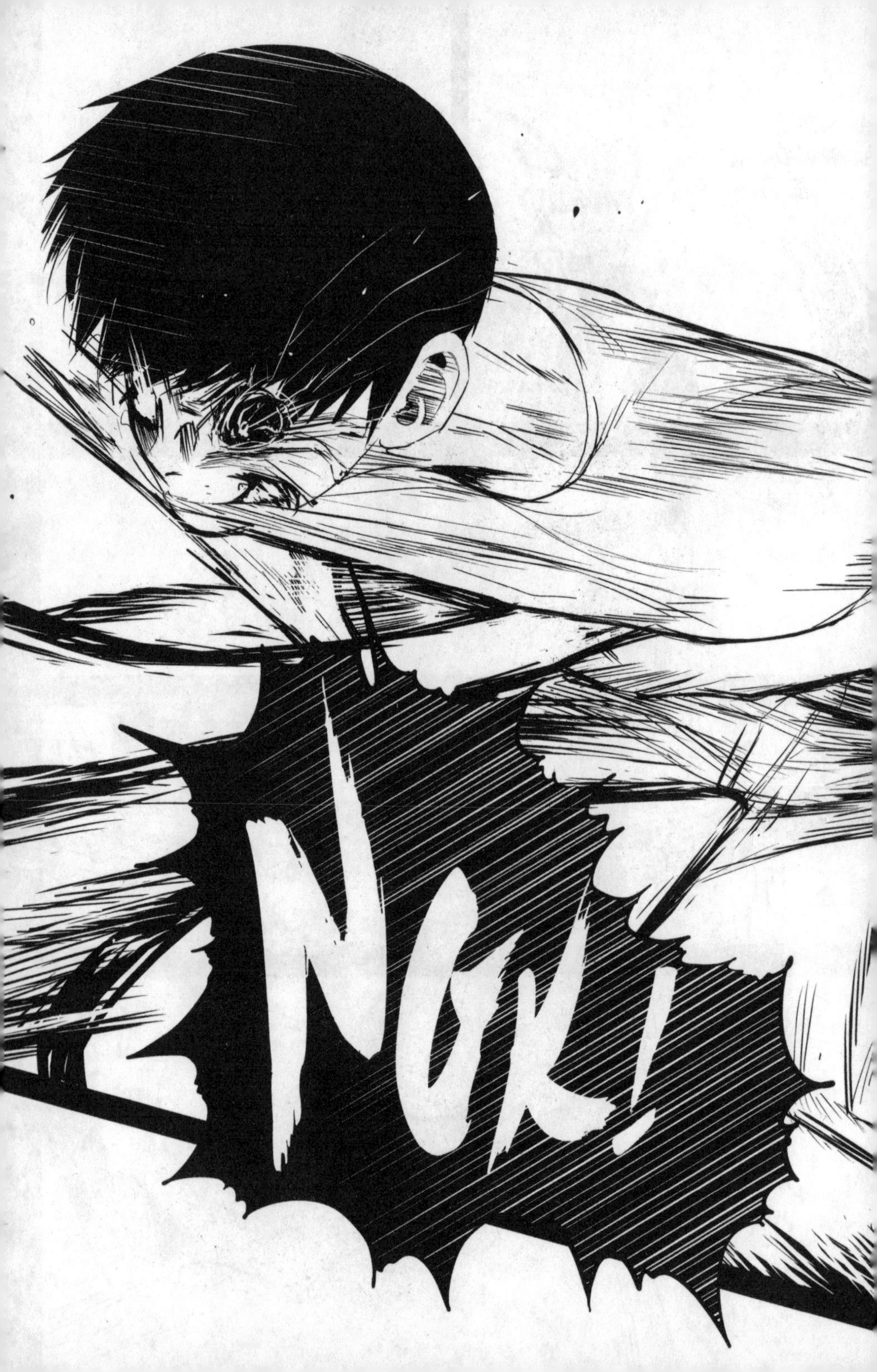
NO!

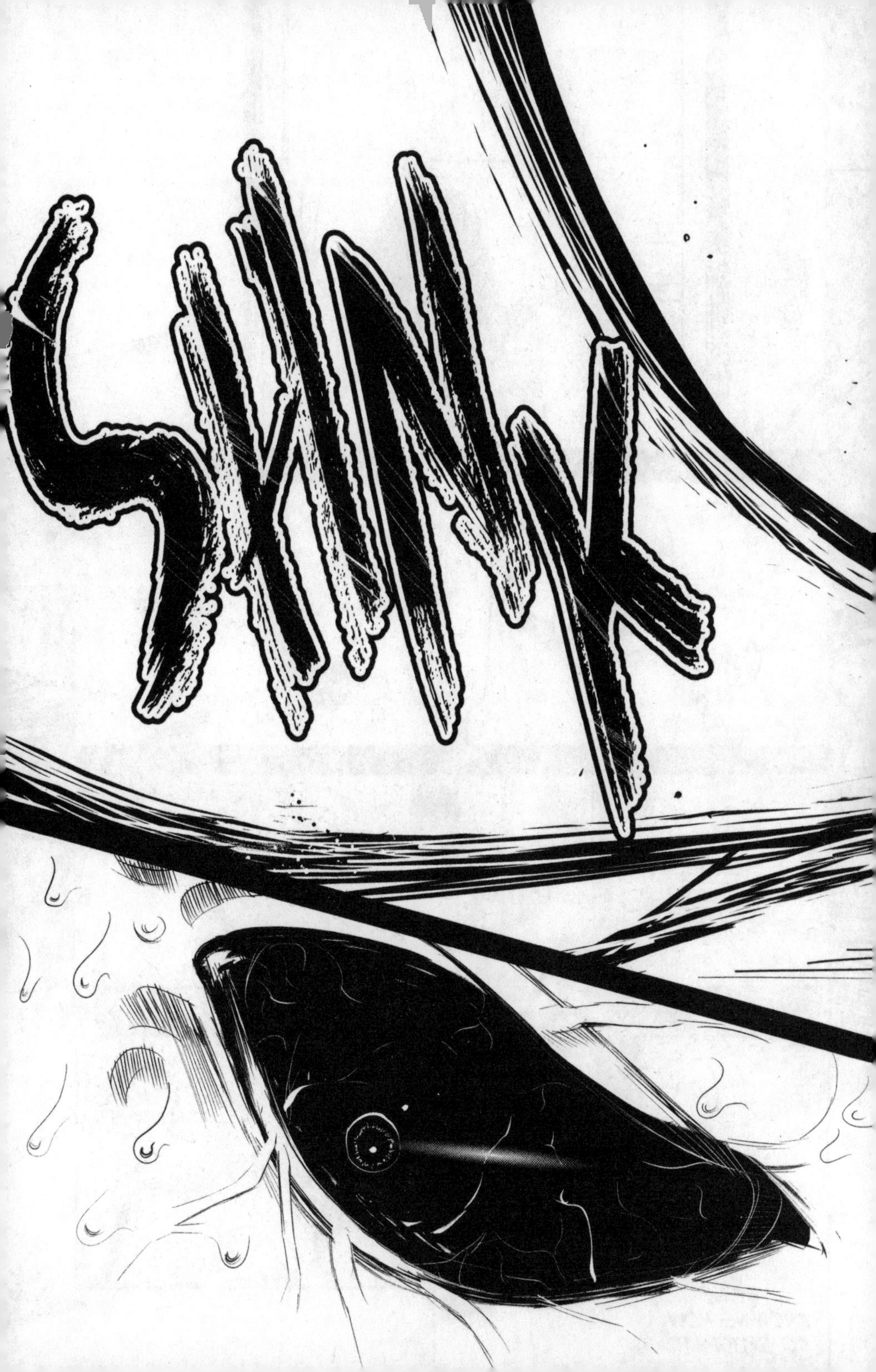
SHINK

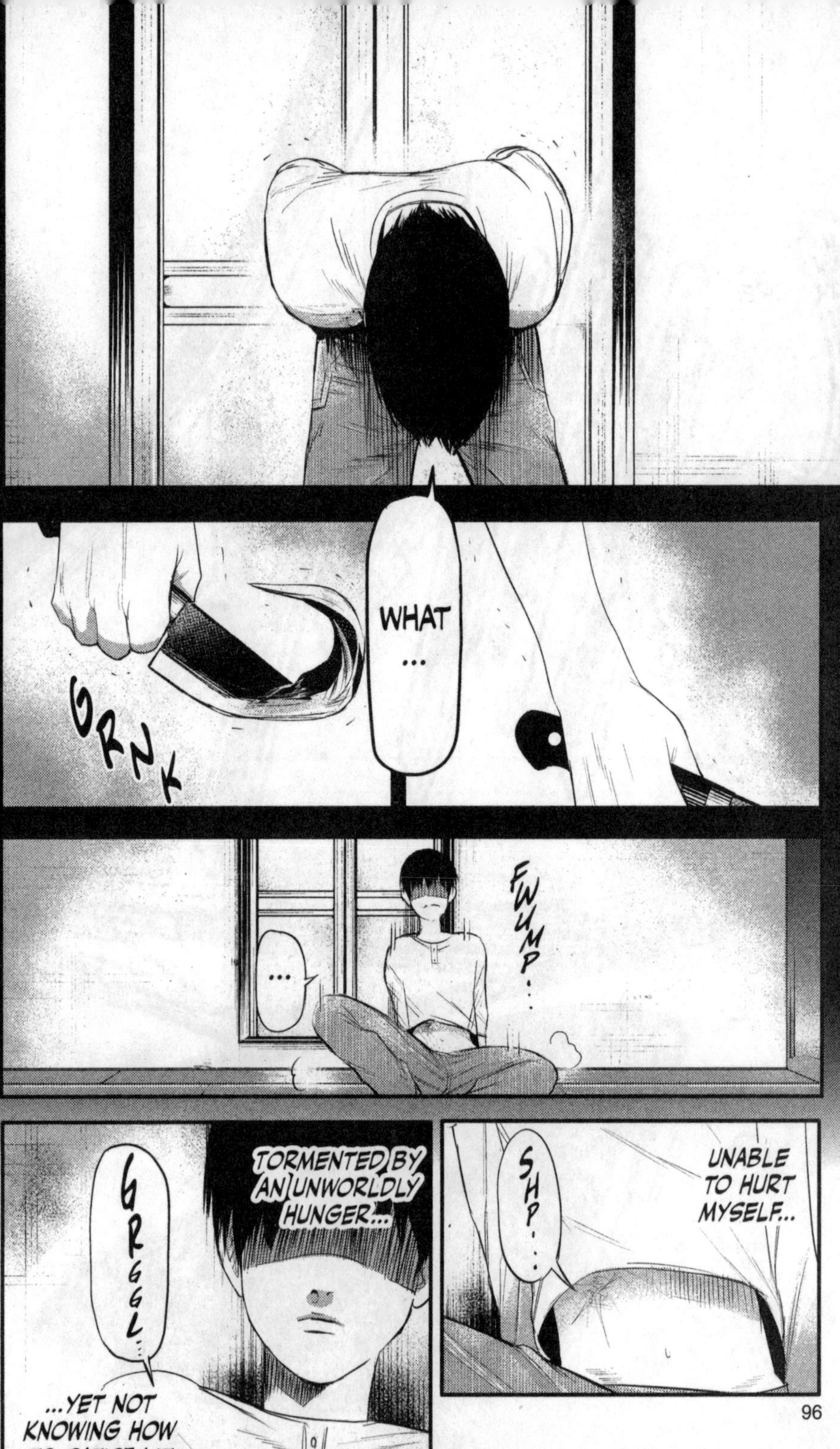
WHAT ...
GRNK
FWUMP...
...
UNABLE TO HURT MYSELF...
SHP...
TORMENTED BY AN UNWORLDLY HUNGER...
GRGGL...
...YET NOT KNOWING HOW TO SATISFY IT.

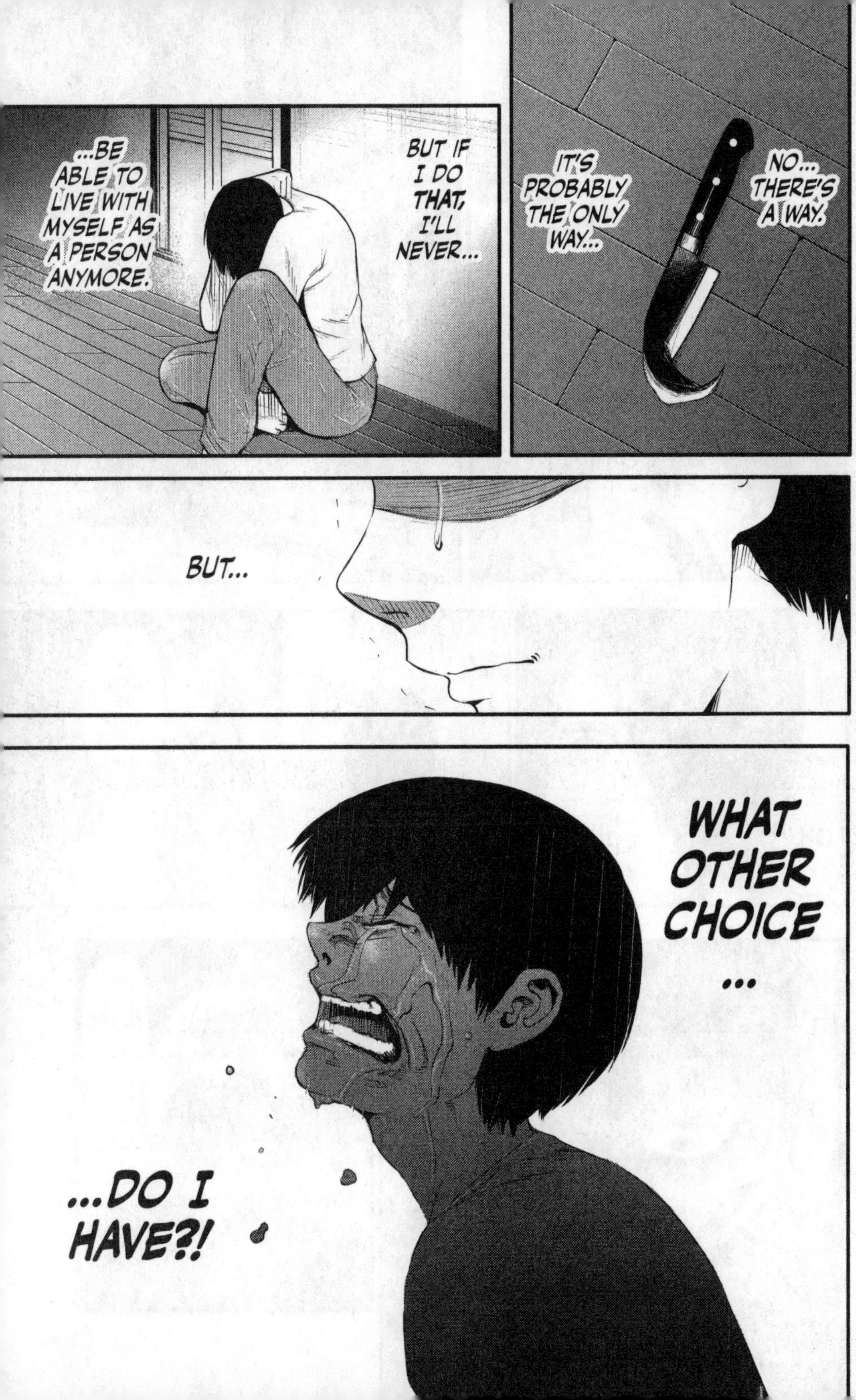
NO... THERE'S A WAY.
IT'S PROBABLY THE ONLY WAY...
BUT IF I DO THAT, I'LL NEVER...
...BE ABLE TO LIVE WITH MYSELF AS A PERSON ANYMORE.
BUT...
WHAT OTHER CHOICE ...
...DO I HAVE?!

I'M SORRY, SIR, WE'RE CLOSED...

OH.

PLEASE HELP ME...

YOU'RE...

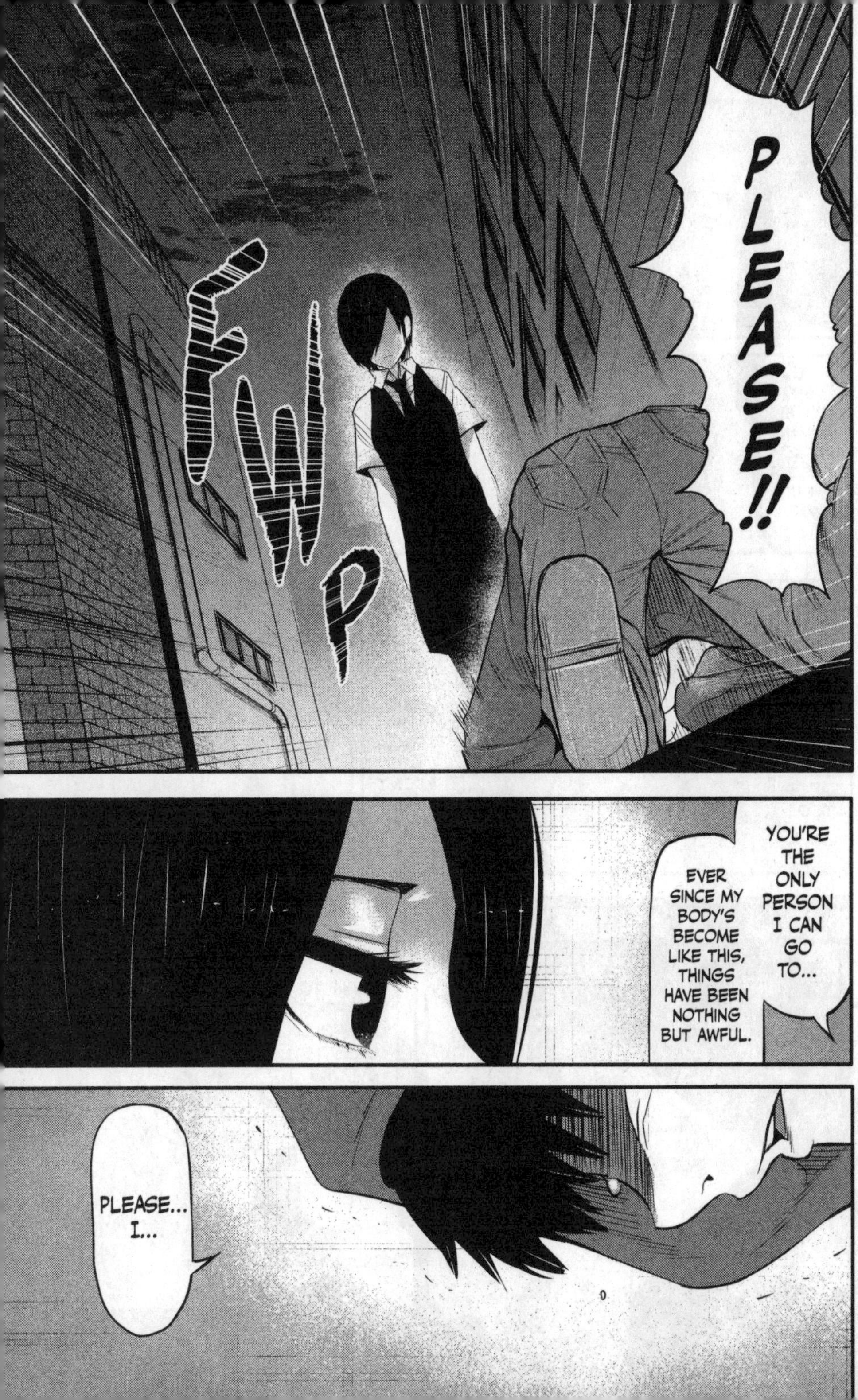
PLEASE!!
FWP
YOU'RE THE ONLY PERSON I CAN GO TO...
EVER SINCE MY BODY'S BECOME LIKE THIS, THINGS HAVE BEEN NOTHING BUT AWFUL.
PLEASE... I...

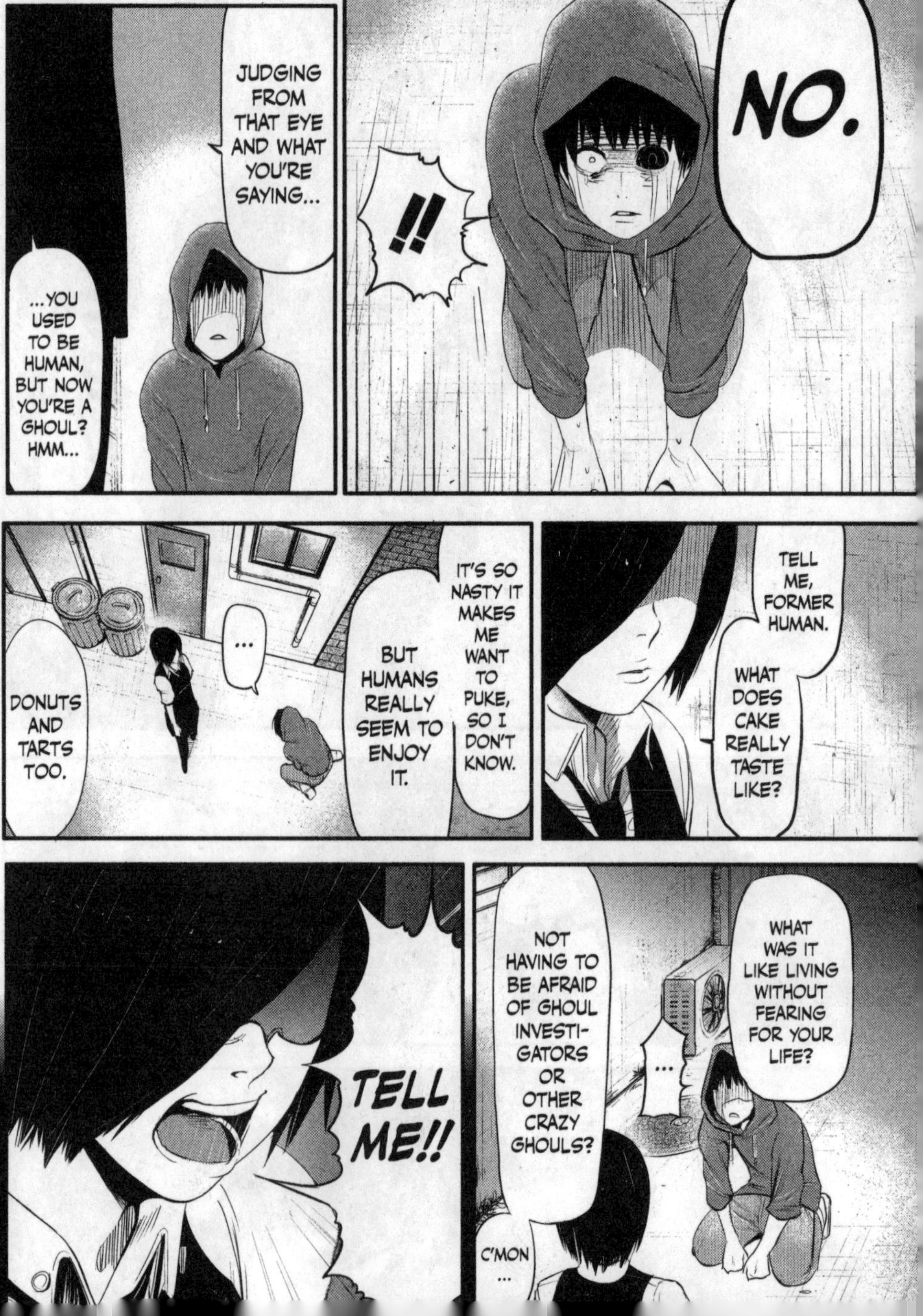
NO.
!!
JUDGING FROM THAT EYE AND WHAT YOU'RE SAYING...
...YOU USED TO BE HUMAN, BUT NOW YOU'RE A GHOUL? HMM...
TELL ME, FORMER HUMAN.
WHAT DOES CAKE REALLY TASTE LIKE?
IT'S SO NASTY IT MAKES ME WANT TO PUKE, SO I DON'T KNOW.
BUT HUMANS REALLY SEEM TO ENJOY IT.
...
DONUTS AND TARTS TOO.
WHAT WAS IT LIKE LIVING WITHOUT FEARING FOR YOUR LIFE?
...
NOT HAVING TO BE AFRAID OF GHOUL INVESTI-GATORS OR OTHER CRAZY GHOULS?
C'MON...
TELL ME!!

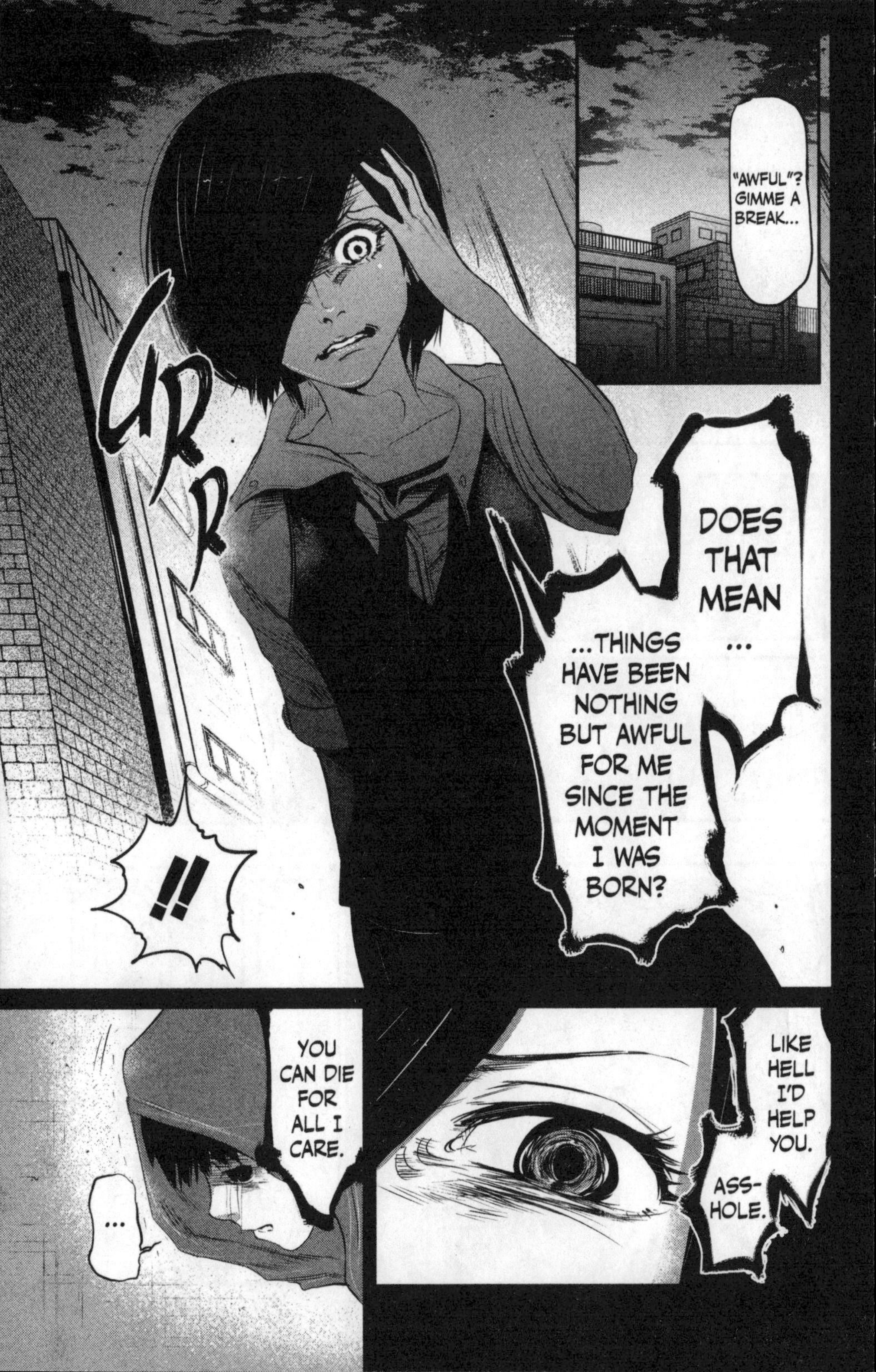
"AWFUL"? GIMME A BREAK...
DOES THAT MEAN ...
...THINGS HAVE BEEN NOTHING BUT AWFUL FOR ME SINCE THE MOMENT I WAS BORN?
URR
!!
LIKE HELL I'D HELP YOU.
ASS-HOLE.
YOU CAN DIE FOR ALL I CARE.
...

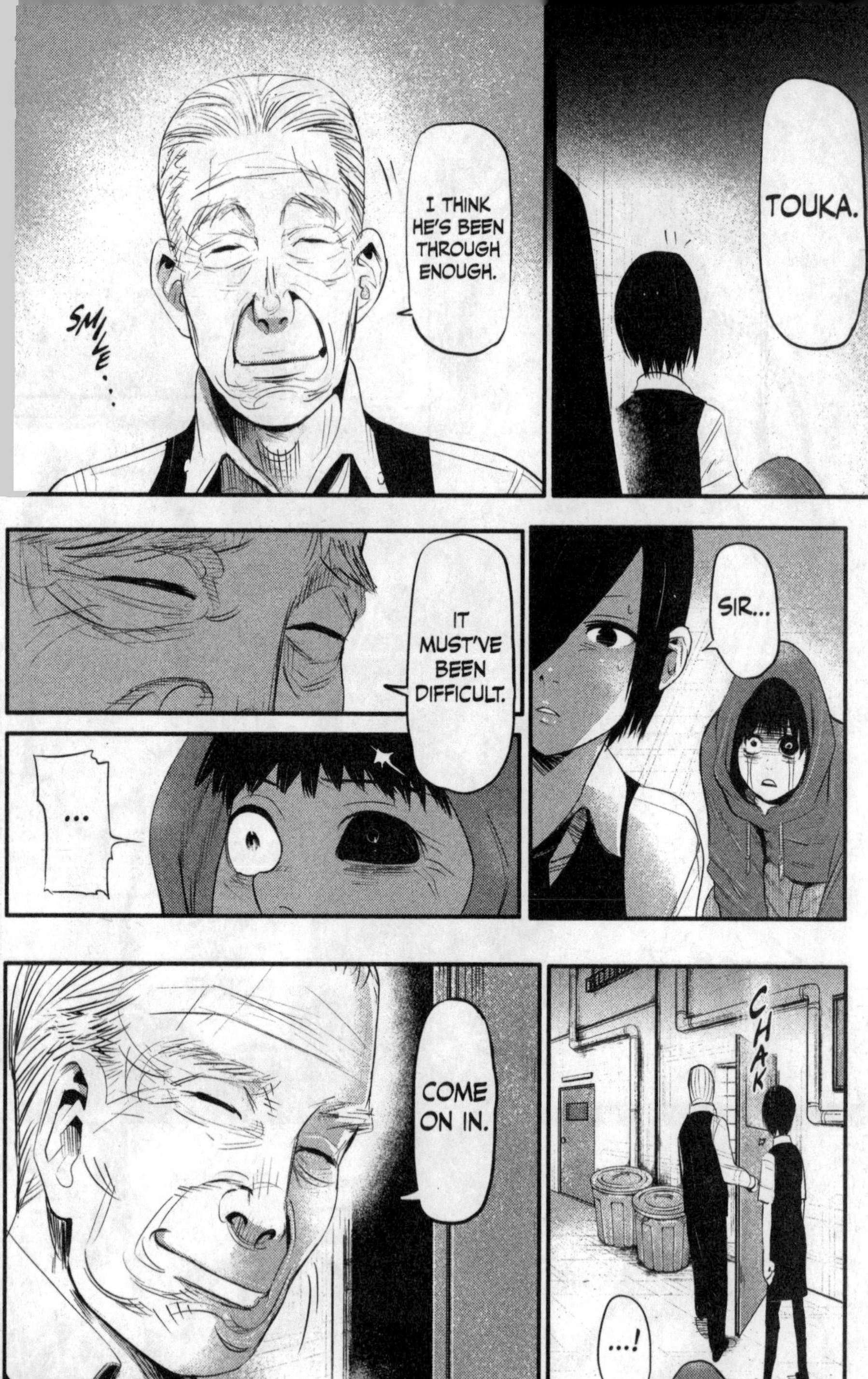
TOUKA.
I THINK HE'S BEEN THROUGH ENOUGH.
SMILE...
SIR...
IT MUST'VE BEEN DIFFICULT.
...
CHAK
...!
COME ON IN.

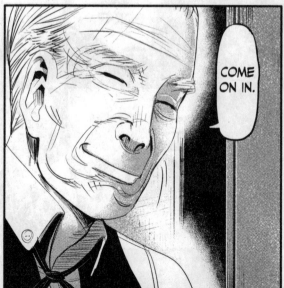

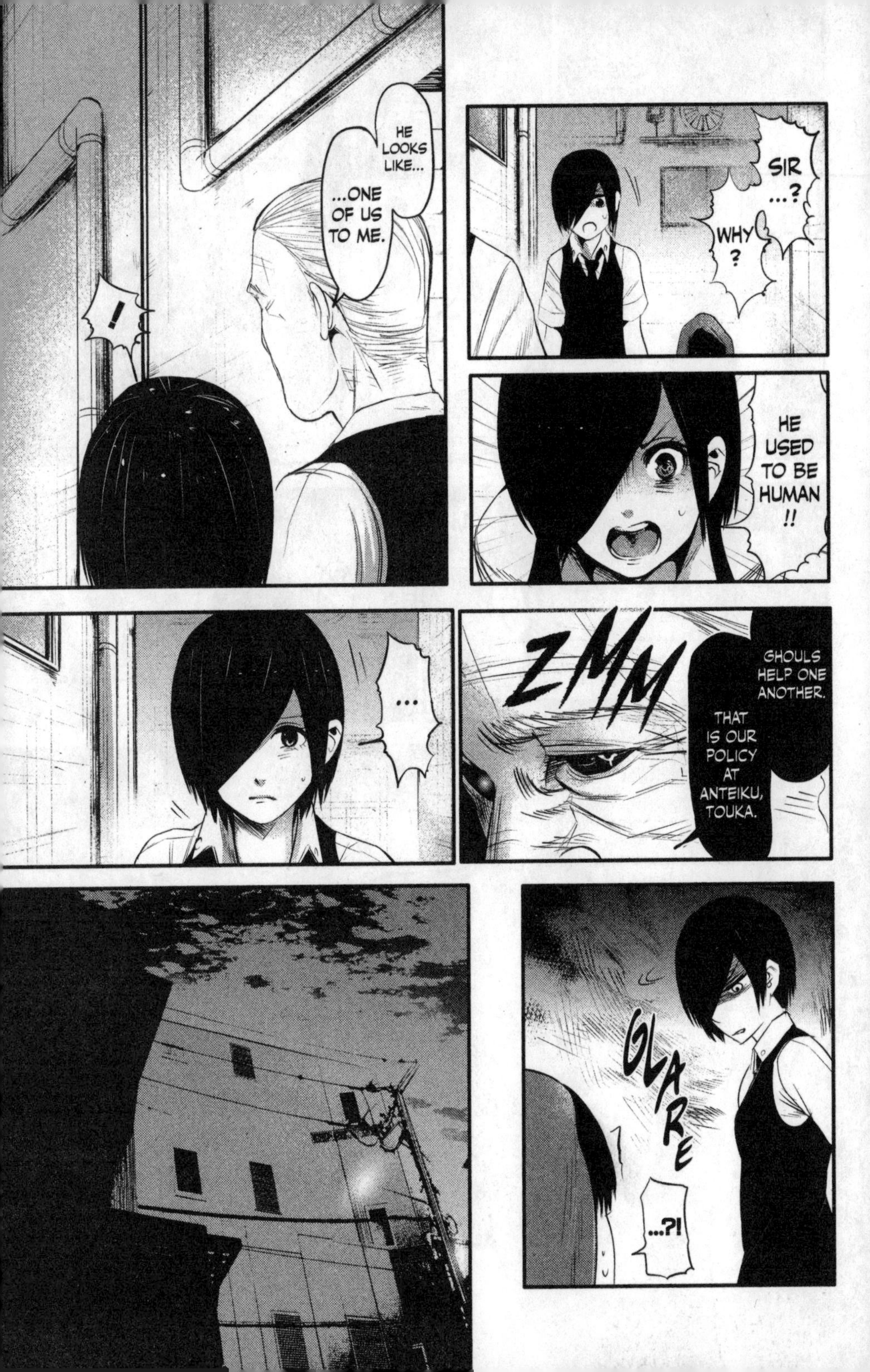
SIR ...?
WHY ?
HE USED TO BE HUMAN !!
HE LOOKS LIKE...
...ONE OF US TO ME.
!
ZMM
GHOULS HELP ONE ANOTHER.
THAT IS OUR POLICY AT ANTEIKU, TOUKA.
...
GLARE
...?!

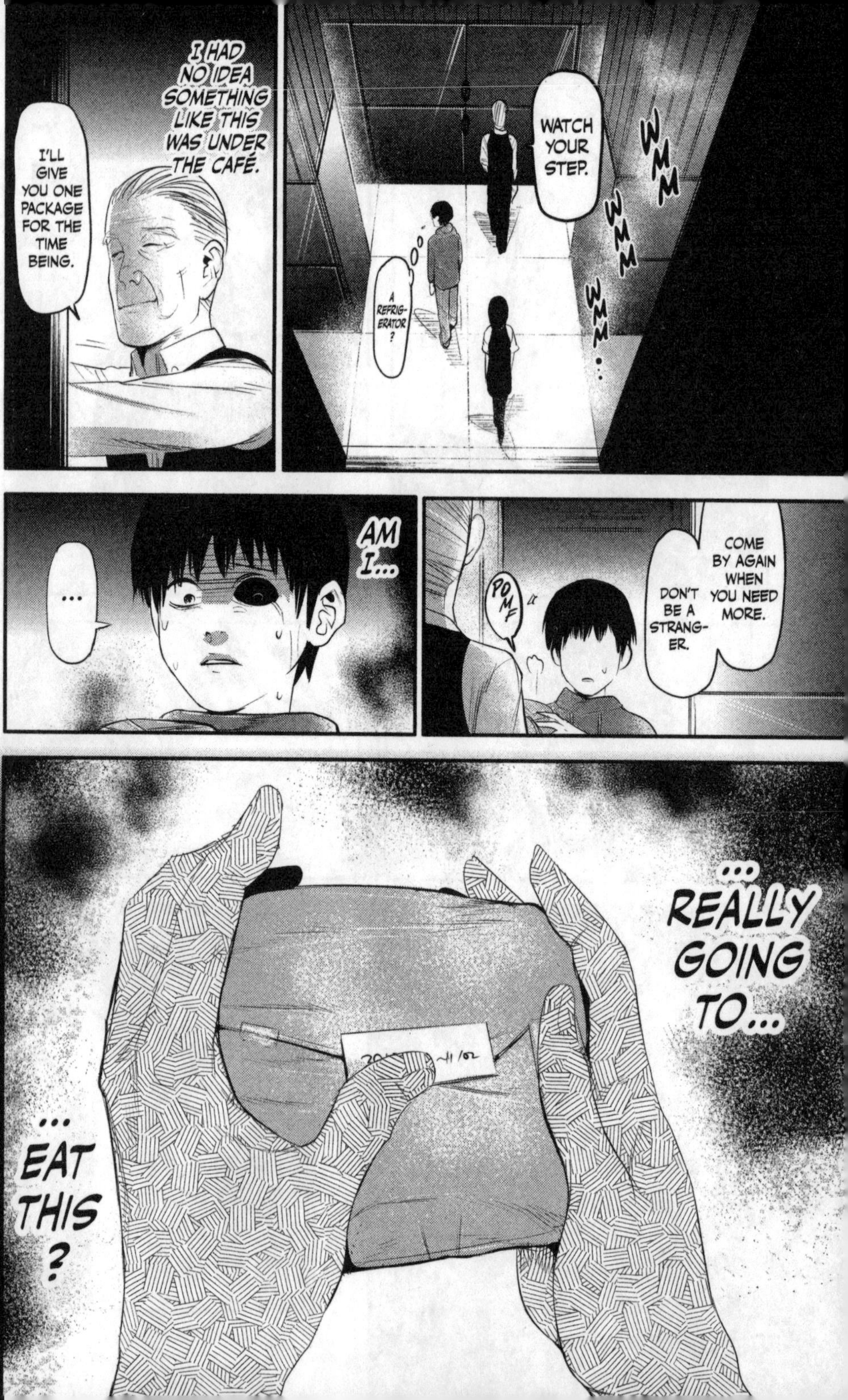
WATCH YOUR STEP.
WMM WMM WMM...
A REFRIG-ERATOR?
I HAD NO IDEA SOMETHING LIKE THIS WAS UNDER THE CAFÉ.
I'LL GIVE YOU ONE PACKAGE FOR THE TIME BEING.
COME BY AGAIN WHEN YOU NEED MORE.
DON'T BE A STRANG-ER.
POMF
AM I...
...
...REALLY GOING TO...
...EAT THIS?

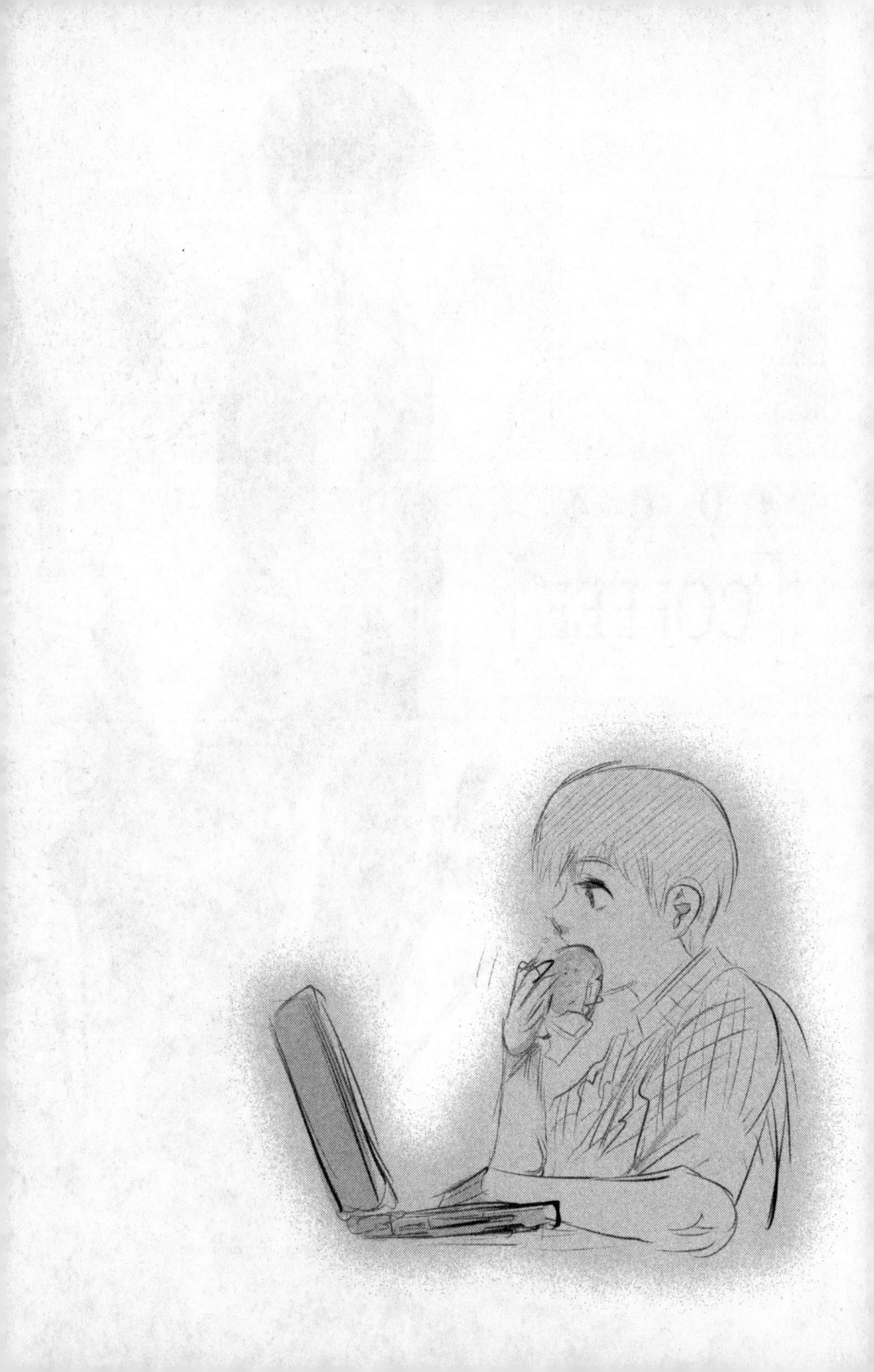

#004

TOKYO GHOUL

[COFFEE]

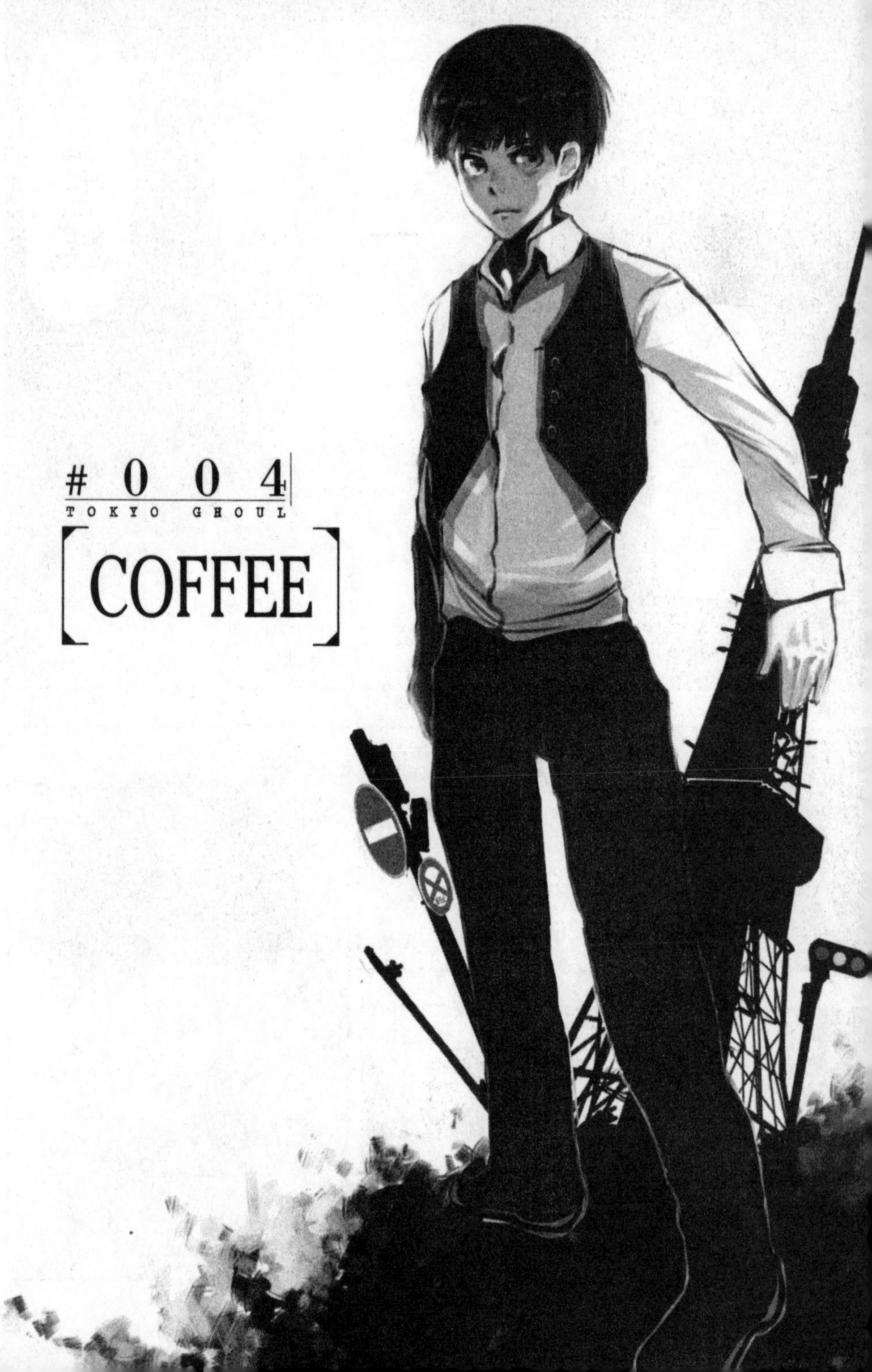

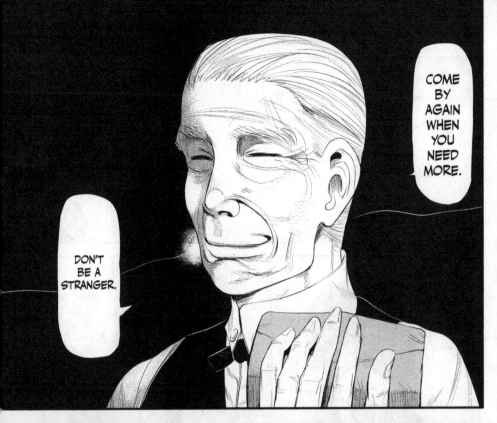

COME BY AGAIN WHEN YOU NEED MORE.

DON'T BE A STRANGER.

...HUMAN FLESH.

TH- THANK YOU...

INSIDE THIS PACKAGE IS...

...
GULP

...

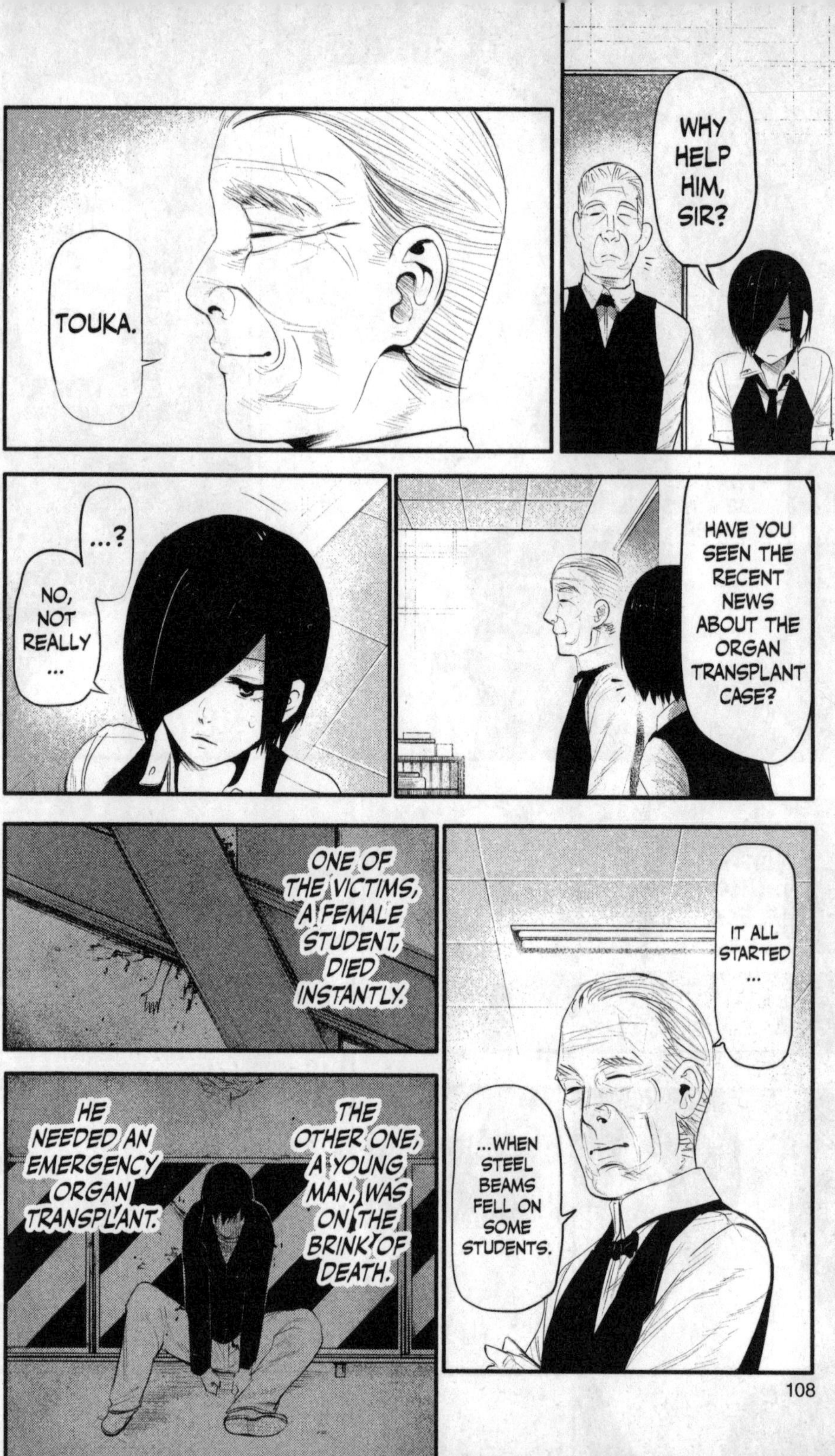
WHY HELP HIM, SIR?
TOUKA.
HAVE YOU SEEN THE RECENT NEWS ABOUT THE ORGAN TRANSPLANT CASE?
...?
NO, NOT REALLY ...
IT ALL STARTED ...
...WHEN STEEL BEAMS FELL ON SOME STUDENTS.
ONE OF THE VICTIMS, A FEMALE STUDENT, DIED INSTANTLY.
THE OTHER ONE, A YOUNG MAN, WAS ON THE BRINK OF DEATH.
HE NEEDED AN EMERGENCY ORGAN TRANSPLANT.

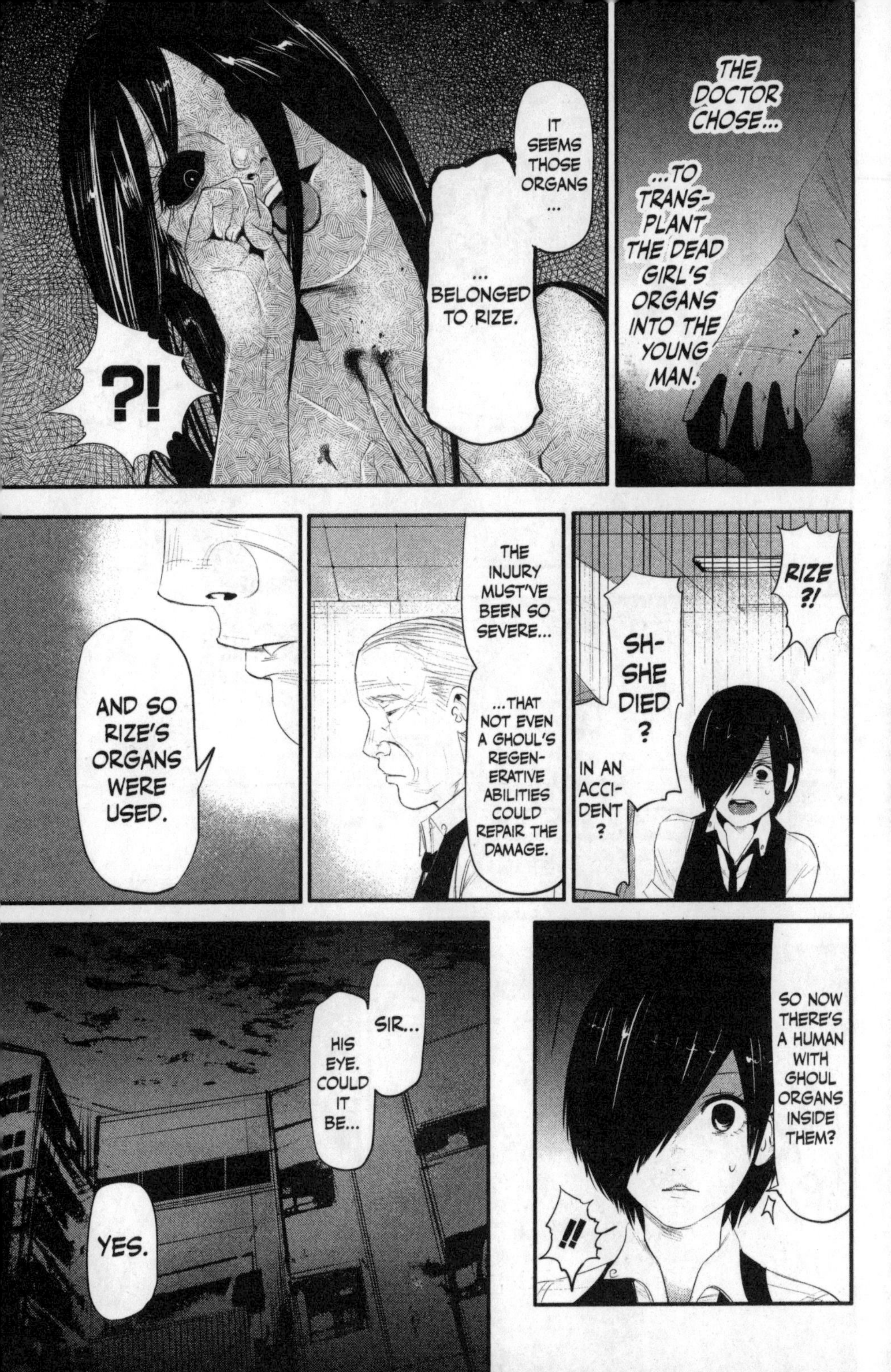
THE DOCTOR CHOSE...
...TO TRANS-PLANT THE DEAD GIRL'S ORGANS INTO THE YOUNG MAN.
IT SEEMS THOSE ORGANS ...
... BELONGED TO RIZE.
?!
RIZE ?!
SH-SHE DIED ?
IN AN ACCI-DENT ?
THE INJURY MUST'VE BEEN SO SEVERE...
...THAT NOT EVEN A GHOUL'S REGEN-ERATIVE ABILITIES COULD REPAIR THE DAMAGE.
AND SO RIZE'S ORGANS WERE USED.
SO NOW THERE'S A HUMAN WITH GHOUL ORGANS INSIDE THEM?
!!
SIR...
HIS EYE. COULD IT BE...
YES.

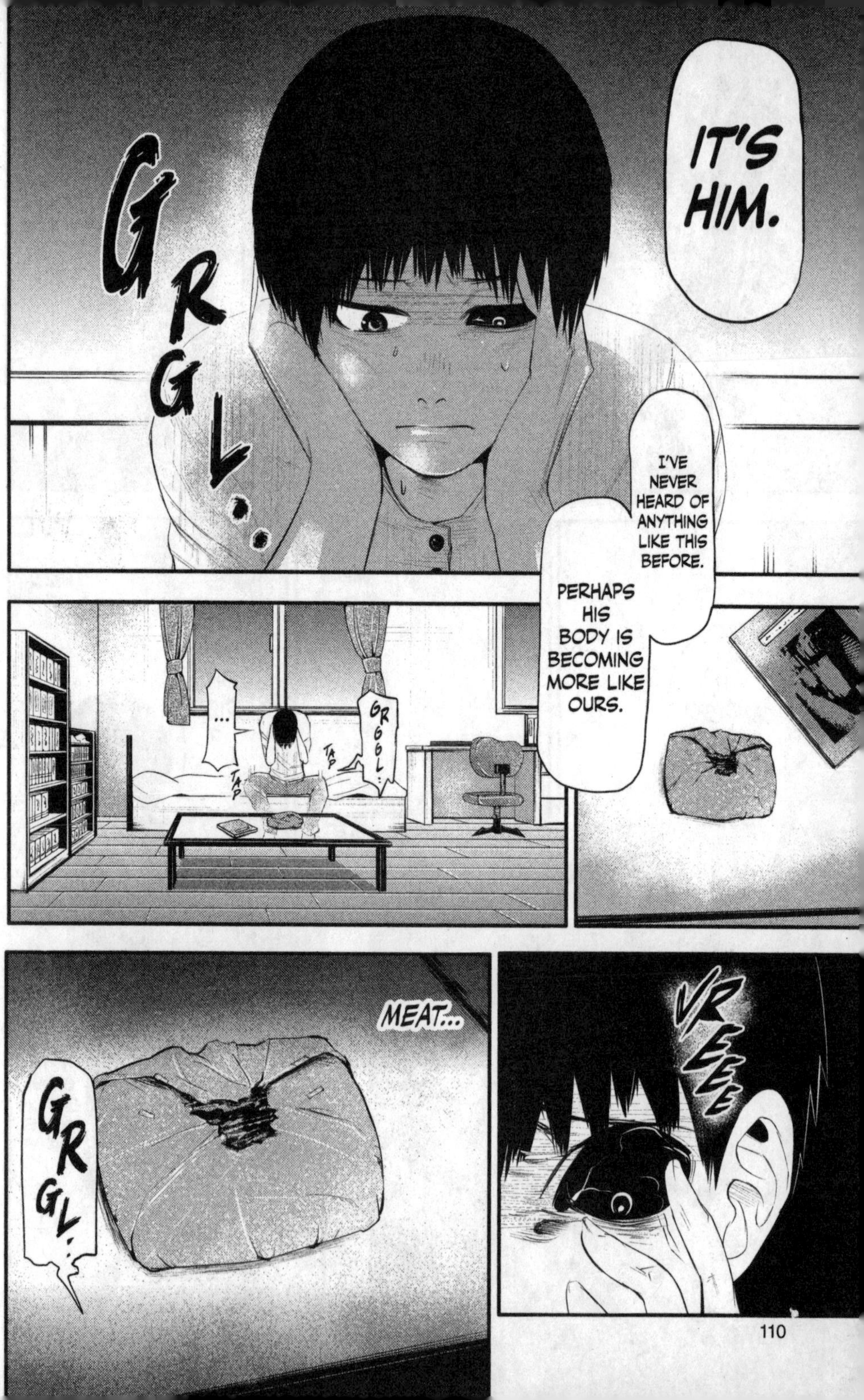
IT'S HIM.
GRGL..
I'VE NEVER HEARD OF ANYTHING LIKE THIS BEFORE.
PERHAPS HIS BODY IS BECOMING MORE LIKE OURS.
GRGGL..
TAP
TAP
...
VREEEE
MEAT...
GRGL..

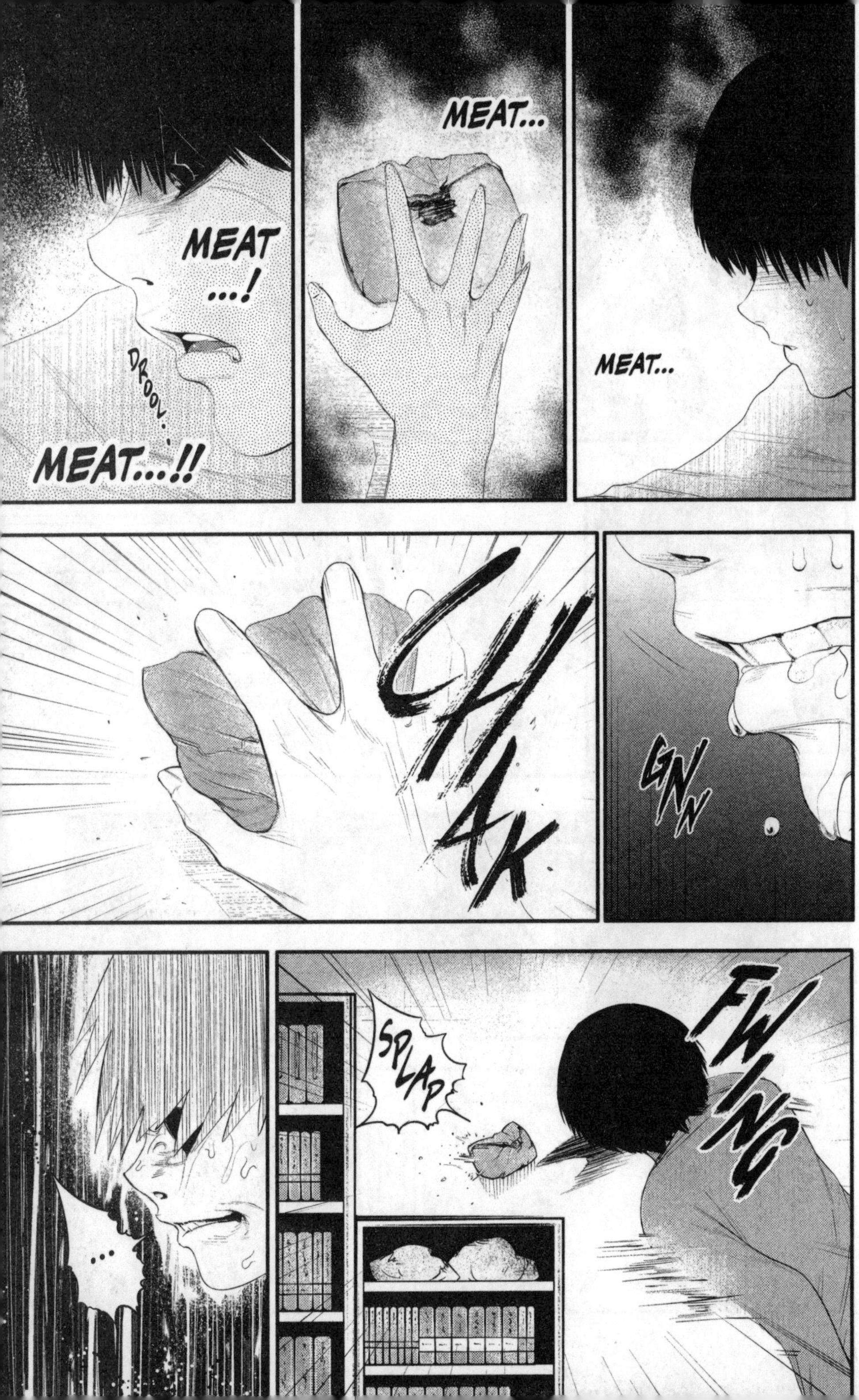
MEAT...
MEAT...
MEAT ...!
DROOL..
MEAT...!!
GNN
CHAK
FWING
SPLAP
...

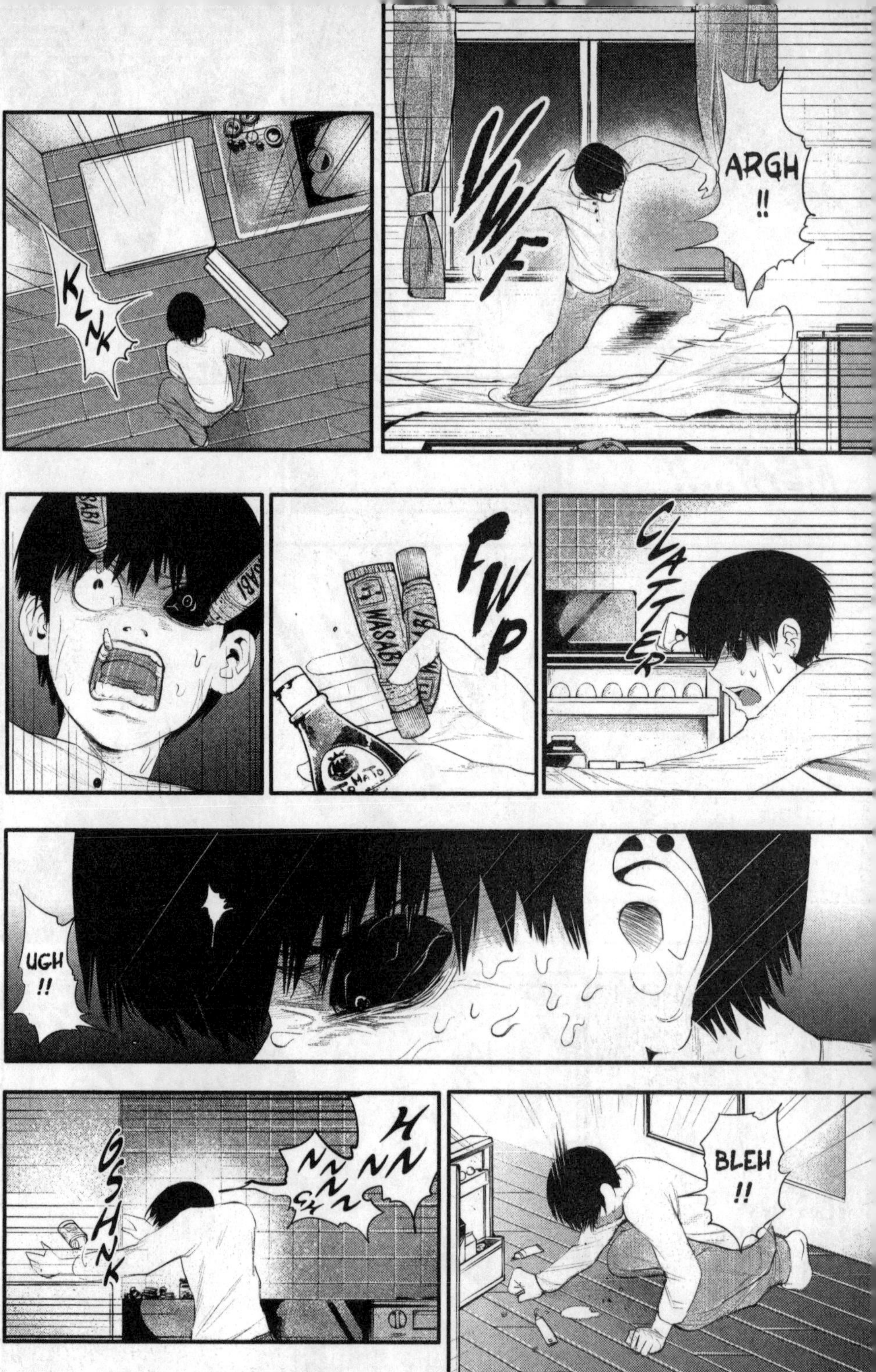
VWF
ARGH!!
KLNK
CLATTER
FWP
WASABI
UGH!!
BLEH!!
HNNNNNNGH
GSHNK

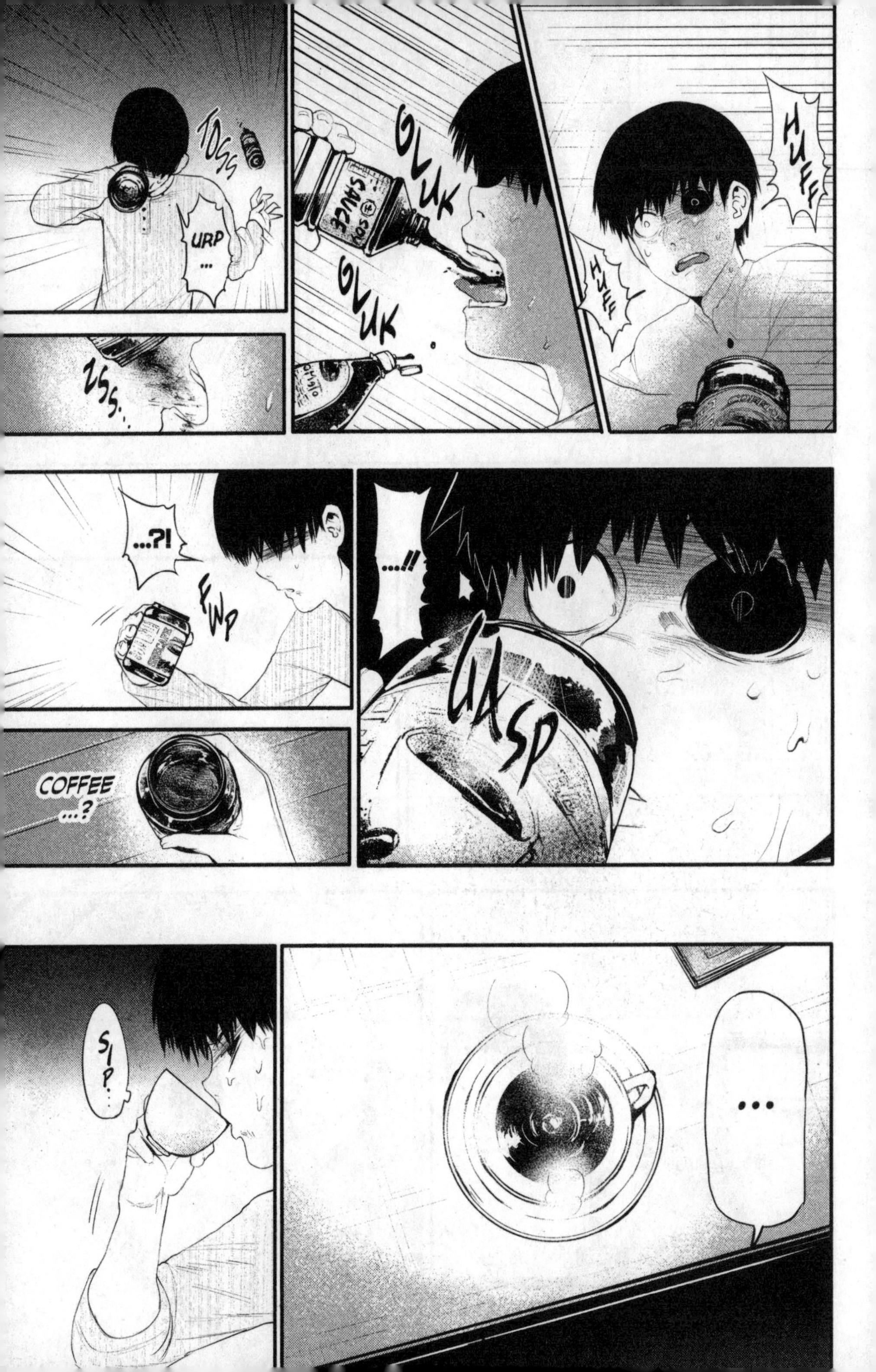
HUFF
HUFF
GLUK
SOY SAUCE
GLUK
TOSS
URP ...
ZSS...
...!!
GASP
...?!
FWP
COFFEE ...?
...
SIP...

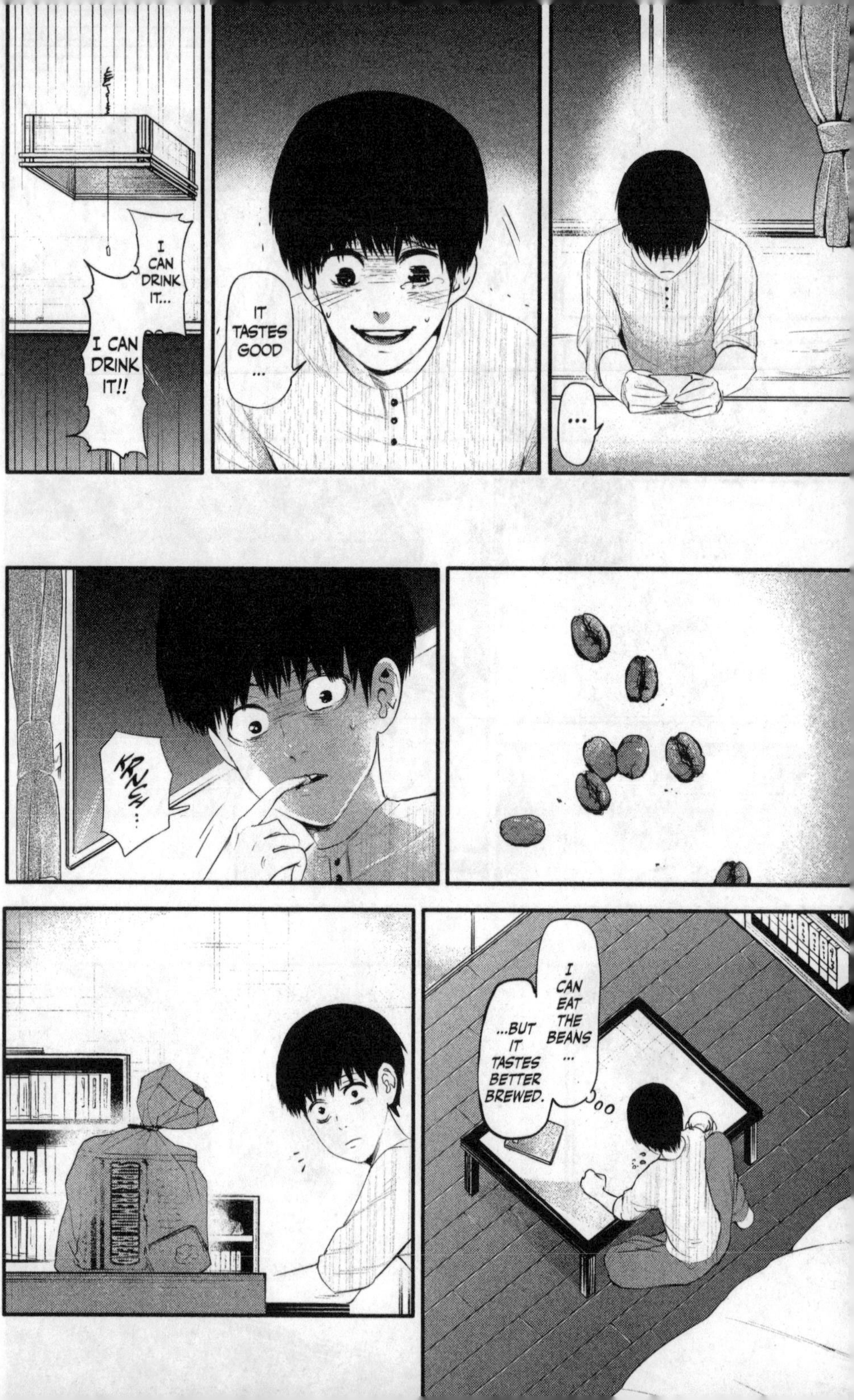
...
IT TASTES GOOD ...
I CAN DRINK IT...
I CAN DRINK IT!!
KRNCH...
I CAN EAT THE BEANS ...
...BUT IT TASTES BETTER BREWED.

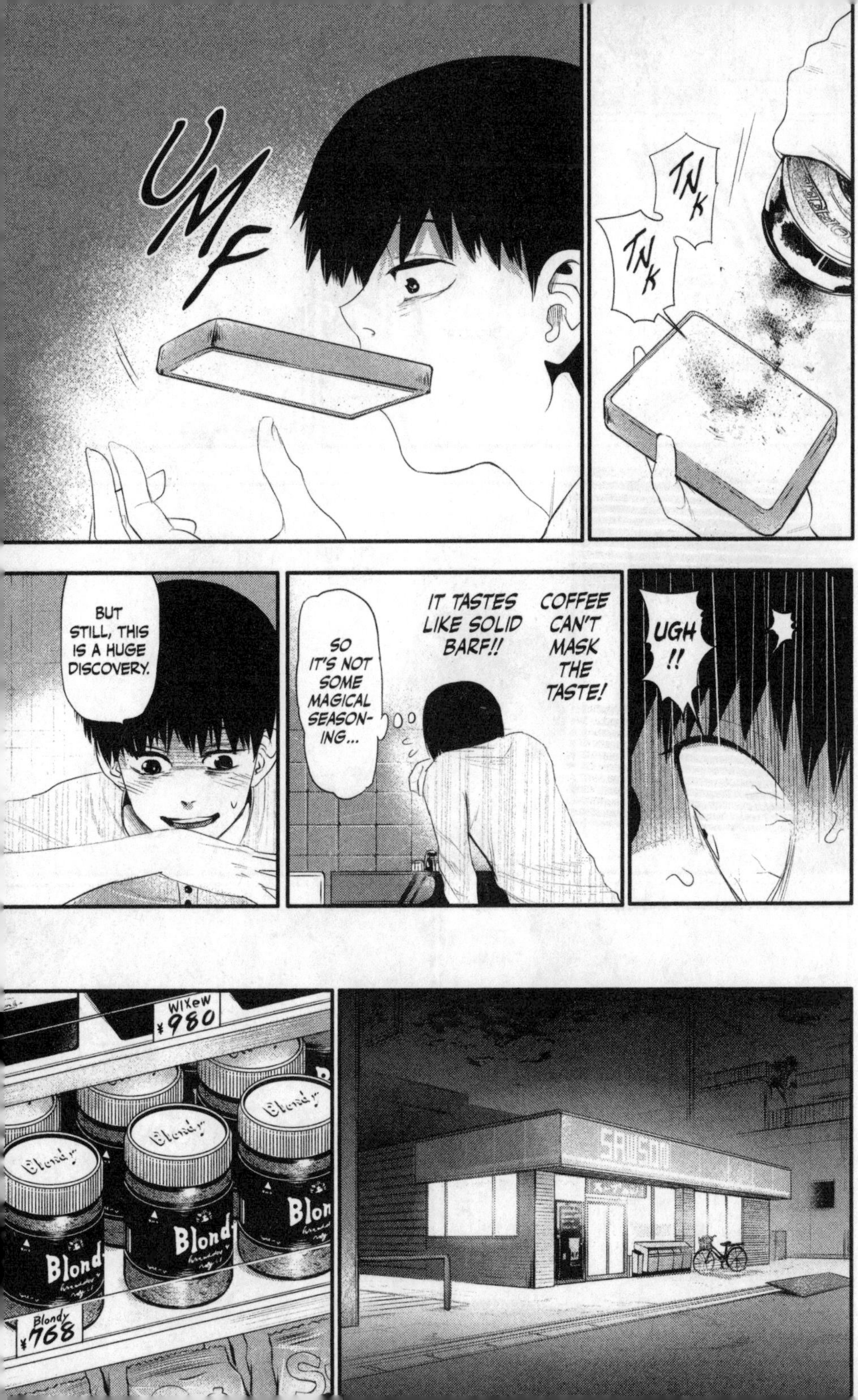
TNK
TNK
UMF
UGH!!
COFFEE CAN'T MASK THE TASTE!
IT TASTES LIKE SOLID BARF!!
SO IT'S NOT SOME MAGICAL SEASON-ING...
BUT STILL, THIS IS A HUGE DISCOVERY.
SAWSON
¥980
Blondy
Blondy
Blondy ¥768

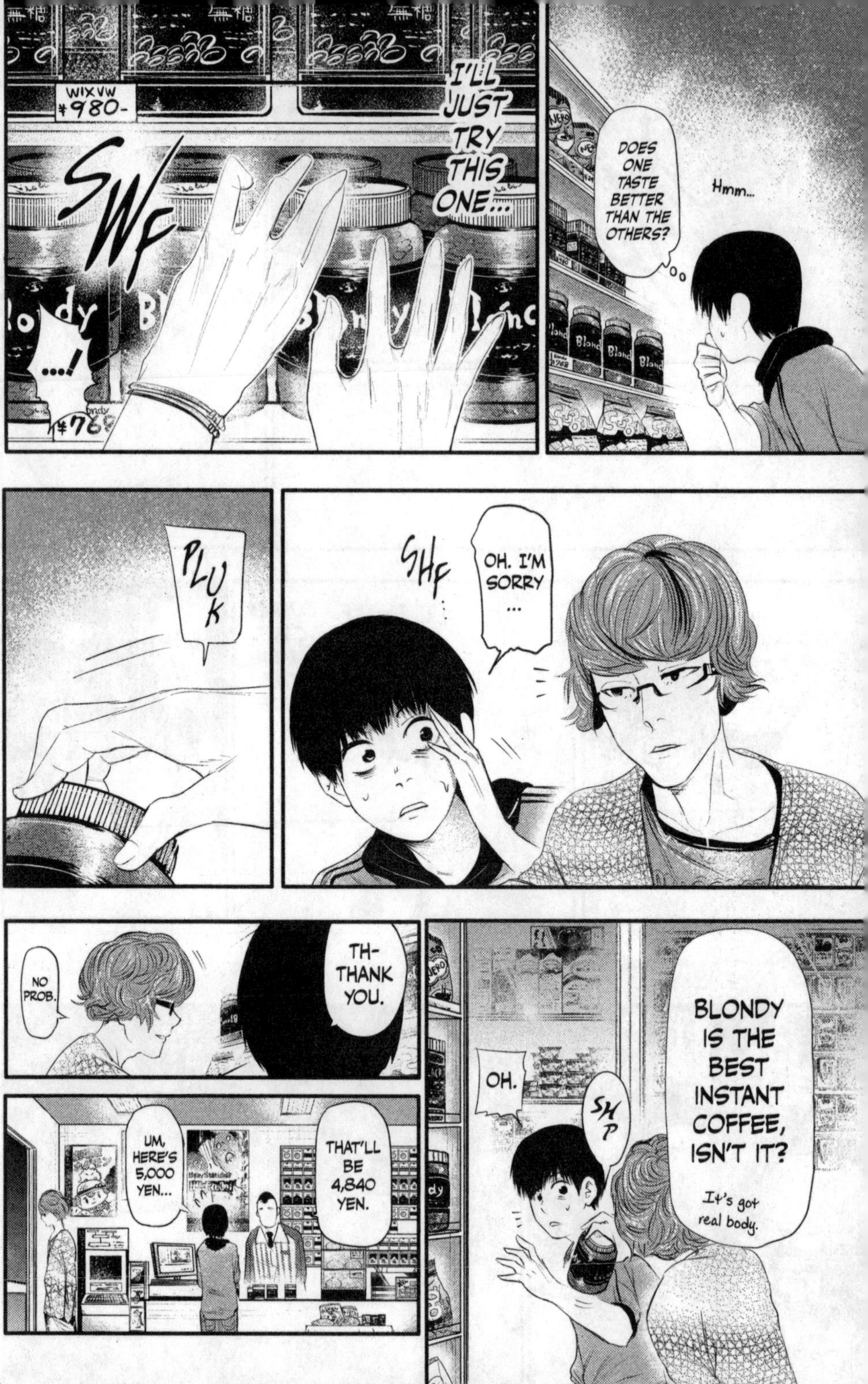
Hmm...
DOES ONE TASTE BETTER THAN THE OTHERS?
I'LL JUST TRY THIS ONE...
WIXVW ¥980-
SWF
...!
SHF
OH. I'M SORRY ...
PLUK
BLONDY IS THE BEST INSTANT COFFEE, ISN'T IT?
It's got real body.
SHP
OH.
TH-THANK YOU.
NO PROB.
THAT'LL BE 4,840 YEN.
UM, HERE'S 5,000 YEN...

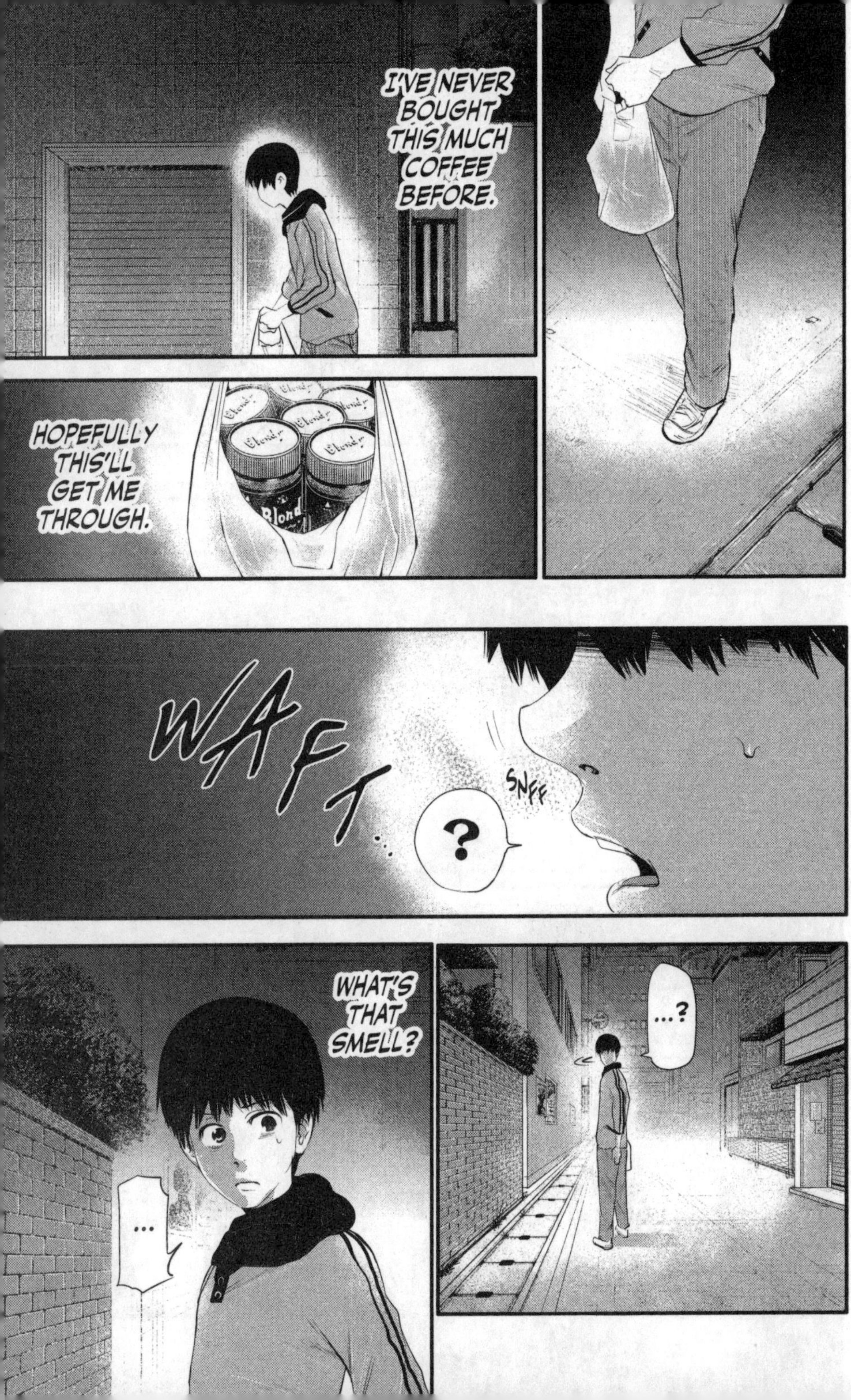
I'VE NEVER BOUGHT THIS MUCH COFFEE BEFORE.
HOPEFULLY THIS'LL GET ME THROUGH.
SNFF
?
WAFT...
...?
WHAT'S THAT SMELL?
...

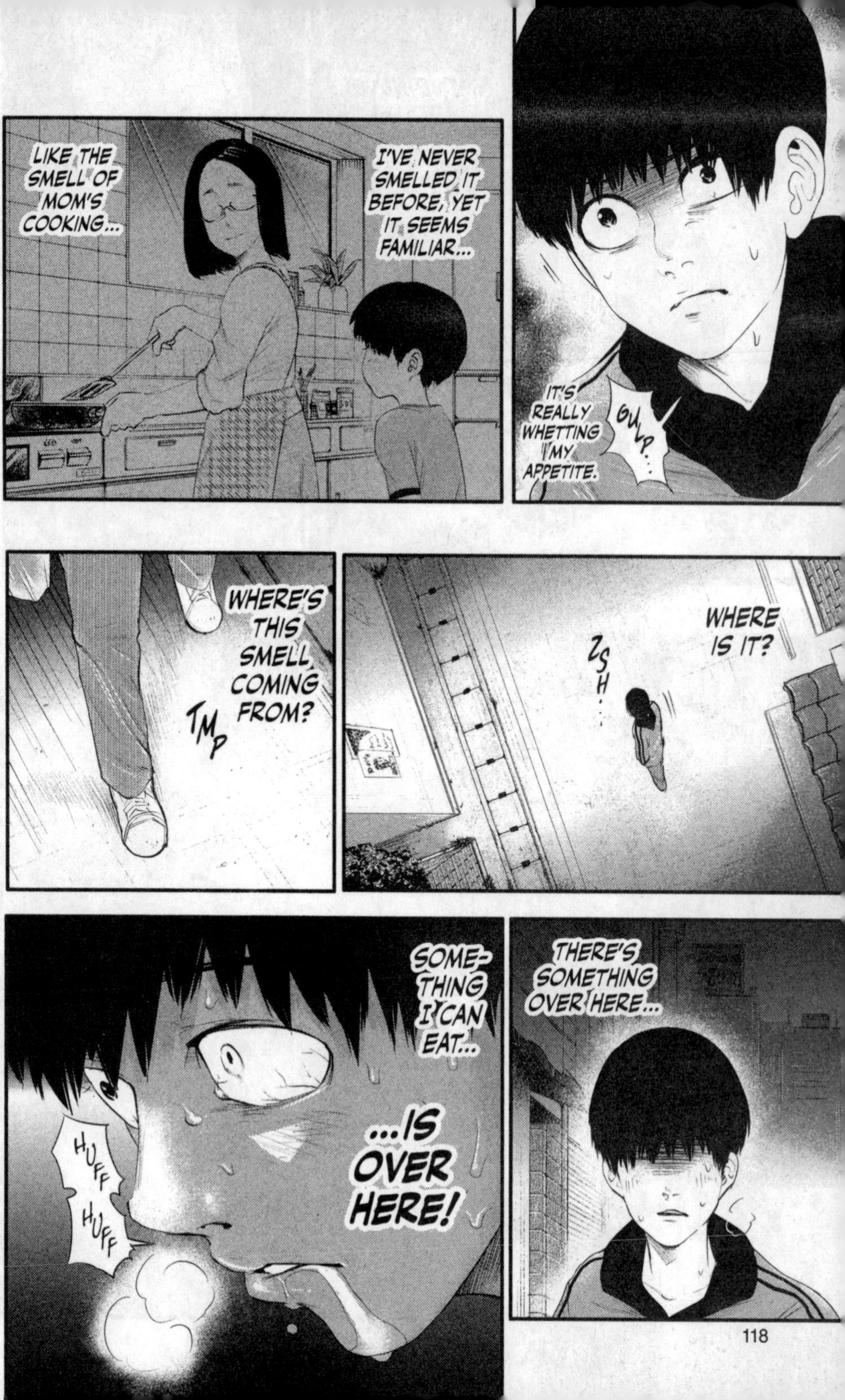
GULP...
IT'S REALLY WHETTING MY APPETITE.
I'VE NEVER SMELLED IT BEFORE, YET IT SEEMS FAMILIAR...
LIKE THE SMELL OF MOM'S COOKING...
WHERE IS IT?
ZSH...
WHERE'S THIS SMELL COMING FROM?
TMP
THERE'S SOMETHING OVER HERE...
SOME-THING I CAN EAT...
...IS OVER HERE!
HUFF HUFF

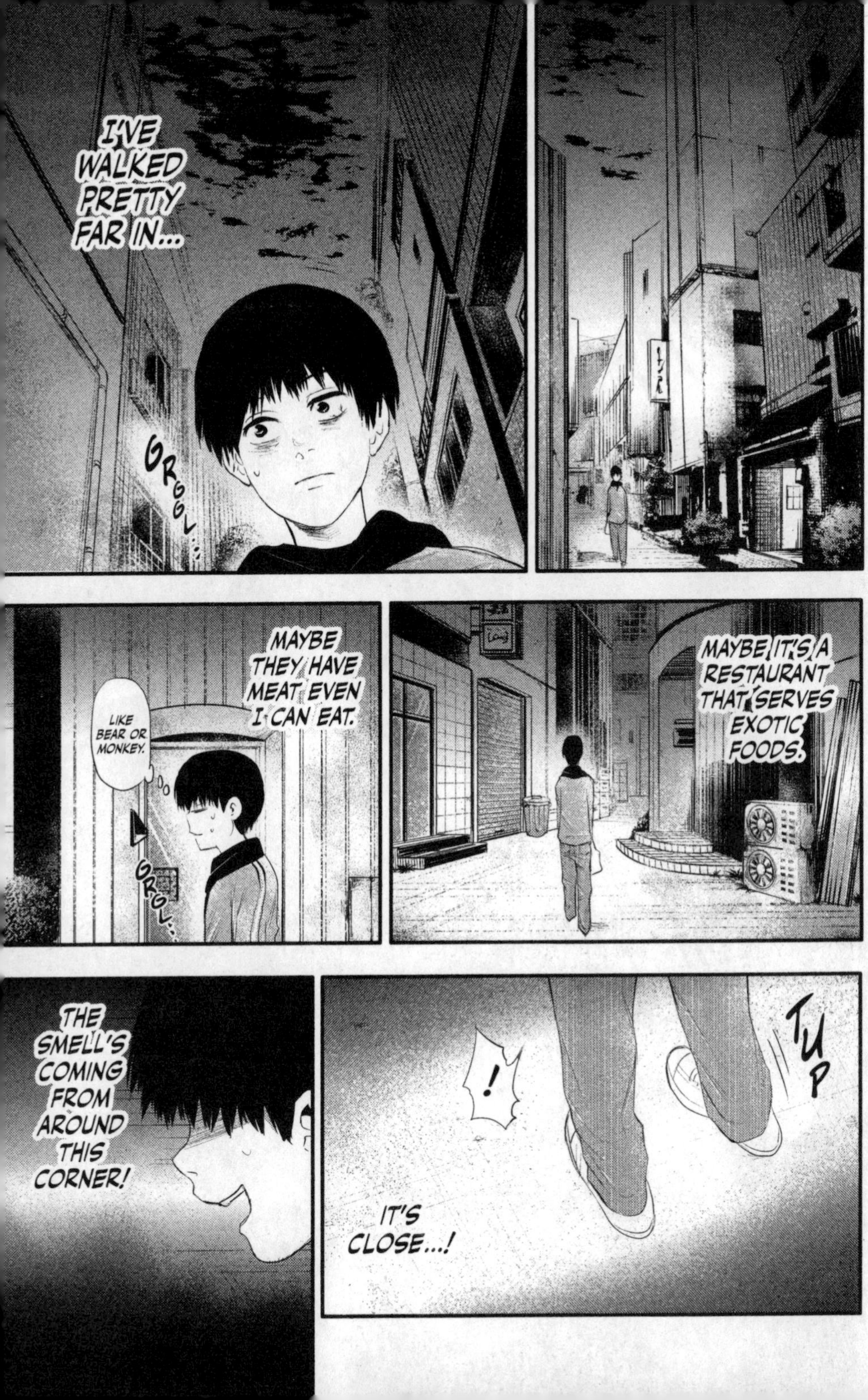
I'VE WALKED PRETTY FAR IN...
GRGGL...
MAYBE IT'S A RESTAURANT THAT SERVES EXOTIC FOODS.
MAYBE THEY HAVE MEAT EVEN I CAN EAT.
LIKE BEAR OR MONKEY.
GRGL...
TUP
!
IT'S CLOSE...!
THE SMELL'S COMING FROM AROUND THIS CORNER!

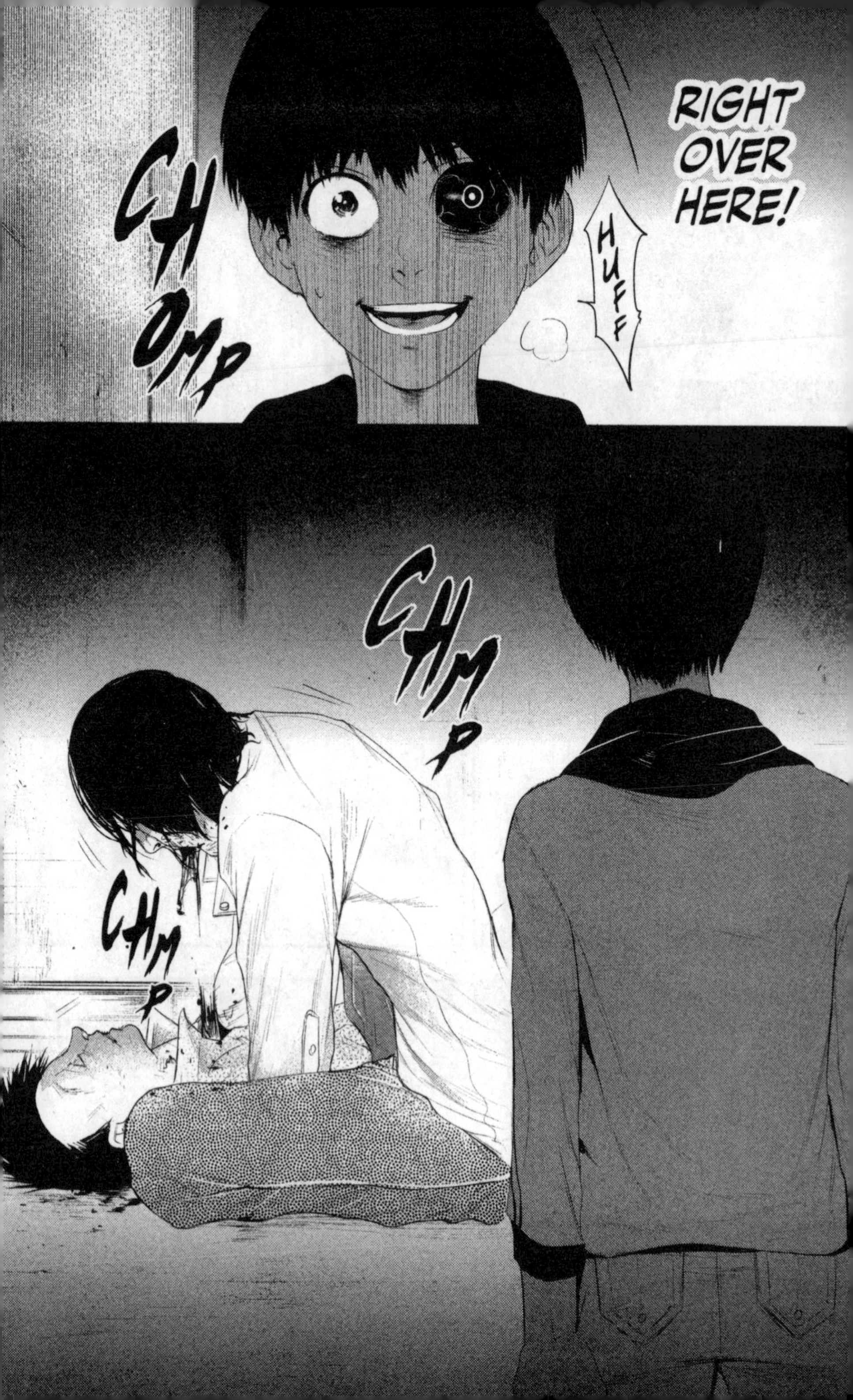
RIGHT OVER HERE!
HUFF
CHOMP
CHMP
CHMP

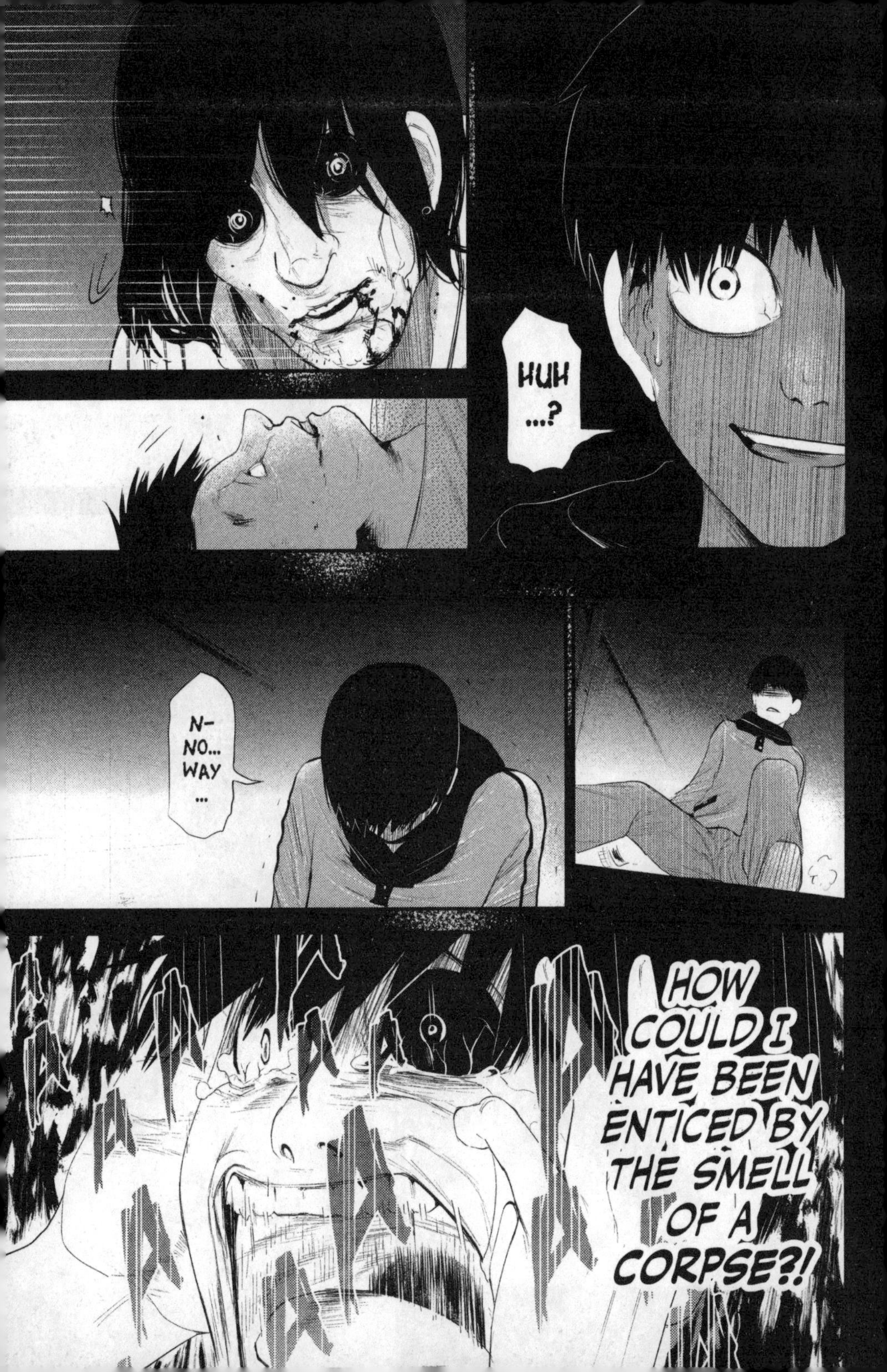
HUH ...?
N-NO... WAY ...
HOW COULD I HAVE BEEN ENTICED BY THE SMELL OF A CORPSE?!

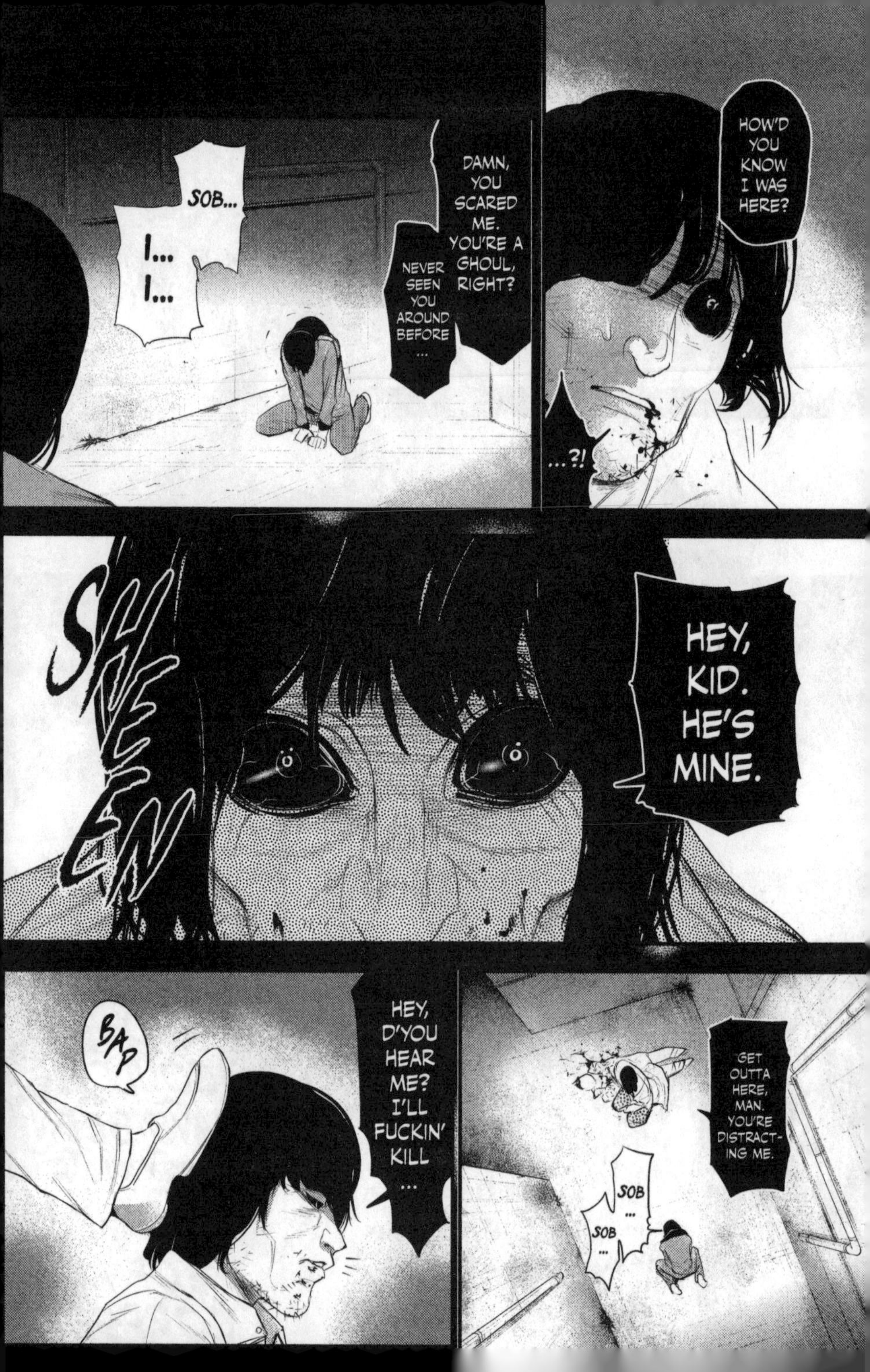
HOW'D YOU KNOW I WAS HERE?
...?!
DAMN, YOU SCARED ME. YOU'RE A GHOUL, RIGHT?
NEVER SEEN YOU AROUND BEFORE...
SOB...
I... I...
HEY, KID. HE'S MINE.
SHEEN
GET OUTTA HERE, MAN. YOU'RE DISTRACTING ME.
SOB...
SOB...
HEY, D'YOU HEAR ME? I'LL FUCKIN' KILL...
BAP

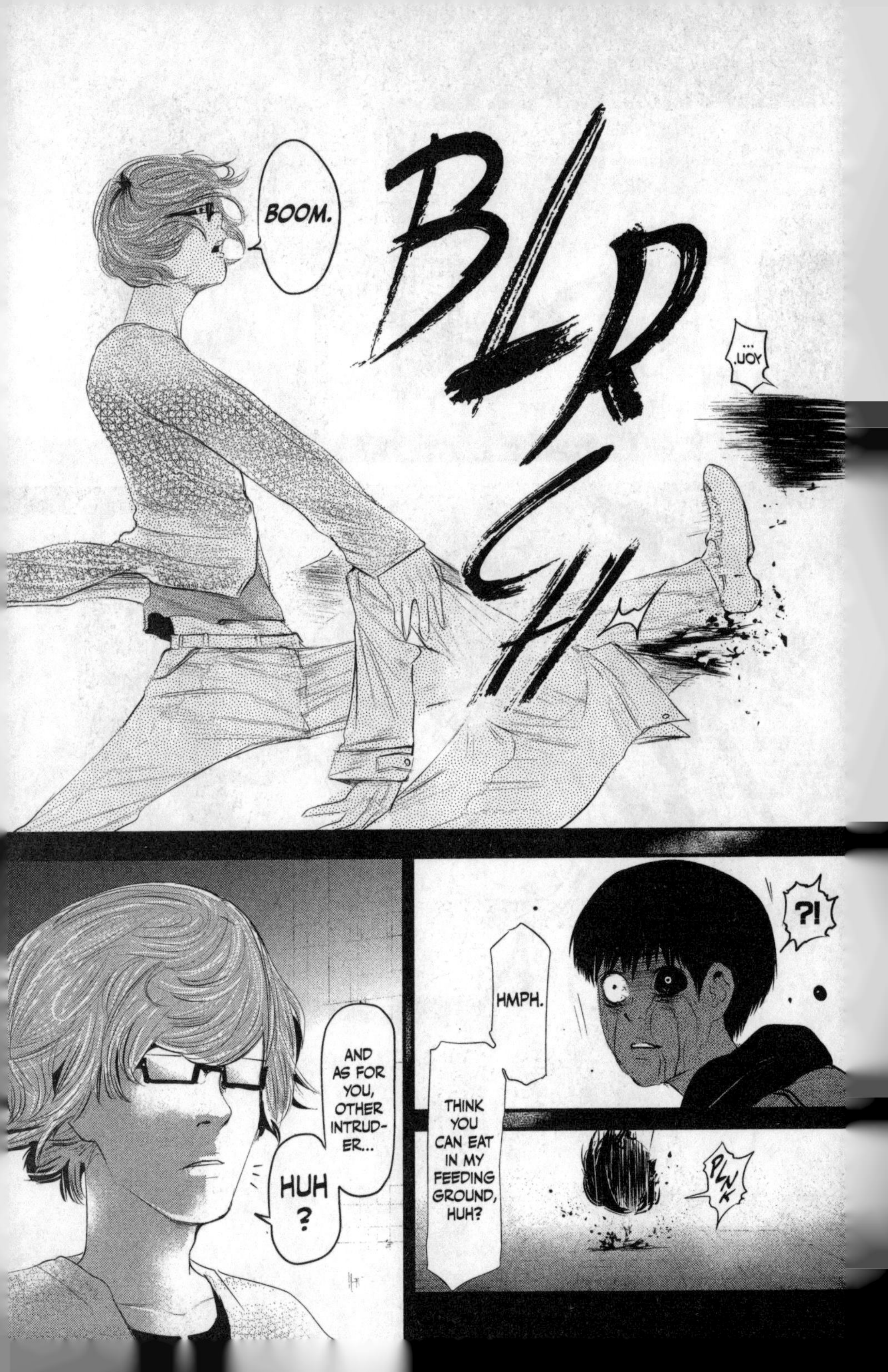

...YOU.
BLRCH
BOOM.
?!
HMPH.
THINK YOU CAN EAT IN MY FEEDING GROUND, HUH?
PLNK
AND AS FOR YOU, OTHER INTRUDER...
HUH?

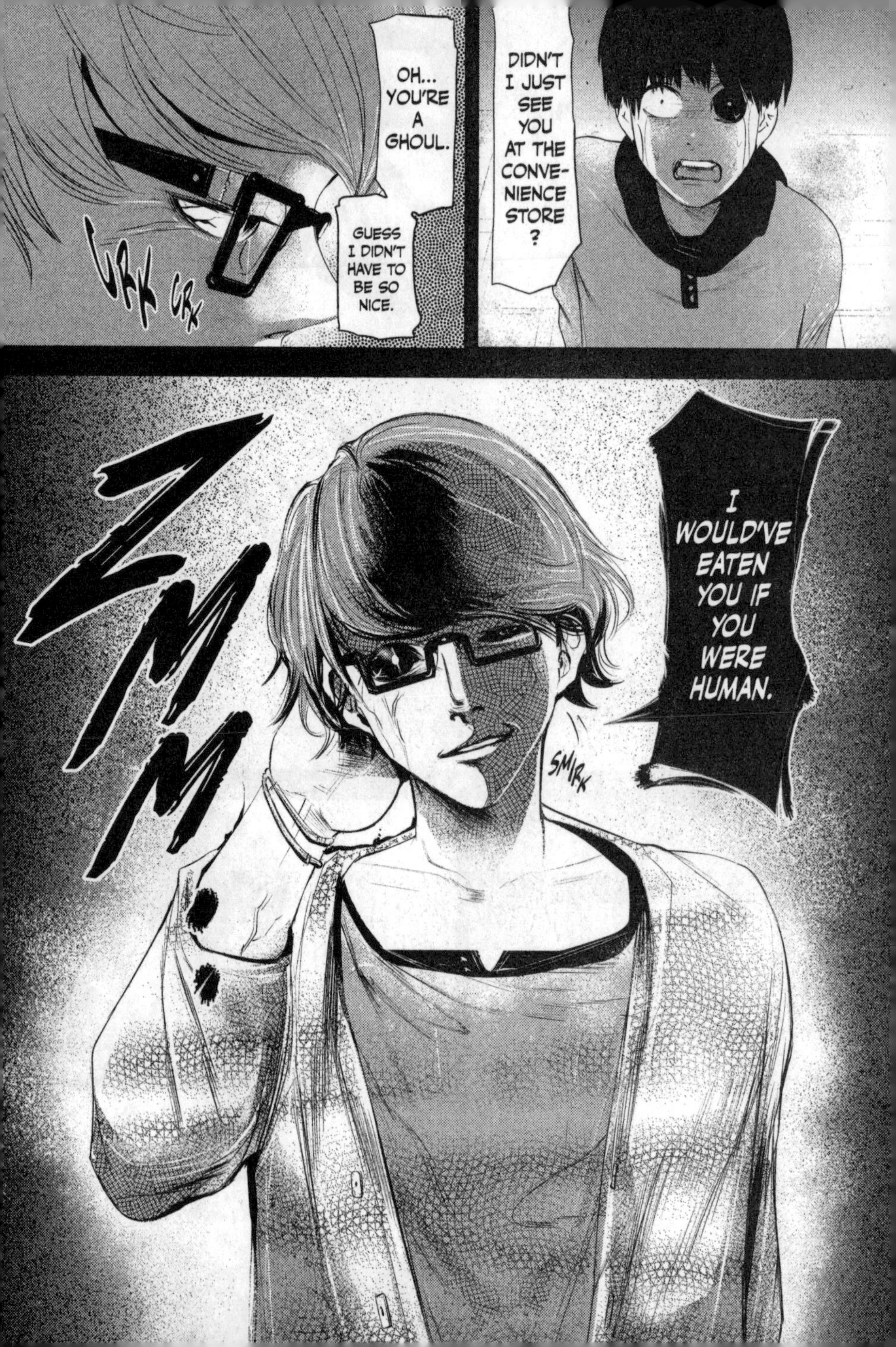
DIDN'T I JUST SEE YOU AT THE CONVENIENCE STORE?
OH... YOU'RE A GHOUL.
GUESS I DIDN'T HAVE TO BE SO NICE.
CRK CRK
I WOULD'VE EATEN YOU IF YOU WERE HUMAN.
SMIRK

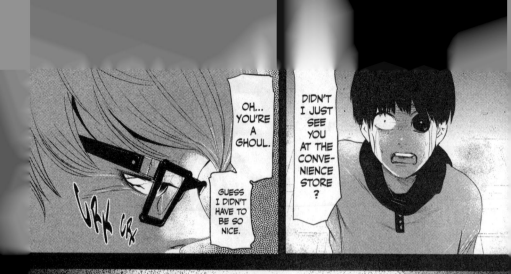

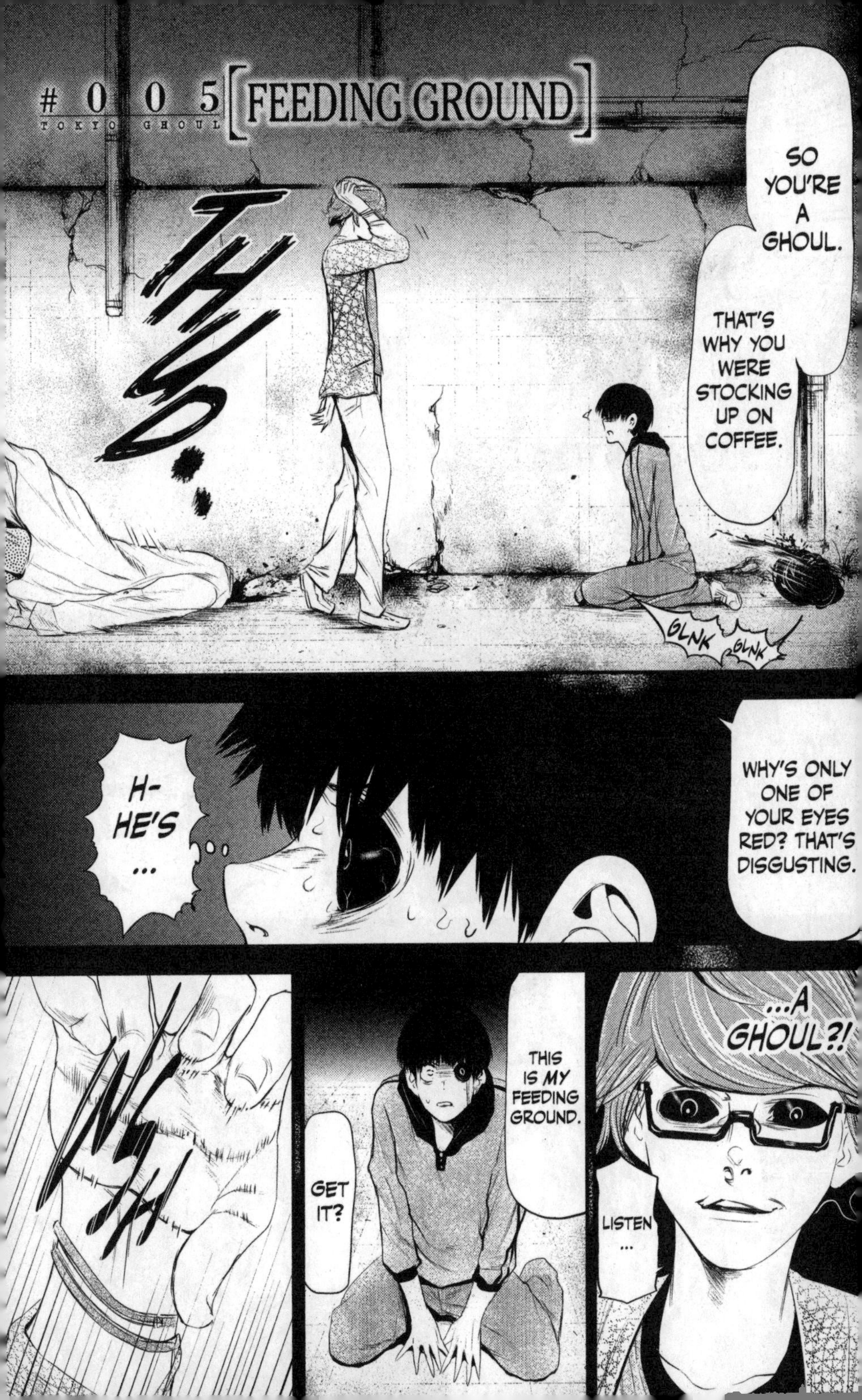

#005 TOKYO GHOUL [FEEDING GROUND]
SO YOU'RE A GHOUL.
THAT'S WHY YOU WERE STOCKING UP ON COFFEE.
GLNK GLNK
THUD
WHY'S ONLY ONE OF YOUR EYES RED? THAT'S DISGUSTING.
H-HE'S ...
...A GHOUL?!
LISTEN ...
THIS IS MY FEEDING GROUND.
GET IT?

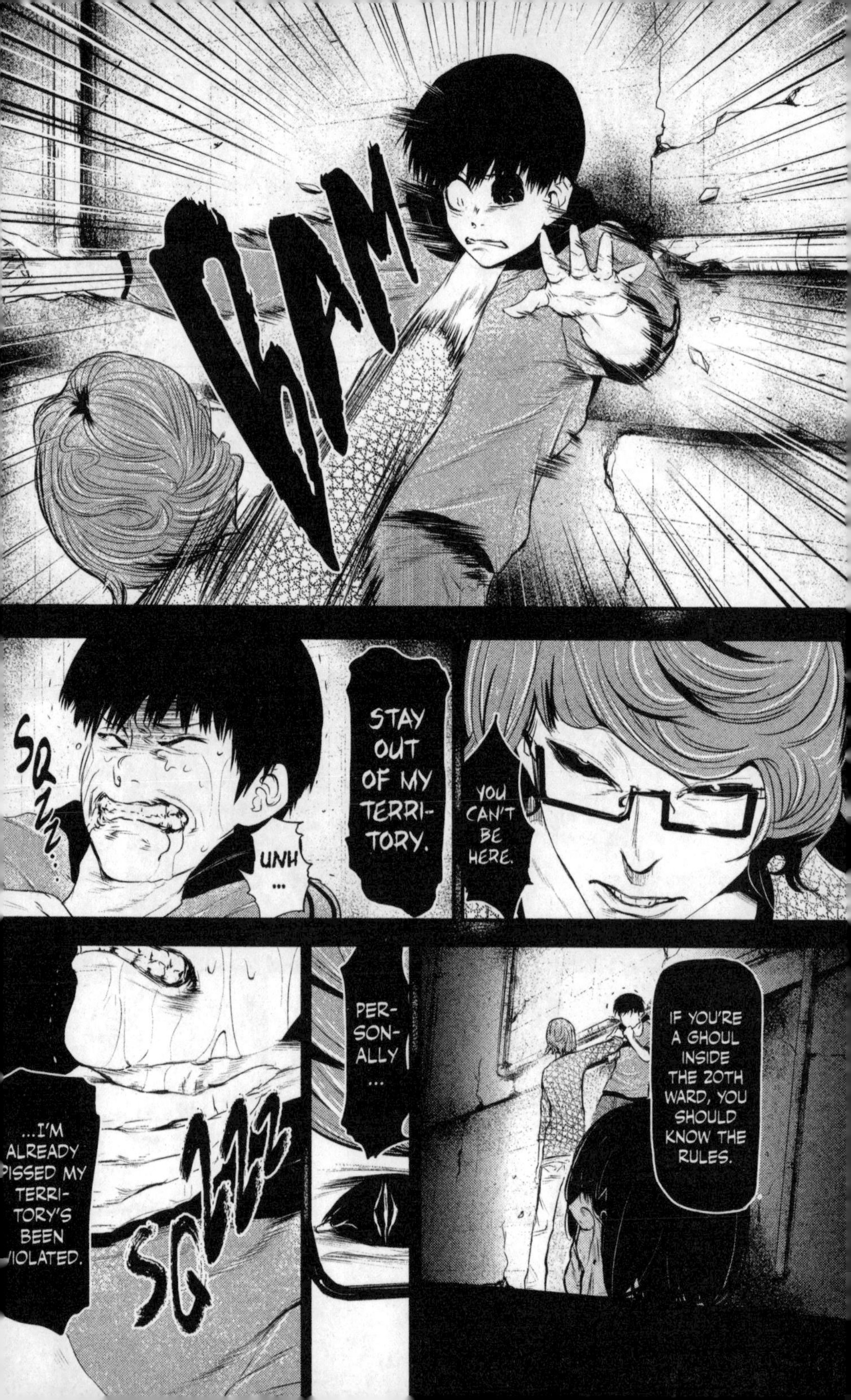
BAM
YOU CAN'T BE HERE.
STAY OUT OF MY TERRI-TORY.
UNH...
SQZZ...
IF YOU'RE A GHOUL INSIDE THE 20TH WARD, YOU SHOULD KNOW THE RULES.
PER-SON-ALLY...
...I'M ALREADY PISSED MY TERRI-TORY'S BEEN VIOLATED.
SQZZZ

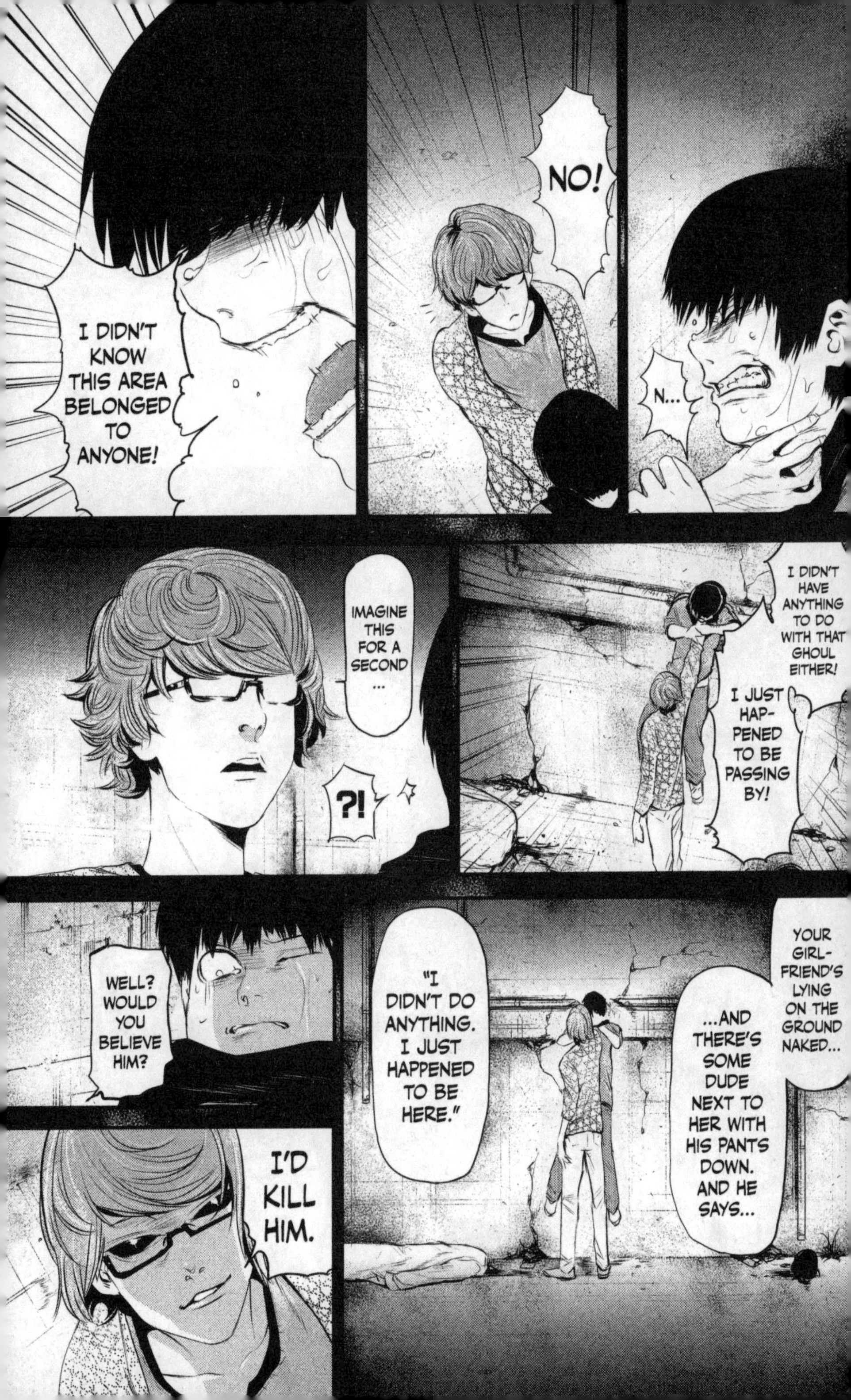
N...
NO!
I DIDN'T KNOW THIS AREA BELONGED TO ANYONE!
I DIDN'T HAVE ANYTHING TO DO WITH THAT GHOUL EITHER!
I JUST HAPPENED TO BE PASSING BY!
IMAGINE THIS FOR A SECOND...
?!
YOUR GIRLFRIEND'S LYING ON THE GROUND NAKED...
...AND THERE'S SOME DUDE NEXT TO HER WITH HIS PANTS DOWN. AND HE SAYS...
"I DIDN'T DO ANYTHING. I JUST HAPPENED TO BE HERE."
WELL? WOULD YOU BELIEVE HIM?
I'D KILL HIM.

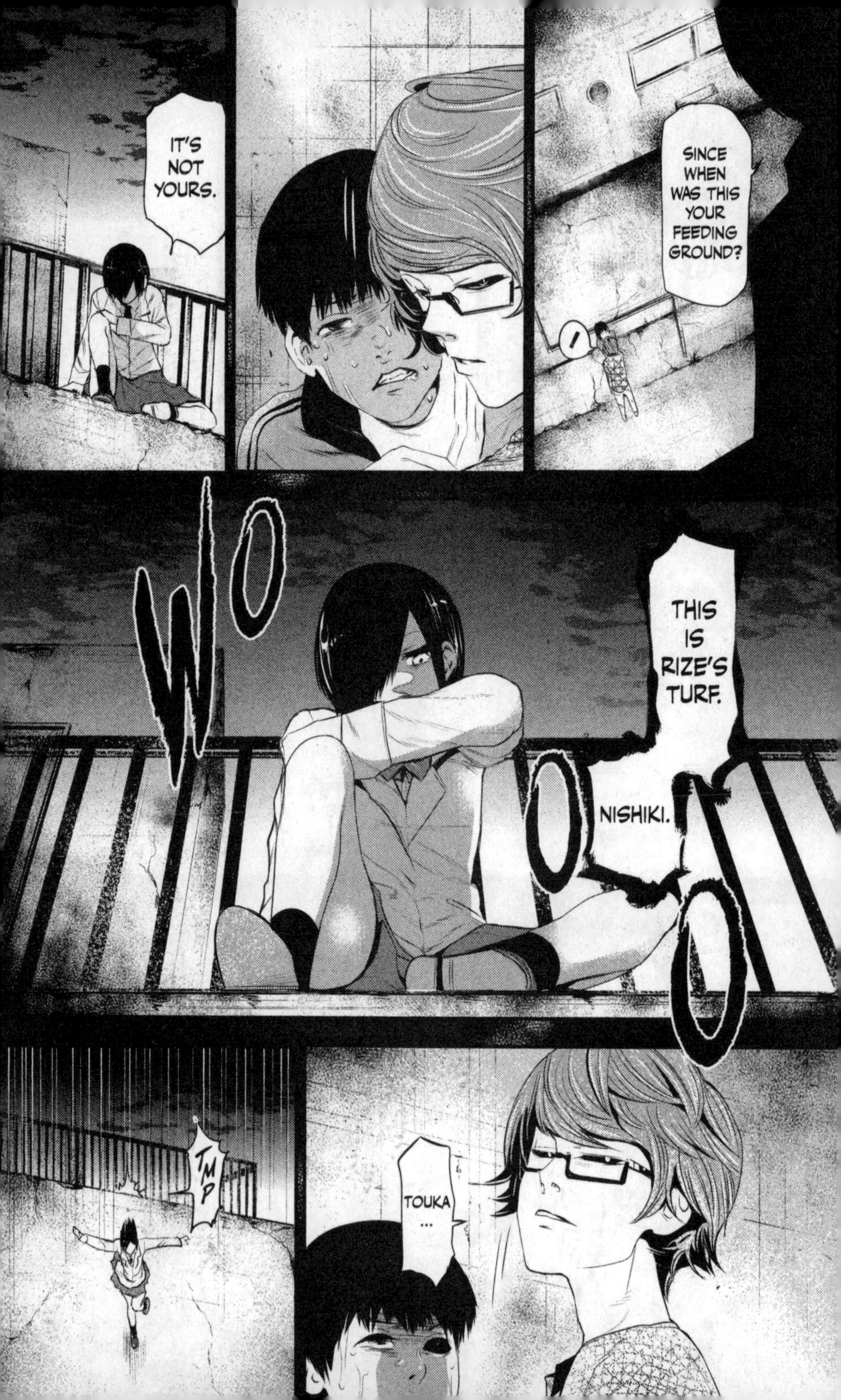
SINCE WHEN WAS THIS YOUR FEEDING GROUND?
!
IT'S NOT YOURS.
THIS IS RIZE'S TURF.
NISHIKI.
WOOO
TOUKA ...
TMP

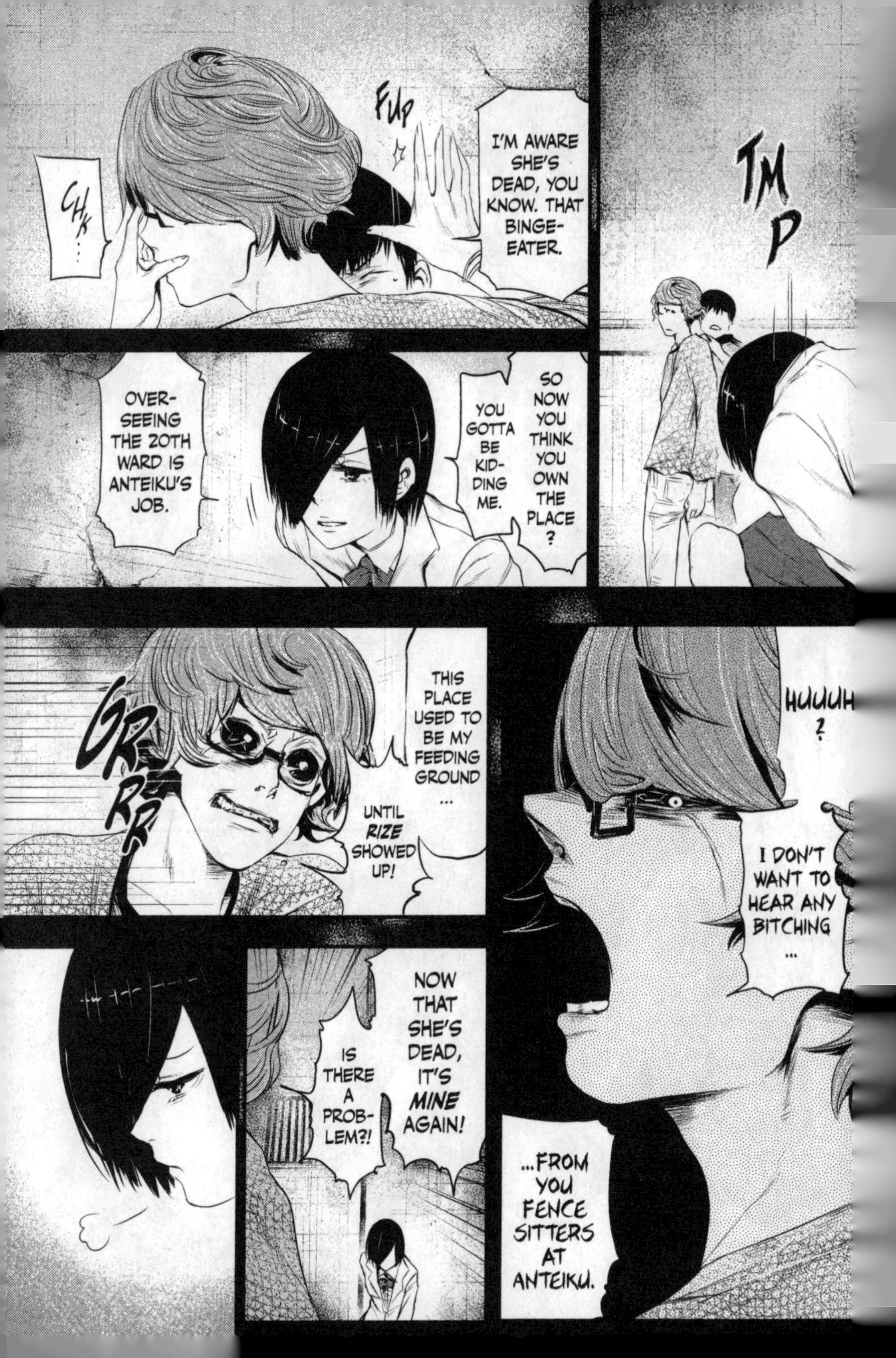
TMP
I'M AWARE SHE'S DEAD, YOU KNOW. THAT BINGE-EATER.
FUP
CHK...
SO NOW YOU THINK YOU OWN THE PLACE?
YOU GOTTA BE KIDDING ME.
OVERSEEING THE 20TH WARD IS ANTEIKU'S JOB.
HUUUH?
I DON'T WANT TO HEAR ANY BITCHING...
...FROM YOU FENCE SITTERS AT ANTEIKU.
THIS PLACE USED TO BE MY FEEDING GROUND...
UNTIL *RIZE* SHOWED UP!
GRRR
NOW THAT SHE'S DEAD, IT'S *MINE* AGAIN!
IS THERE A PROBLEM?!

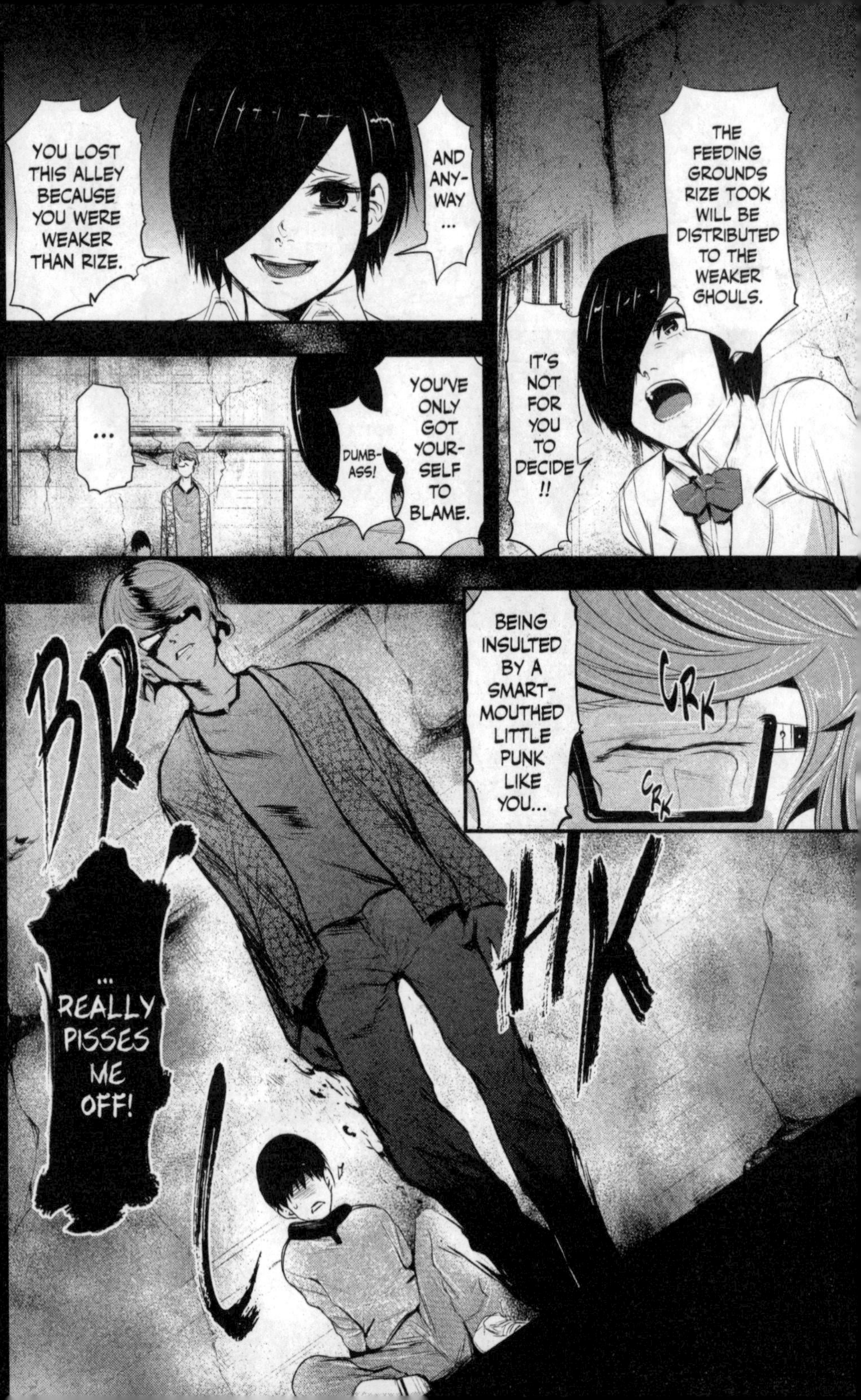
THE FEEDING GROUNDS RIZE TOOK WILL BE DISTRIBUTED TO THE WEAKER GHOULS.
IT'S NOT FOR YOU TO DECIDE !!
AND ANYWAY ...
YOU LOST THIS ALLEY BECAUSE YOU WERE WEAKER THAN RIZE.
YOU'VE ONLY GOT YOURSELF TO BLAME.
DUMB-ASS!
...
BEING INSULTED BY A SMART-MOUTHED LITTLE PUNK LIKE YOU...
CRK
CRK
... REALLY PISSES ME OFF!
BR
HK

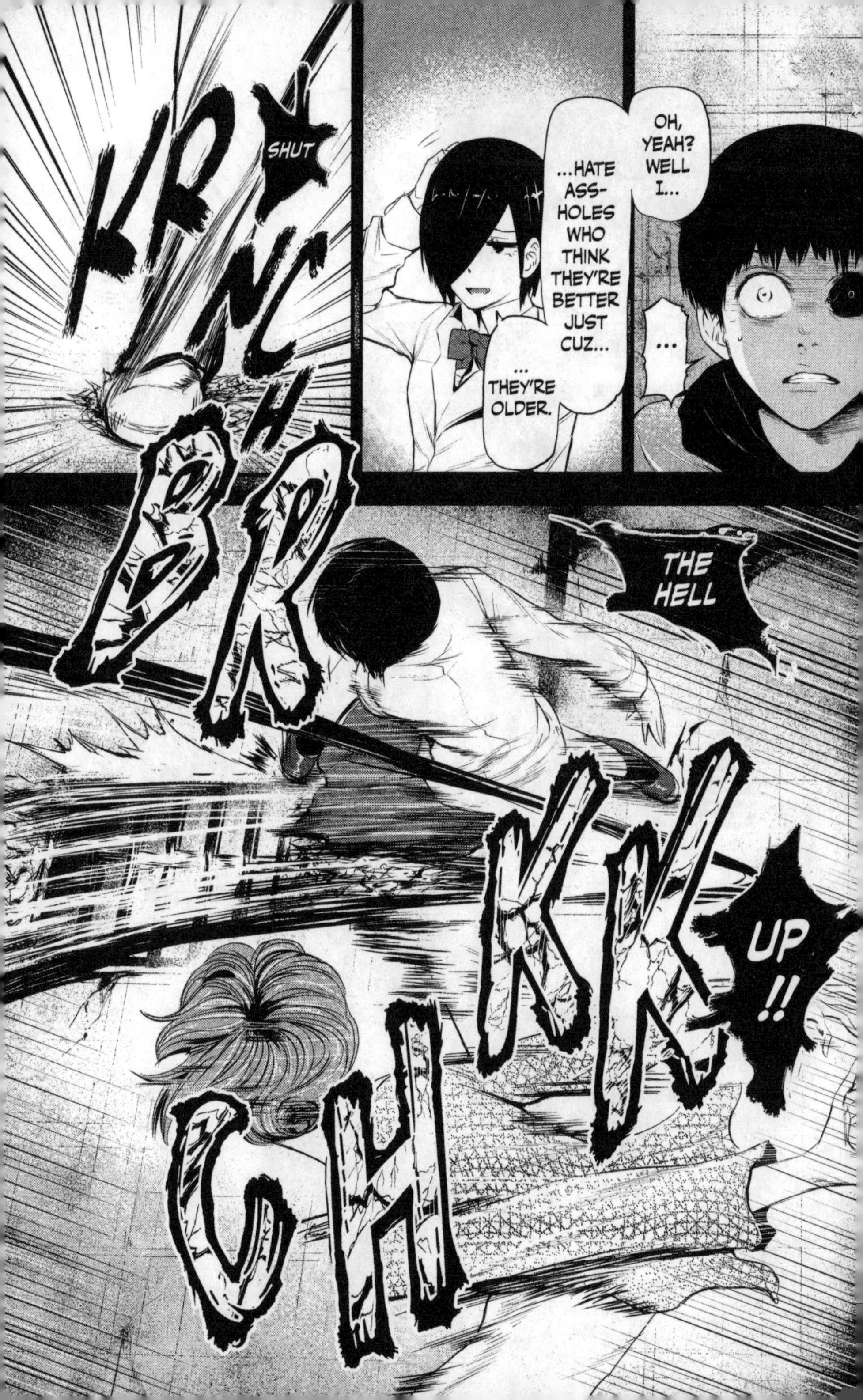
OH, YEAH? WELL I...
...
...HATE ASS-HOLES WHO THINK THEY'RE BETTER JUST CUZ...
... THEY'RE OLDER.
KRNCH
SHUT
THE HELL
UP !!

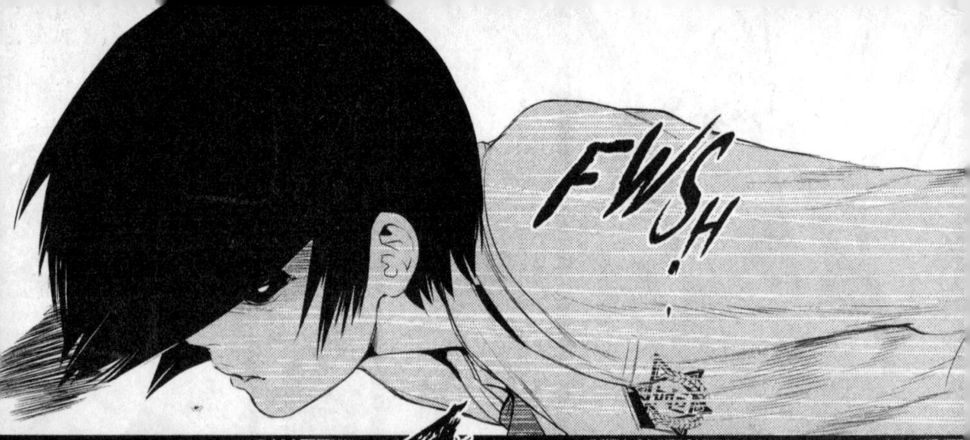
FWSH!

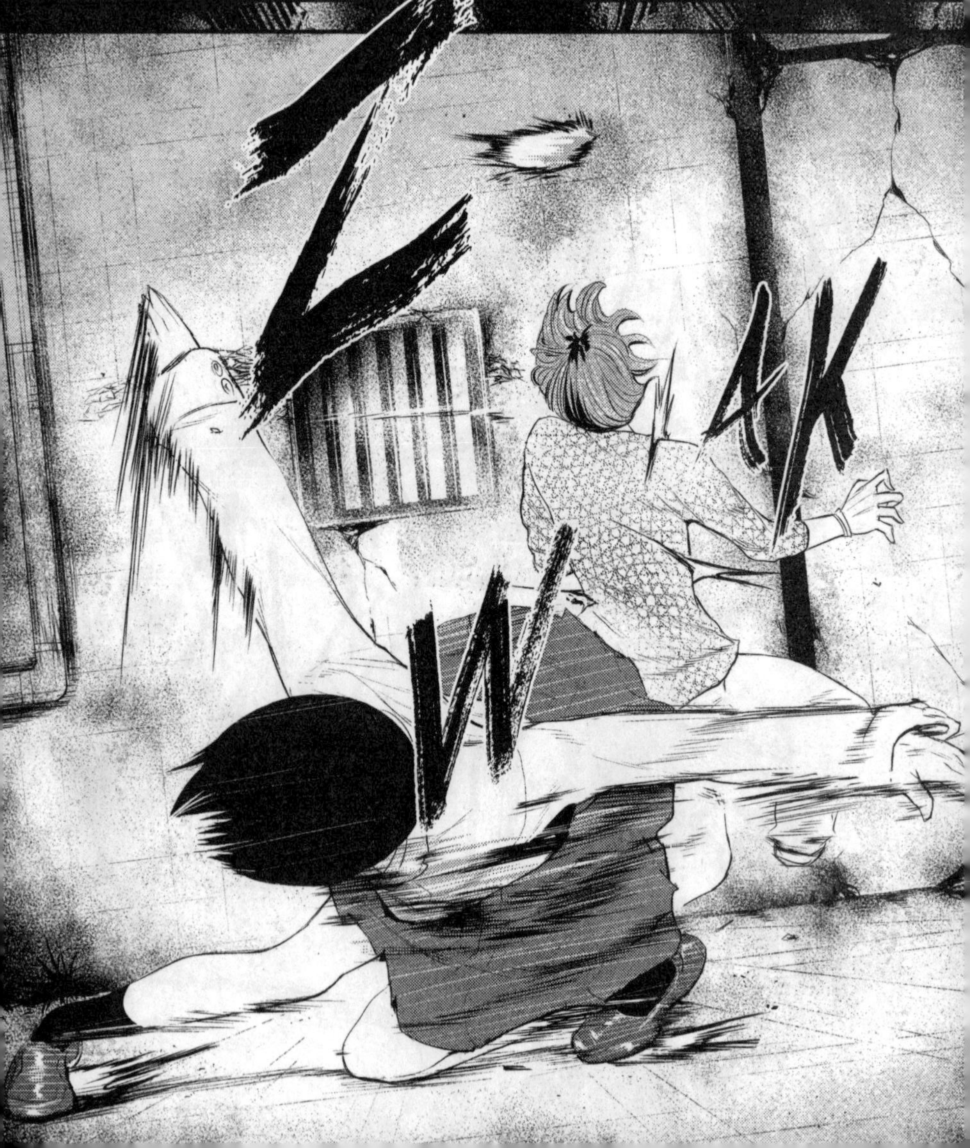
ZWAK

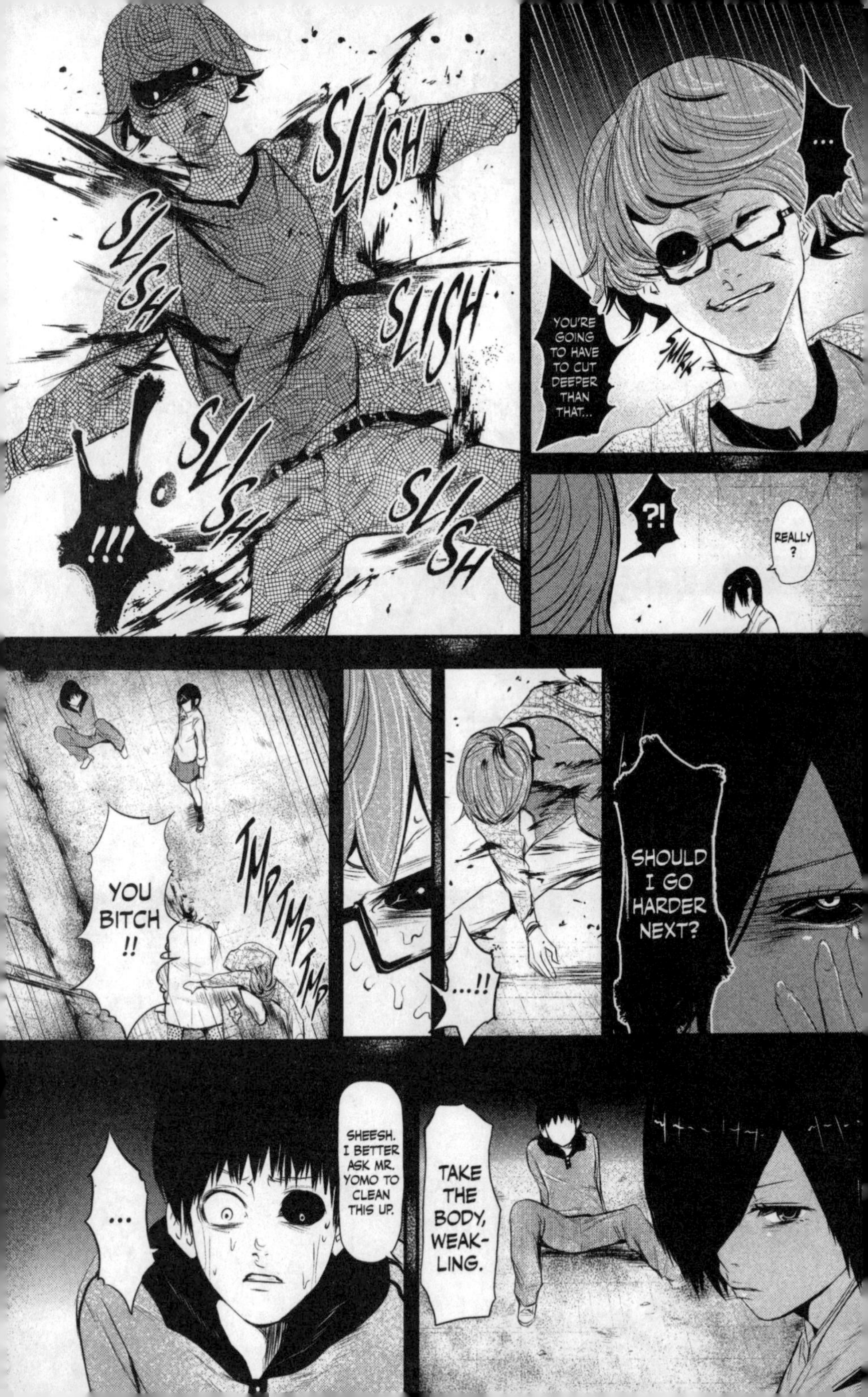
...
YOU'RE GOING TO HAVE TO CUT DEEPER THAN THAT...
?!
REALLY?
SLISH
SLISH
SLISH
SLISH
SLISH
!!!
SHOULD I GO HARDER NEXT?
...!!
YOU BITCH!!
TMP TMP TMP TMP
TAKE THE BODY, WEAK-LING.
SHEESH. I BETTER ASK MR. YOMO TO CLEAN THIS UP.
...

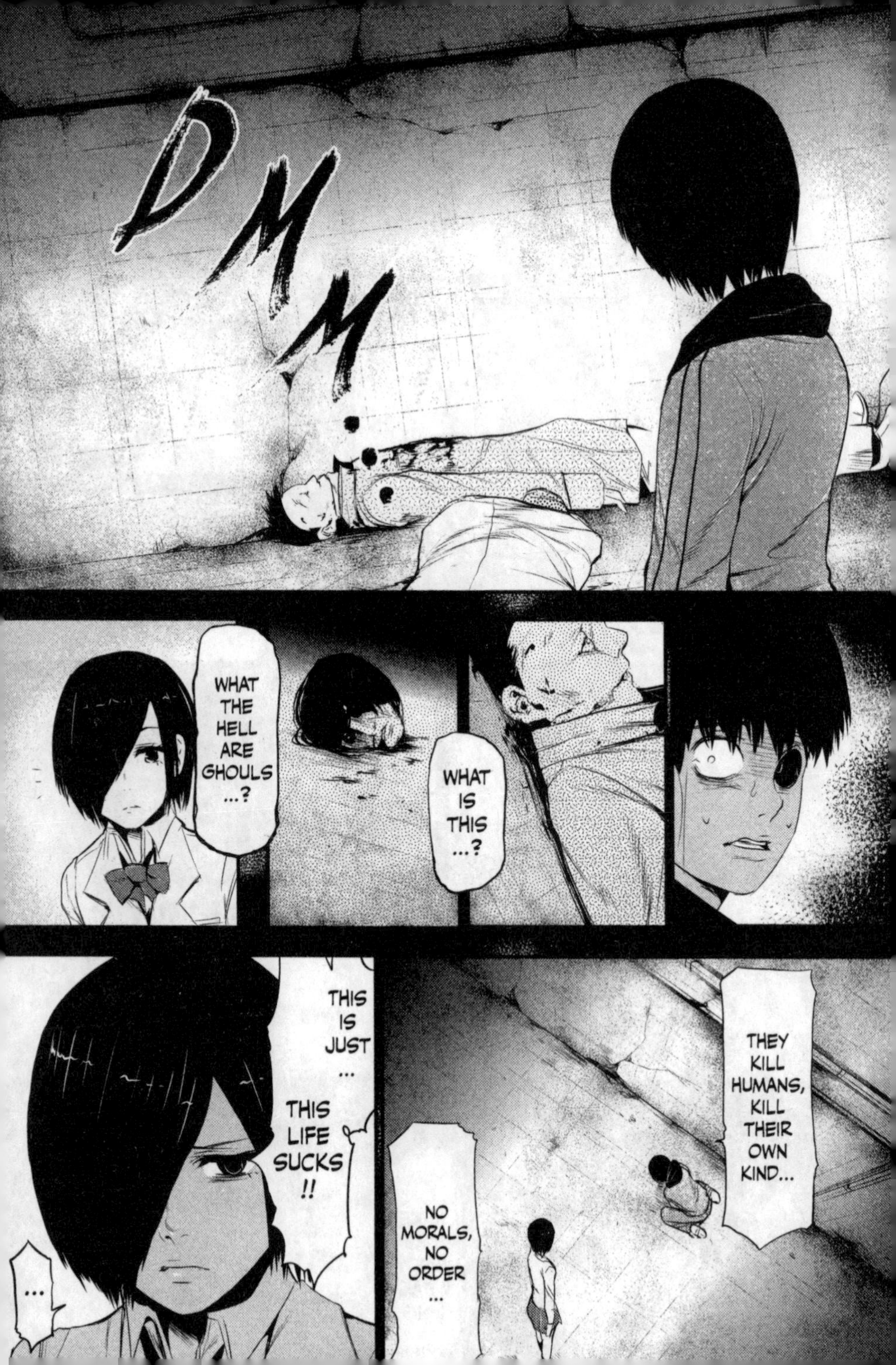
DMM
WHAT IS THIS ...?
WHAT THE HELL ARE GHOULS ...?
THEY KILL HUMANS, KILL THEIR OWN KIND...
NO MORALS, NO ORDER ...
THIS IS JUST ...
THIS LIFE SUCKS !!
...

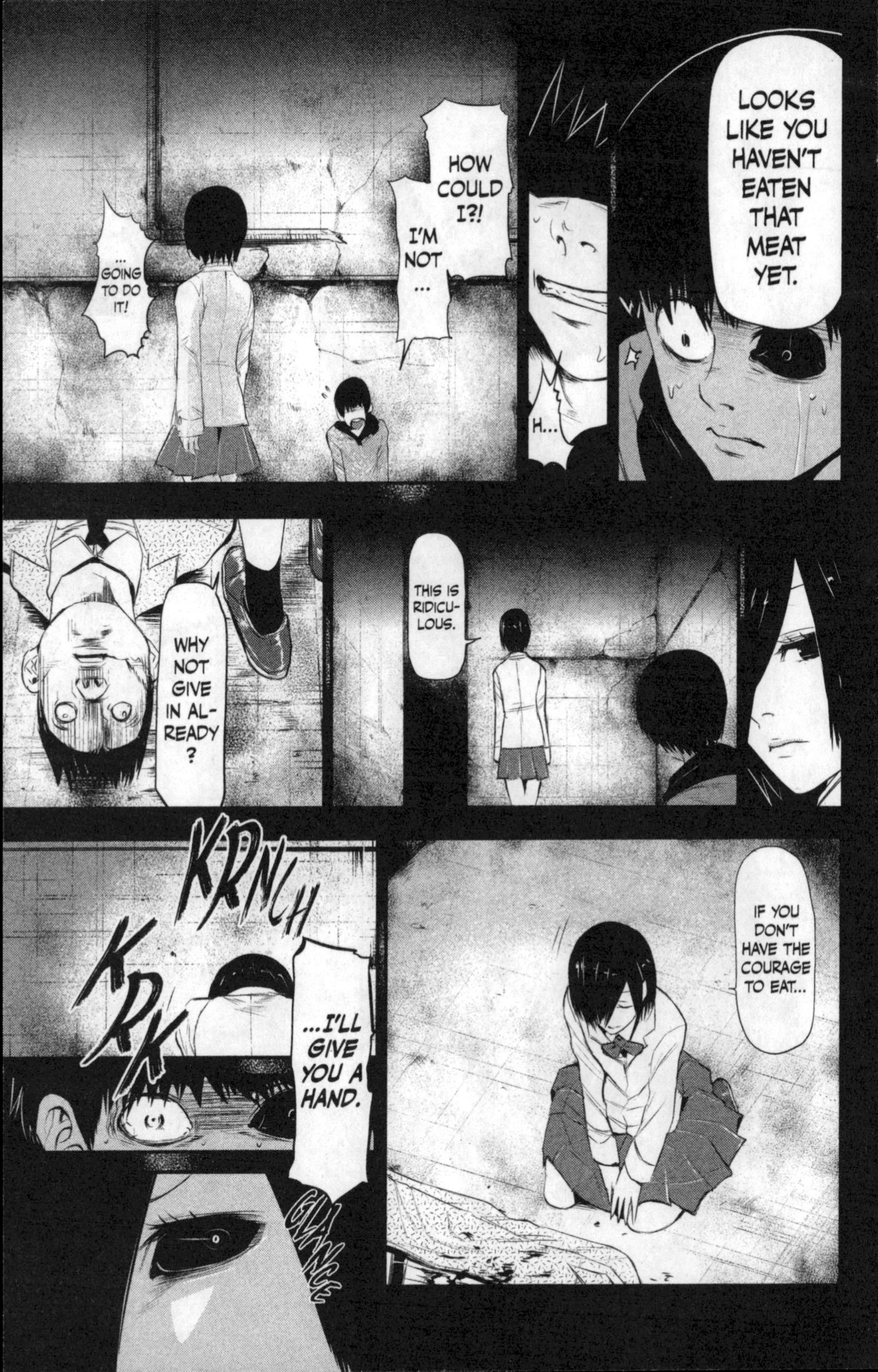
LOOKS LIKE YOU HAVEN'T EATEN THAT MEAT YET.
H...
HOW COULD I?!
I'M NOT ...
... GOING TO DO IT!
THIS IS RIDICU-LOUS.
WHY NOT GIVE IN AL-READY ?
IF YOU DON'T HAVE THE COURAGE TO EAT...
KRNCH
KRK
...I'LL GIVE YOU A HAND.
GLANCE

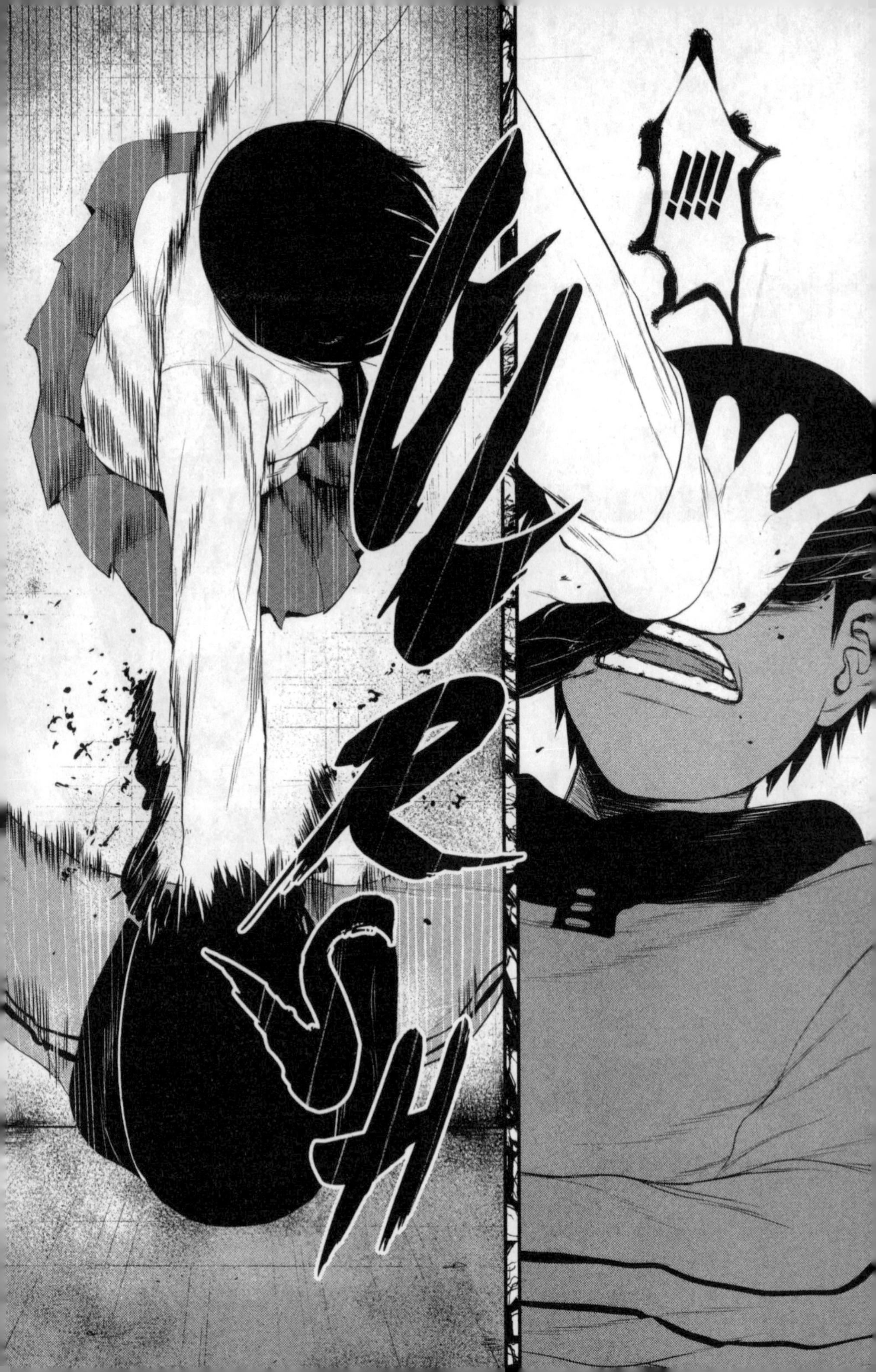
!!!!

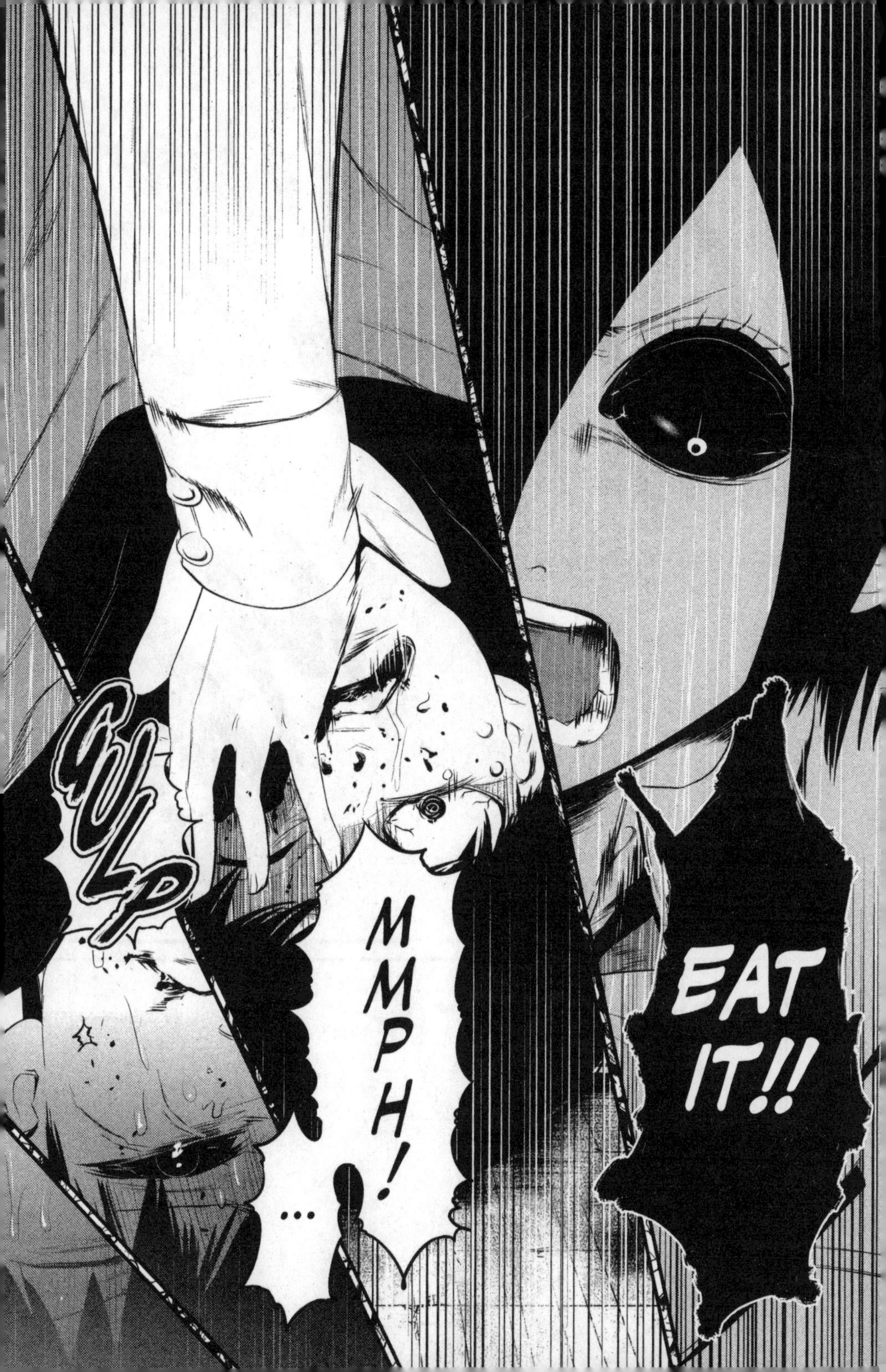
EAT IT!!
MMPH!
...
GULP

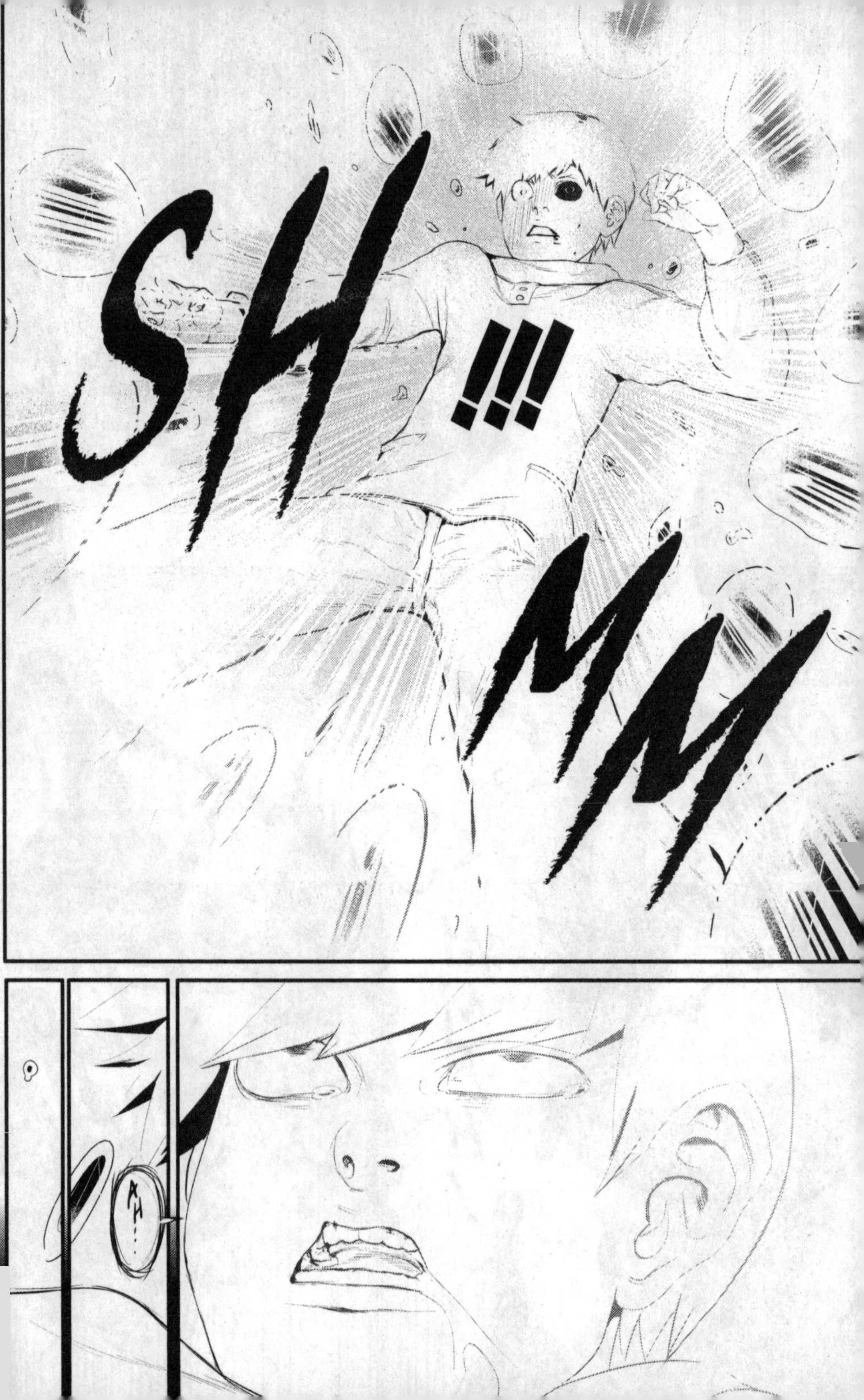
SH
!!!
MM
AH...

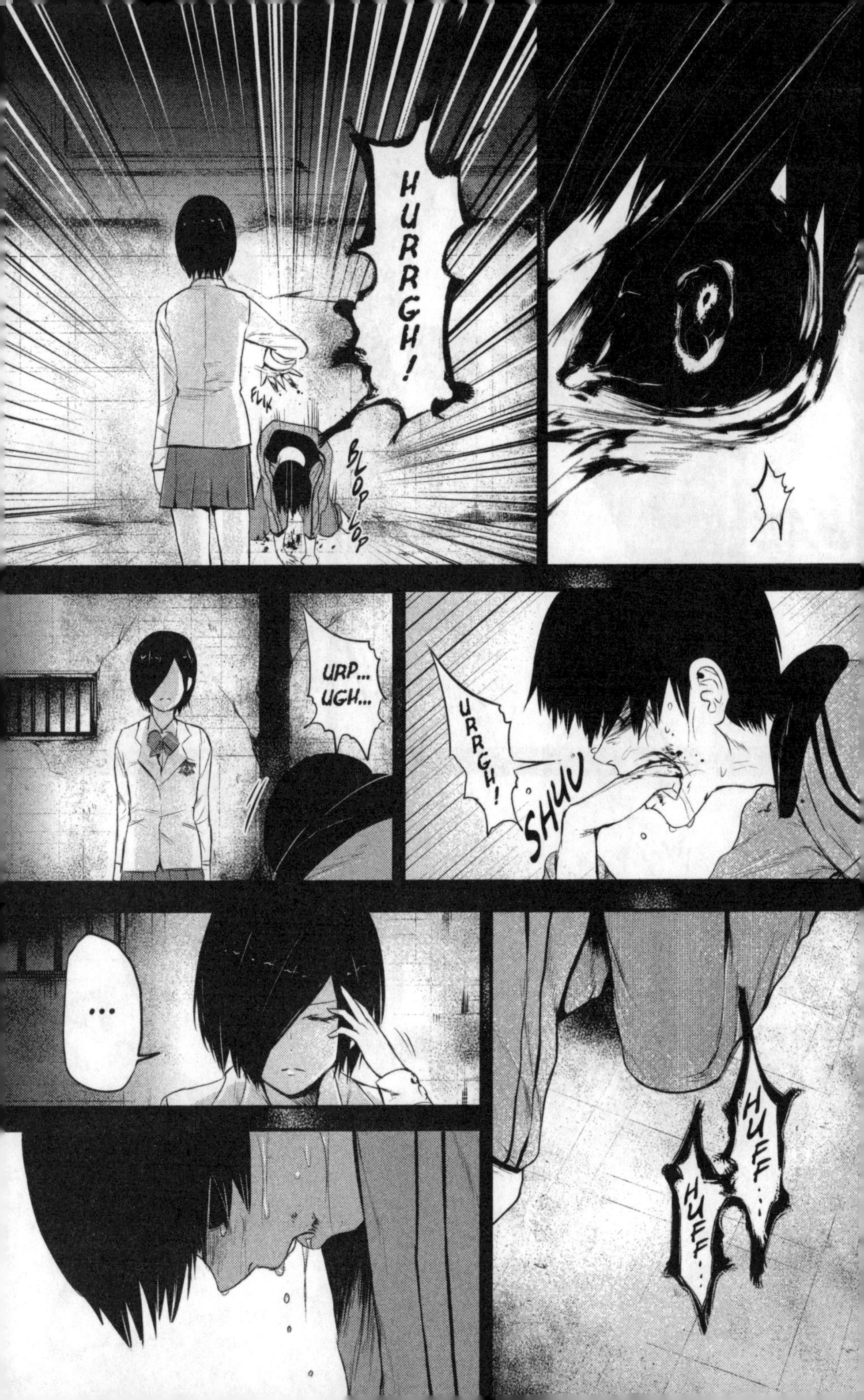
HURRRGH!
FLIK
BLOOP LOP
URRGH!
SHUU
URP... UGH...
HUFF... HUFF...
...

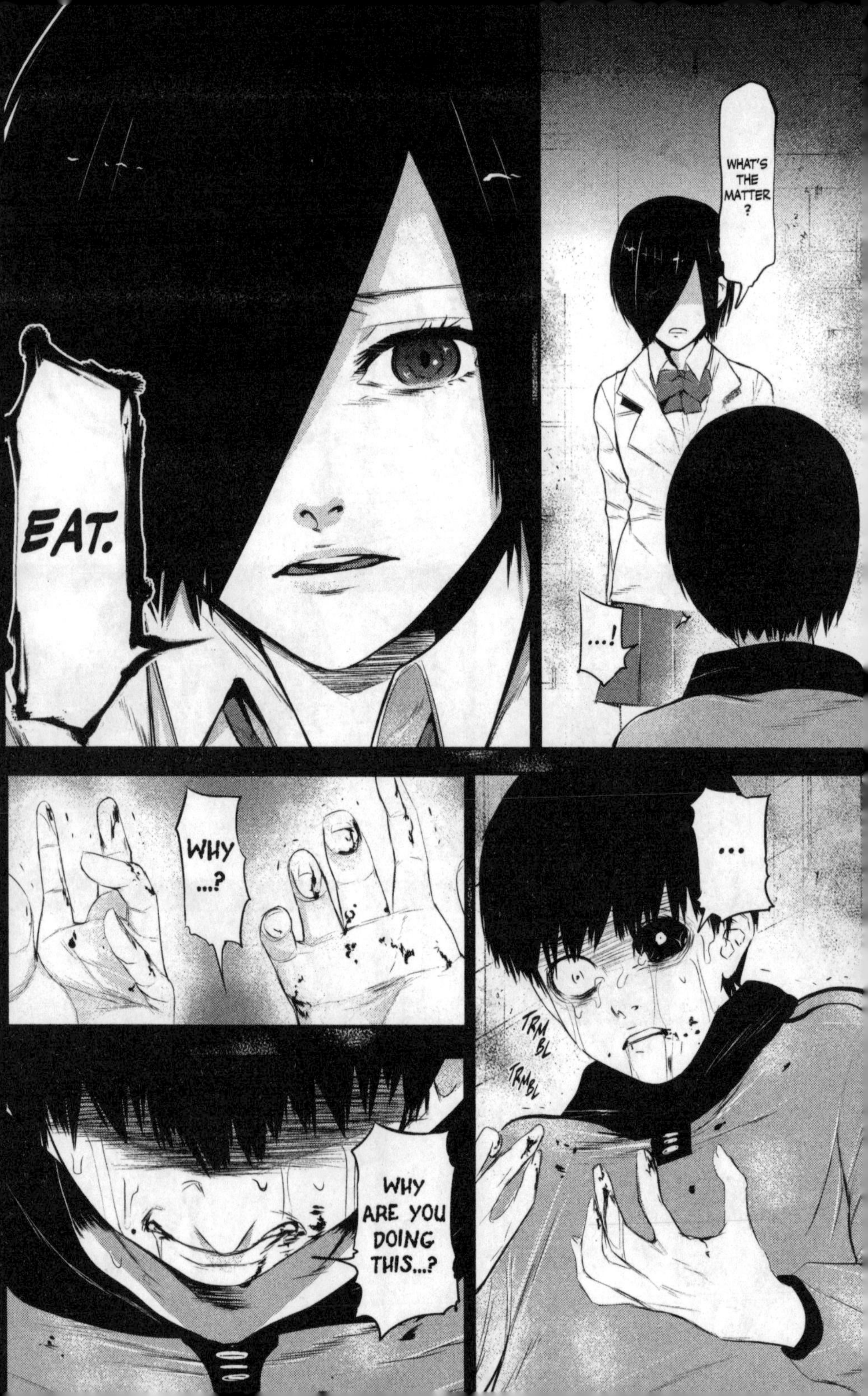
WHAT'S THE MATTER?
...!
EAT.
...
TRMBL
TRMBL
WHY ...?
WHY ARE YOU DOING THIS...?

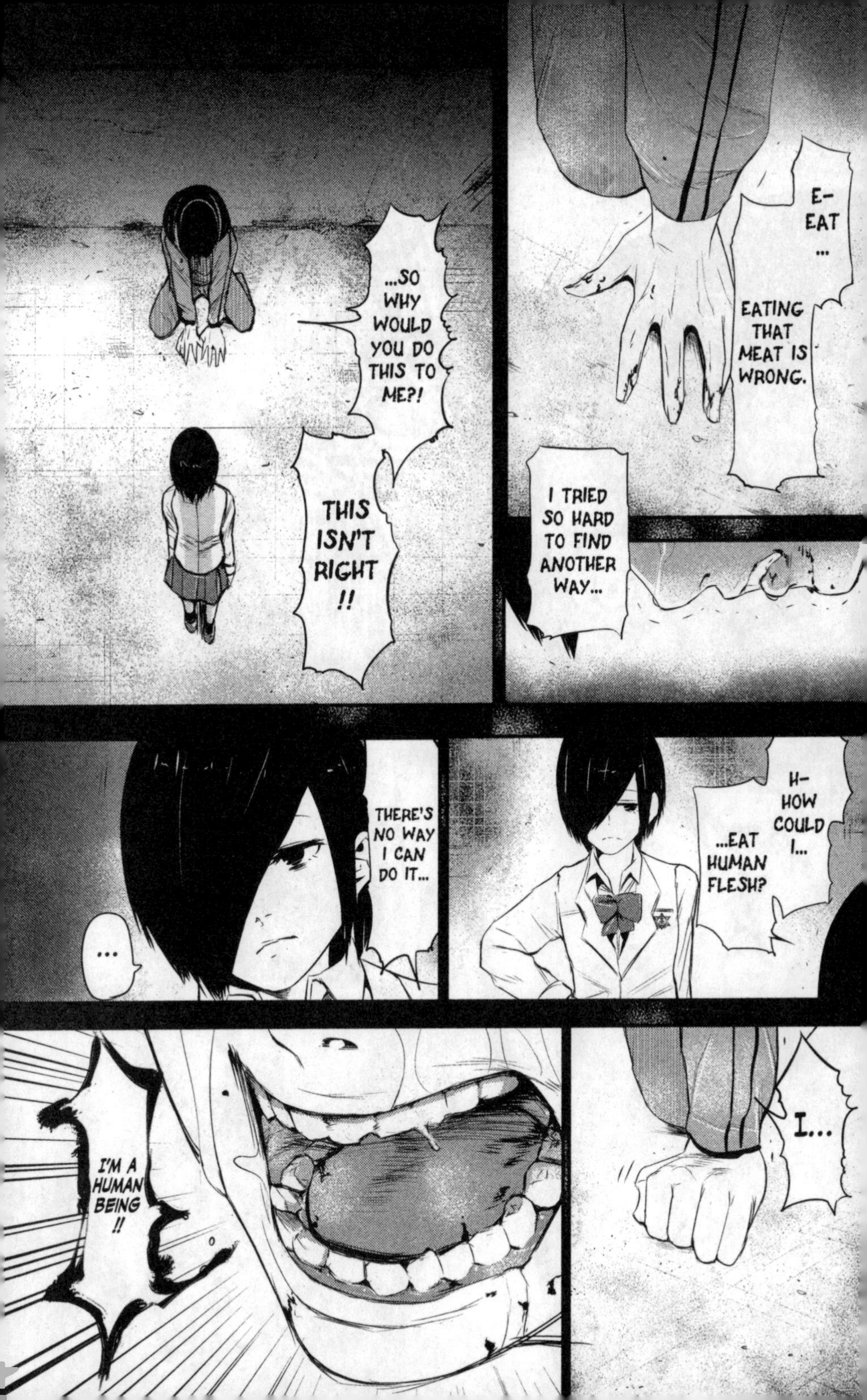
E- EAT ...
EATING THAT MEAT IS WRONG.
I TRIED SO HARD TO FIND ANOTHER WAY...
...SO WHY WOULD YOU DO THIS TO ME?!
THIS ISN'T RIGHT !!
H- HOW COULD I...
...EAT HUMAN FLESH?
THERE'S NO WAY I CAN DO IT...
...
I...
I'M A HUMAN BEING !!

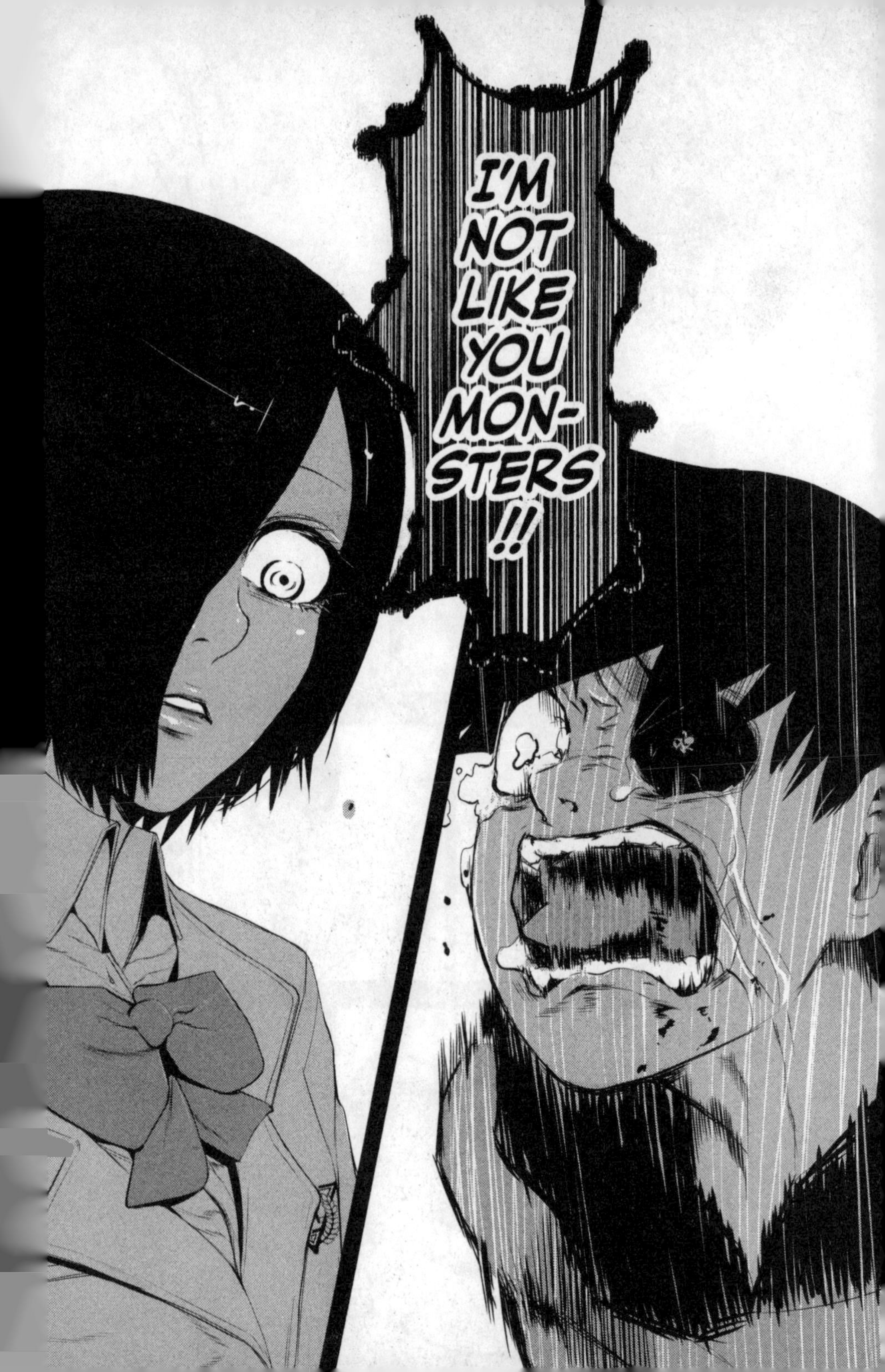
I'M NOT LIKE YOU MON-STERS!!

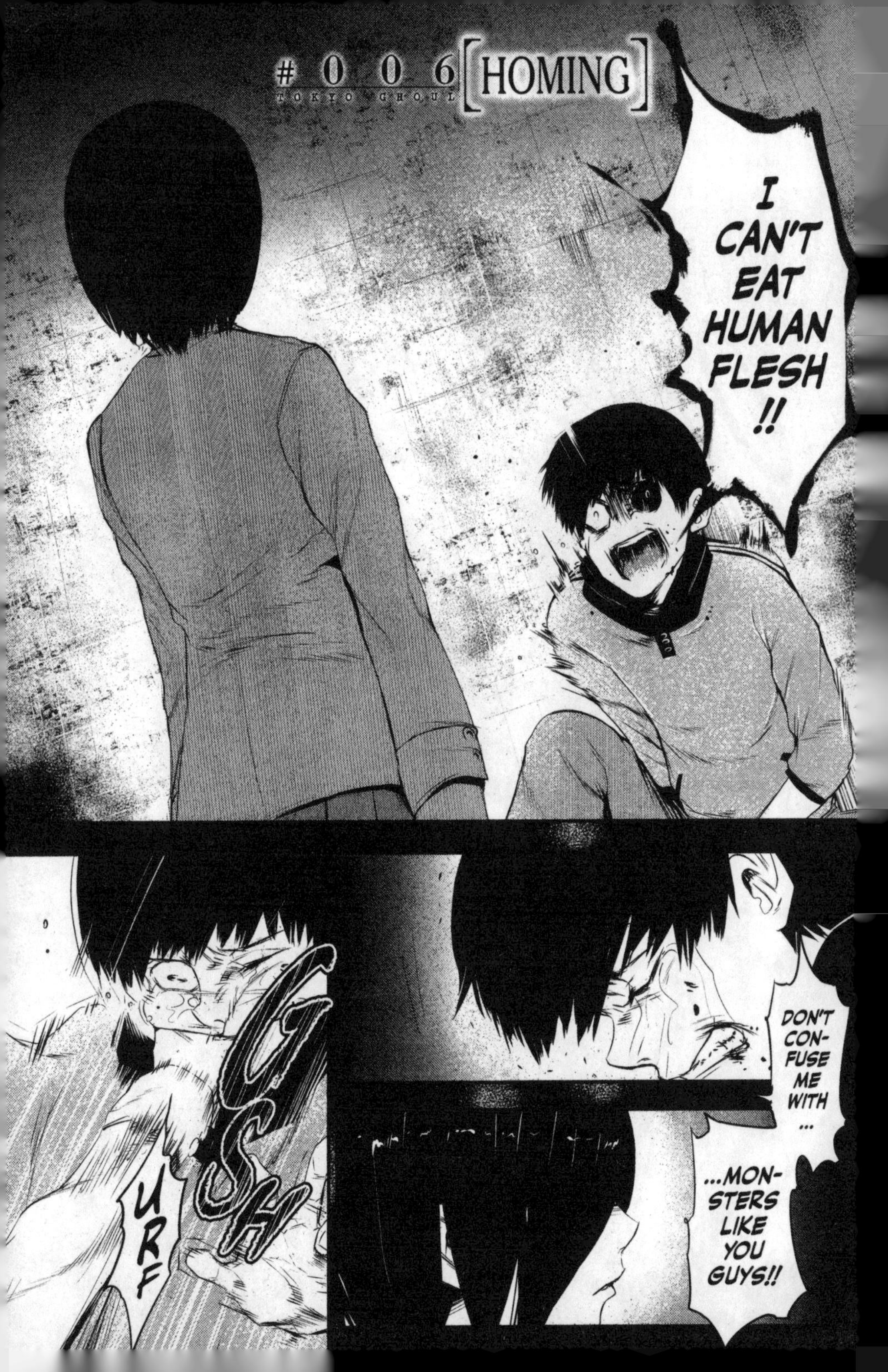
#006 [HOMING]
TOKYO GHOUL
I CAN'T EAT HUMAN FLESH!!
DON'T CONFUSE ME WITH...
...MONSTERS LIKE YOU GUYS!!
GUSH
URF

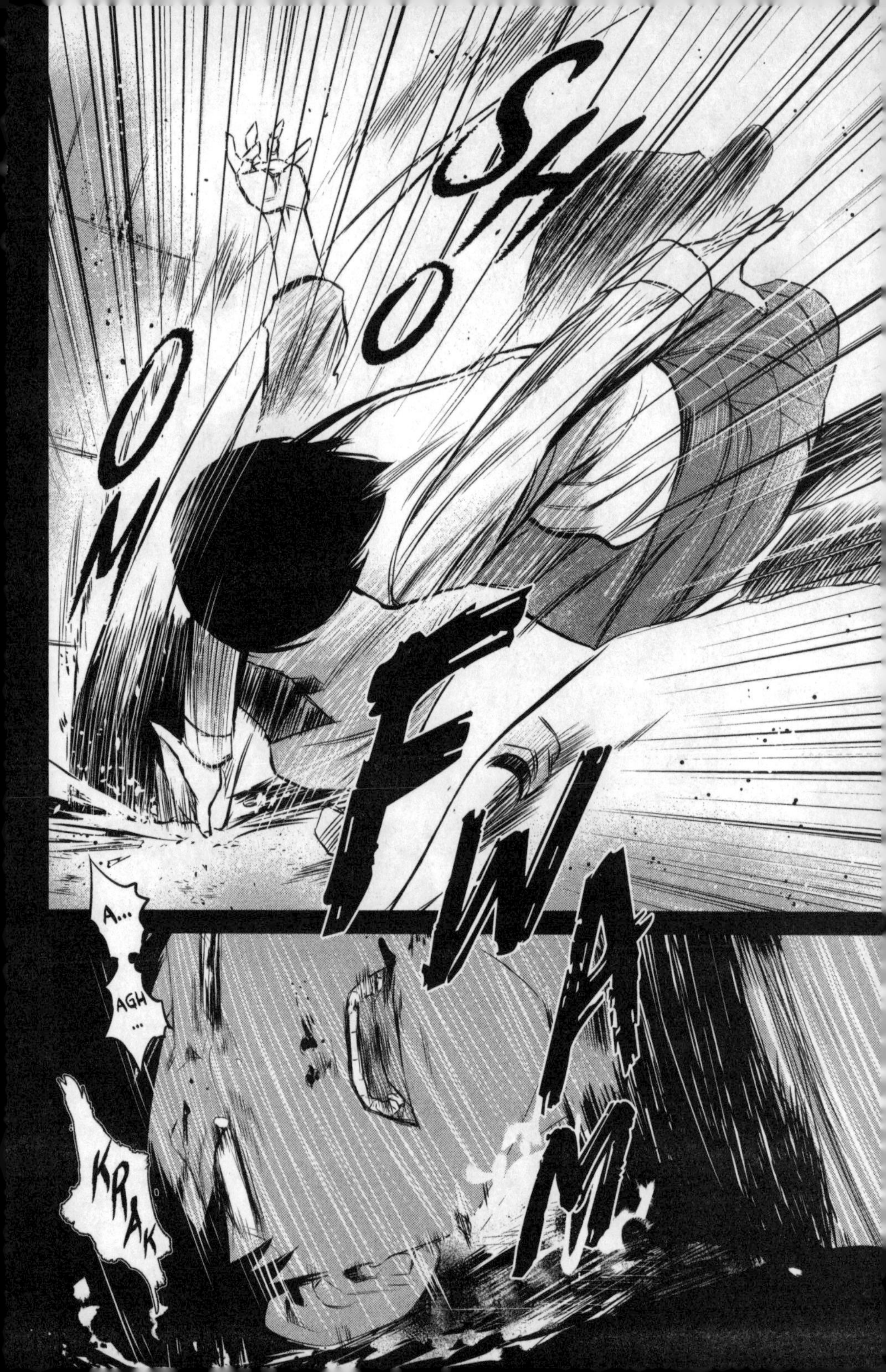
SHOOOM
FWAM
A... AGH...
KRAK

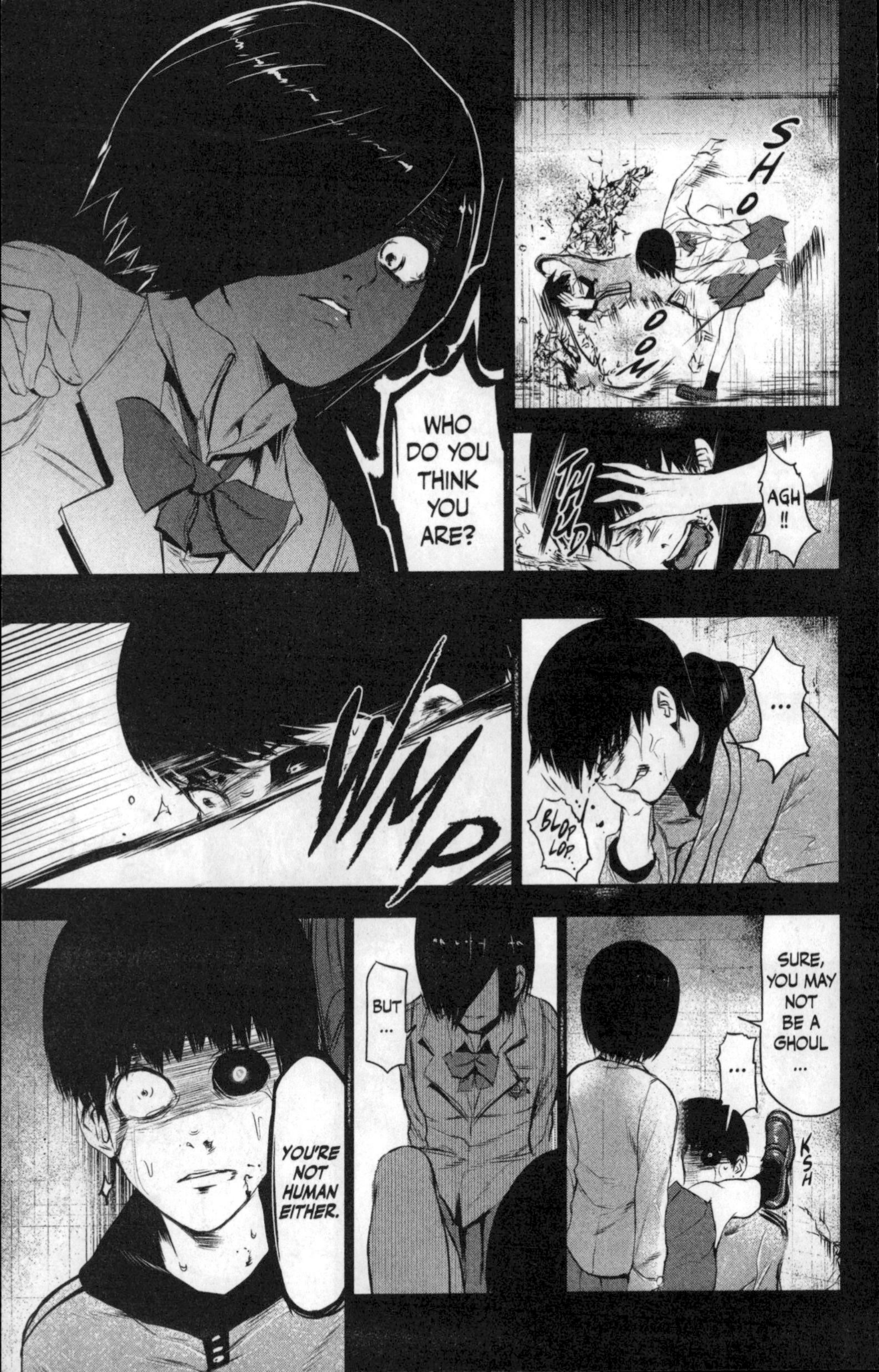

SHOOOOM
THUD
AGH!!
WHO DO YOU THINK YOU ARE?
...
BLOP LOP...
WMP
SURE, YOU MAY NOT BE A GHOUL...
...
KSH
BUT...
YOU'RE NOT HUMAN EITHER.

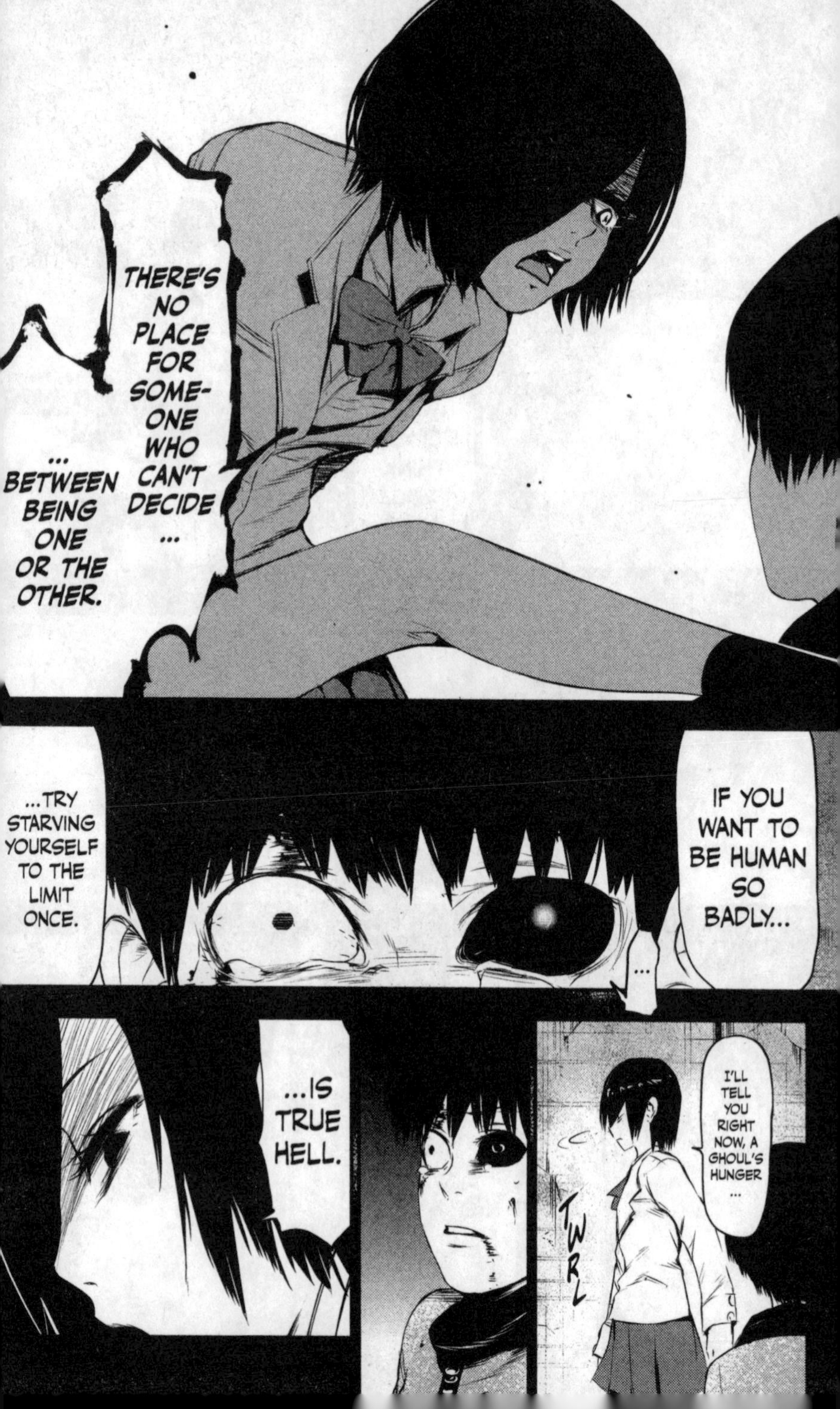
THERE'S NO PLACE FOR SOME-ONE WHO CAN'T DECIDE...
...BETWEEN BEING ONE OR THE OTHER.
IF YOU WANT TO BE HUMAN SO BADLY...
...
...TRY STARVING YOURSELF TO THE LIMIT ONCE.
I'LL TELL YOU RIGHT NOW, A GHOUL'S HUNGER...
TWRL
...IS TRUE HELL.

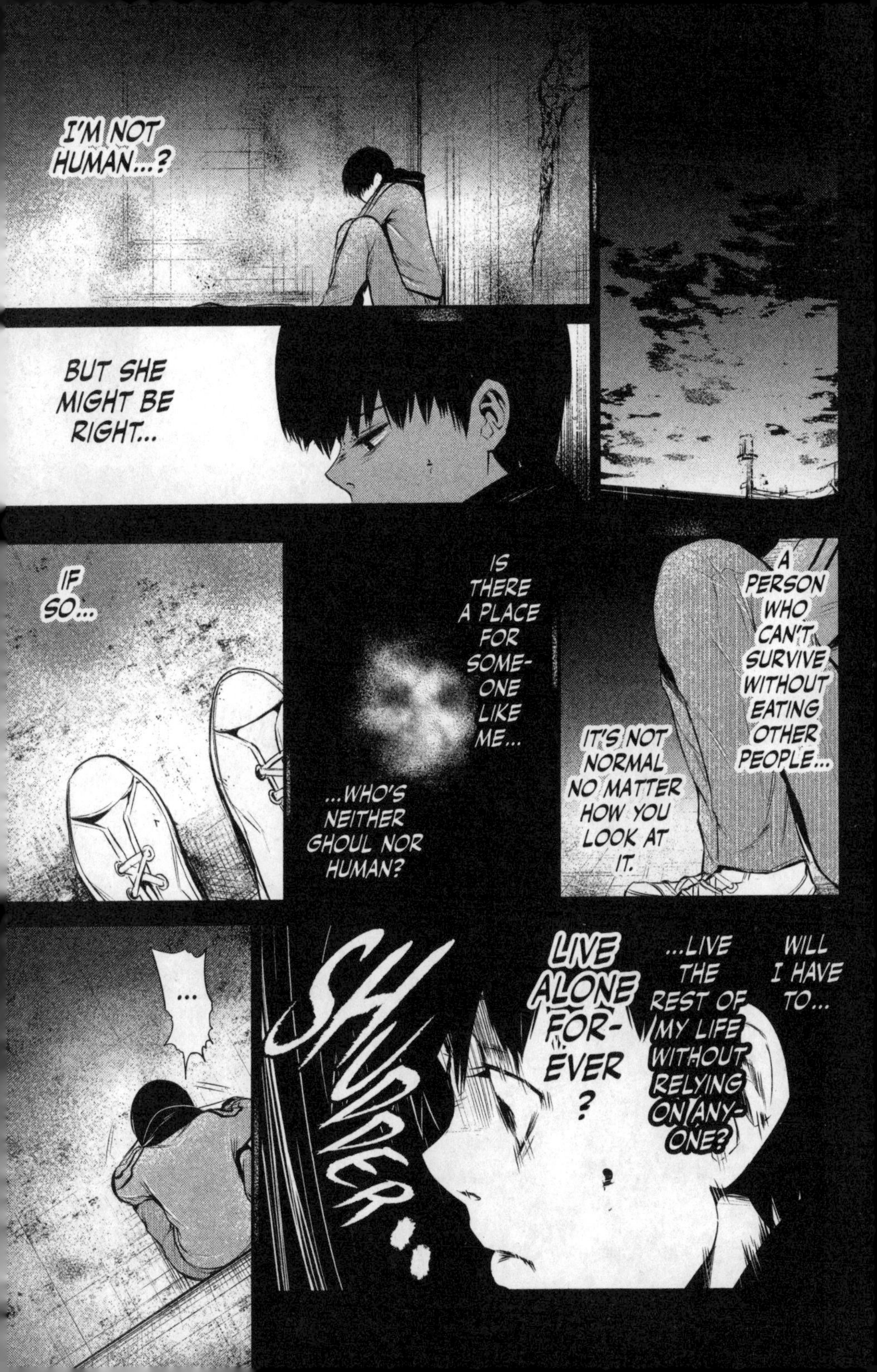
I'M NOT HUMAN...?
BUT SHE MIGHT BE RIGHT...
A PERSON WHO CAN'T SURVIVE WITHOUT EATING OTHER PEOPLE...
IT'S NOT NORMAL NO MATTER HOW YOU LOOK AT IT.
IS THERE A PLACE FOR SOMEONE LIKE ME...
...WHO'S NEITHER GHOUL NOR HUMAN?
IF SO...
WILL I HAVE TO...
...LIVE THE REST OF MY LIFE WITHOUT RELYING ON ANYONE?
LIVE ALONE FOREVER?
SHIVER...
...

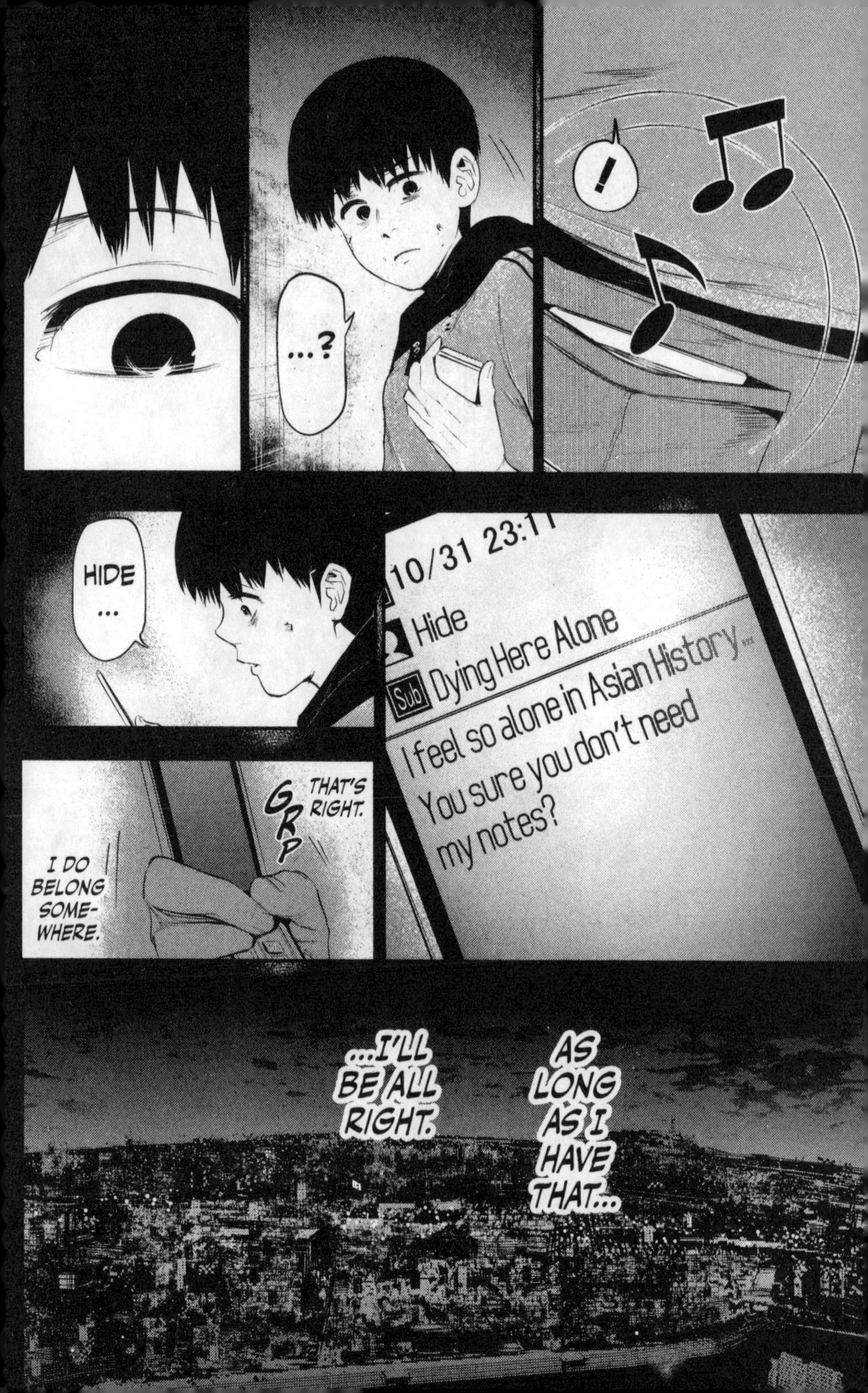
!
...?
10/31 23:11
Hide
Sub Dying Here Alone
I feel so alone in Asian History
You sure you don't need my notes?
HIDE ...
GRP
THAT'S RIGHT.
I DO BELONG SOMEWHERE.
AS LONG AS I HAVE THAT...
...I'LL BE ALL RIGHT.

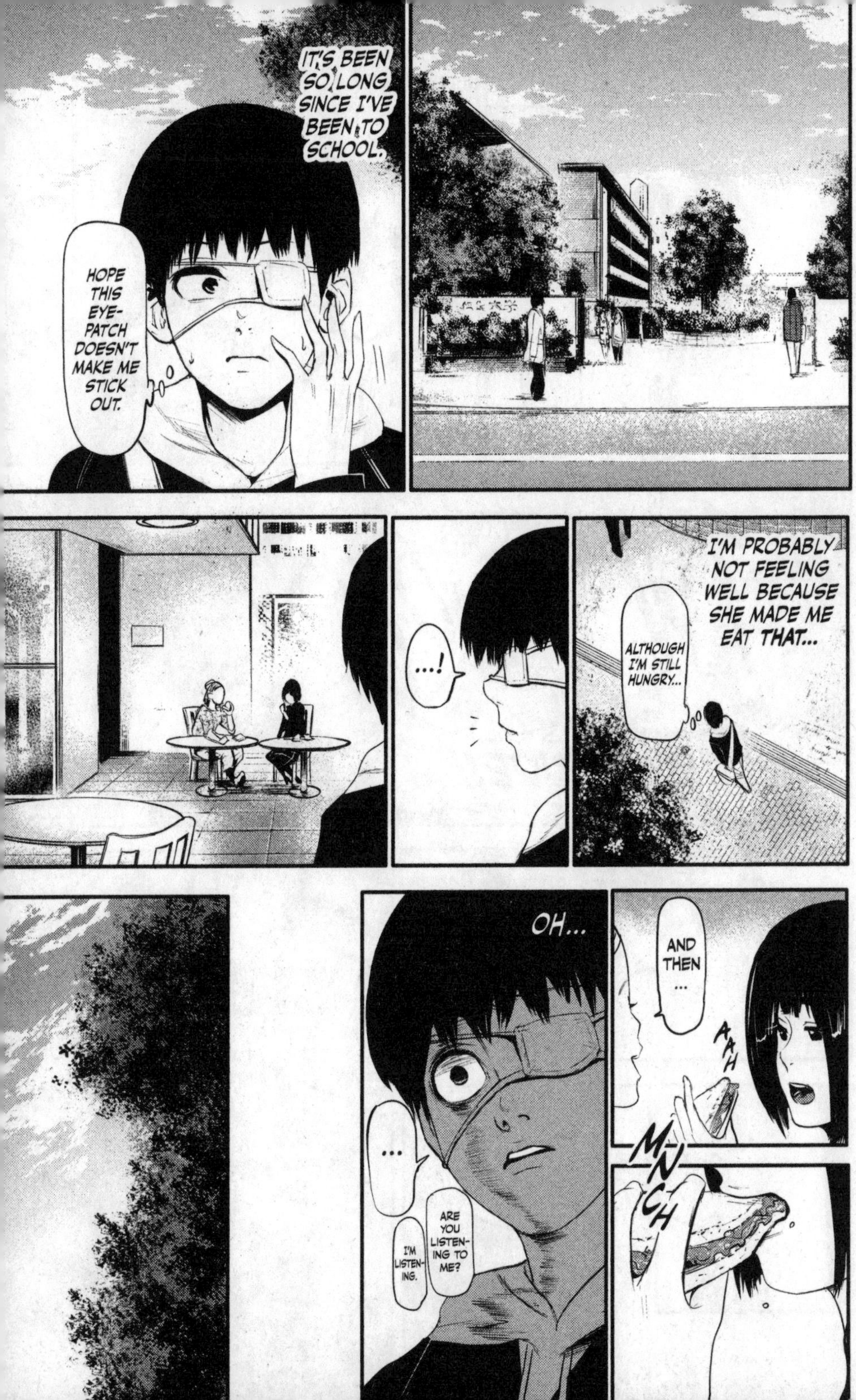
IT'S BEEN SO LONG SINCE I'VE BEEN TO SCHOOL.
HOPE THIS EYE-PATCH DOESN'T MAKE ME STICK OUT.
I'M PROBABLY NOT FEELING WELL BECAUSE SHE MADE ME EAT THAT...
ALTHOUGH I'M STILL HUNGRY...
...!
AND THEN ...
AAH
MNCH
OH...
...
ARE YOU LISTENING TO ME?
I'M LISTENING.

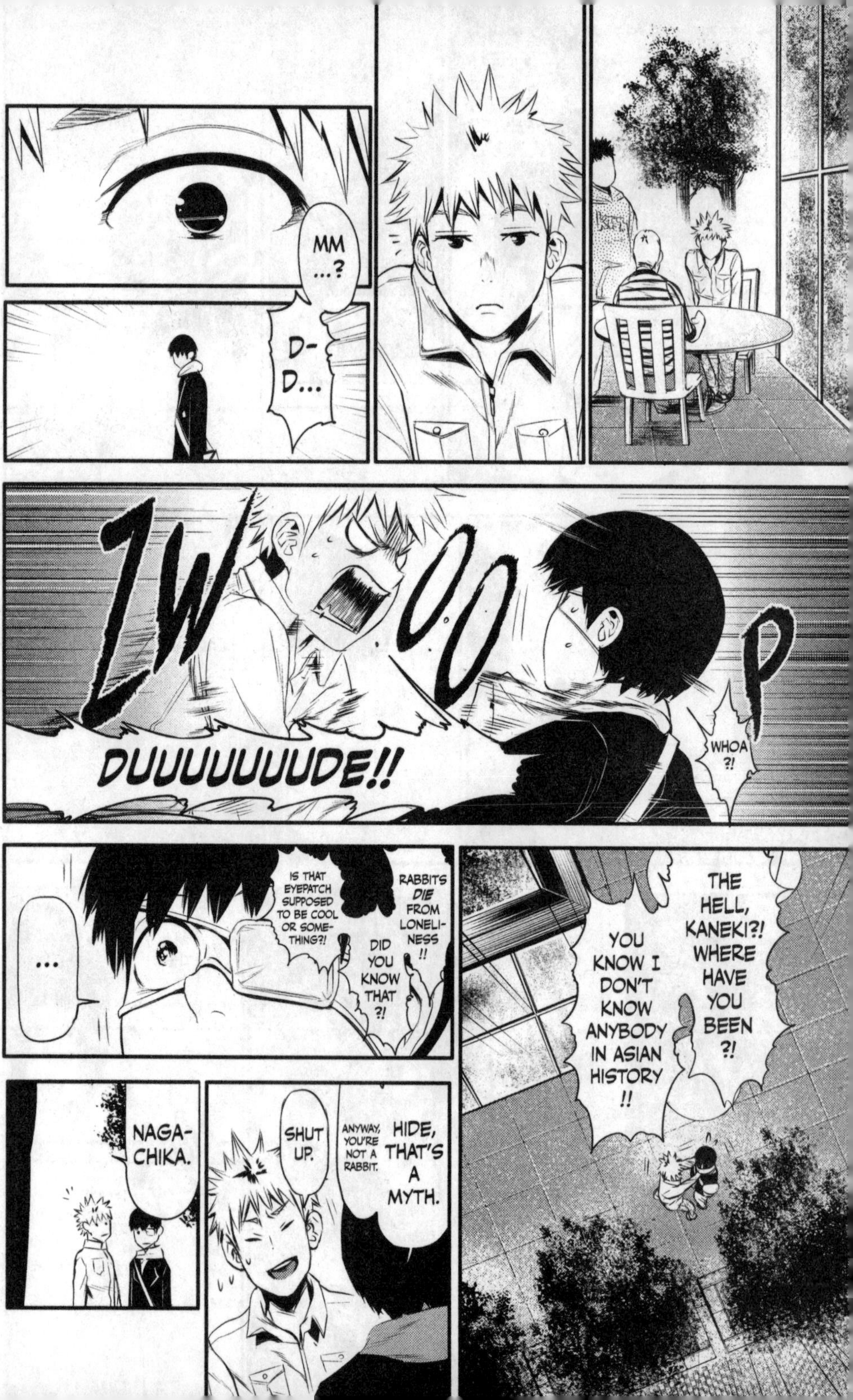
MM ...?
D- D...
ZWOOP
DUUUUUUUDE!!
WHOA ?!
THE HELL, KANEKI?! WHERE HAVE YOU BEEN ?!
YOU KNOW I DON'T KNOW ANYBODY IN ASIAN HISTORY !!
RABBITS DIE FROM LONELINESS !!
DID YOU KNOW THAT ?!
IS THAT EYEPATCH SUPPOSED TO BE COOL OR SOME-THING?!
...
HIDE, THAT'S A MYTH.
ANYWAY, YOU'RE NOT A RABBIT.
SHUT UP.
NAGA-CHIKA.

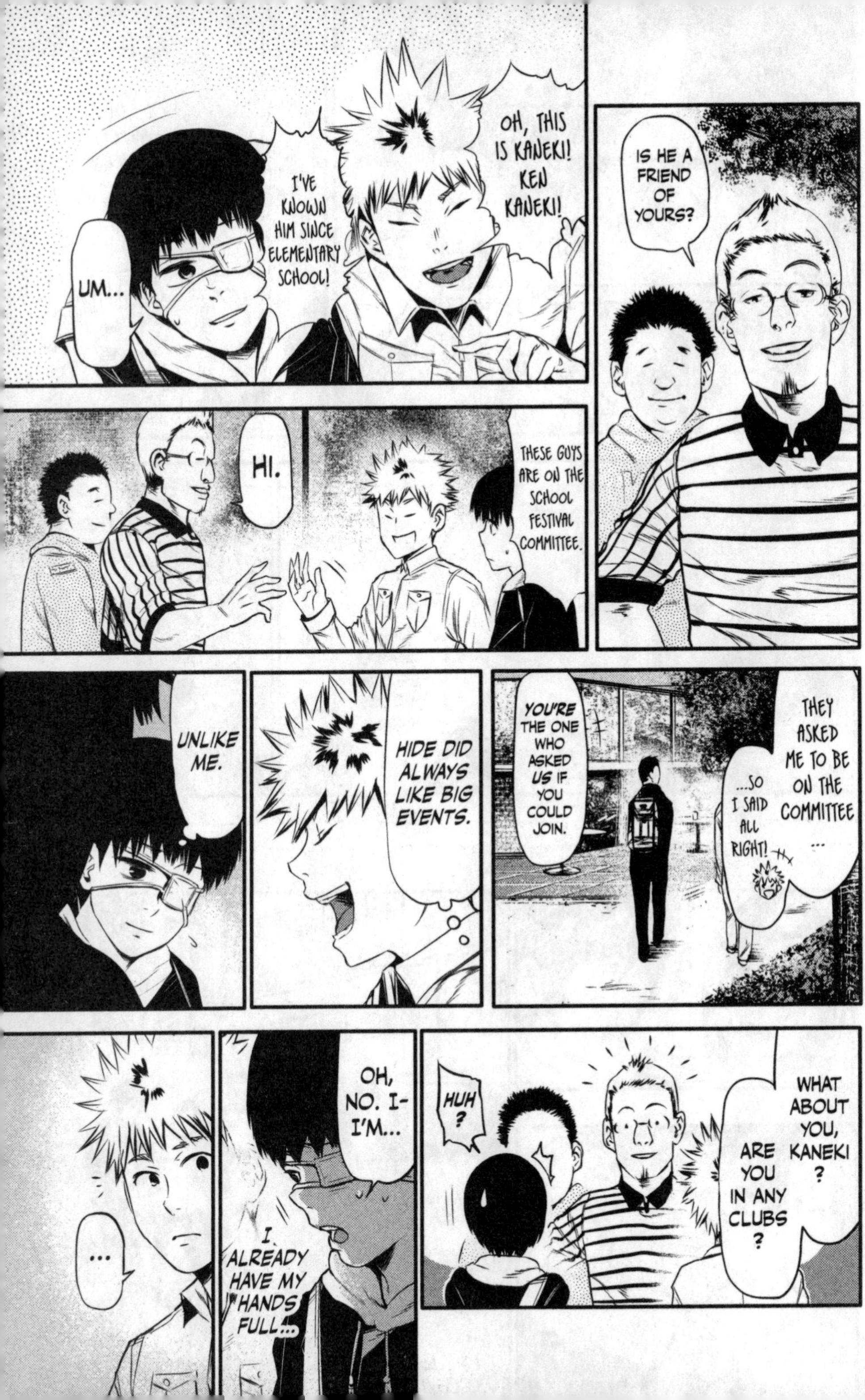
IS HE A FRIEND OF YOURS?
OH, THIS IS KANEKI! KEN KANEKI!
I'VE KNOWN HIM SINCE ELEMENTARY SCHOOL!
UM...
THESE GUYS ARE ON THE SCHOOL FESTIVAL COMMITTEE.
HI.
THEY ASKED ME TO BE ON THE COMMITTEE ...
...SO I SAID ALL RIGHT!
YOU'RE THE ONE WHO ASKED US IF YOU COULD JOIN.
HIDE DID ALWAYS LIKE BIG EVENTS.
UNLIKE ME.
WHAT ABOUT YOU, KANEKI?
ARE YOU IN ANY CLUBS?
HUH?
OH, NO. I-I'M...
I. ALREADY HAVE MY HANDS FULL...
...

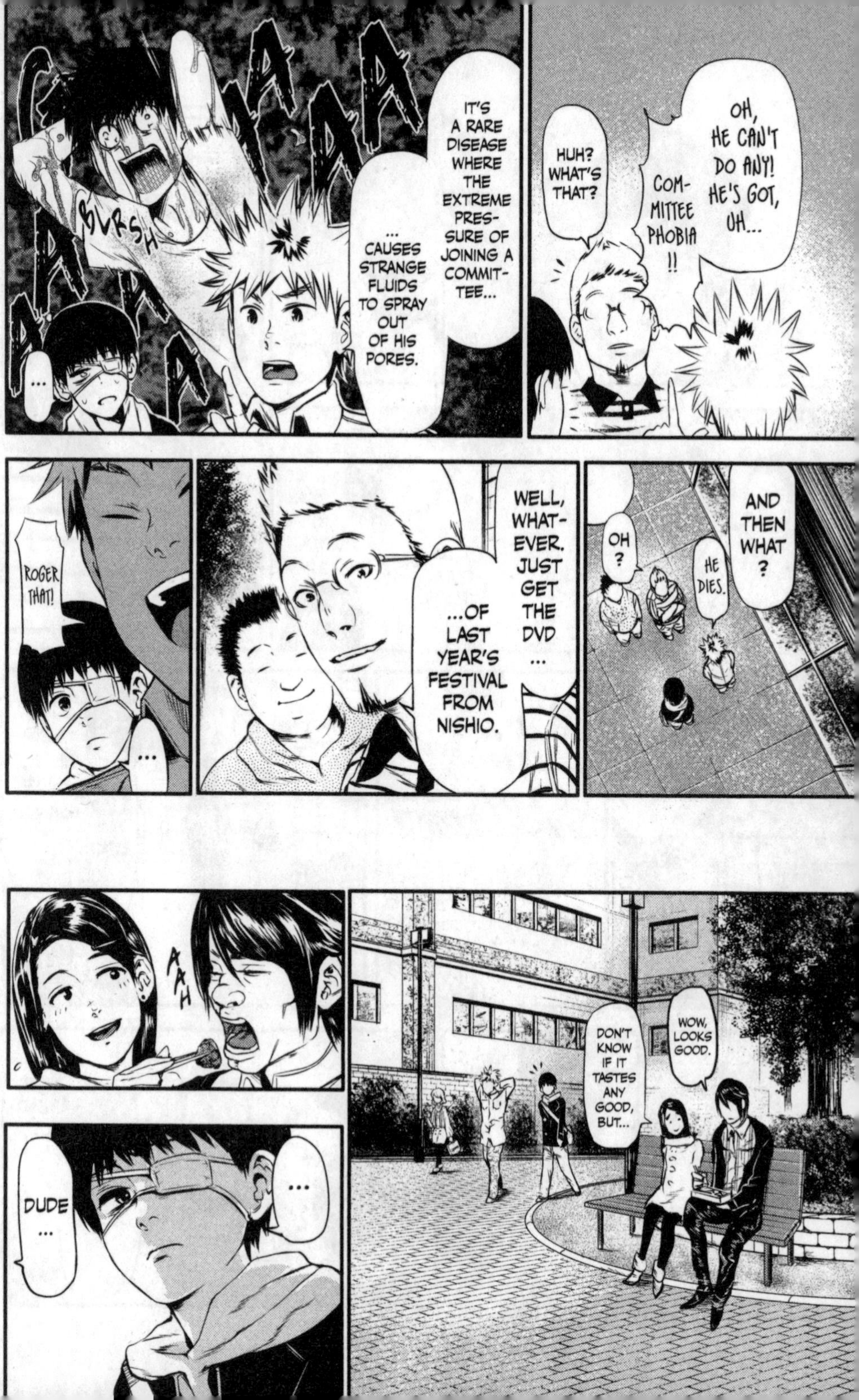
OH, HE CAN'T DO ANY! HE'S GOT, UH...
COMMITTEE PHOBIA!!
HUH? WHAT'S THAT?
IT'S A RARE DISEASE WHERE THE EXTREME PRESSURE OF JOINING A COMMITTEE...
... CAUSES STRANGE FLUIDS TO SPRAY OUT OF HIS PORES.
...
AND THEN WHAT?
HE DIES.
OH?
WELL, WHATEVER. JUST GET THE DVD...
...OF LAST YEAR'S FESTIVAL FROM NISHIO.
ROGER THAT!
...
WOW, LOOKS GOOD.
DON'T KNOW IF IT TASTES ANY GOOD, BUT...
AAH
...
DUDE...

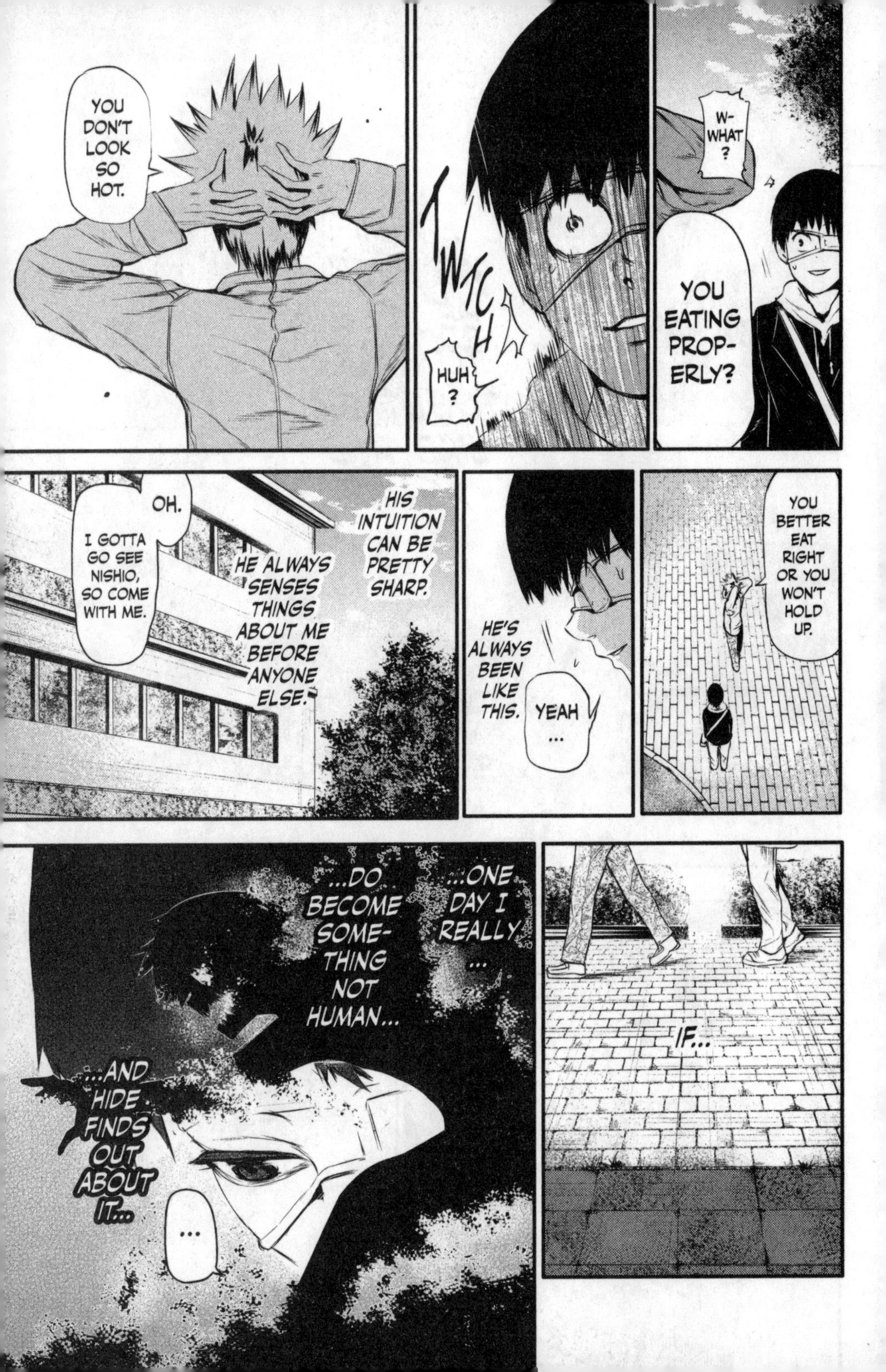

W-WHAT?
YOU EATING PROP-ERLY?
TWITCH
HUH?
YOU DON'T LOOK SO HOT.
YOU BETTER EAT RIGHT OR YOU WON'T HOLD UP.
HE'S ALWAYS BEEN LIKE THIS.
YEAH...
HIS INTUITION CAN BE PRETTY SHARP.
HE ALWAYS SENSES THINGS ABOUT ME BEFORE ANYONE ELSE.
OH.
I GOTTA GO SEE NISHIO, SO COME WITH ME.
IF...
...ONE DAY I REALLY...
...DO BECOME SOME-THING NOT HUMAN...
...AND HIDE FINDS OUT ABOUT IT...
...

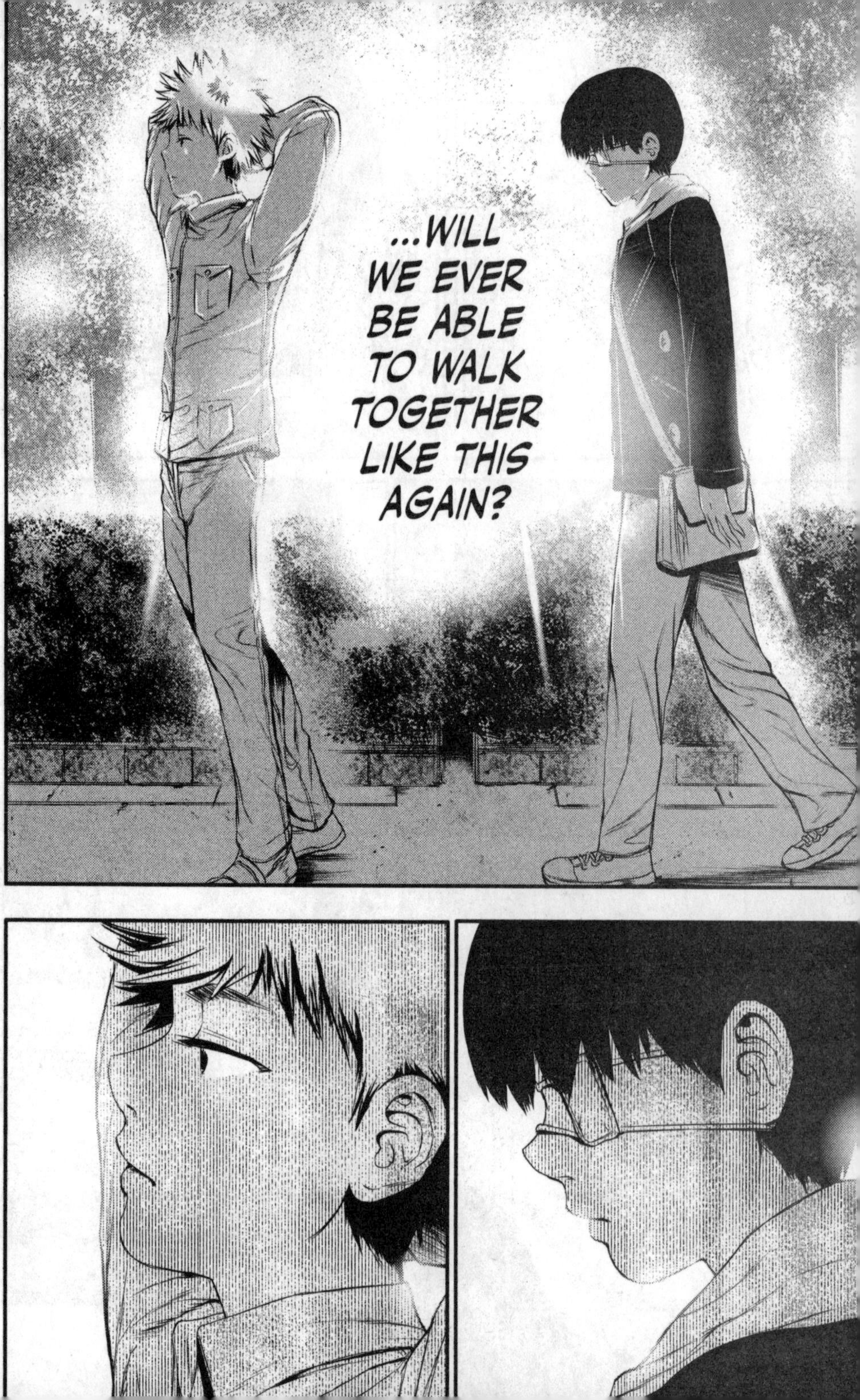
...WILL
WE EVER
BE ABLE
TO WALK
TOGETHER
LIKE THIS
AGAIN?

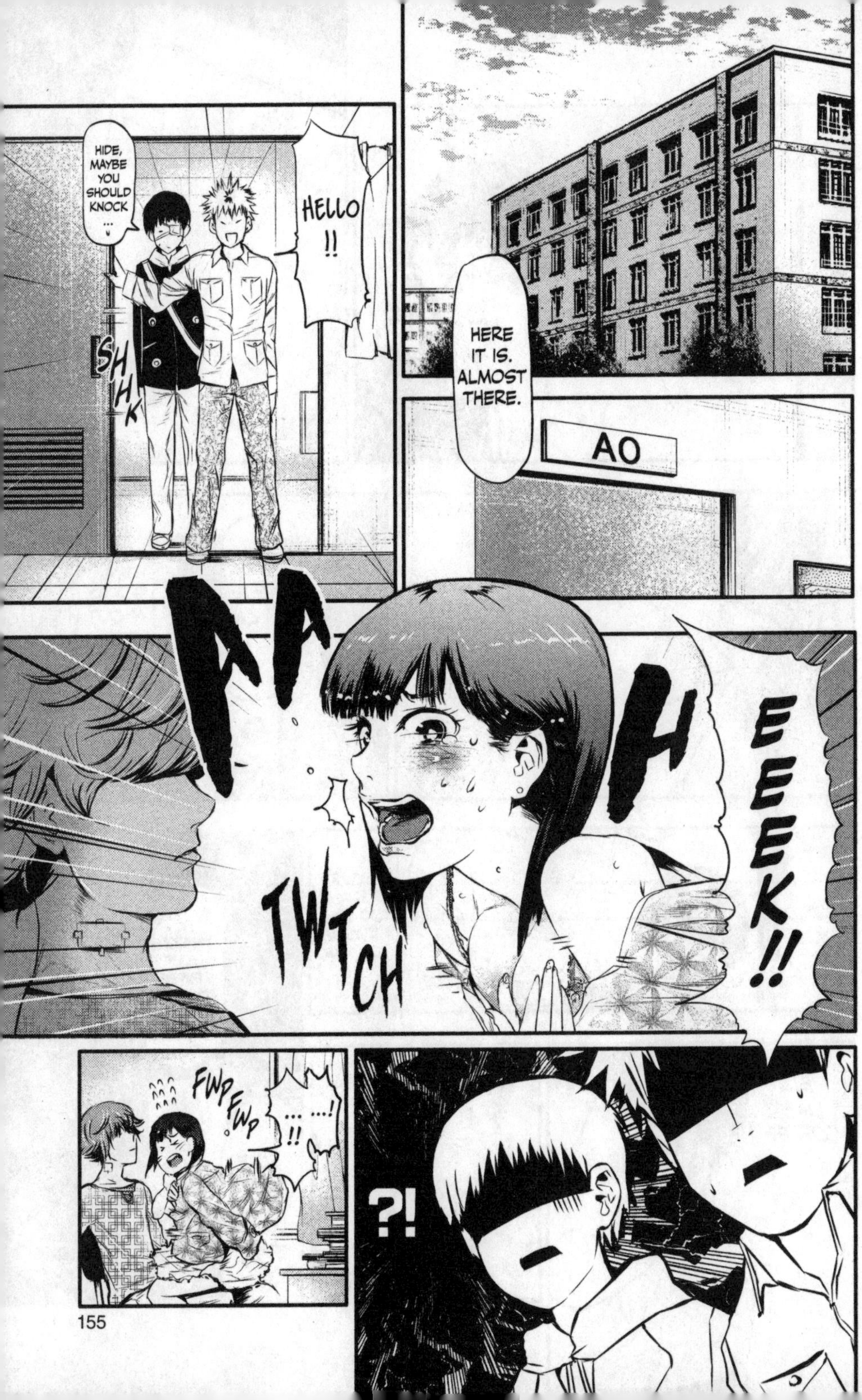
HERE IT IS. ALMOST THERE.
AO
HELLO!!
HIDE, MAYBE YOU SHOULD KNOCK...
SHHK
EEEEK!!
AAH
TWTCH
?!
... ...!
!!
FWP FWP

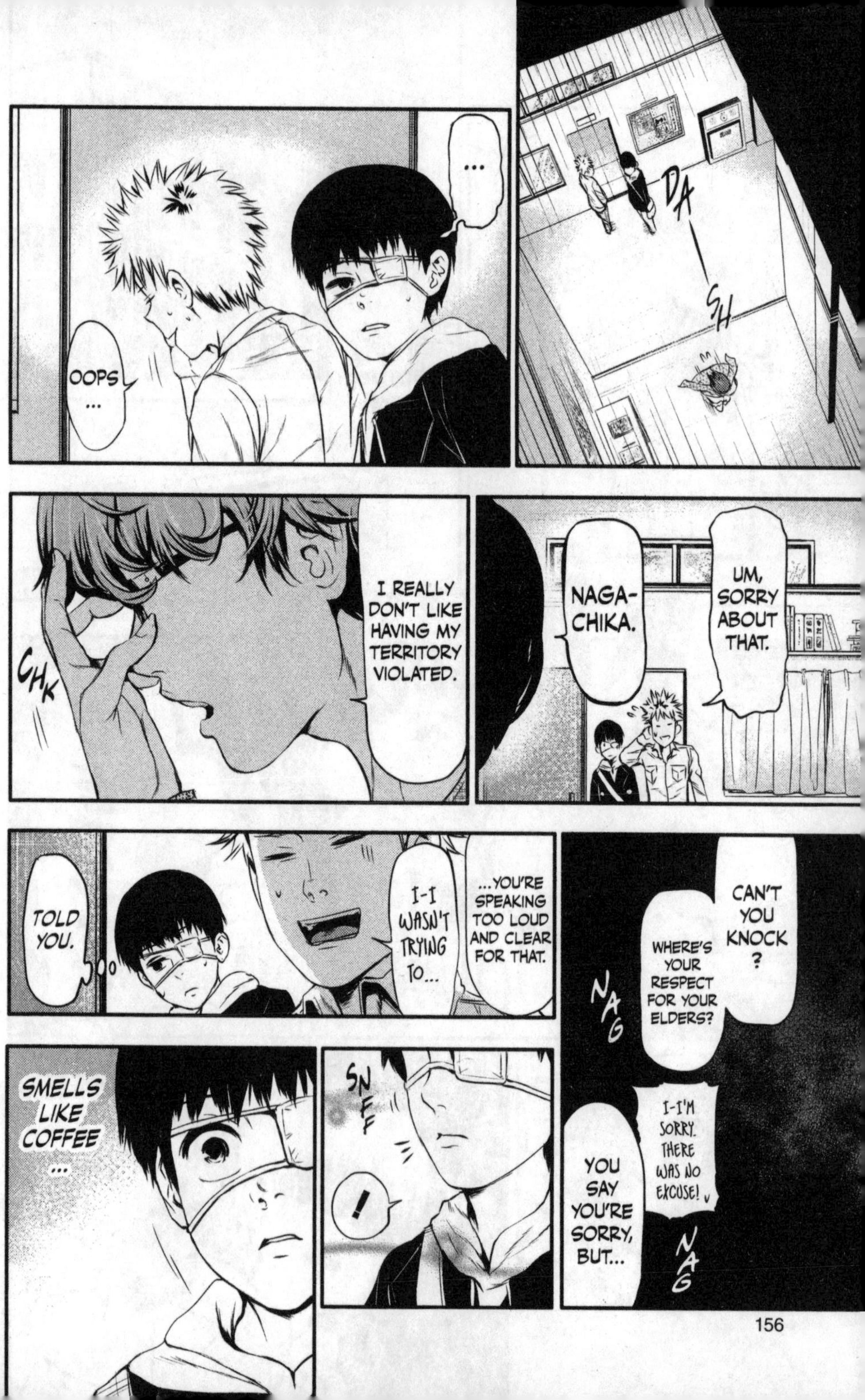

DA
SH
...
OOPS ...
UM, SORRY ABOUT THAT.
NAGA-CHIKA.
I REALLY DON'T LIKE HAVING MY TERRITORY VIOLATED.
CHK
CAN'T YOU KNOCK?
WHERE'S YOUR RESPECT FOR YOUR ELDERS?
NAG
I-I'M SORRY. THERE WAS NO EXCUSE!
YOU SAY YOU'RE SORRY, BUT...
NAG
...YOU'RE SPEAKING TOO LOUD AND CLEAR FOR THAT.
I-I WASN'T TRYING TO...
TOLD YOU.
SNFF
!
SMELLS LIKE COFFEE ...

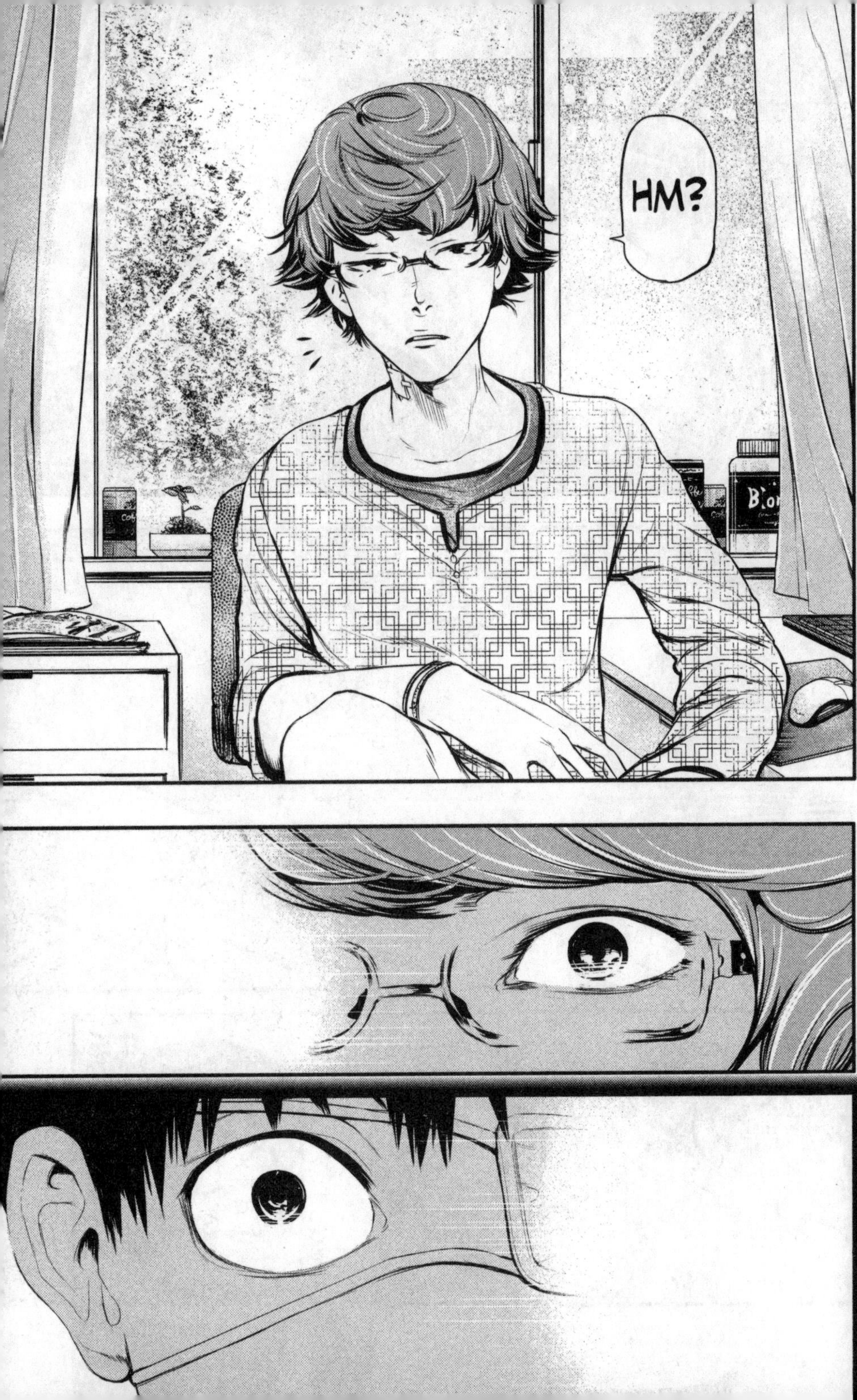
HM?

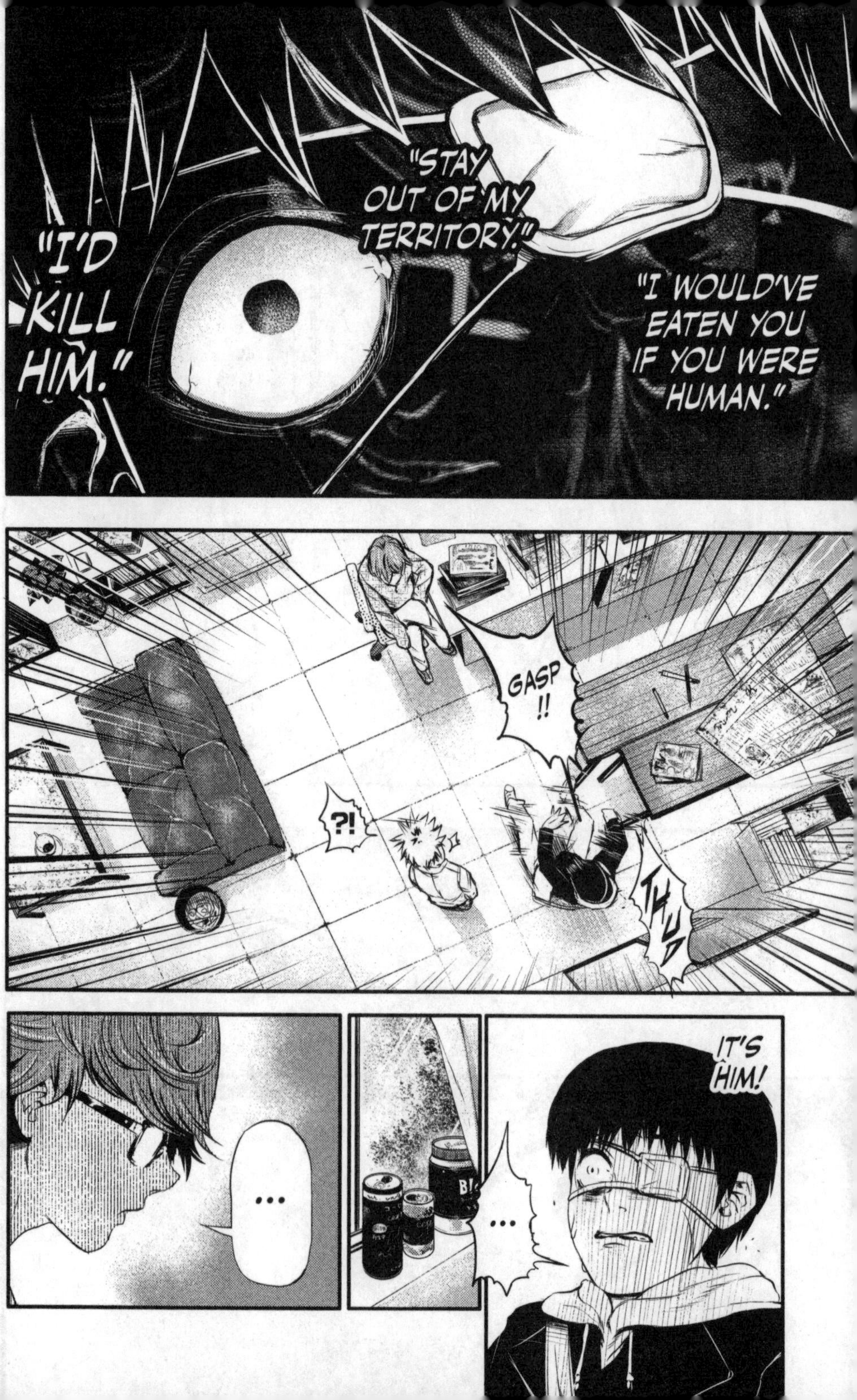
"STAY OUT OF MY TERRITORY."
"I WOULD'VE EATEN YOU IF YOU WERE HUMAN."
"I'D KILL HIM."
GASP !!
?!
THUD
IT'S HIM!
...
...

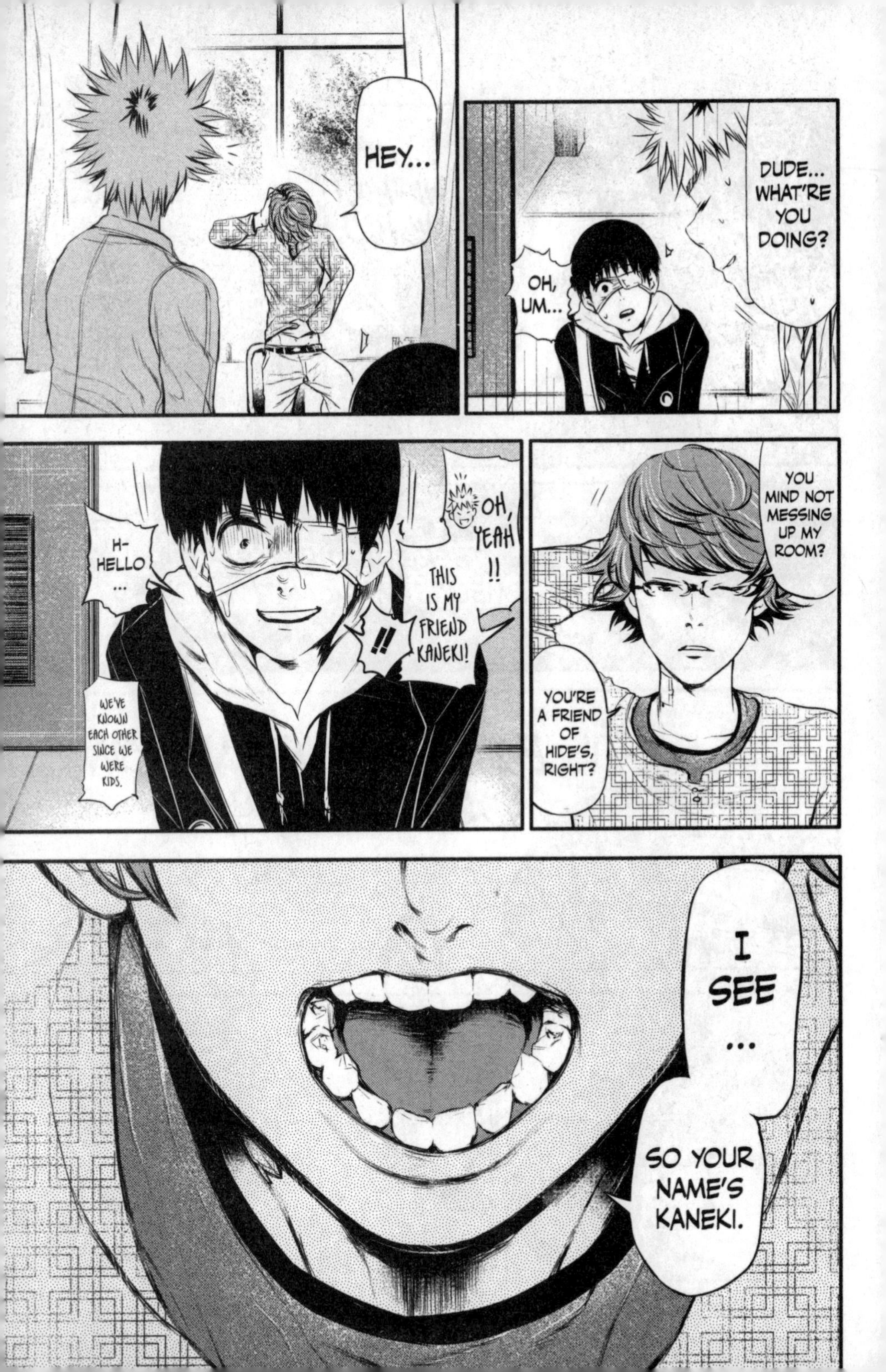
DUDE... WHAT'RE YOU DOING?
OH, UM...
HEY...
YOU MIND NOT MESSING UP MY ROOM?
YOU'RE A FRIEND OF HIDE'S, RIGHT?
OH, YEAH !!
THIS IS MY FRIEND KANEKI!
!!
H-HELLO ...
WE'VE KNOWN EACH OTHER SINCE WE WERE KIDS.
I SEE ...
SO YOUR NAME'S KANEKI.

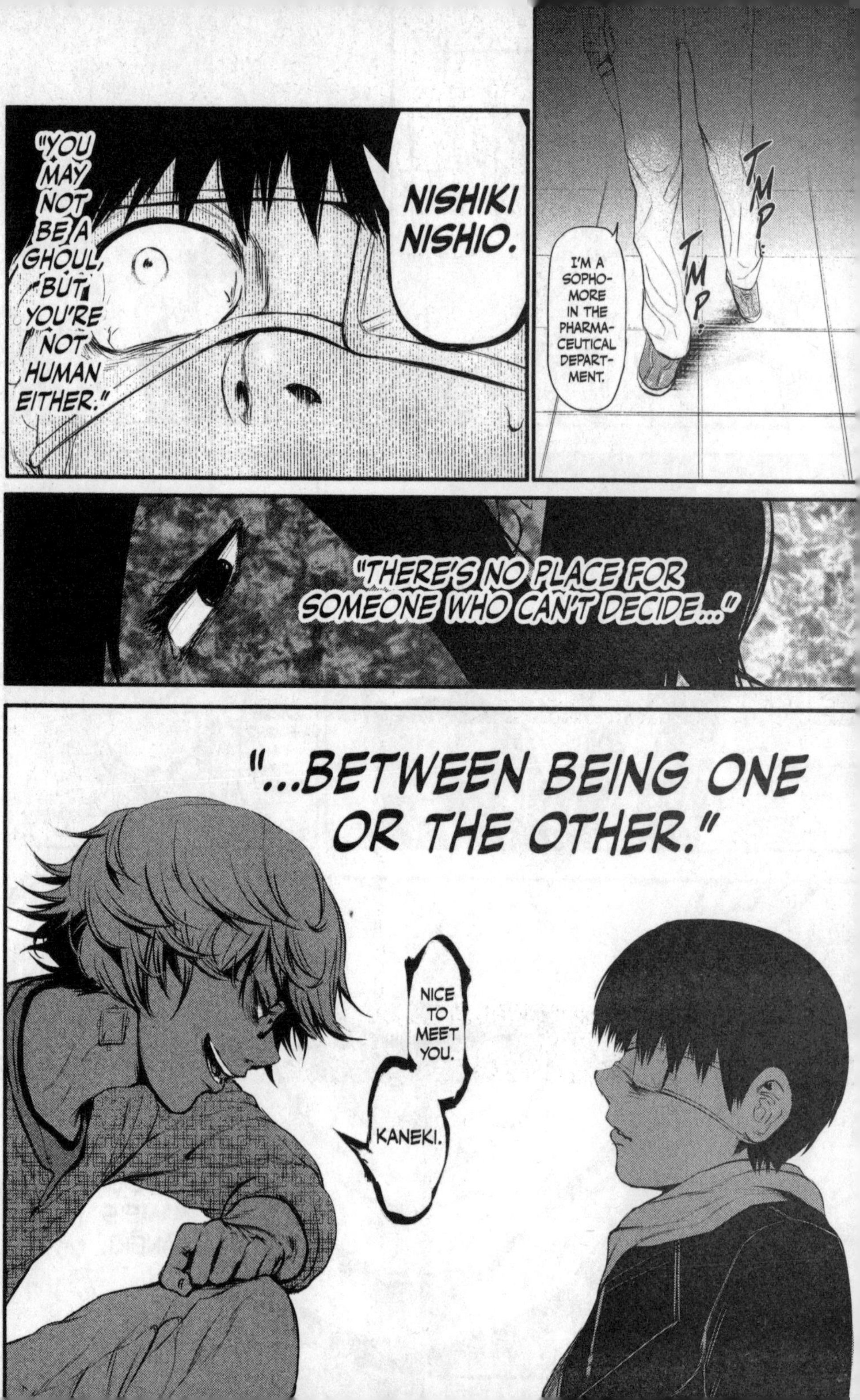
TMP.
TMP.
I'M A SOPHOMORE IN THE PHARMACEUTICAL DEPARTMENT.
NISHIKI NISHIO.
"YOU MAY NOT BE A GHOUL, BUT YOU'RE NOT HUMAN EITHER."
"THERE'S NO PLACE FOR SOMEONE WHO CAN'T DECIDE..."
"...BETWEEN BEING ONE OR THE OTHER."
NICE TO MEET YOU.
KANEKI.

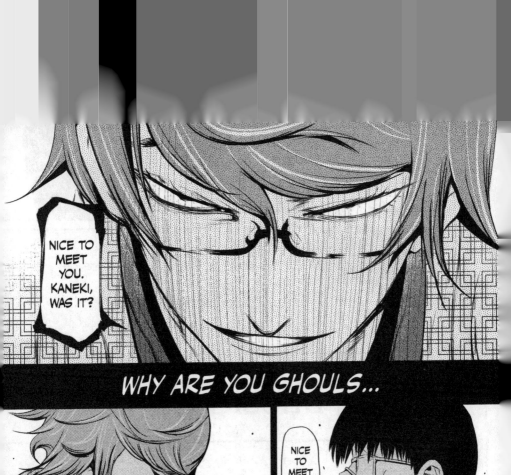

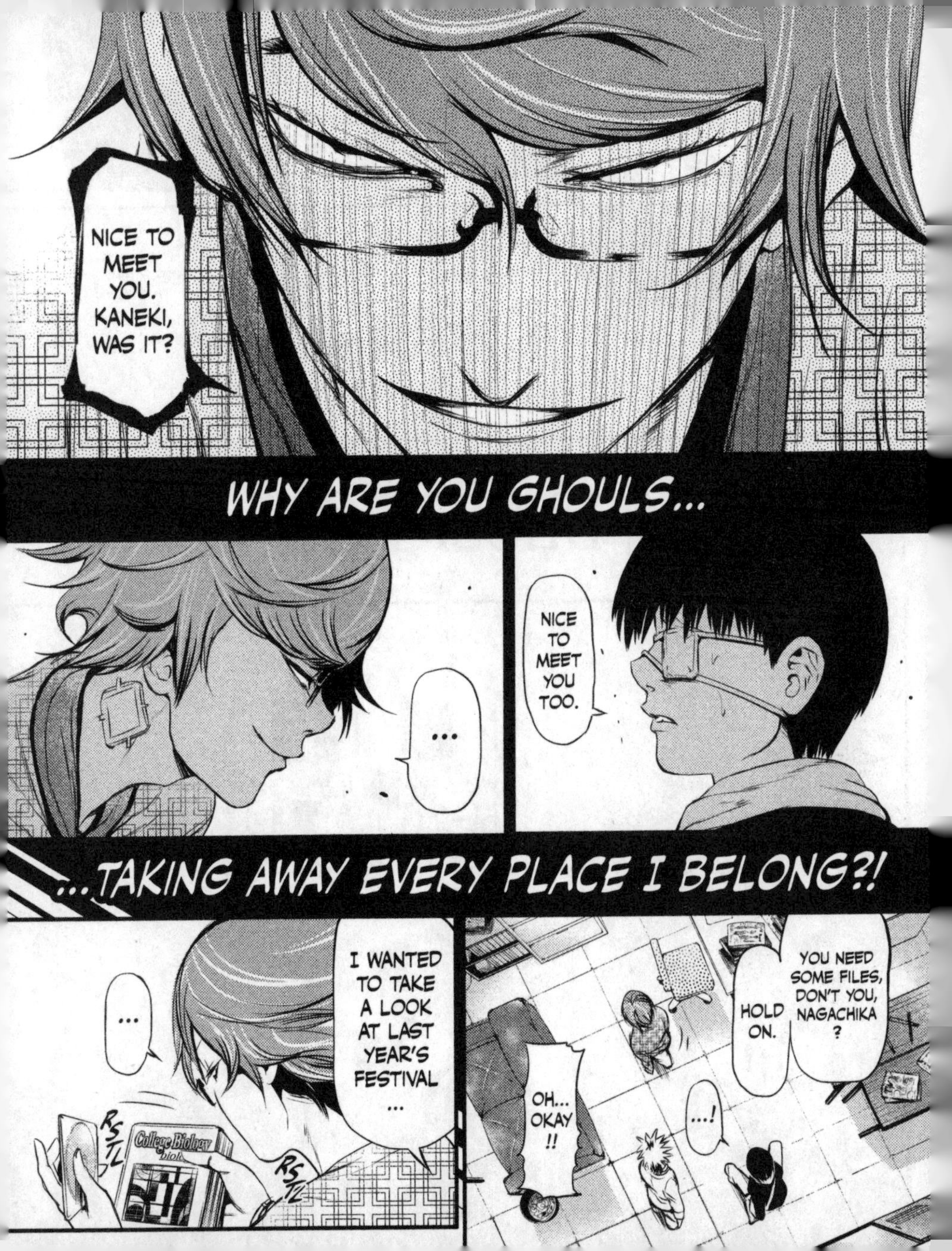
NICE TO MEET YOU. KANEKI, WAS IT?
WHY ARE YOU GHOULS...
NICE TO MEET YOU TOO.
...
...TAKING AWAY EVERY PLACE I BELONG?!
YOU NEED SOME FILES, DON'T YOU, NAGACHIKA?
HOLD ON.
...!
OH... OKAY!!
I WANTED TO TAKE A LOOK AT LAST YEAR'S FESTIVAL...
...
RSTL
RSTL
College Biology

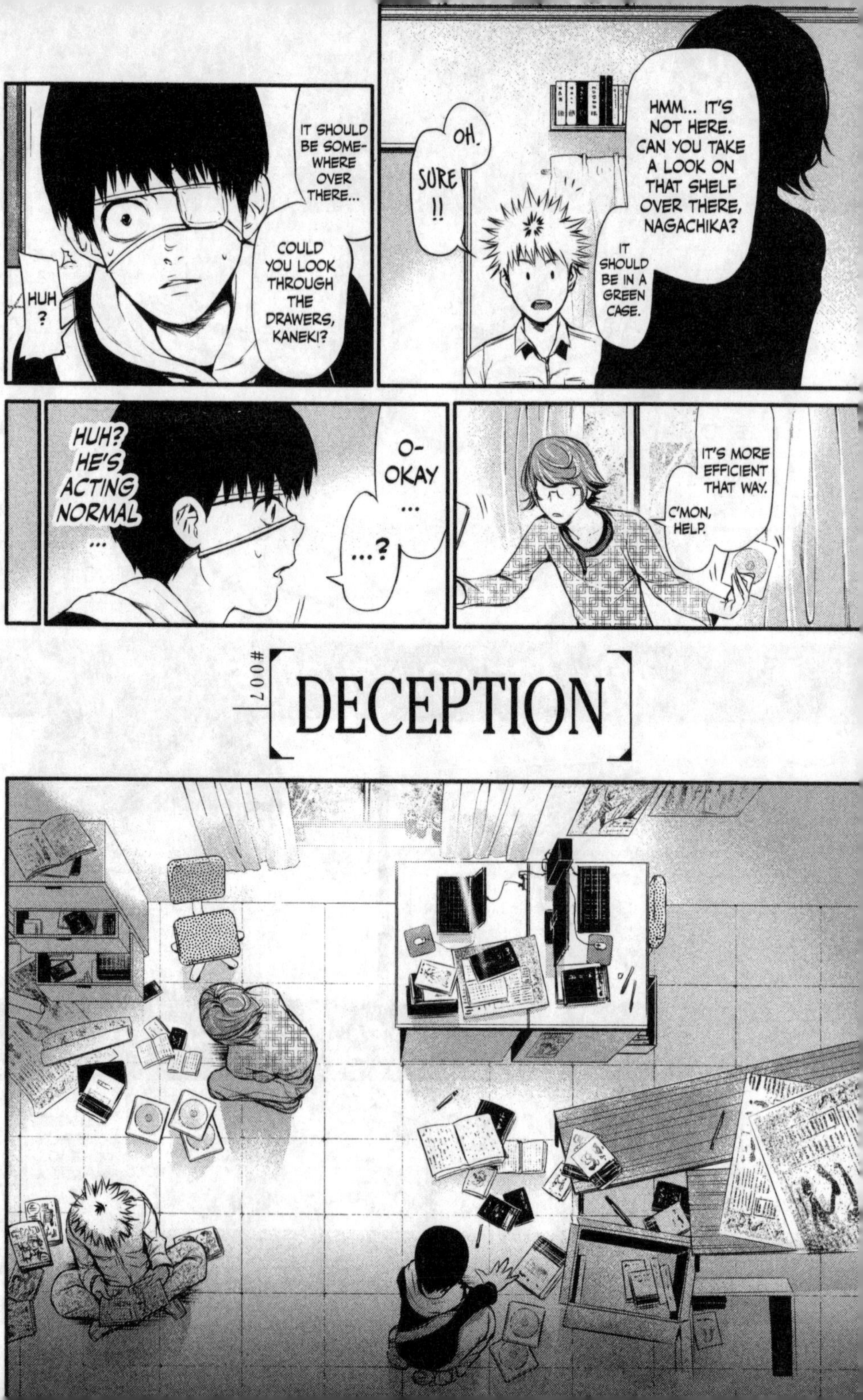

HMM... IT'S NOT HERE. CAN YOU TAKE A LOOK ON THAT SHELF OVER THERE, NAGACHIKA?
IT SHOULD BE IN A GREEN CASE.
OH.
SURE!!
IT SHOULD BE SOME-WHERE OVER THERE...
COULD YOU LOOK THROUGH THE DRAWERS, KANEKI?
HUH?
IT'S MORE EFFICIENT THAT WAY.
C'MON, HELP.
O-OKAY...
...?
HUH? HE'S ACTING NORMAL...
#007
DECEPTION

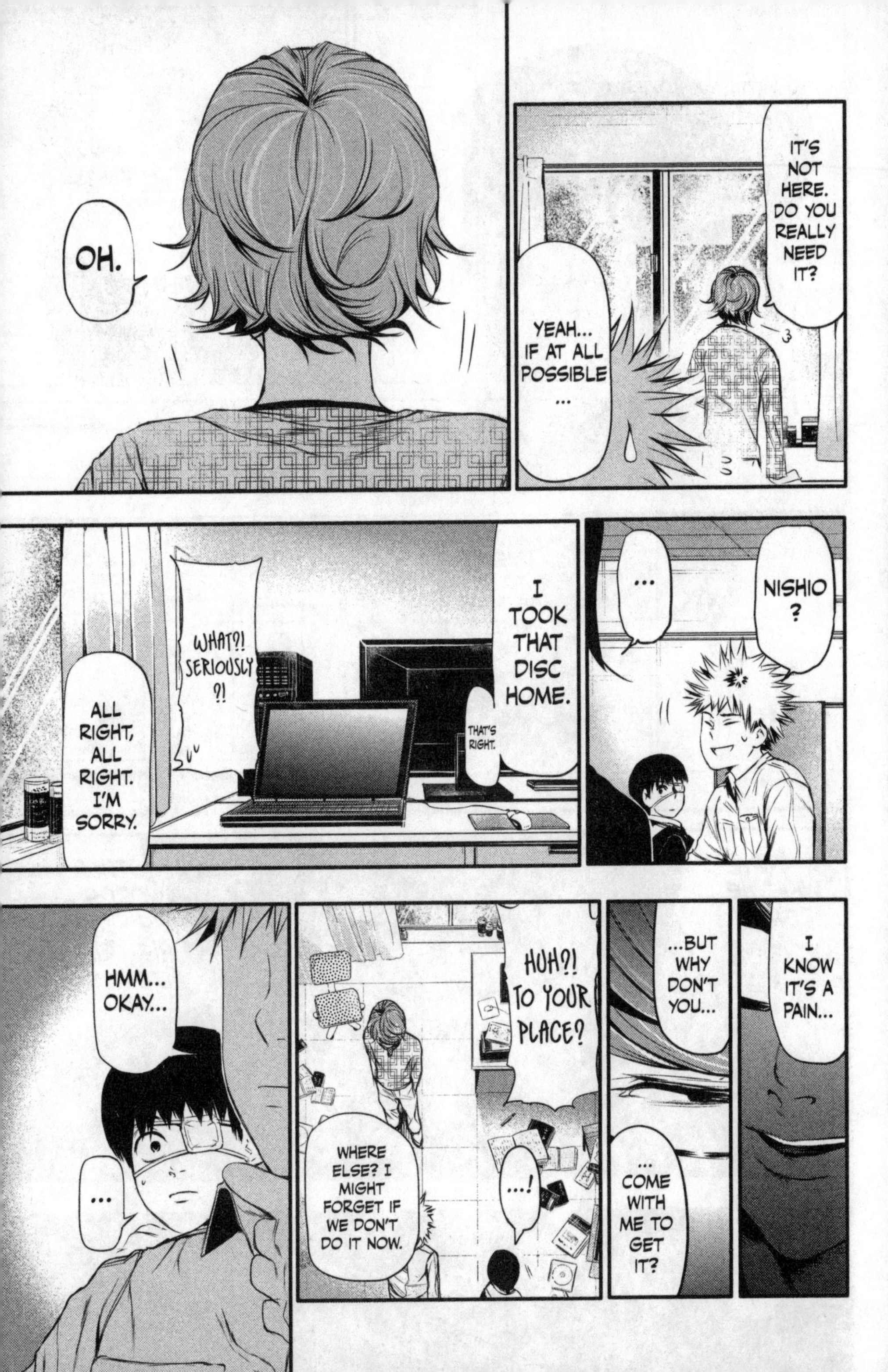
IT'S NOT HERE. DO YOU REALLY NEED IT?
YEAH... IF AT ALL POSSIBLE ...
OH.
NISHIO ?
...
I TOOK THAT DISC HOME.
THAT'S RIGHT.
WHAT?! SERIOUSLY ?!
ALL RIGHT, ALL RIGHT. I'M SORRY.
I KNOW IT'S A PAIN...
...BUT WHY DON'T YOU...
... COME WITH ME TO GET IT?
HUH?! TO YOUR PLACE?
WHERE ELSE? I MIGHT FORGET IF WE DON'T DO IT NOW.
...!
HMM... OKAY...
...

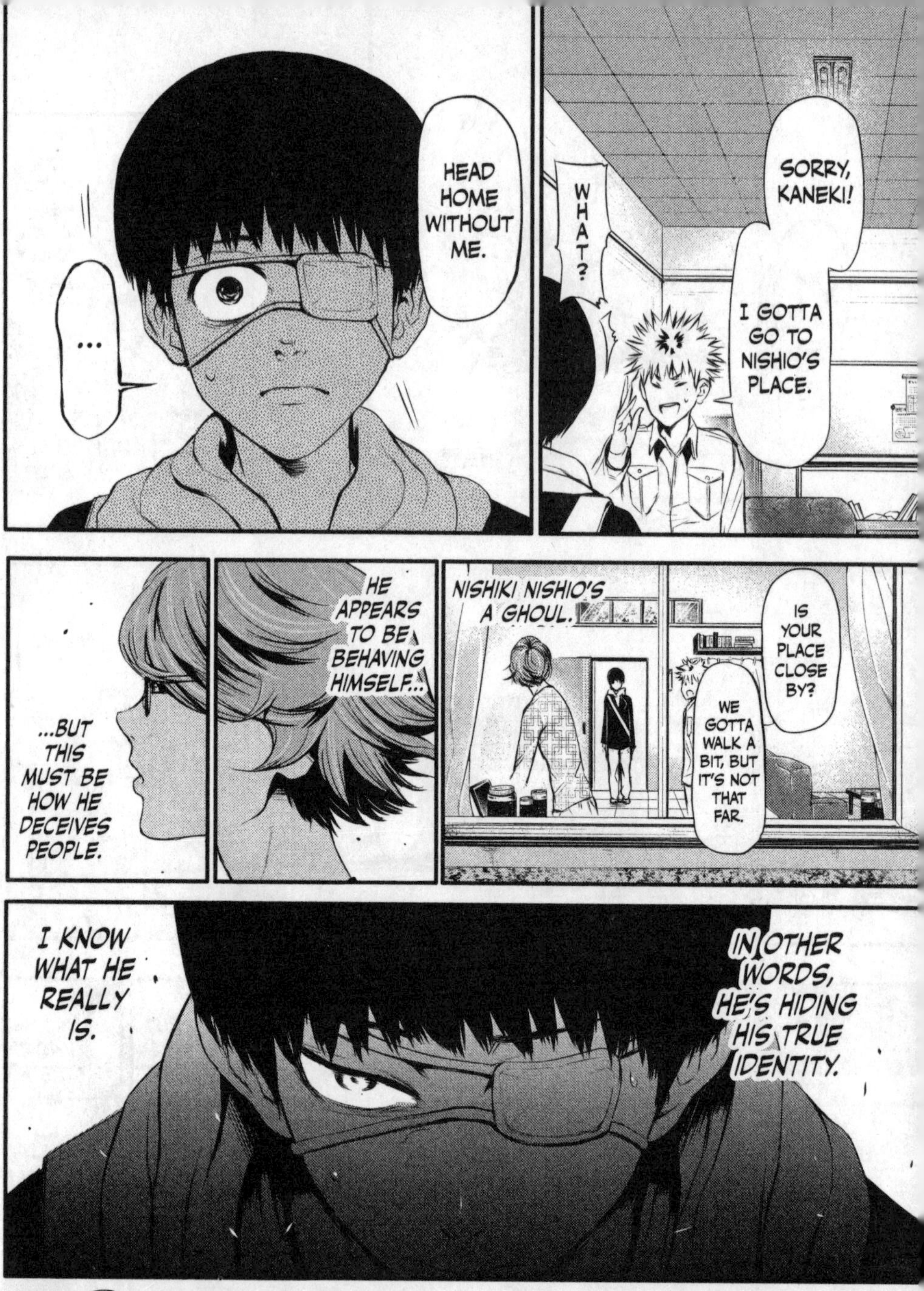
SORRY, KANEKI!
I GOTTA GO TO NISHIO'S PLACE.
WHAT?
HEAD HOME WITHOUT ME.
...
IS YOUR PLACE CLOSE BY?
WE GOTTA WALK A BIT, BUT IT'S NOT THAT FAR.
NISHIKI NISHIO'S A GHOUL.
HE APPEARS TO BE BEHAVING HIMSELF...
...BUT THIS MUST BE HOW HE DECEIVES PEOPLE.
IN OTHER WORDS, HE'S HIDING HIS TRUE IDENTITY.
I KNOW WHAT HE REALLY IS.

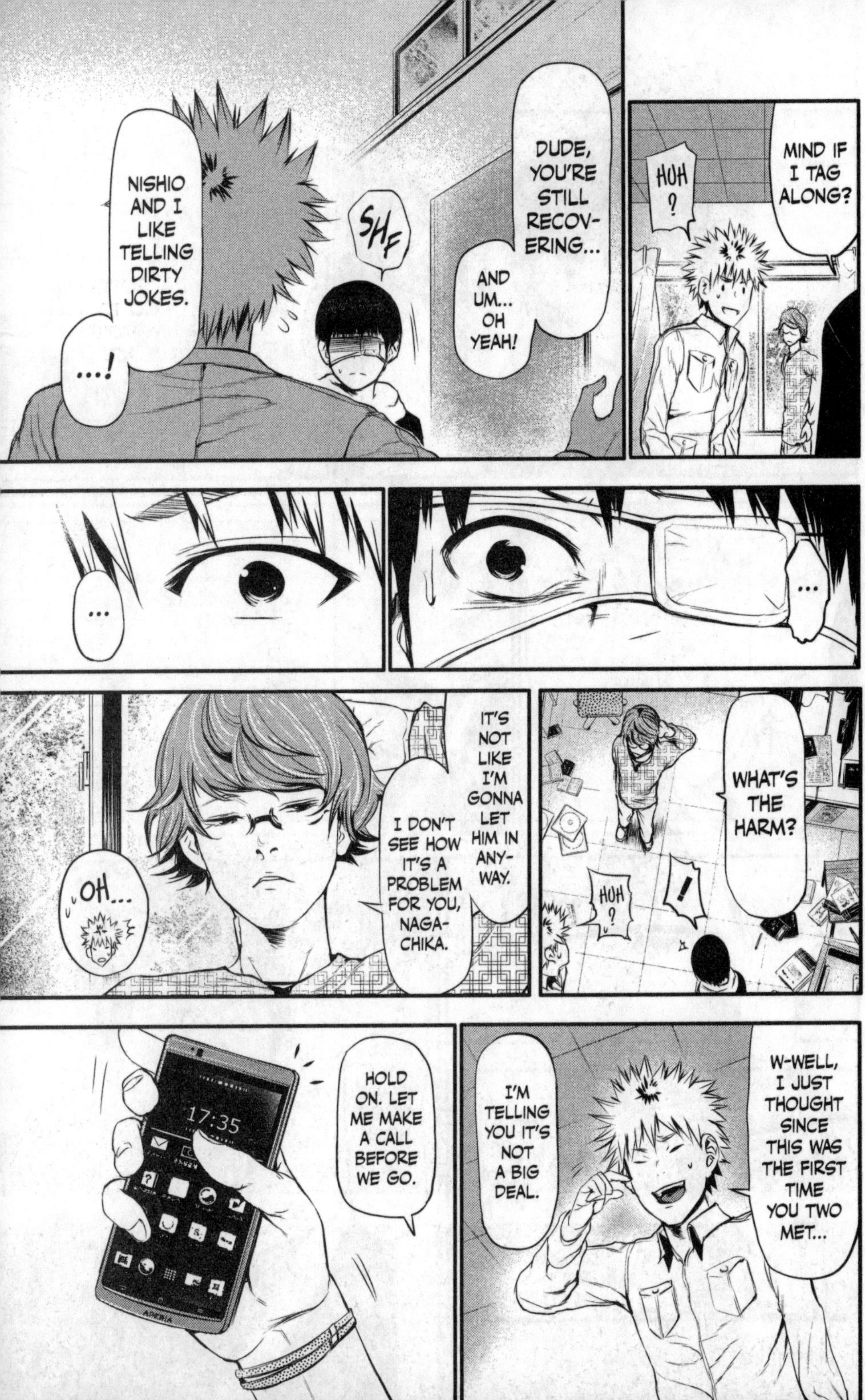
MIND IF I TAG ALONG?
HUH?
DUDE, YOU'RE STILL RECOV-ERING...
AND UM... OH YEAH!
SHF
NISHIO AND I LIKE TELLING DIRTY JOKES.
...!
...
...
WHAT'S THE HARM?
!
HUH?
IT'S NOT LIKE I'M GONNA LET HIM IN ANY-WAY.
I DON'T SEE HOW IT'S A PROBLEM FOR YOU, NAGA-CHIKA.
OH...
W-WELL, I JUST THOUGHT SINCE THIS WAS THE FIRST TIME YOU TWO MET...
I'M TELLING YOU IT'S NOT A BIG DEAL.
HOLD ON. LET ME MAKE A CALL BEFORE WE GO.
17:35

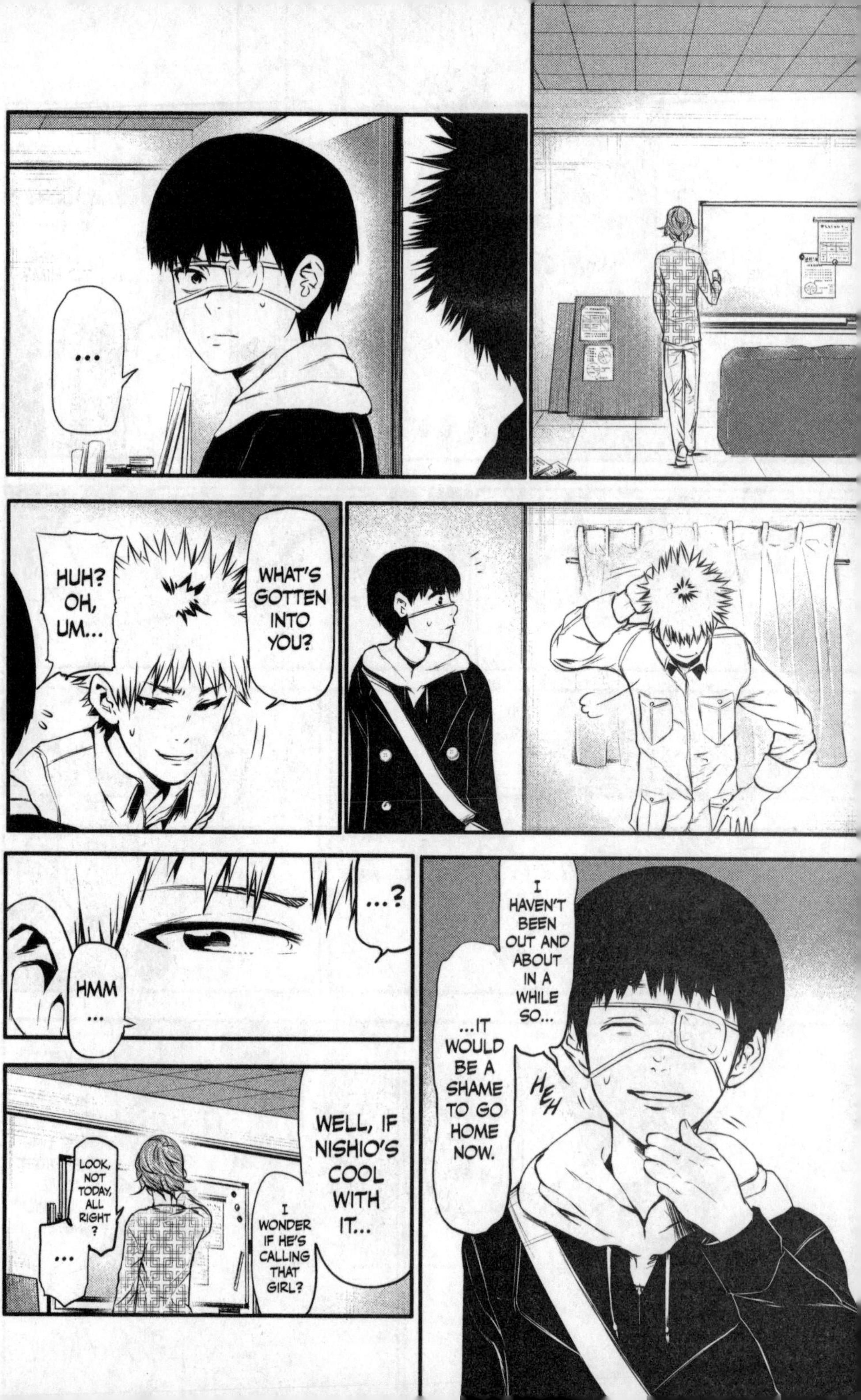
...
WHAT'S GOTTEN INTO YOU?
HUH? OH, UM...
I HAVEN'T BEEN OUT AND ABOUT IN A WHILE SO...
...IT WOULD BE A SHAME TO GO HOME NOW.
HEH
...?
HMM ...
WELL, IF NISHIO'S COOL WITH IT...
I WONDER IF HE'S CALLING THAT GIRL?
LOOK, NOT TODAY, ALL RIGHT?
...

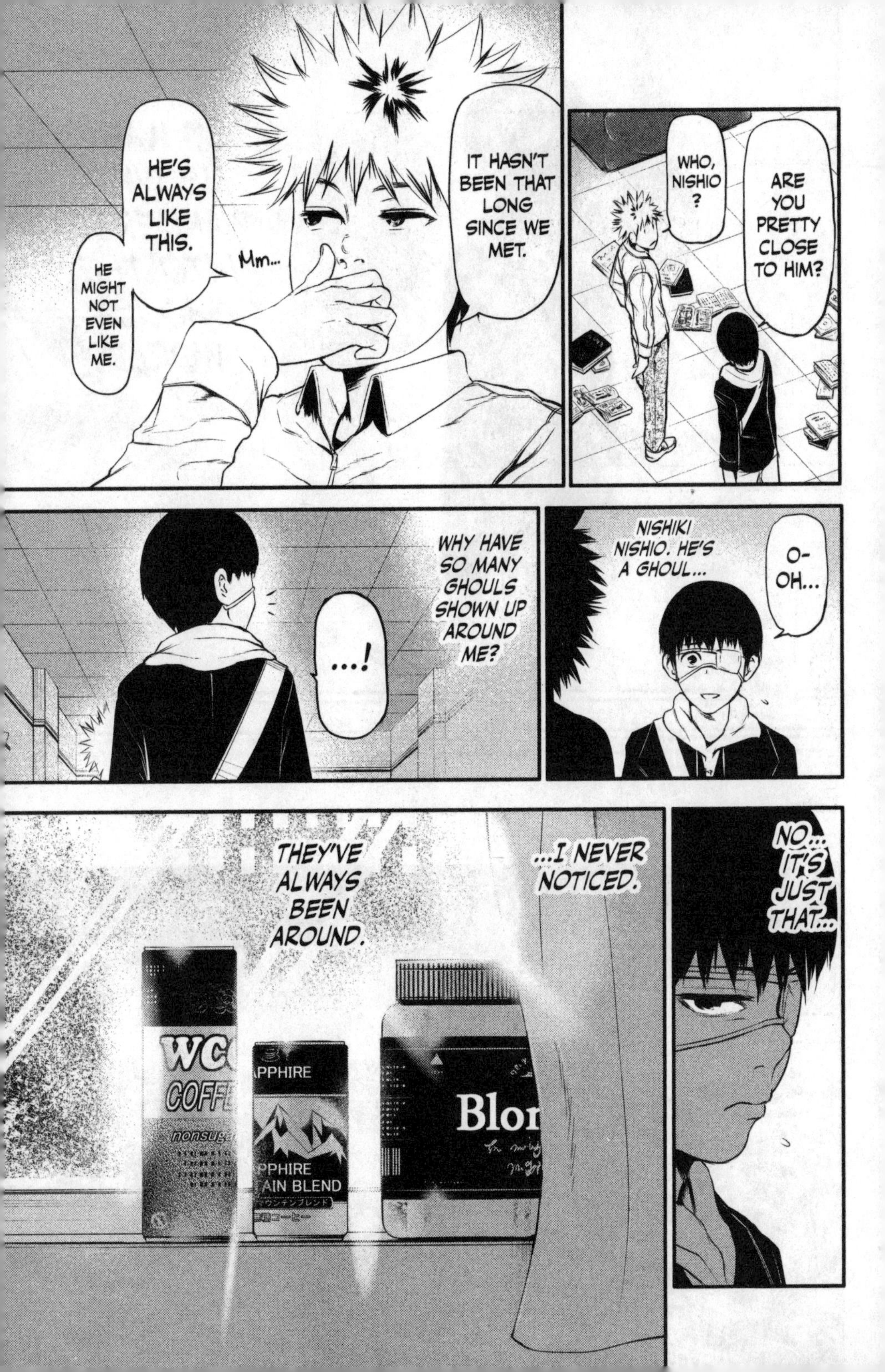
ARE YOU PRETTY CLOSE TO HIM?
WHO, NISHIO?
IT HASN'T BEEN THAT LONG SINCE WE MET.
Mm...
HE'S ALWAYS LIKE THIS.
HE MIGHT NOT EVEN LIKE ME.
O-OH...
NISHIKI NISHIO. HE'S A GHOUL...
WHY HAVE SO MANY GHOULS SHOWN UP AROUND ME?
...!
NO... IT'S JUST THAT...
...I NEVER NOTICED.
THEY'VE ALWAYS BEEN AROUND.

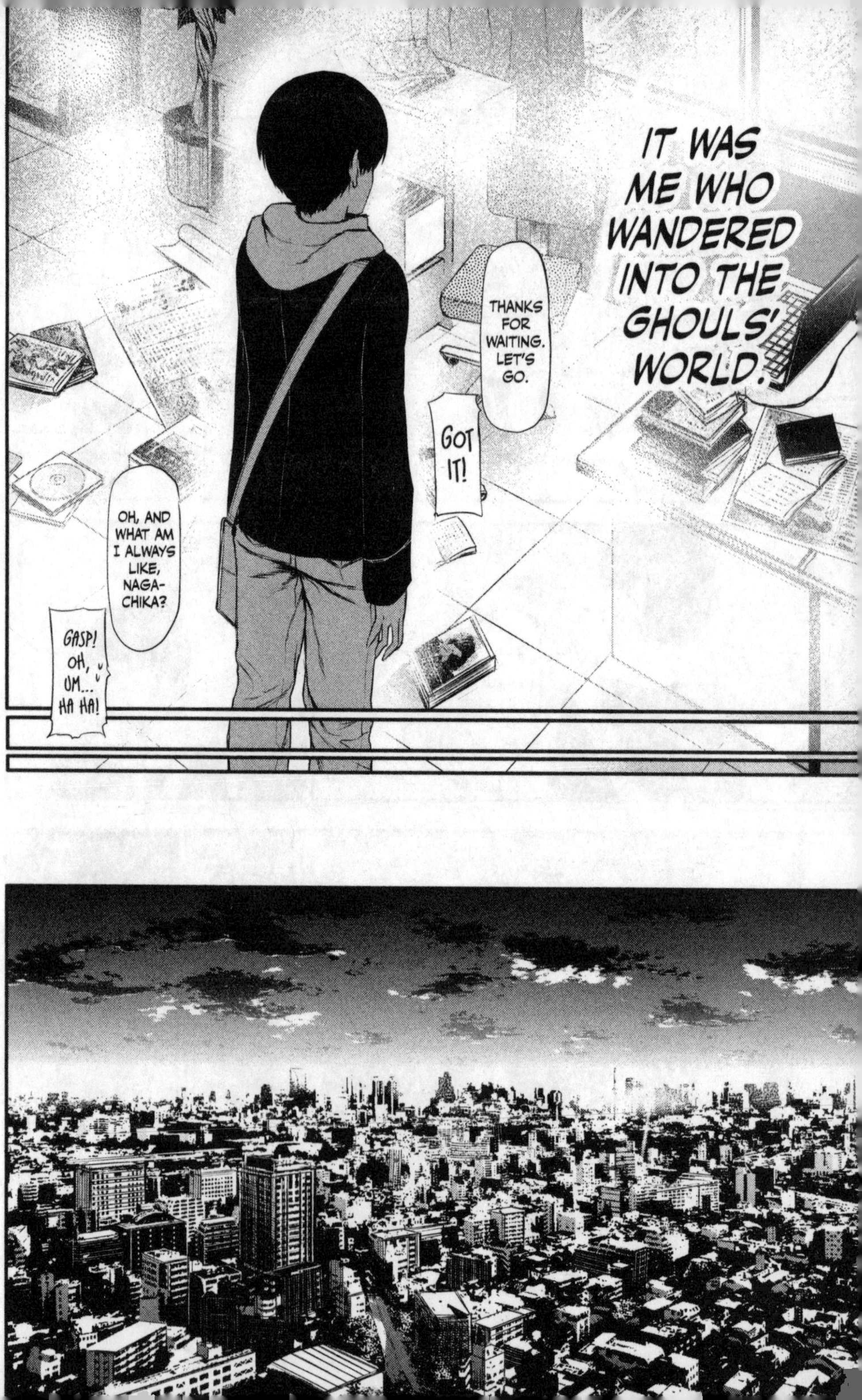
IT WAS ME WHO WANDERED INTO THE GHOULS' WORLD.
THANKS FOR WAITING. LET'S GO.
GOT IT!
OH, AND WHAT AM I ALWAYS LIKE, NAGA-CHIKA?
GASP! OH, UM... HA HA!

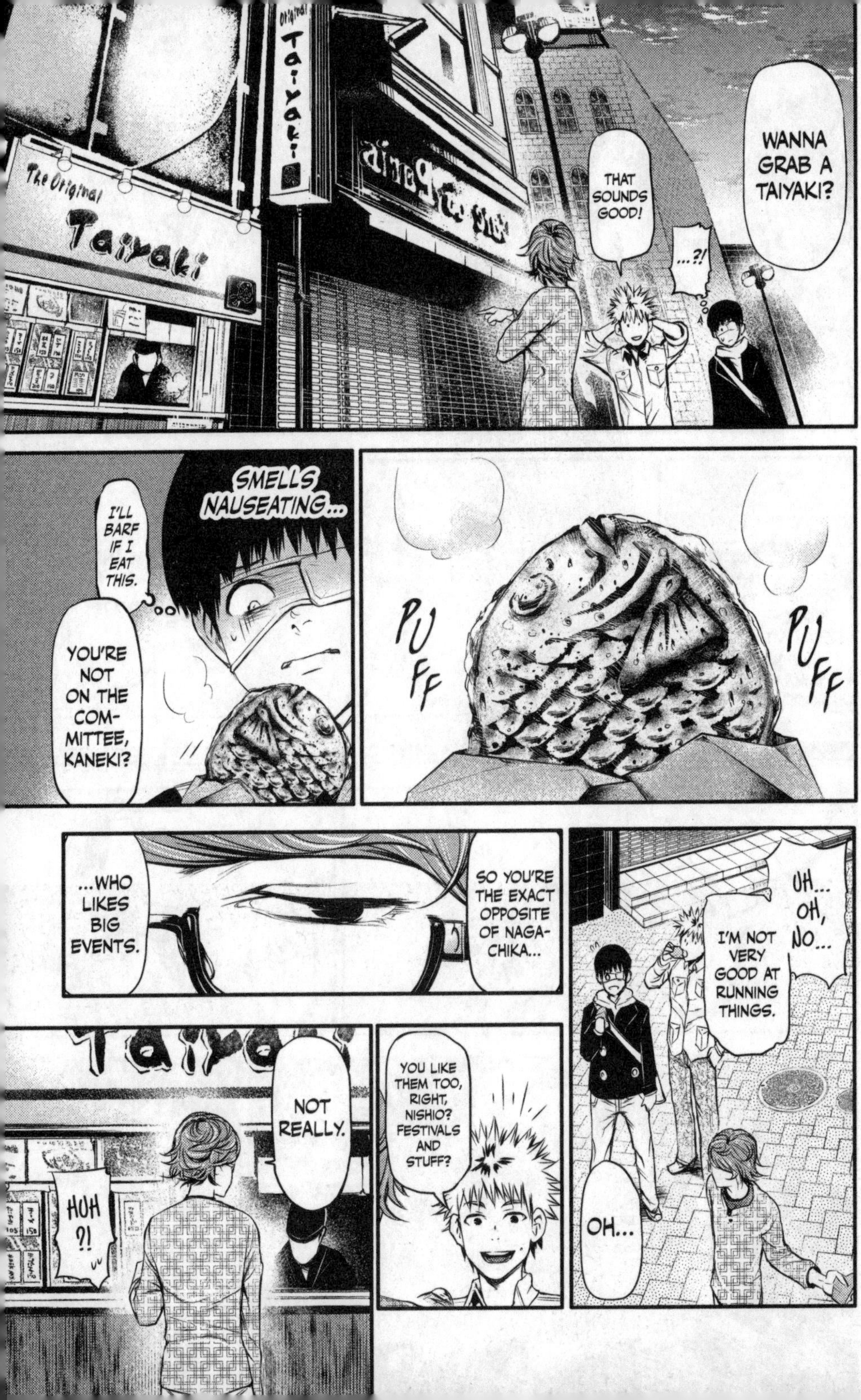

WANNA GRAB A TAIYAKI?
...?!
THAT SOUNDS GOOD!
Original Taiyaki
The Original Taiyaki
PUFF
PUFF
SMELLS NAUSEATING...
I'LL BARF IF I EAT THIS.
YOU'RE NOT ON THE COM-MITTEE, KANEKI?
UH... OH, NO...
I'M NOT VERY GOOD AT RUNNING THINGS.
OH...
SO YOU'RE THE EXACT OPPOSITE OF NAGA-CHIKA...
...WHO LIKES BIG EVENTS.
YOU LIKE THEM TOO, RIGHT, NISHIO? FESTIVALS AND STUFF?
NOT REALLY.
HUH ?!

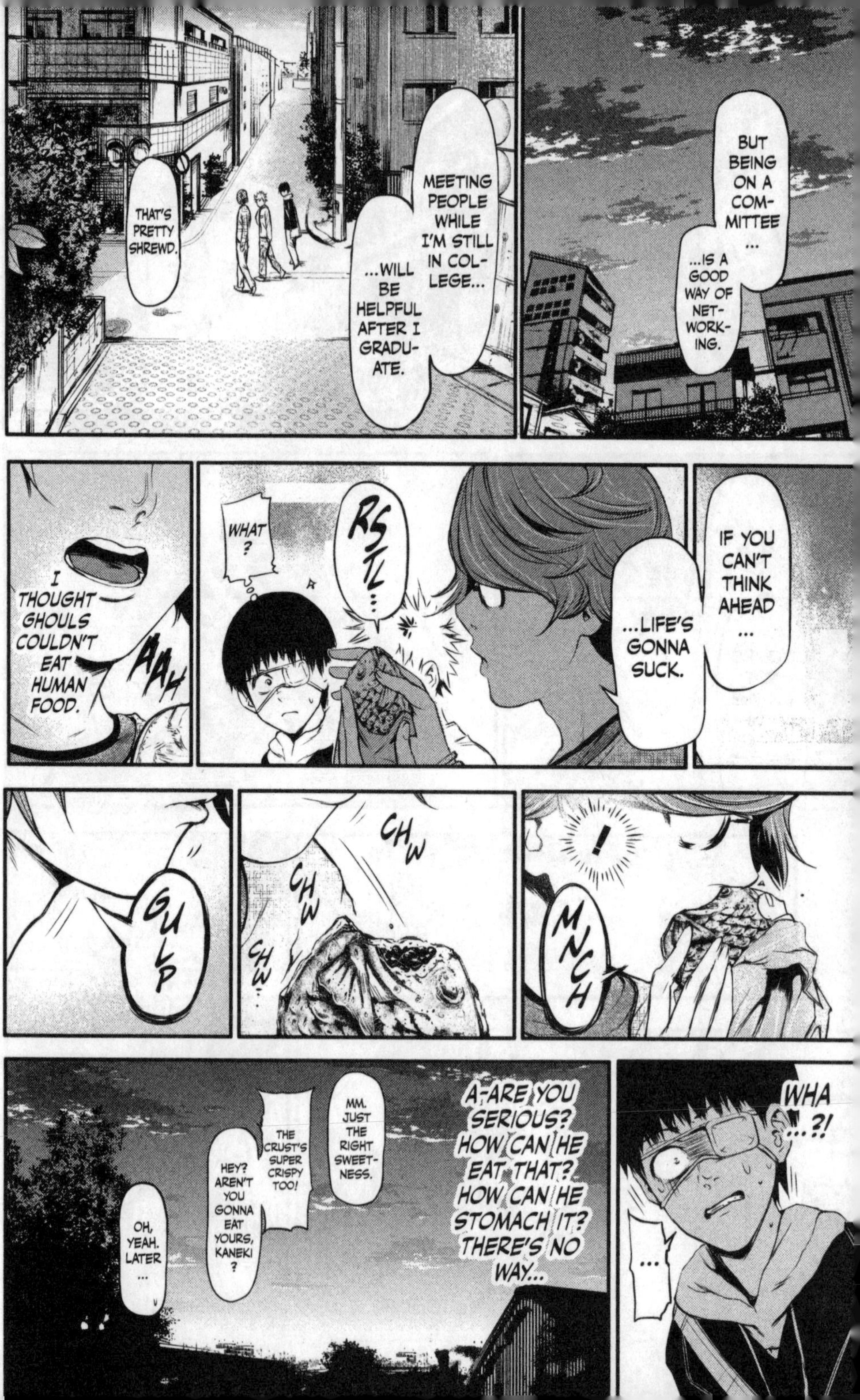

BUT BEING ON A COMMITTEE...
...IS A GOOD WAY OF NETWORKING.
MEETING PEOPLE WHILE I'M STILL IN COLLEGE...
...WILL BE HELPFUL AFTER I GRADUATE.
THAT'S PRETTY SHREWD.
IF YOU CAN'T THINK AHEAD...
...LIFE'S GONNA SUCK.
RSTL...
WHAT?
AAAH
I THOUGHT GHOULS COULDN'T EAT HUMAN FOOD.
!
MNCH
CHW
CHW
CHW...
GULP
WHA...?!
...
A-ARE YOU SERIOUS? HOW CAN HE EAT THAT? HOW CAN HE STOMACH IT? THERE'S NO WAY...
MM. JUST THE RIGHT SWEETNESS.
THE CRUST'S SUPER CRISPY TOO!
HEY? AREN'T YOU GONNA EAT YOURS, KANEKI?
OH, YEAH. LATER...

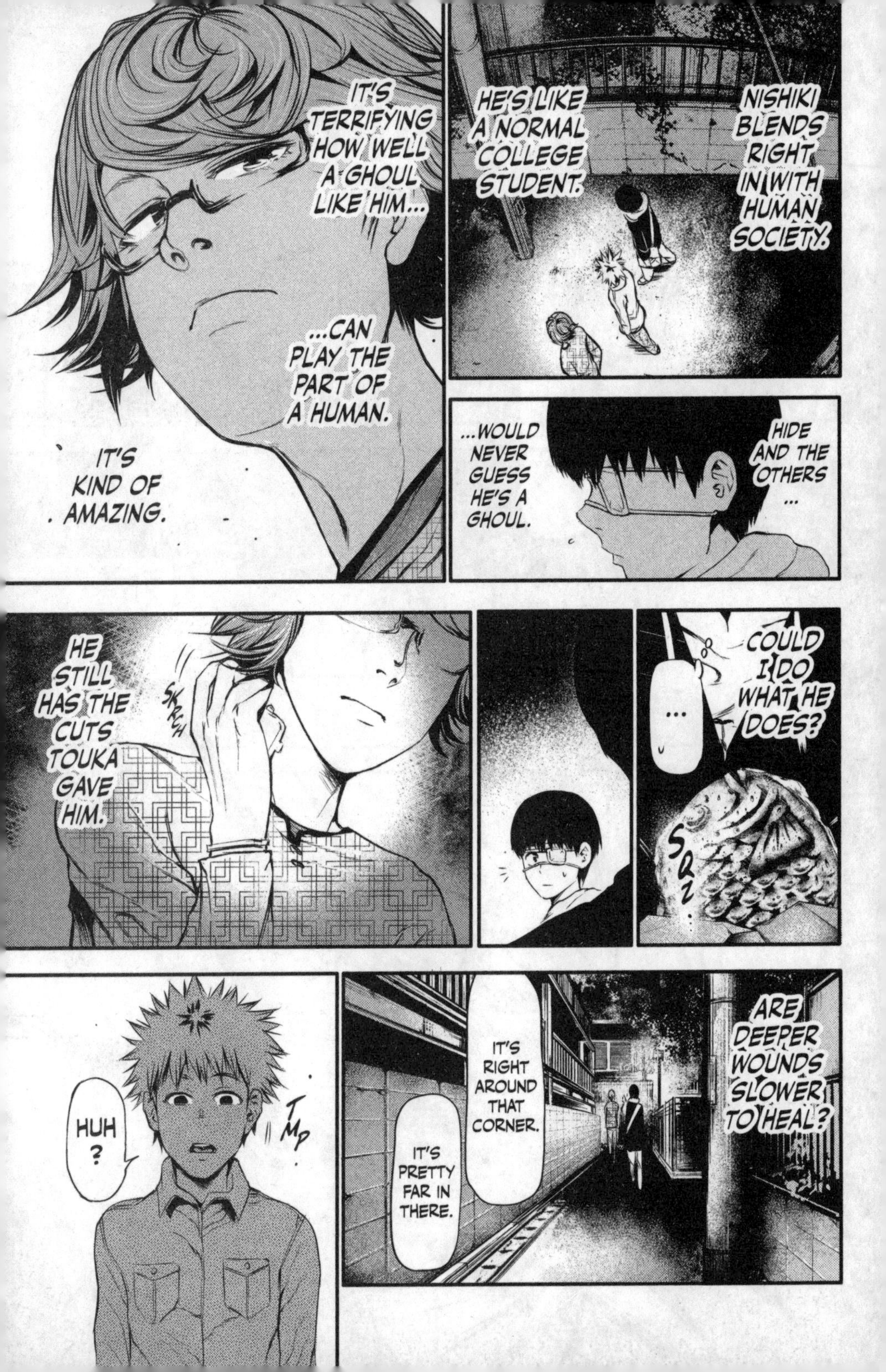
NISHIKI BLENDS RIGHT IN WITH HUMAN SOCIETY.
HE'S LIKE A NORMAL COLLEGE STUDENT.
HIDE AND THE OTHERS ...
...WOULD NEVER GUESS HE'S A GHOUL.
IT'S TERRIFYING HOW WELL A GHOUL LIKE HIM...
...CAN PLAY THE PART OF A HUMAN.
IT'S KIND OF AMAZING.
COULD I DO WHAT HE DOES?
SQZ
...
HE STILL HAS THE CUTS TOUKA GAVE HIM.
SKRCH
ARE DEEPER WOUNDS SLOWER TO HEAL?
IT'S RIGHT AROUND THAT CORNER.
IT'S PRETTY FAR IN THERE.
TMP
HUH?

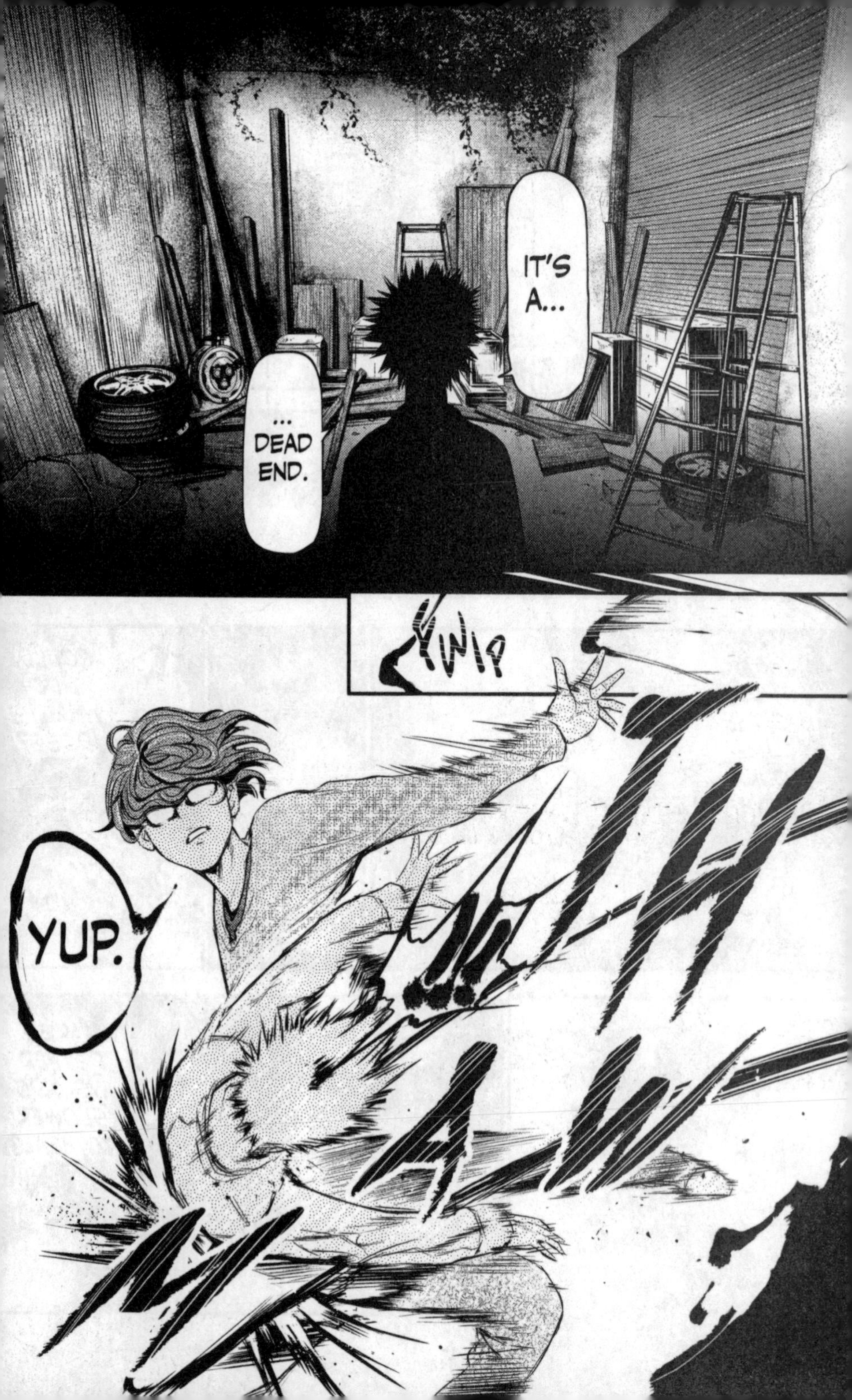
IT'S A...
... DEAD END.
YUP.

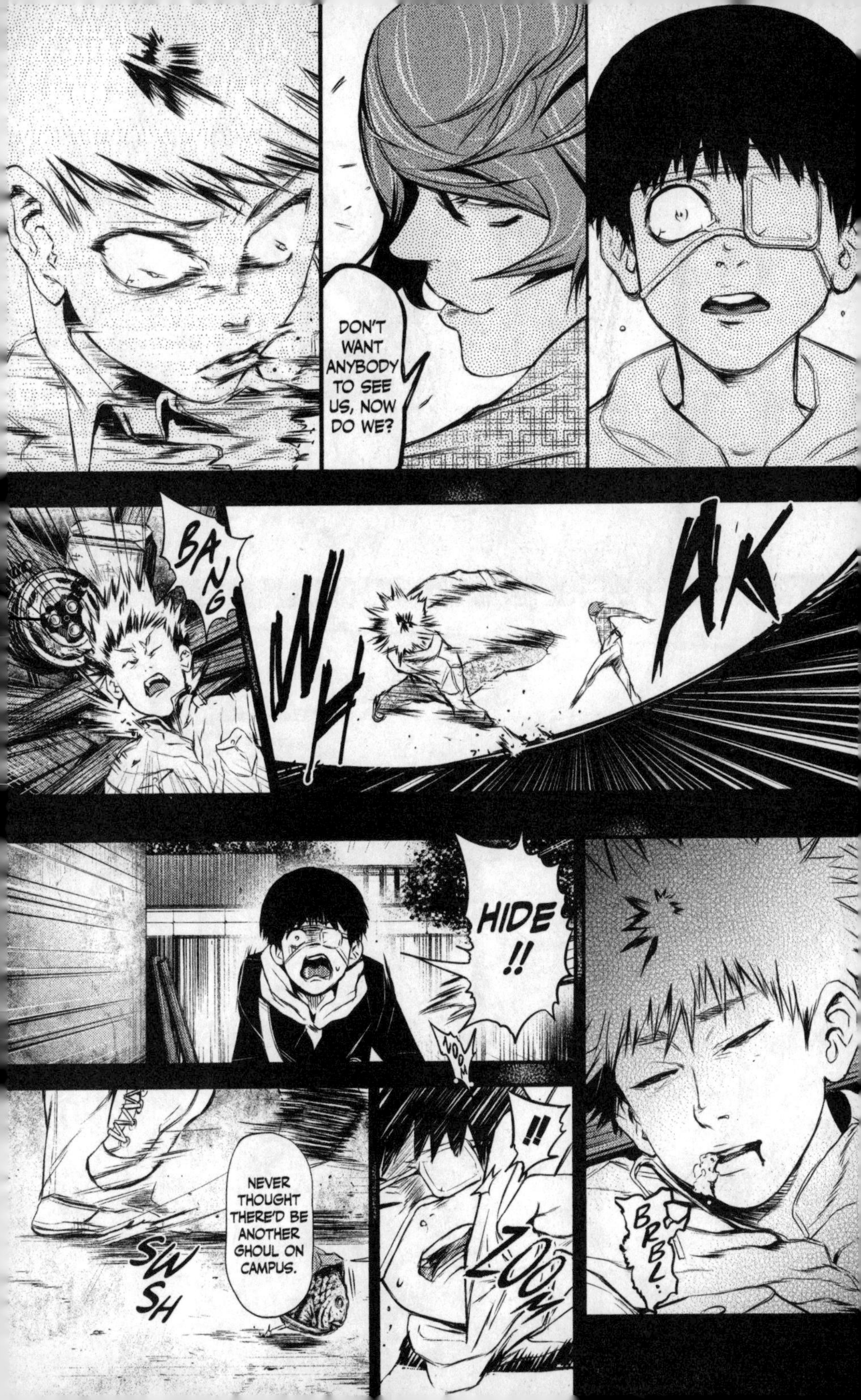
DON'T WANT ANYBODY TO SEE US, NOW DO WE?
WHAK
BANG
BRBL...
HIDE!!
VOOM
!!
ZOOM
NEVER THOUGHT THERE'D BE ANOTHER GHOUL ON CAMPUS.
SWSH

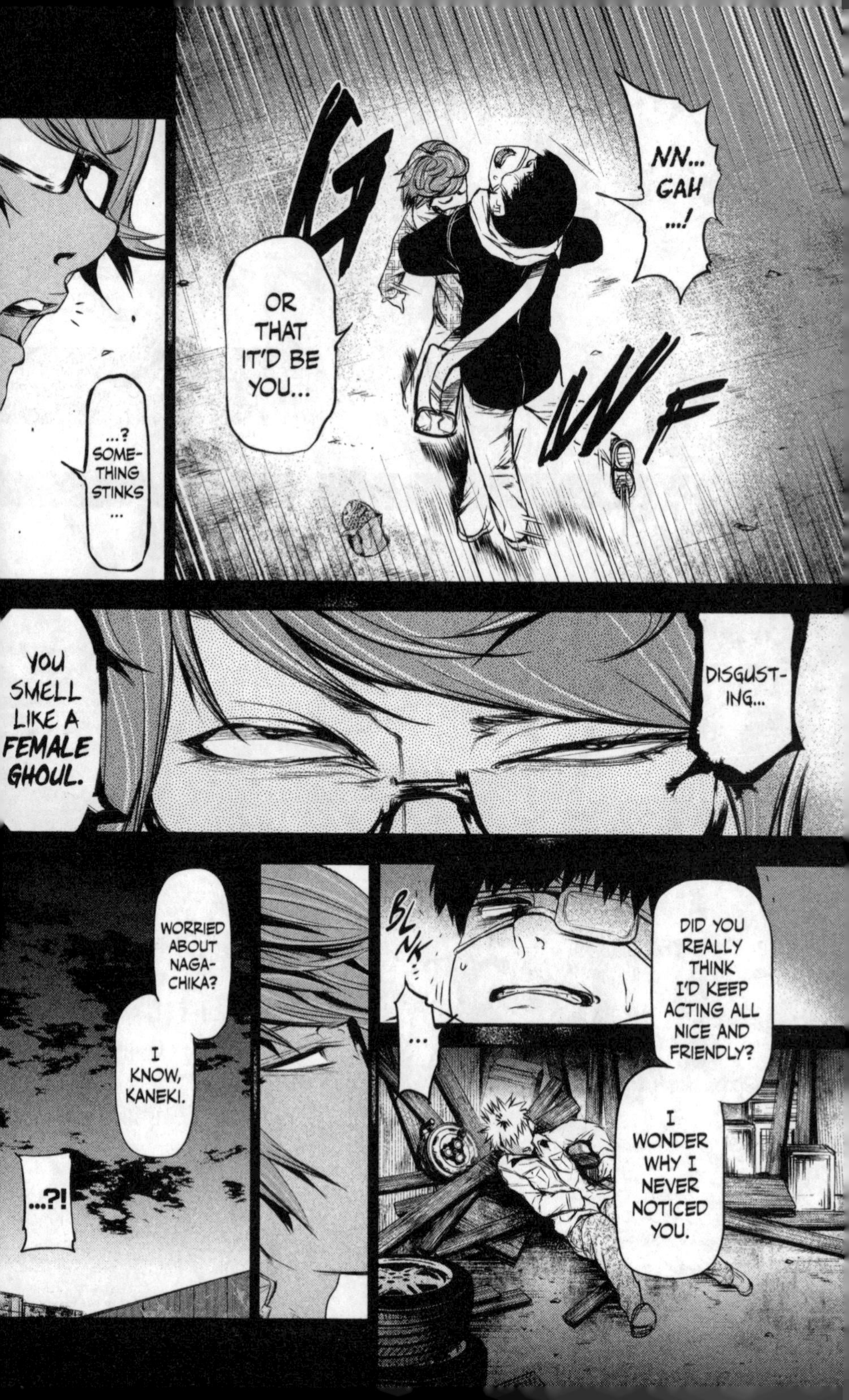
NN... GAH ...!
G
WF
OR THAT IT'D BE YOU...
...? SOME-THING STINKS ...
DISGUST-ING...
YOU SMELL LIKE A **FEMALE GHOUL.**
DID YOU REALLY THINK I'D KEEP ACTING ALL NICE AND FRIENDLY?
BLNK
...
I WONDER WHY I NEVER NOTICED YOU.
WORRIED ABOUT NAGA-CHIKA?
I KNOW, KANEKI.
...?!

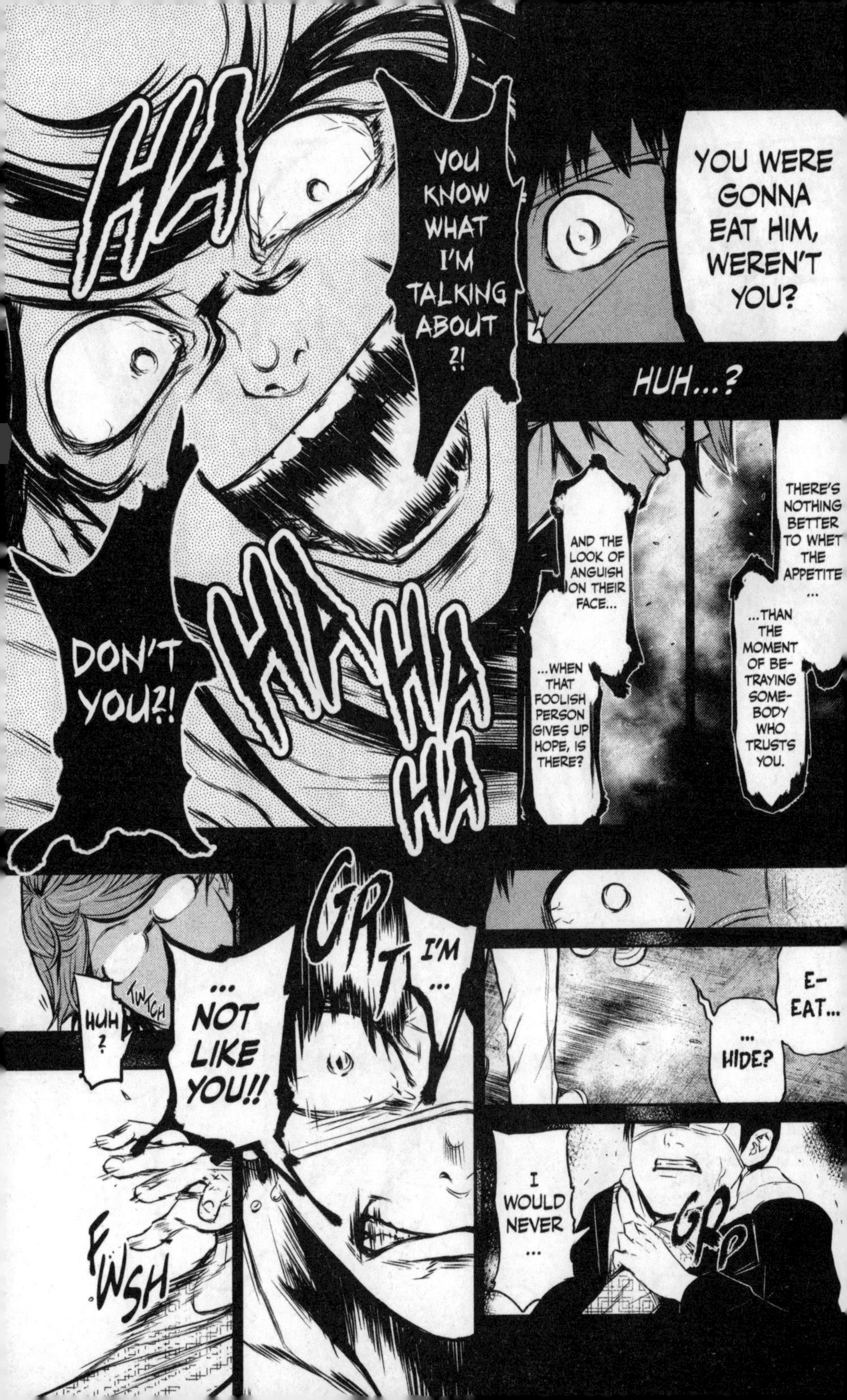
YOU WERE GONNA EAT HIM, WEREN'T YOU?
HUH...?
THERE'S NOTHING BETTER TO WHET THE APPETITE...
...THAN THE MOMENT OF BE-TRAYING SOME-BODY WHO TRUSTS YOU.
AND THE LOOK OF ANGUISH ON THEIR FACE...
...WHEN THAT FOOLISH PERSON GIVES UP HOPE, IS THERE?
HA
YOU KNOW WHAT I'M TALKING ABOUT?!
HA HA HA
DON'T YOU?!
E-EAT...
...HIDE?
I WOULD NEVER...
I'M...
...NOT LIKE YOU!!
TWICH
HUH?
FWSH

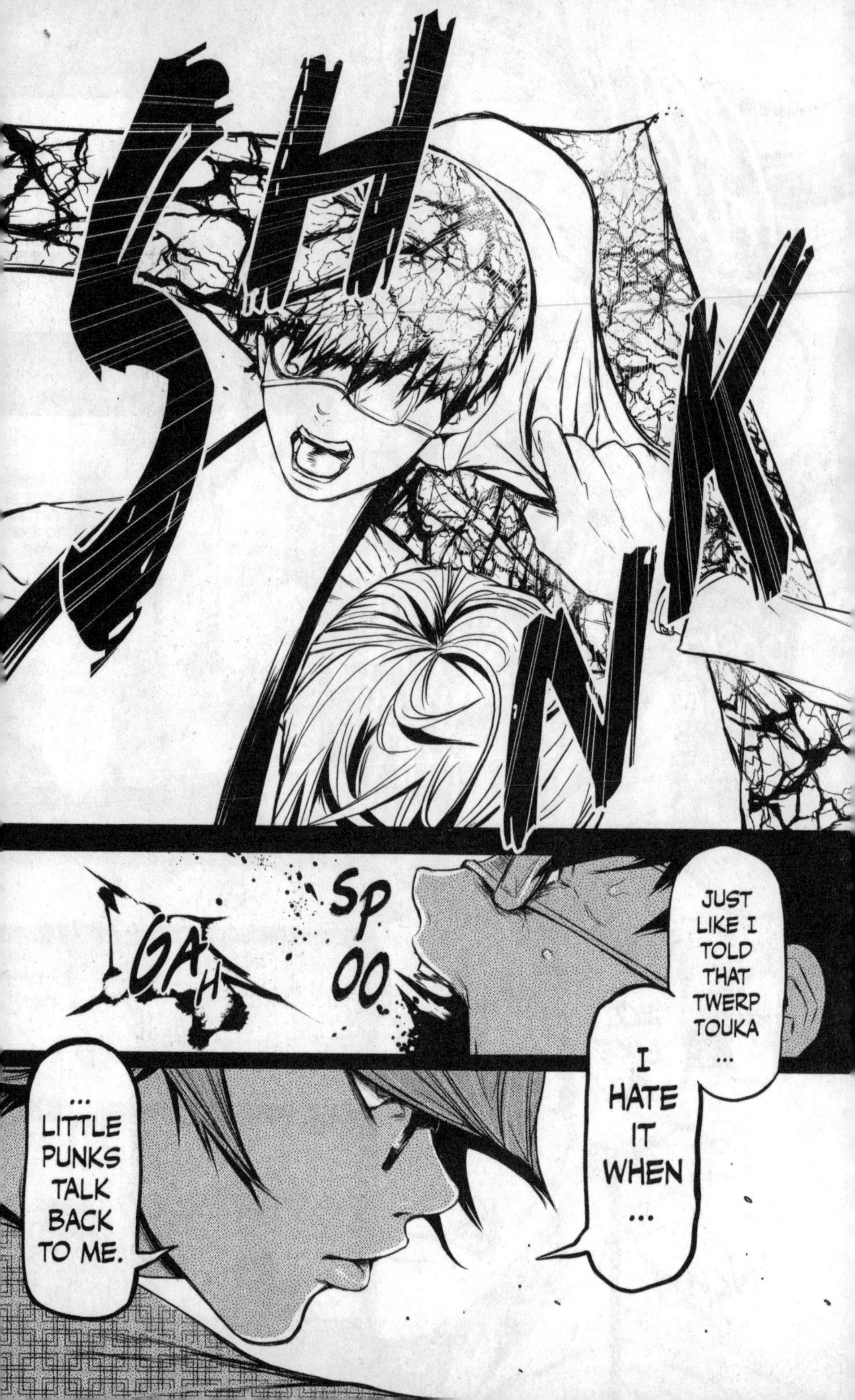
JUST LIKE I TOLD THAT TWERP TOUKA ...
SPOO
GAH
I HATE IT WHEN ...
... LITTLE PUNKS TALK BACK TO ME.

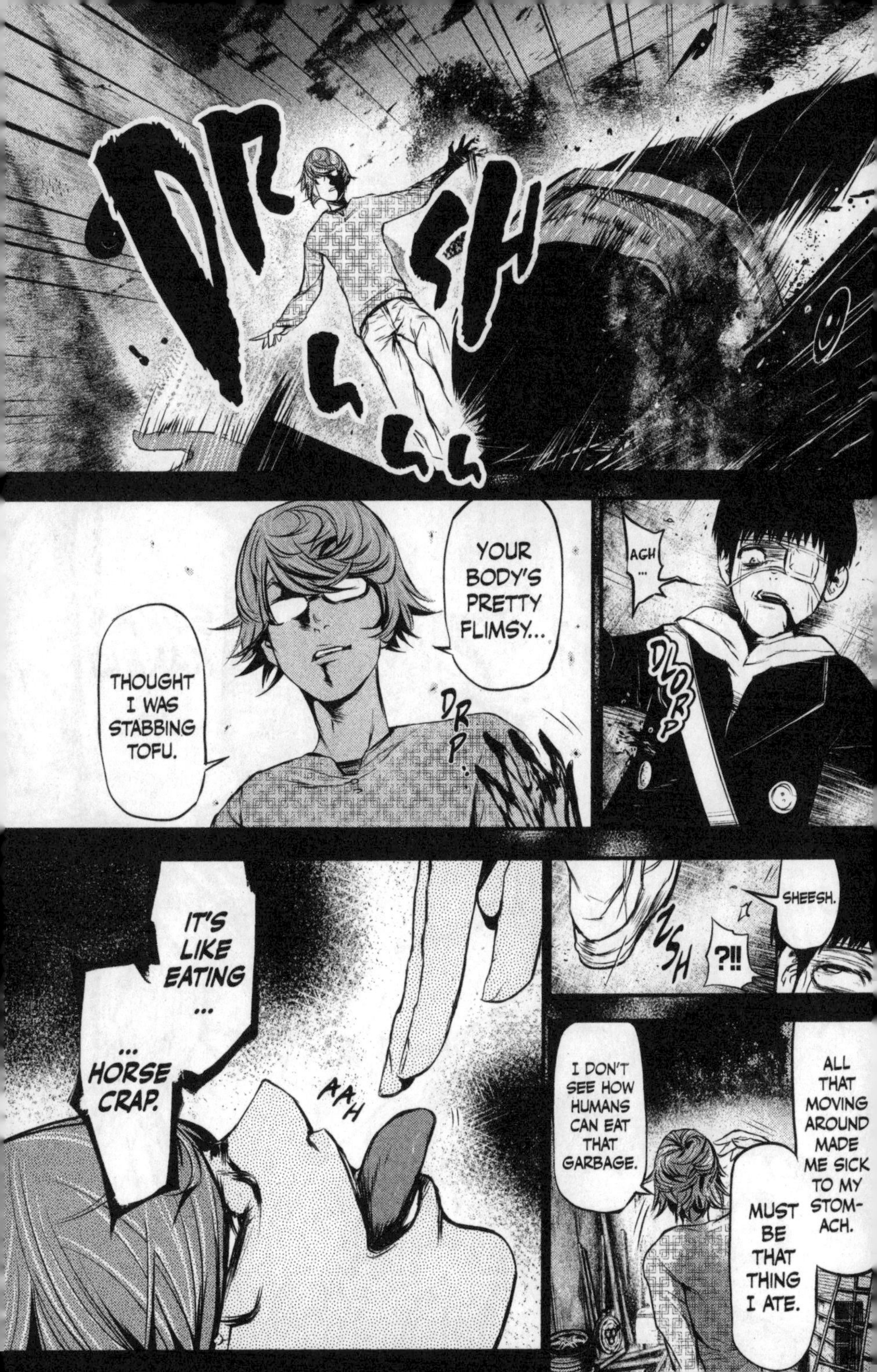
DRSH
AGH ...
DLORP
YOUR BODY'S PRETTY FLIMSY...
THOUGHT I WAS STABBING TOFU.
DRP
SHEESH.
?!!
WUSH
ALL THAT MOVING AROUND MADE ME SICK TO MY STOM-ACH.
MUST BE THAT THING I ATE.
I DON'T SEE HOW HUMANS CAN EAT THAT GARBAGE.
IT'S LIKE EATING ...
... HORSE CRAP.
AAH

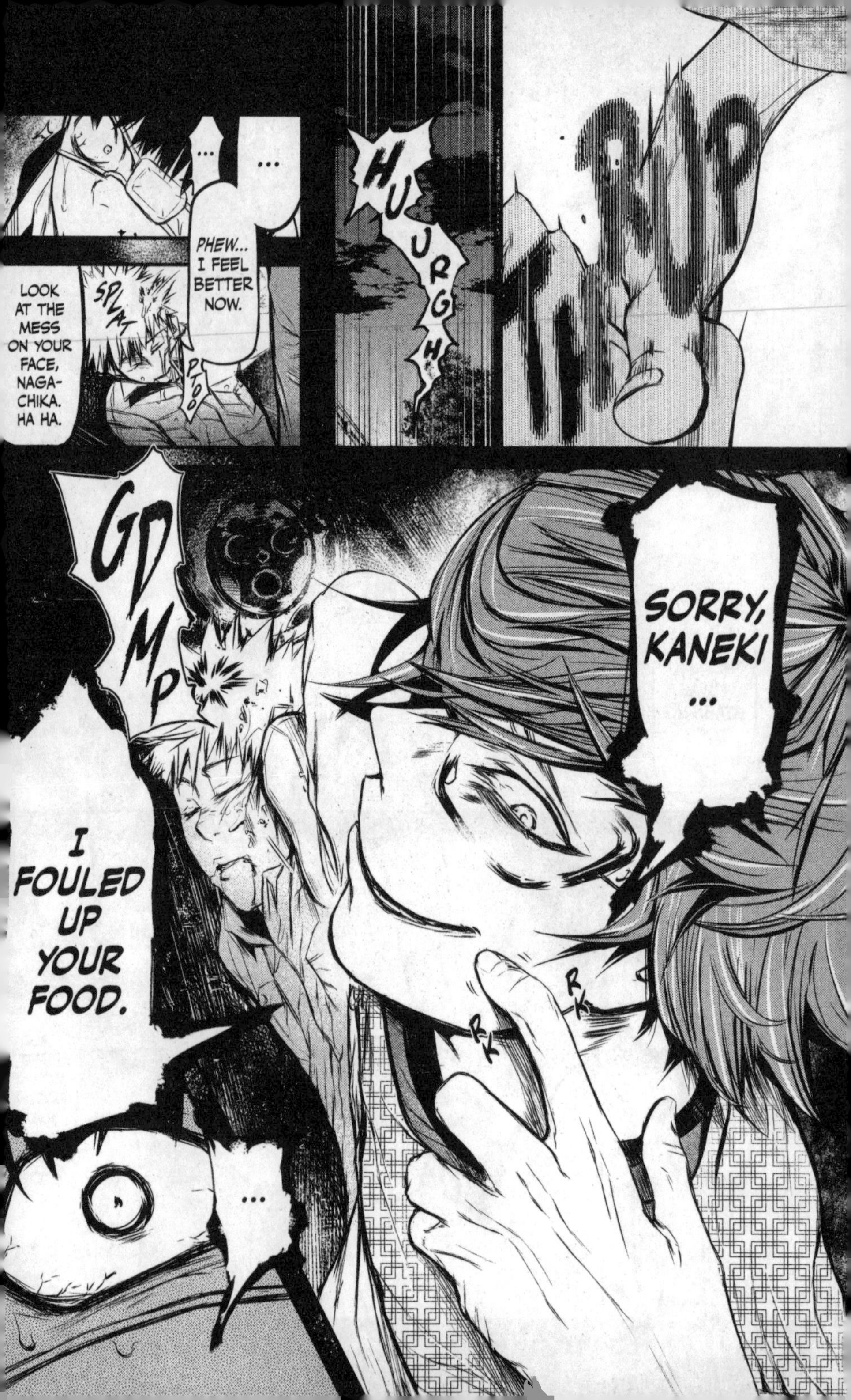
THRUP
HUURGHH
...
...
PHEW... I FEEL BETTER NOW.
SPLAT
PTOO
LOOK AT THE MESS ON YOUR FACE, NAGA-CHIKA. HA HA.
SORRY, KANEKI ...
RK
RK
GDMP
I FOULED UP YOUR FOOD.
...

#008 [KAGUNE]

TOKYO GHOUL

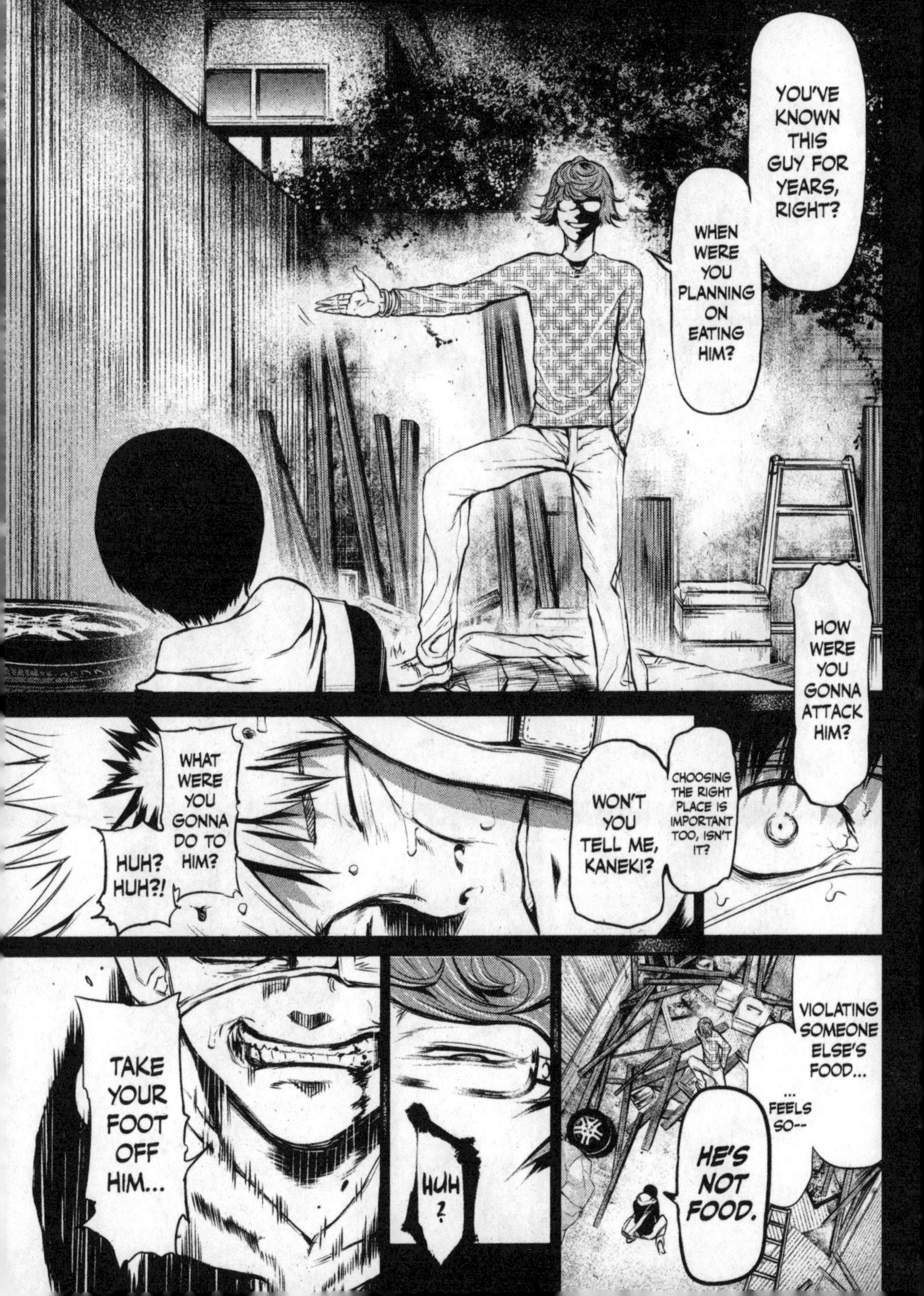

YOU'VE KNOWN THIS GUY FOR YEARS, RIGHT?
WHEN WERE YOU PLANNING ON EATING HIM?
HOW WERE YOU GONNA ATTACK HIM?
CHOOSING THE RIGHT PLACE IS IMPORTANT TOO, ISN'T IT?
WON'T YOU TELL ME, KANEKI?
WHAT WERE YOU GONNA DO TO HIM?
HUH? HUH?!
VIOLATING SOMEONE ELSE'S FOOD...
...FEELS SO--
HE'S NOT FOOD.
HUH?
TAKE YOUR FOOT OFF HIM...

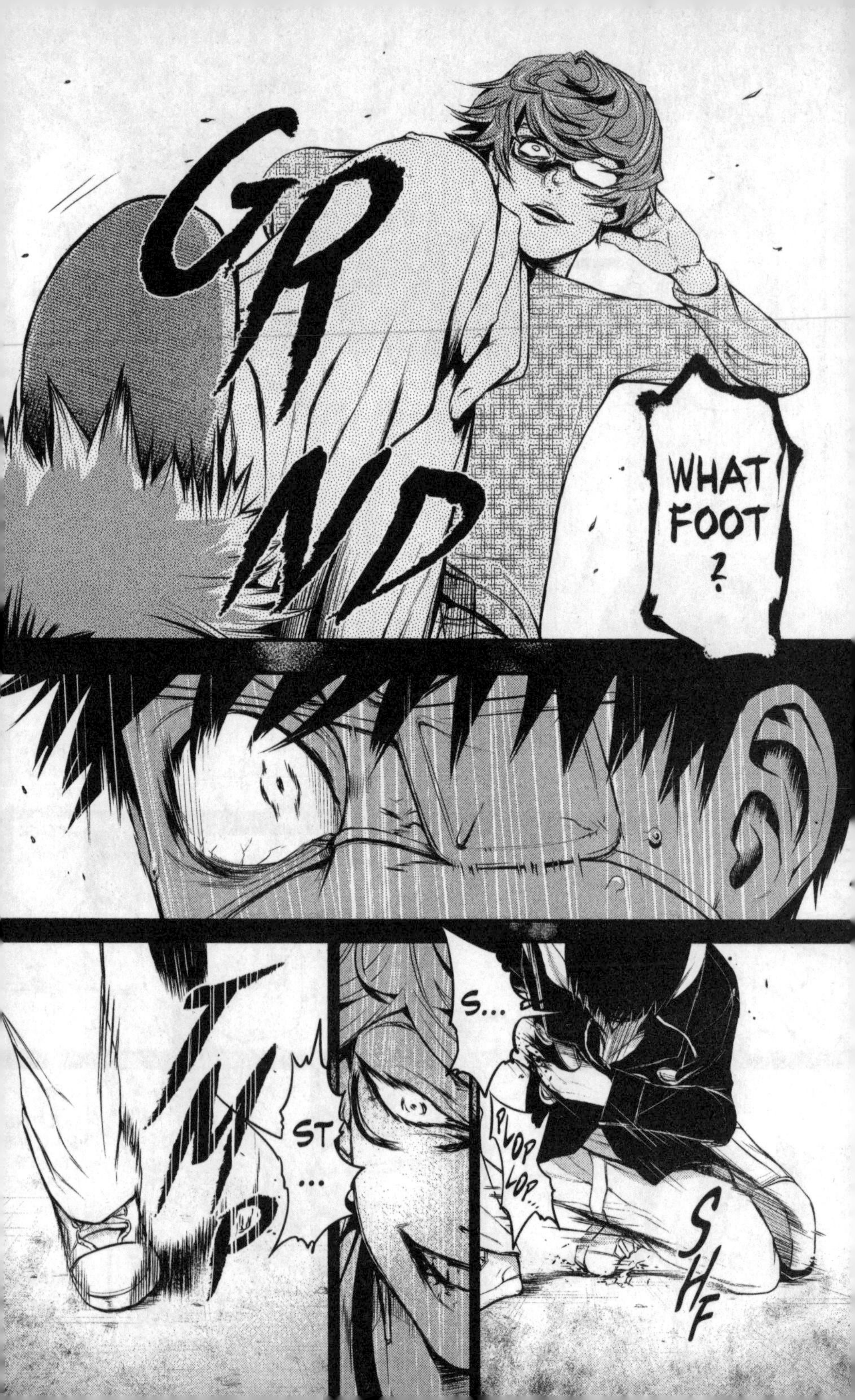
WHAT FOOT ?
GR
ND
S...
PLOP LOP...
SHF
ST
...

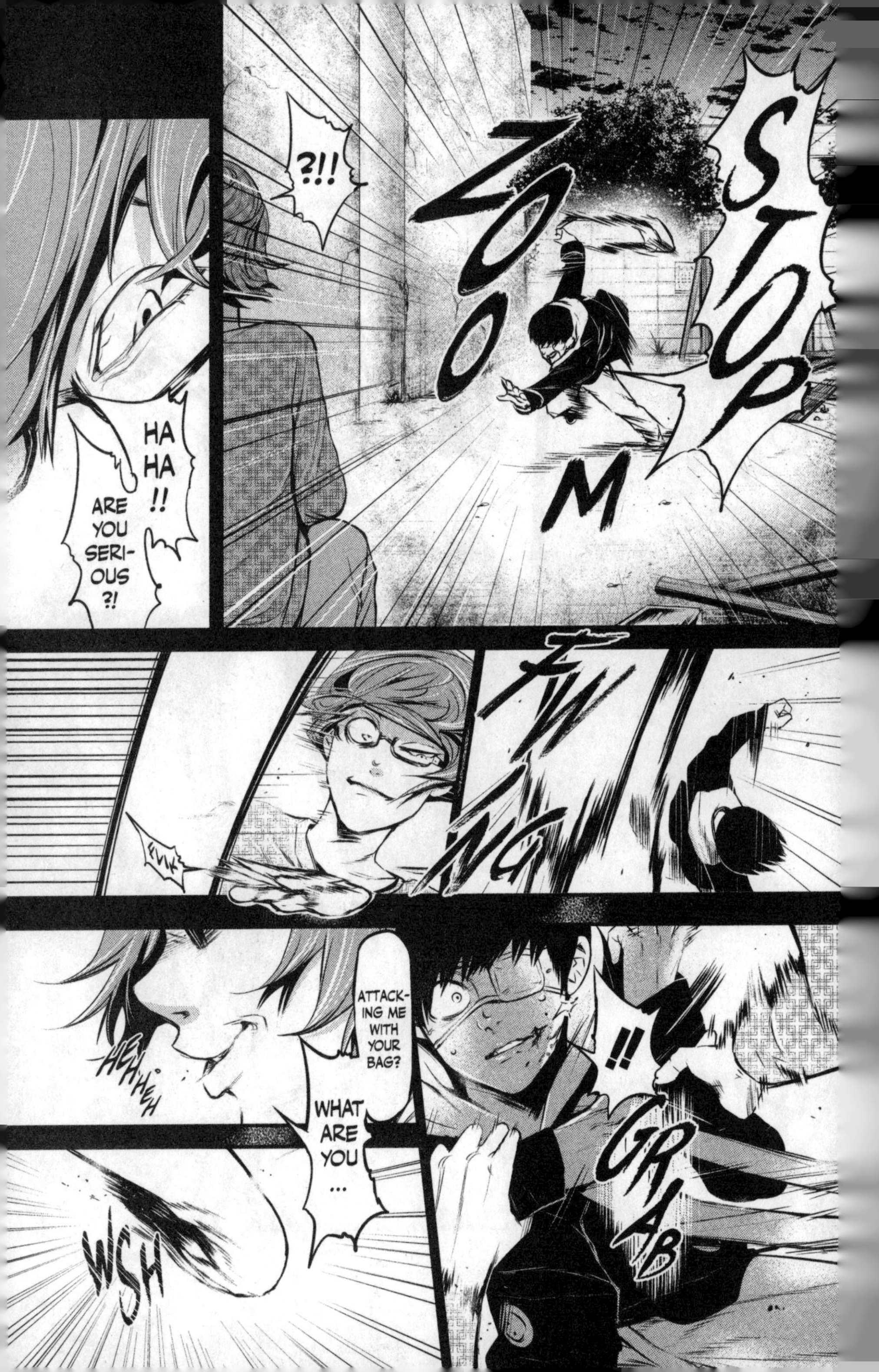
STOP
ZOOM
?!!
HA HA!!
ARE YOU SERIOUS?!
FWING
!!
GRAB
ATTACKING ME WITH YOUR BAG?
WHAT ARE YOU ...
HEH HEH
WSH

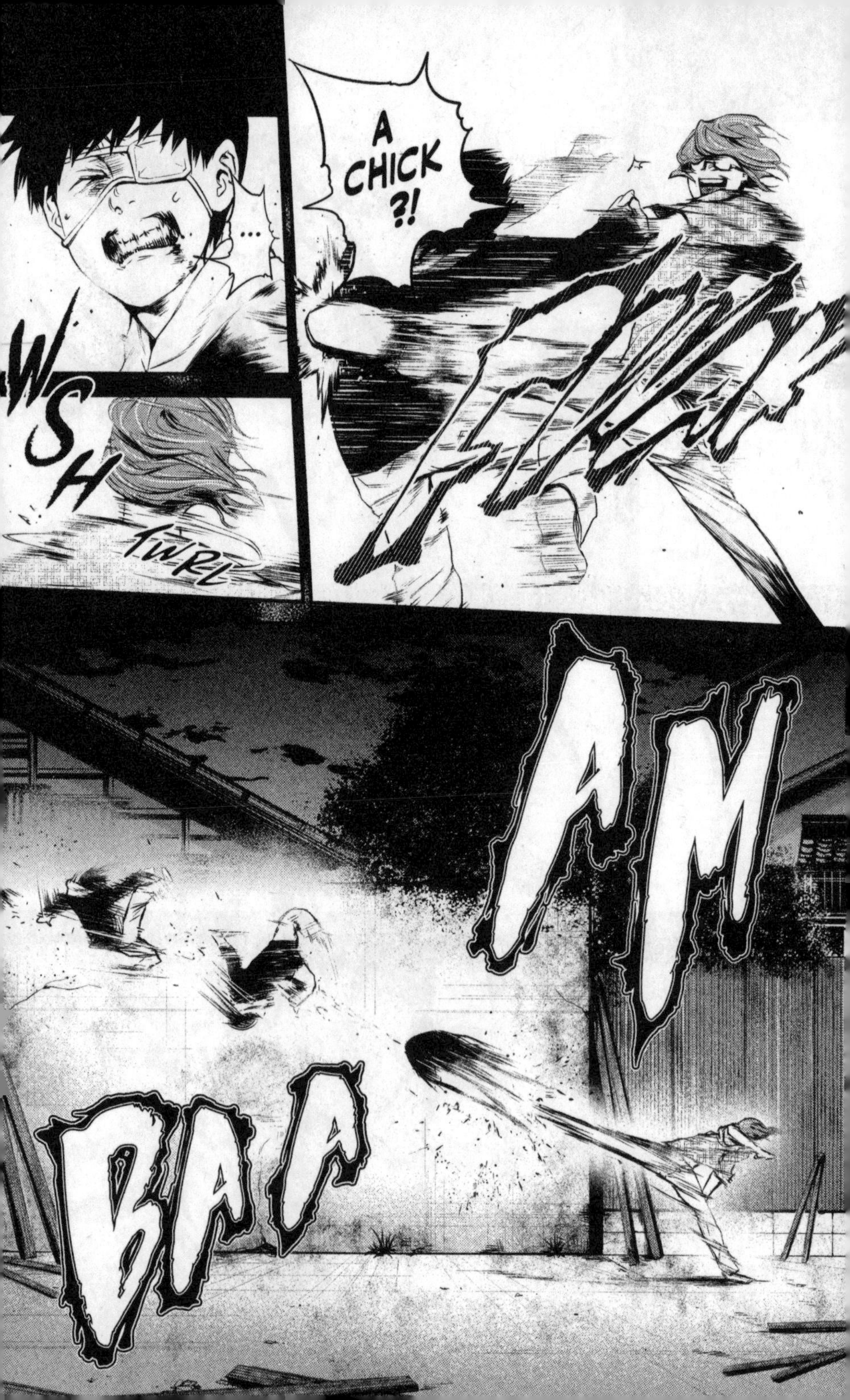

A CHICK ?!
...
WSH
TWRL
BA
AM

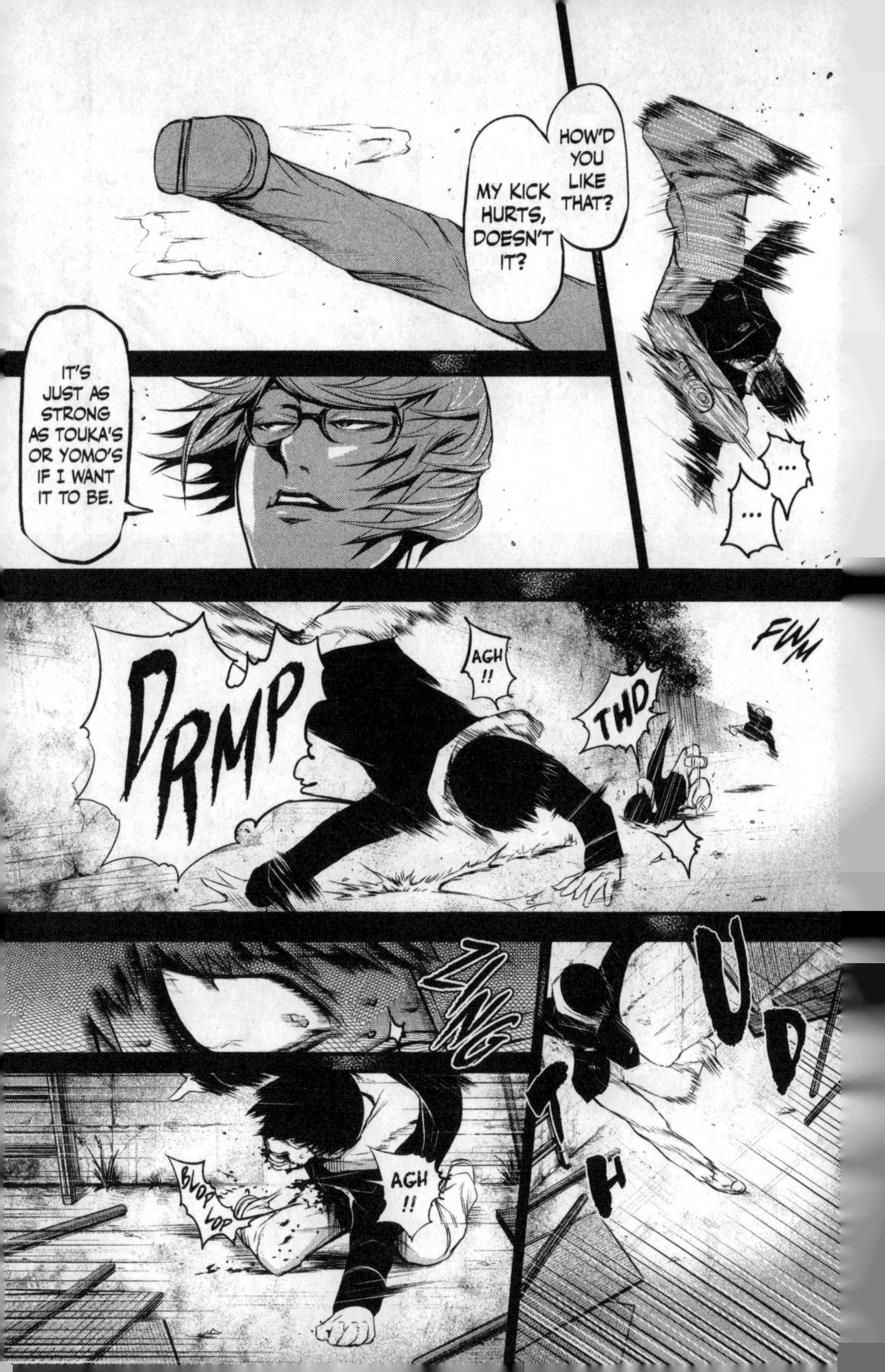
...
...
HOW'D YOU LIKE THAT?
MY KICK HURTS, DOESN'T IT?
IT'S JUST AS STRONG AS TOUKA'S OR YOMO'S IF I WANT IT TO BE.
FWM
THD
AGH !!
DRMP
THUD
ZING
AGH !!
BLOP LOP

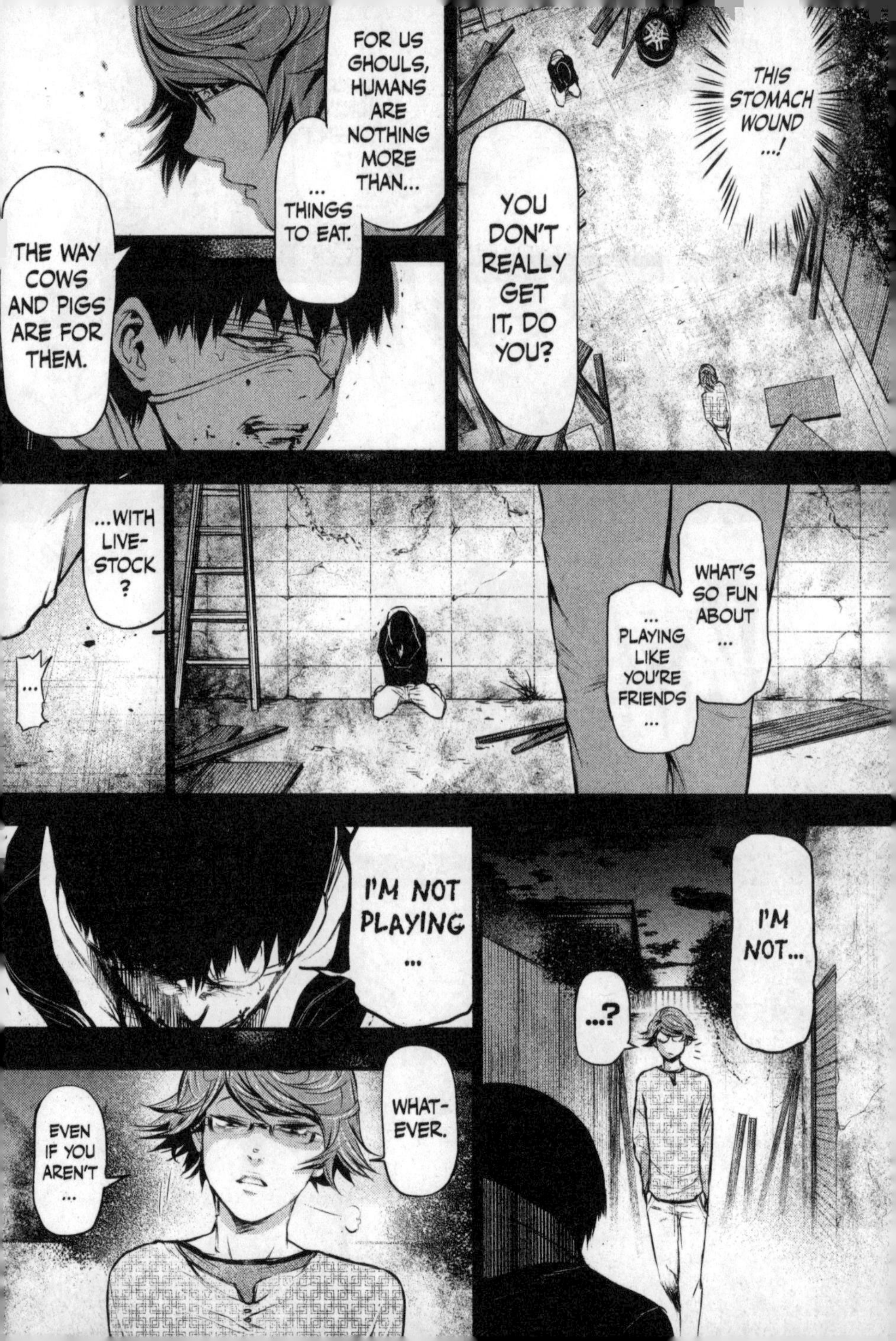
THIS STOMACH WOUND ...!
YOU DON'T REALLY GET IT, DO YOU?
FOR US GHOULS, HUMANS ARE NOTHING MORE THAN...
... THINGS TO EAT.
THE WAY COWS AND PIGS ARE FOR THEM.
WHAT'S SO FUN ABOUT ...
... PLAYING LIKE YOU'RE FRIENDS ...
...WITH LIVE-STOCK ?
...
I'M NOT...
...?
I'M NOT PLAYING ...
WHAT-EVER.
EVEN IF YOU AREN'T ...

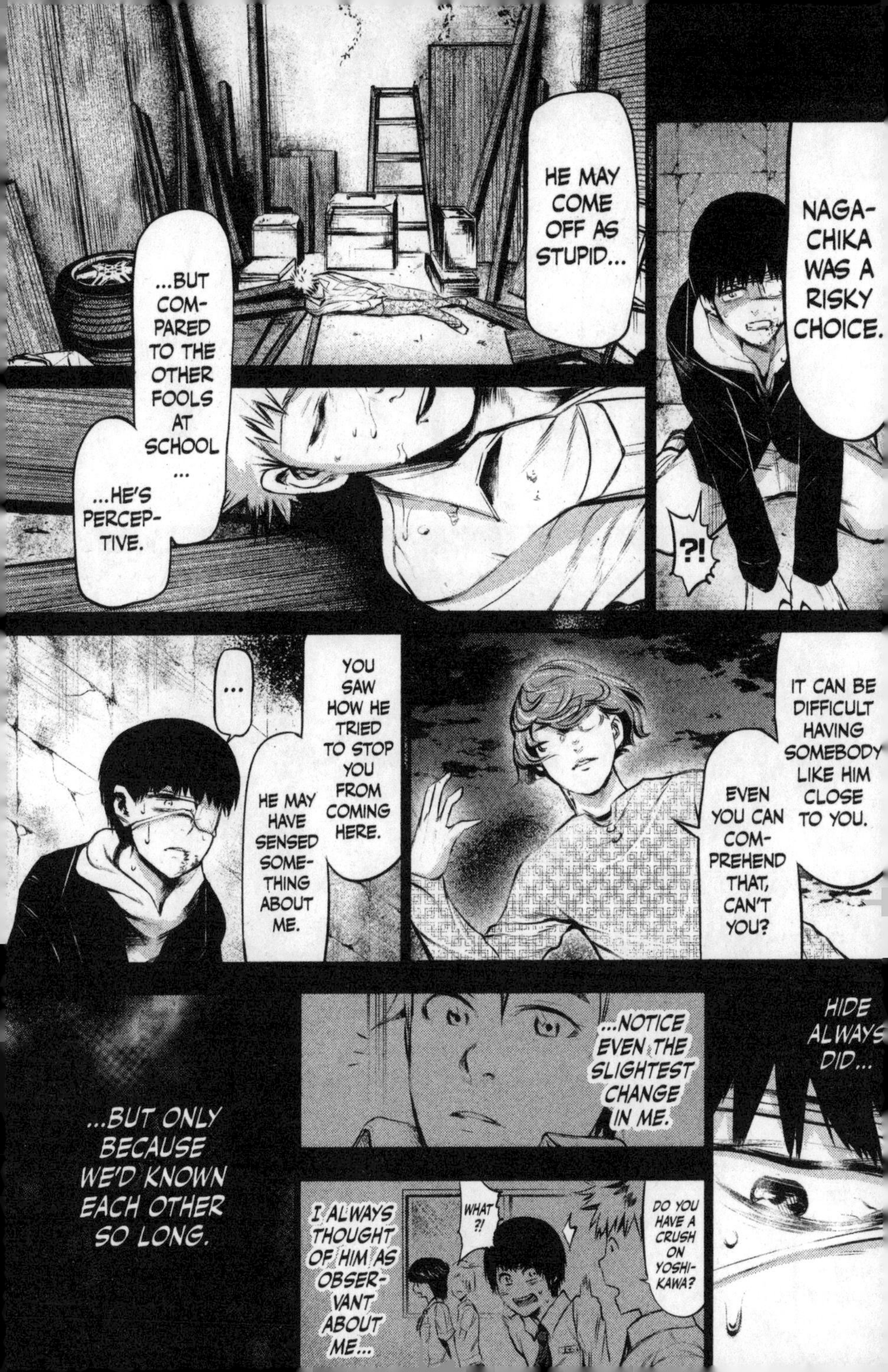
NAGACHIKA WAS A RISKY CHOICE.
?!
HE MAY COME OFF AS STUPID...
...BUT COMPARED TO THE OTHER FOOLS AT SCHOOL...
...HE'S PERCEPTIVE.
IT CAN BE DIFFICULT HAVING SOMEBODY LIKE HIM CLOSE TO YOU.
EVEN YOU CAN COMPREHEND THAT, CAN'T YOU?
YOU SAW HOW HE TRIED TO STOP YOU FROM COMING HERE.
HE MAY HAVE SENSED SOMETHING ABOUT ME.
...
HIDE ALWAYS DID...
...NOTICE EVEN THE SLIGHTEST CHANGE IN ME.
DO YOU HAVE A CRUSH ON YOSHIKAWA?
WHAT?!
I ALWAYS THOUGHT OF HIM AS OBSERVANT ABOUT ME...
...BUT ONLY BECAUSE WE'D KNOWN EACH OTHER SO LONG.

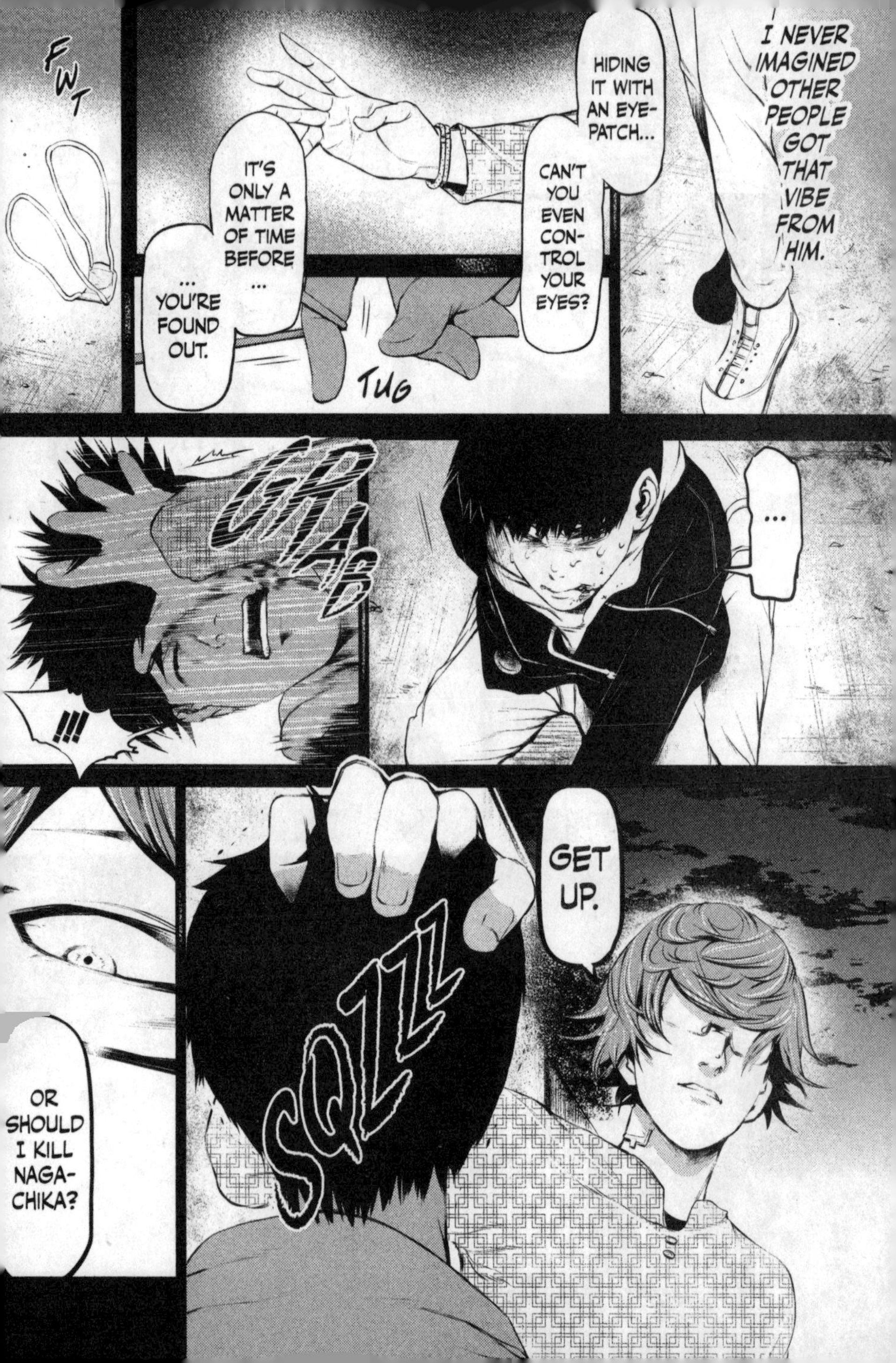
I NEVER IMAGINED OTHER PEOPLE GOT THAT VIBE FROM HIM.
HIDING IT WITH AN EYE-PATCH...
CAN'T YOU EVEN CON-TROL YOUR EYES?
TUG
IT'S ONLY A MATTER OF TIME BEFORE...
...YOU'RE FOUND OUT.
FWT
...
GRAB
!!!
GET UP.
SQZZZ
OR SHOULD I KILL NAGA-CHIKA?

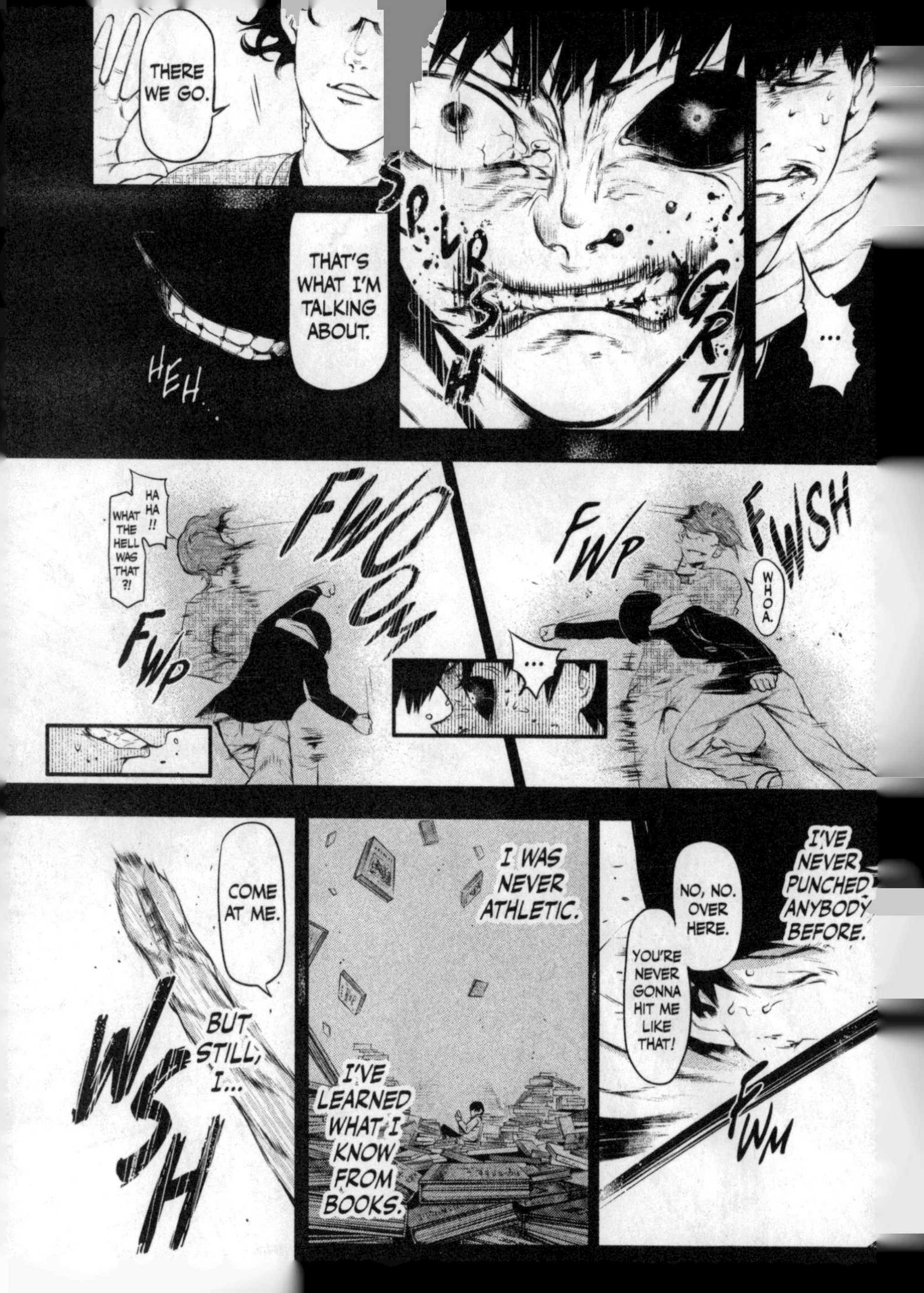
...
GRT
SPLRSH
THERE WE GO.
THAT'S WHAT I'M TALKING ABOUT.
HEH...
FWSH
WHOA.
FWP
...
FWOOM
HA HA!!
WHAT THE HELL WAS THAT?!
FWP
I'VE NEVER PUNCHED ANYBODY BEFORE.
NO, NO. OVER HERE.
YOU'RE NEVER GONNA HIT ME LIKE THAT!
FWM
I WAS NEVER ATHLETIC.
I'VE LEARNED WHAT I KNOW FROM BOOKS.
COME AT ME.
BUT STILL, I...
WSH

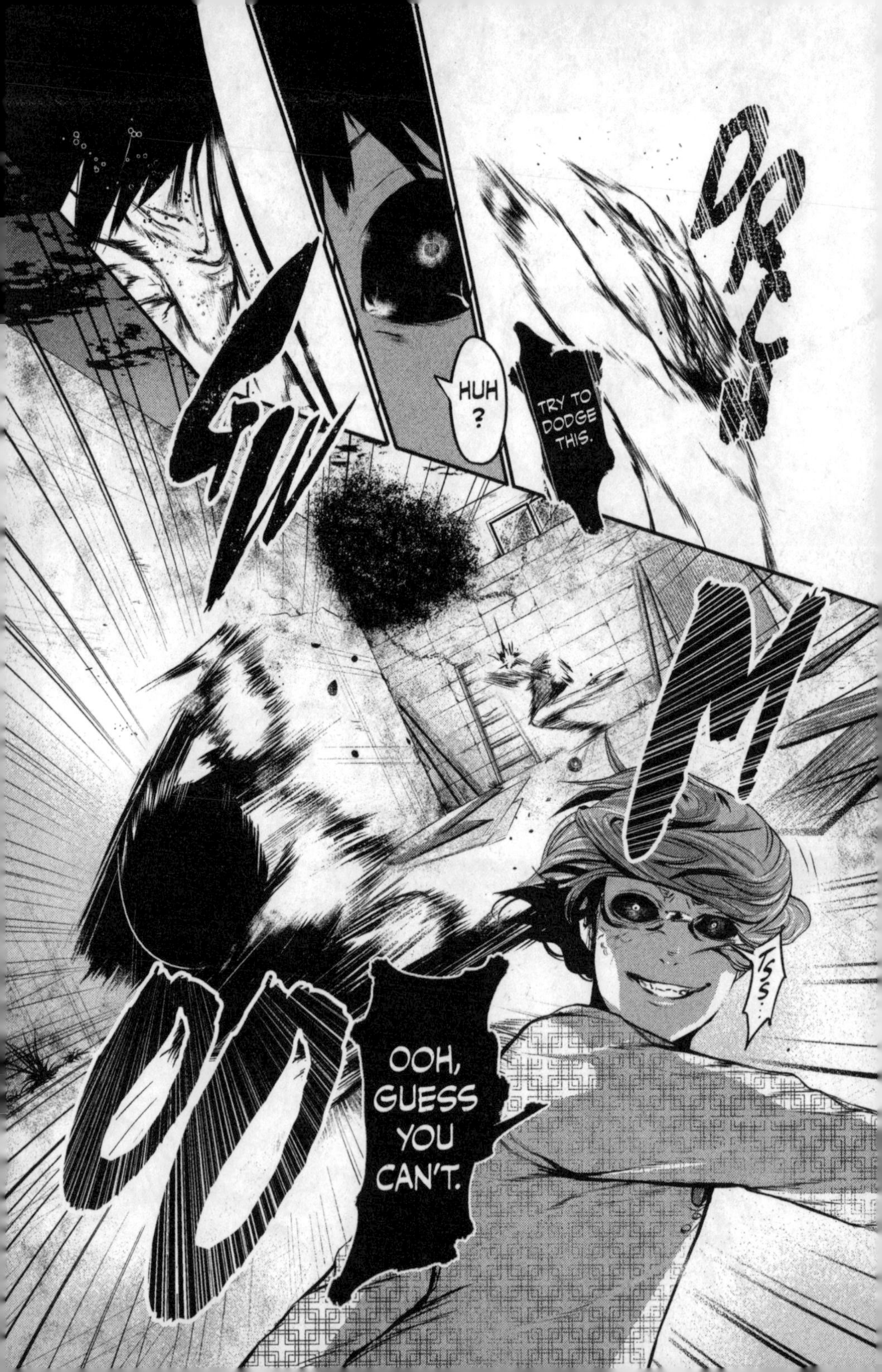
TRY TO DODGE THIS.
HUH?
TSS...
OOH, GUESS YOU CAN'T.

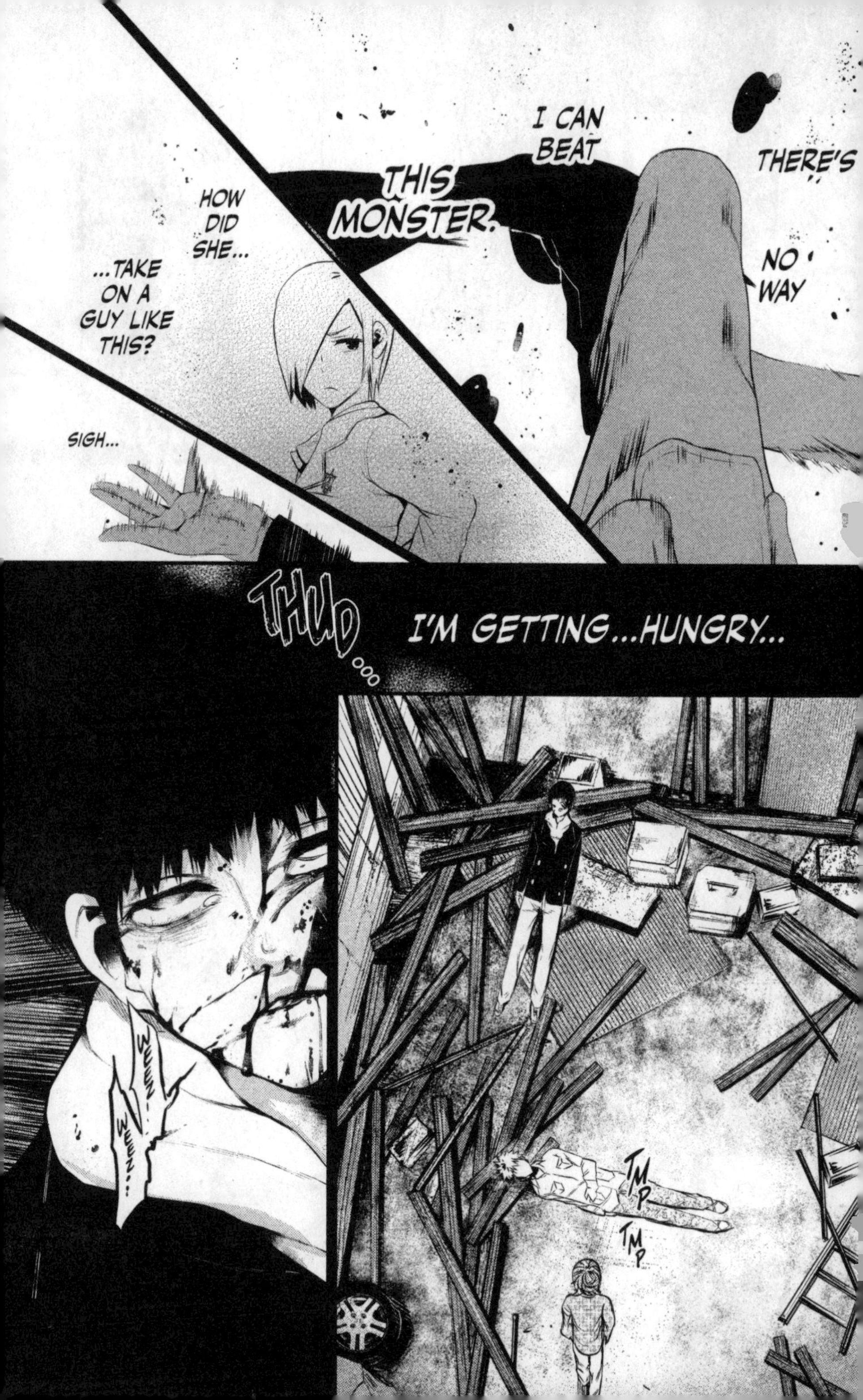
THERE'S NO WAY
I CAN BEAT THIS MONSTER.
HOW DID SHE...
...TAKE ON A GUY LIKE THIS?
SIGH...
I'M GETTING...HUNGRY...
THUD
TMP
TMP
WEEZ
WEEZ

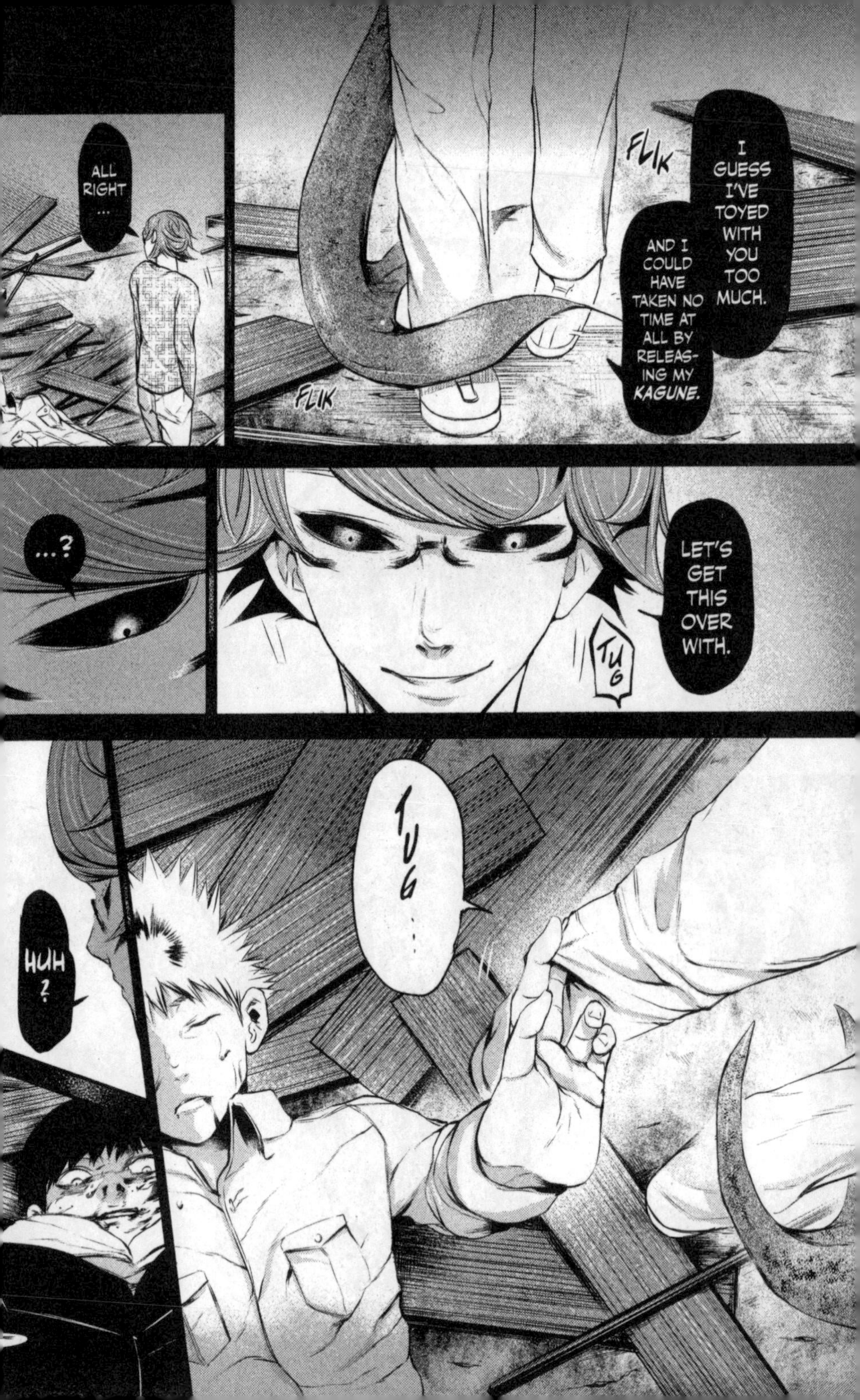
FLIK
I GUESS I'VE TOYED WITH YOU TOO MUCH.
AND I COULD HAVE TAKEN NO TIME AT ALL BY RELEAS-ING MY *KAGUNE.*
FLIK
ALL RIGHT ...
LET'S GET THIS OVER WITH.
TUG
...?
TUG ...
HUH?

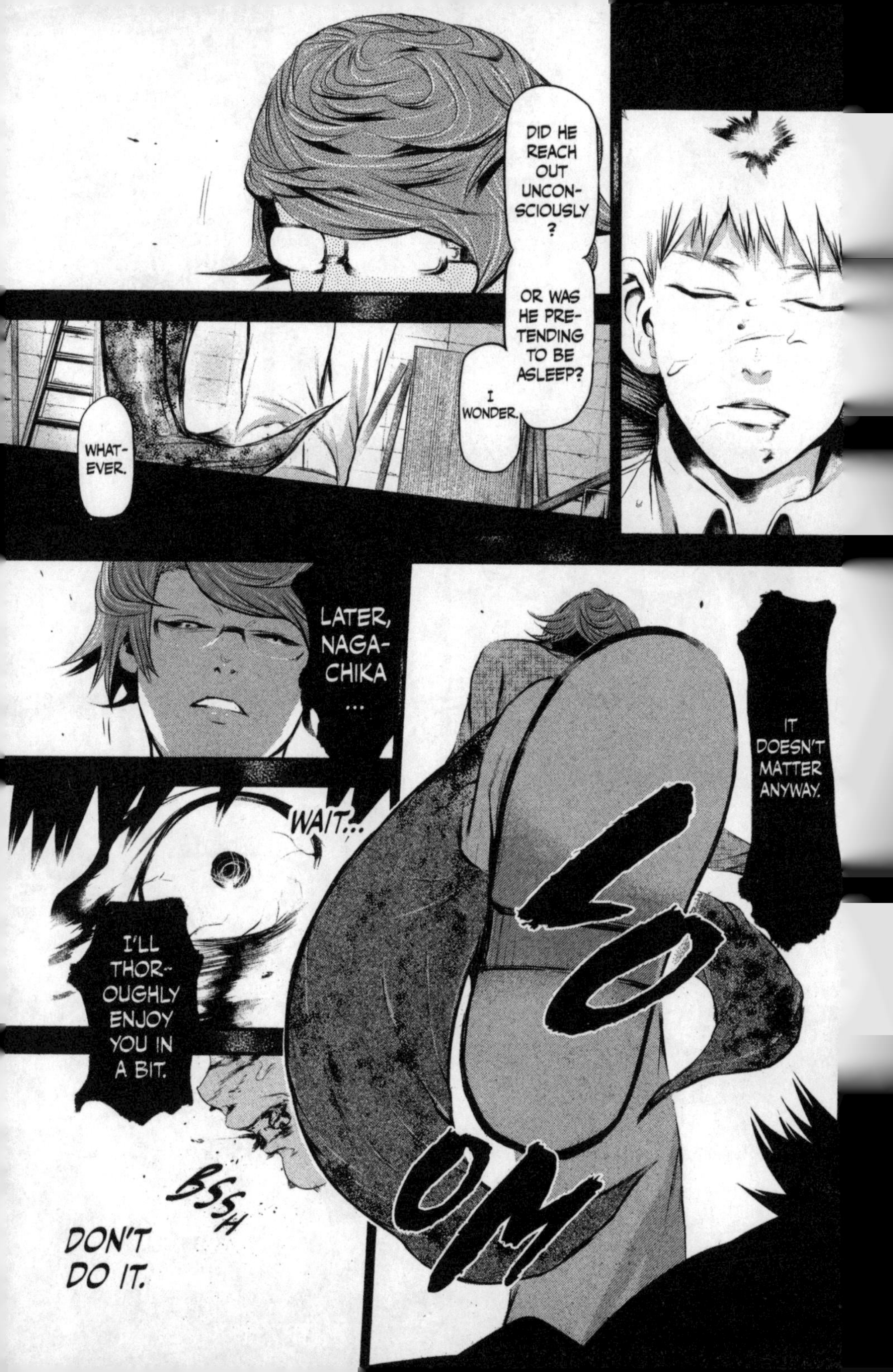
DID HE REACH OUT UNCONSCIOUSLY?
OR WAS HE PRETENDING TO BE ASLEEP?
I WONDER.
WHATEVER.
IT DOESN'T MATTER ANYWAY.
LATER, NAGACHIKA...
WAIT...
I'LL THOROUGHLY ENJOY YOU IN A BIT.
BSSH
DON'T DO IT.

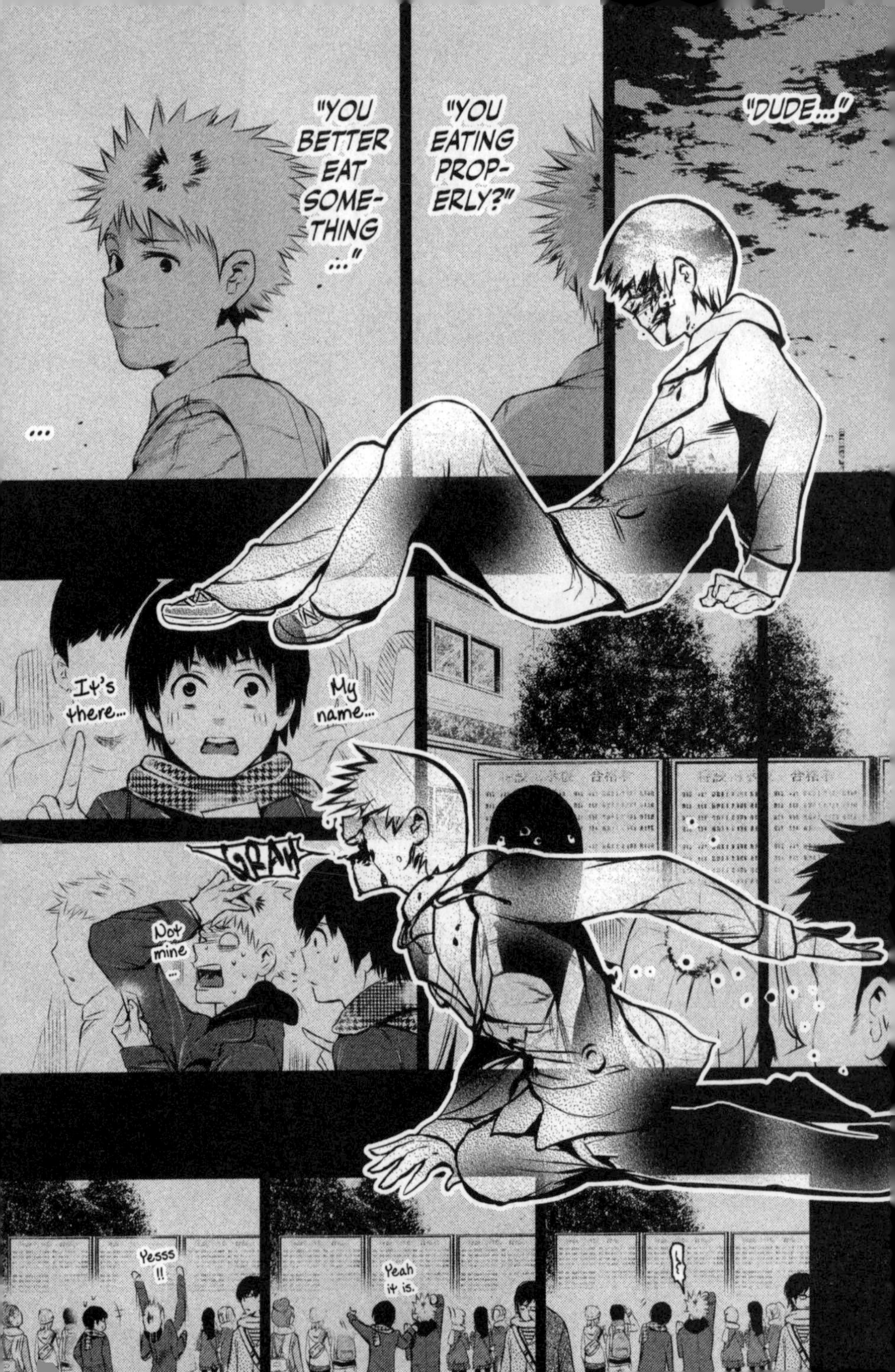
"DUDE..."
"YOU EATING PROPERLY?"
"YOU BETTER EAT SOMETHING ..."
...
My name...
It's there...
GRAH
Not mine ...
!
Yeah it is.
Yesss !!

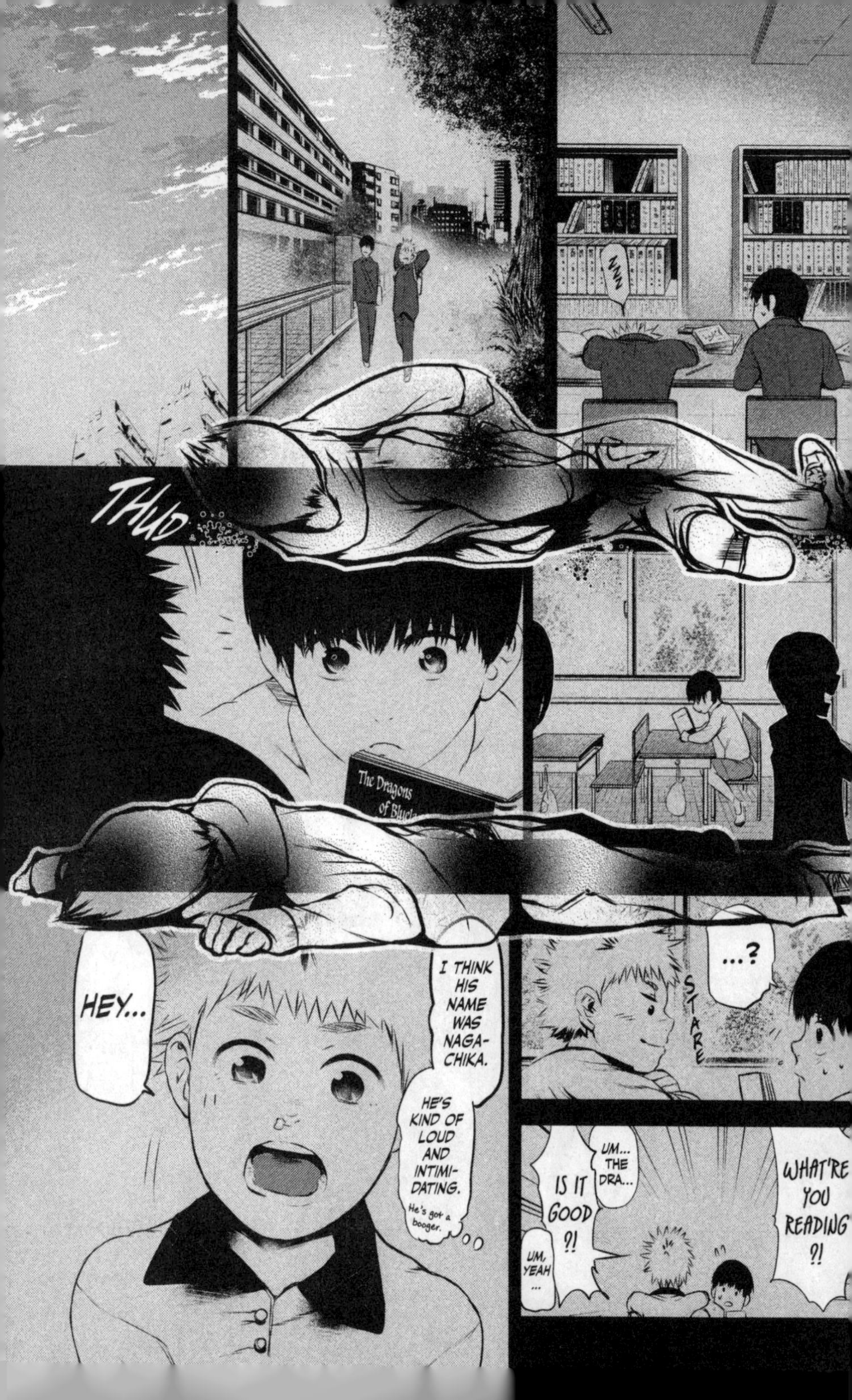
ZZZ
THUD
The Dragons
...?
STARE
WHAT'RE YOU READING ?!
UM... THE DRA...
IS IT GOOD ?!
UM, YEAH ...
HEY...
I THINK HIS NAME WAS NAGA-CHIKA.
HE'S KIND OF LOUD AND INTIMI-DATING.
He's got a booger.

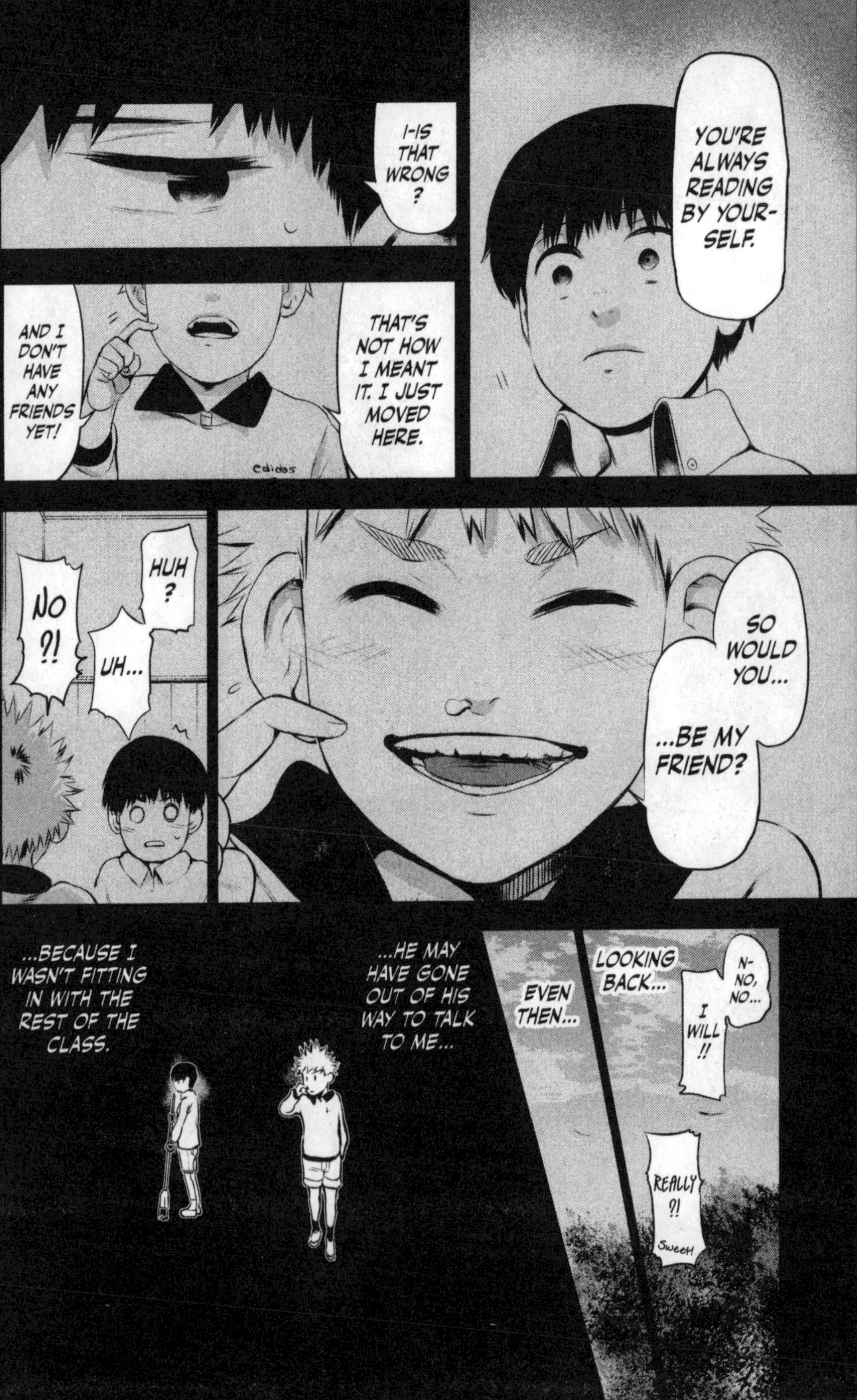
YOU'RE ALWAYS READING BY YOUR-SELF.
I-IS THAT WRONG?
THAT'S NOT HOW I MEANT IT. I JUST MOVED HERE.
AND I DON'T HAVE ANY FRIENDS YET!
edidas
SO WOULD YOU...
...BE MY FRIEND?
HUH?
NO?!
UH...
N-NO, NO...
I WILL!!
REALLY?!
Sweet!
LOOKING BACK...
EVEN THEN...
...HE MAY HAVE GONE OUT OF HIS WAY TO TALK TO ME...
...BECAUSE I WASN'T FITTING IN WITH THE REST OF THE CLASS.

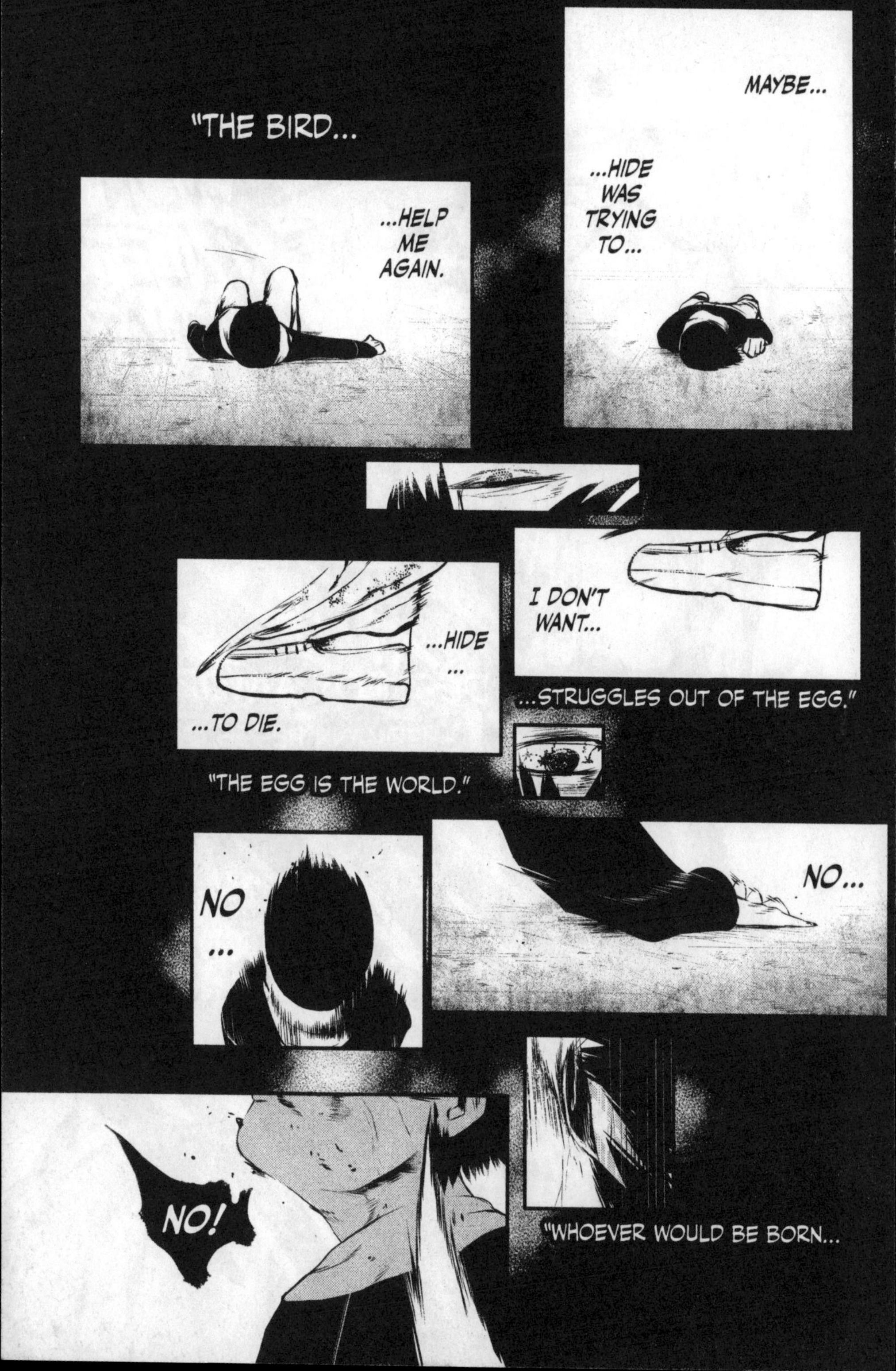

"THE BIRD...

...HELP
ME
AGAIN.

MAYBE...

...HIDE
WAS
TRYING
TO...

...HIDE
...

...TO DIE.

I DON'T
WANT...

...STRUGGLES OUT OF THE EGG."

"THE EGG IS THE WORLD."

NO
...

NO...

NO!

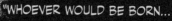

"WHOEVER WOULD BE BORN...

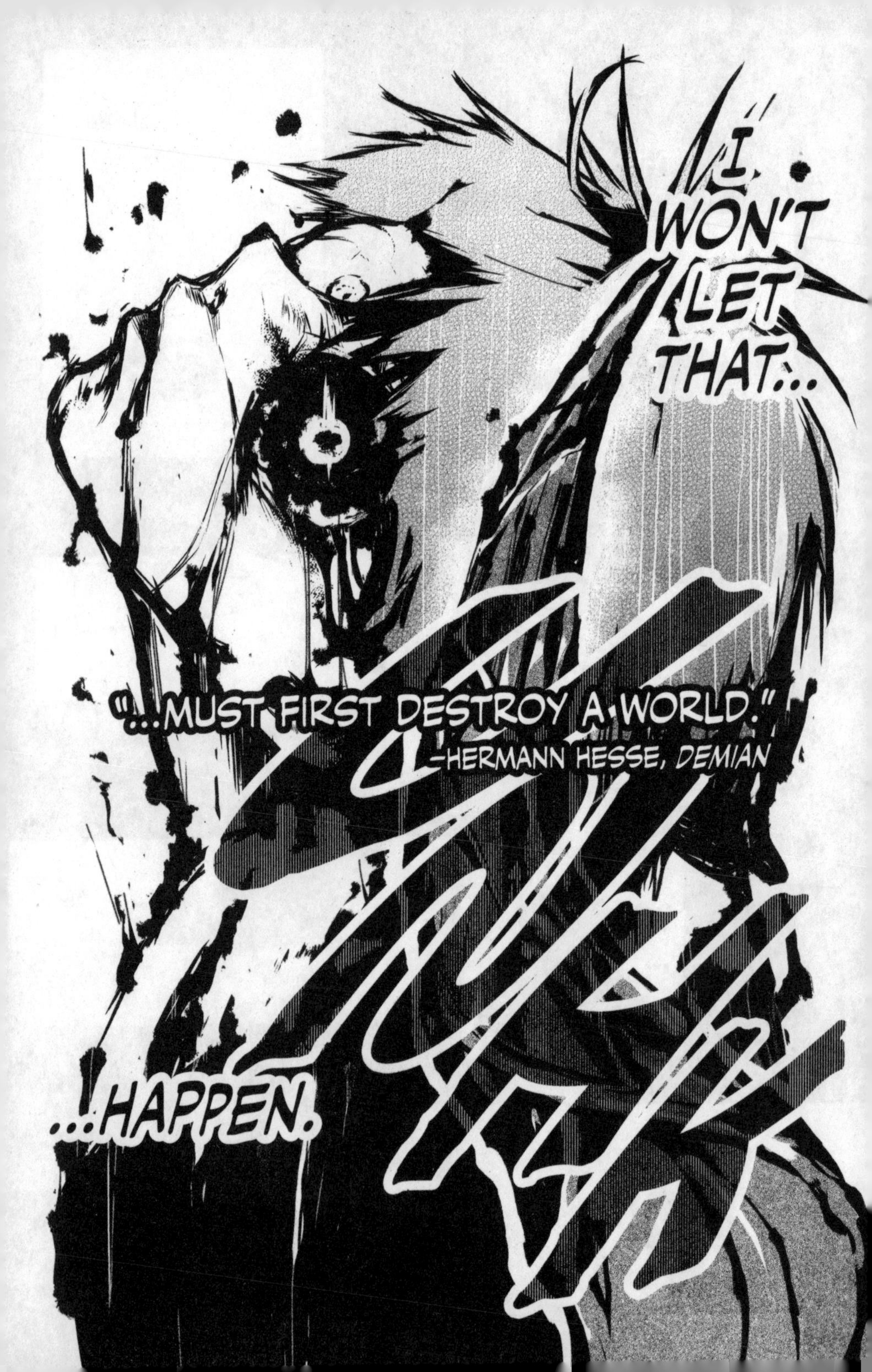

I WON'T LET THAT...
"...MUST FIRST DESTROY A WORLD."
–HERMANN HESSE, *DEMIAN*
...HAPPEN.

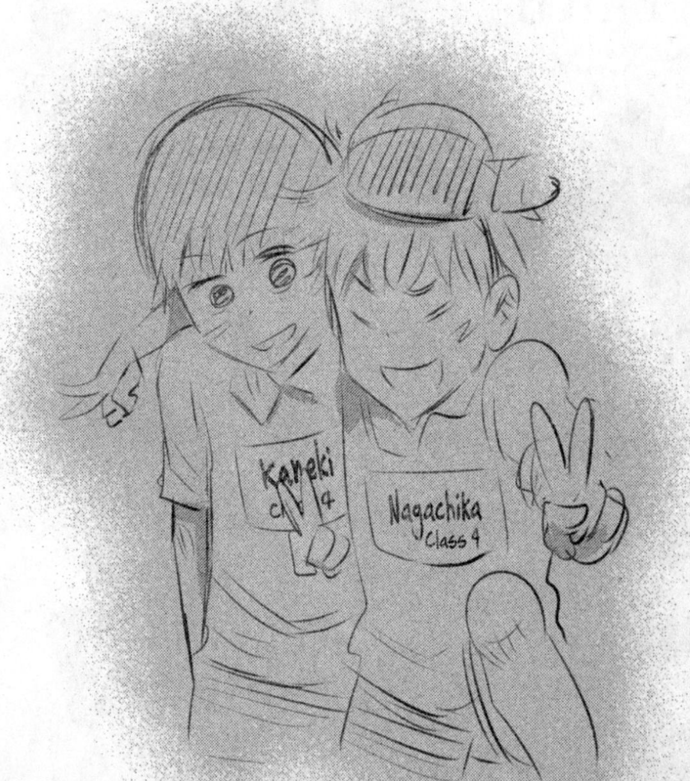
Nagachika
Class 4

#009 [HATCH]

TOKYO GHOUL

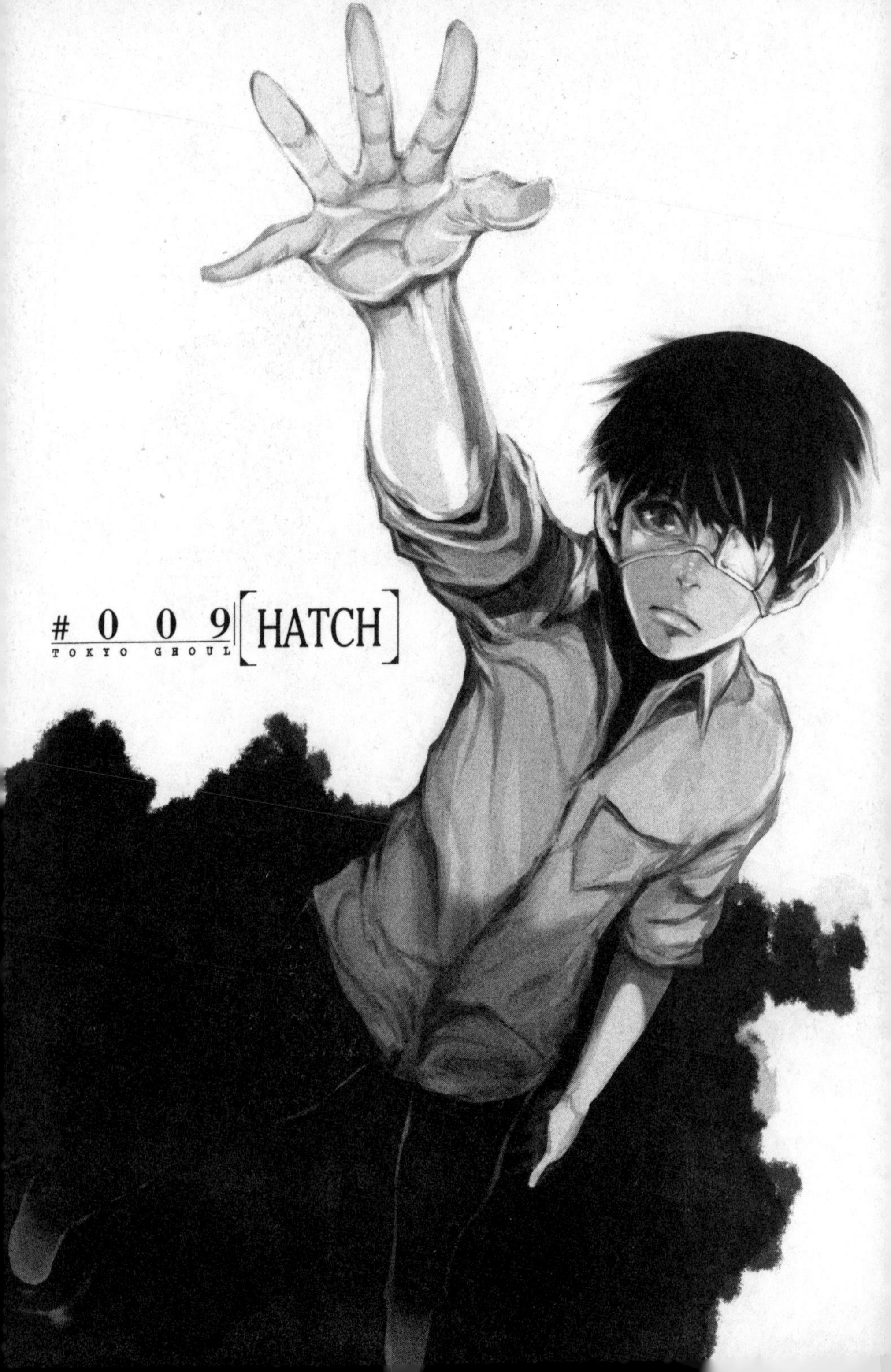

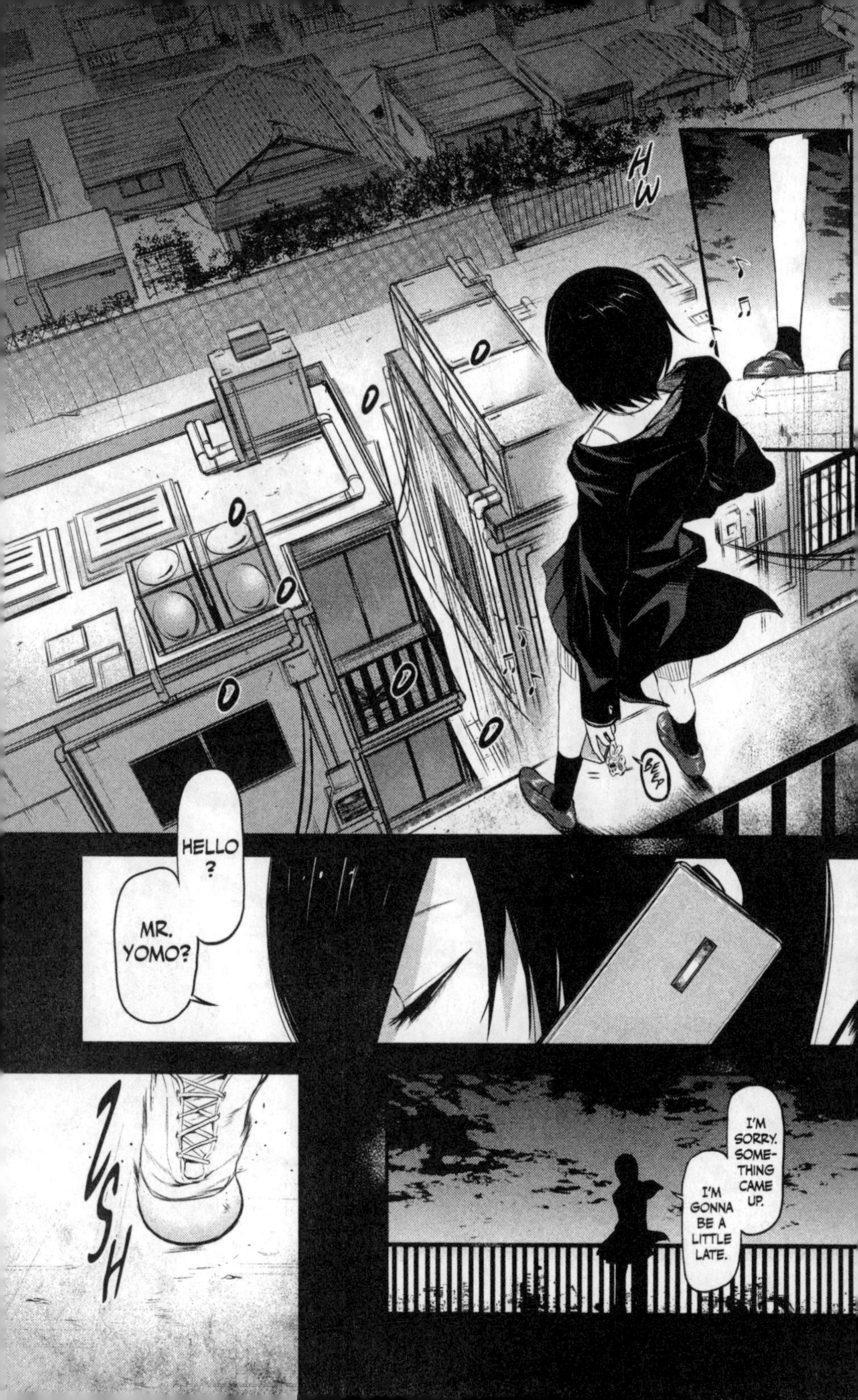
HW
BEEP
HELLO?
MR. YOMO?
I'M SORRY. SOMETHING CAME UP.
I'M GONNA BE A LITTLE LATE.

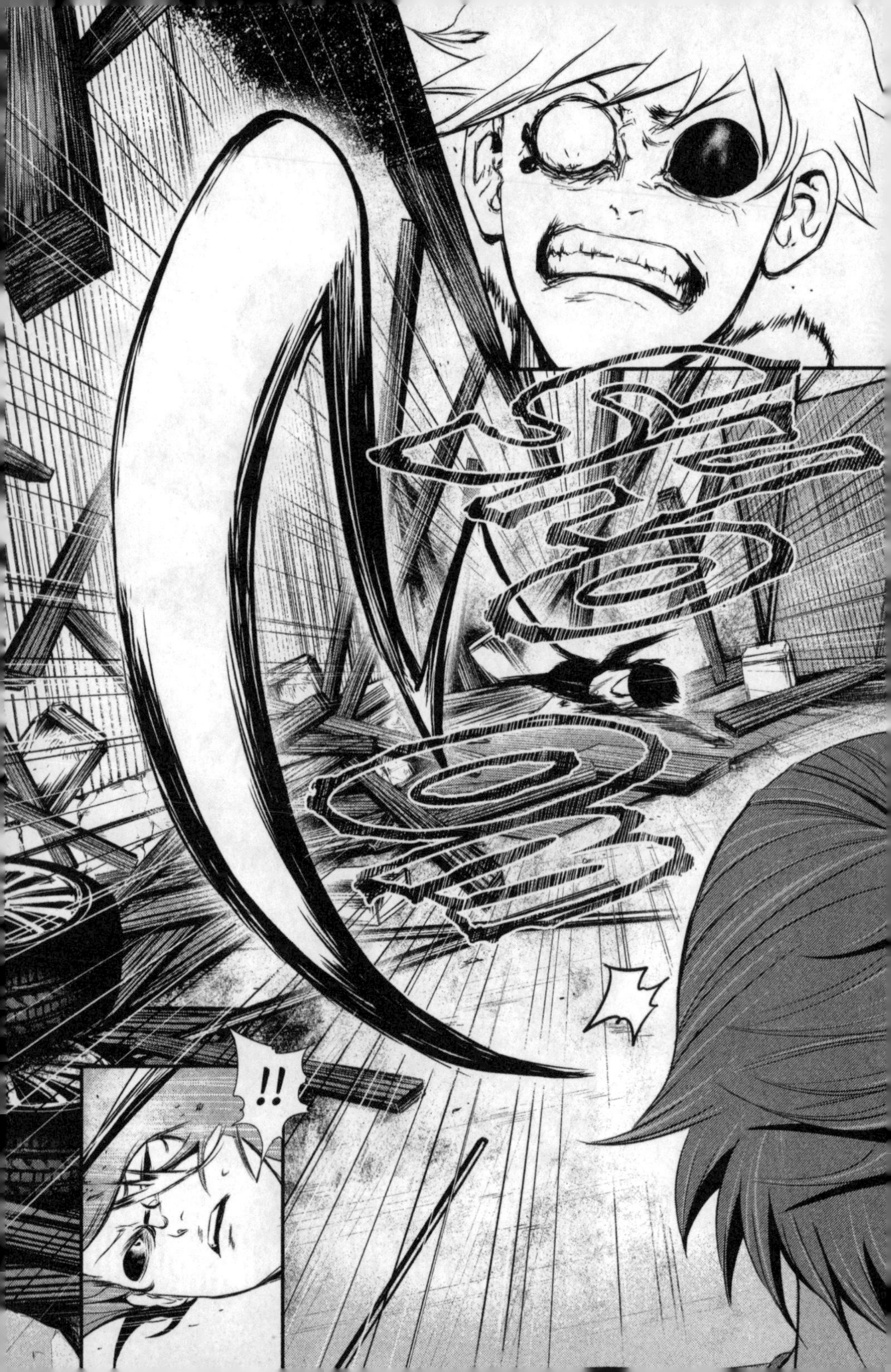
!!

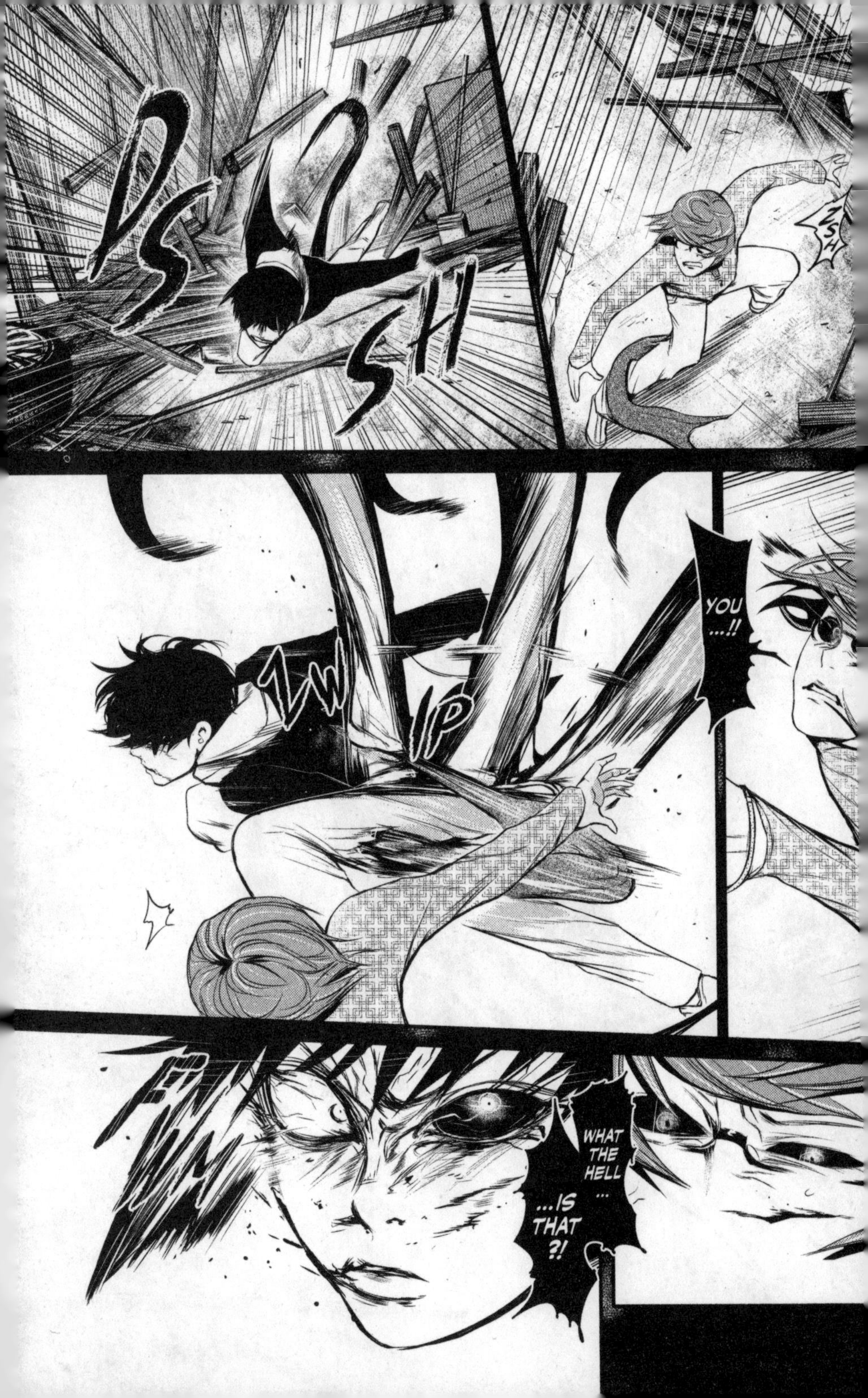
ZSH
YOU ...!!
ZWIP
WHAT THE HELL ...
...IS THAT ?!

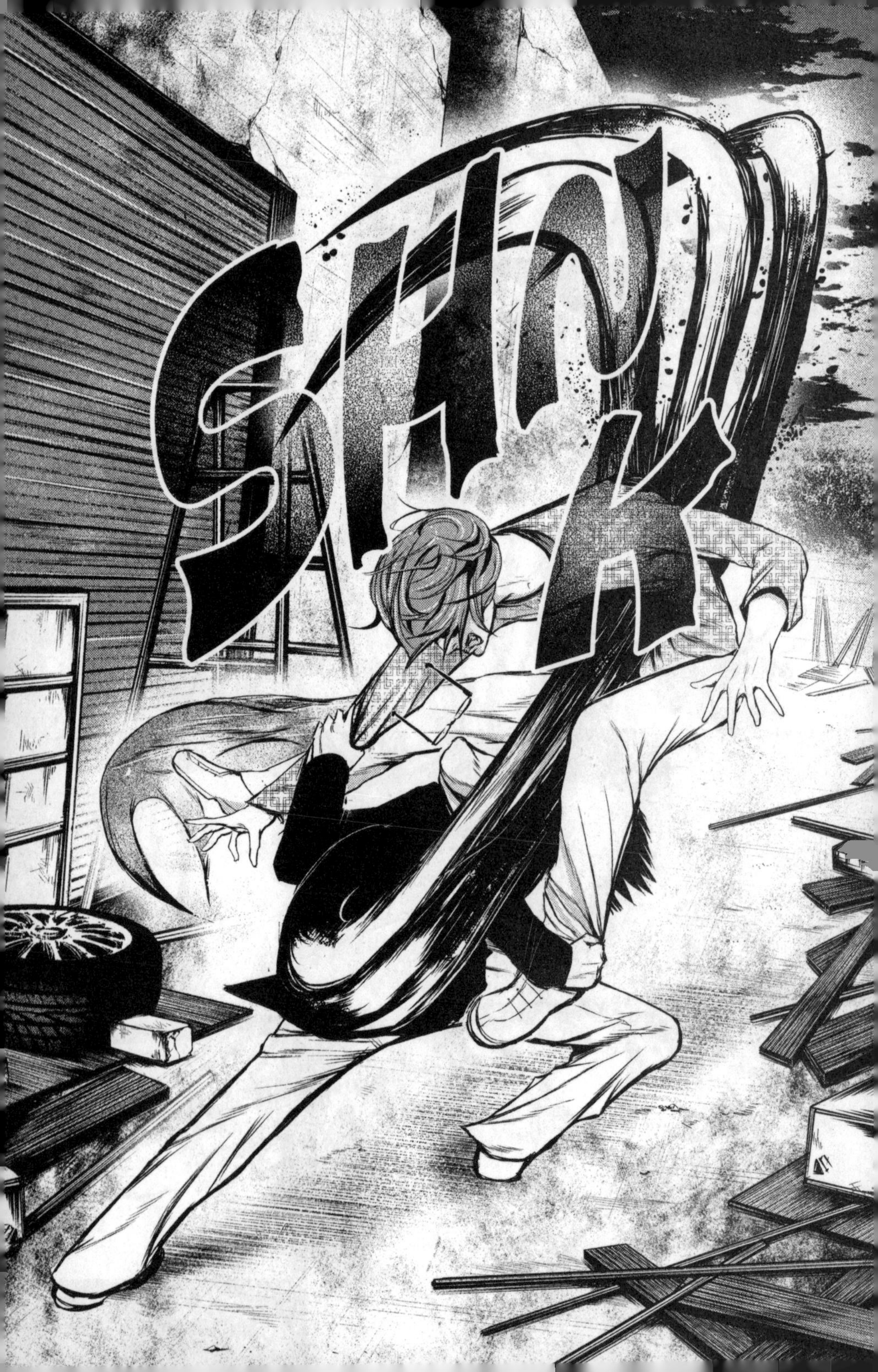
SHICK

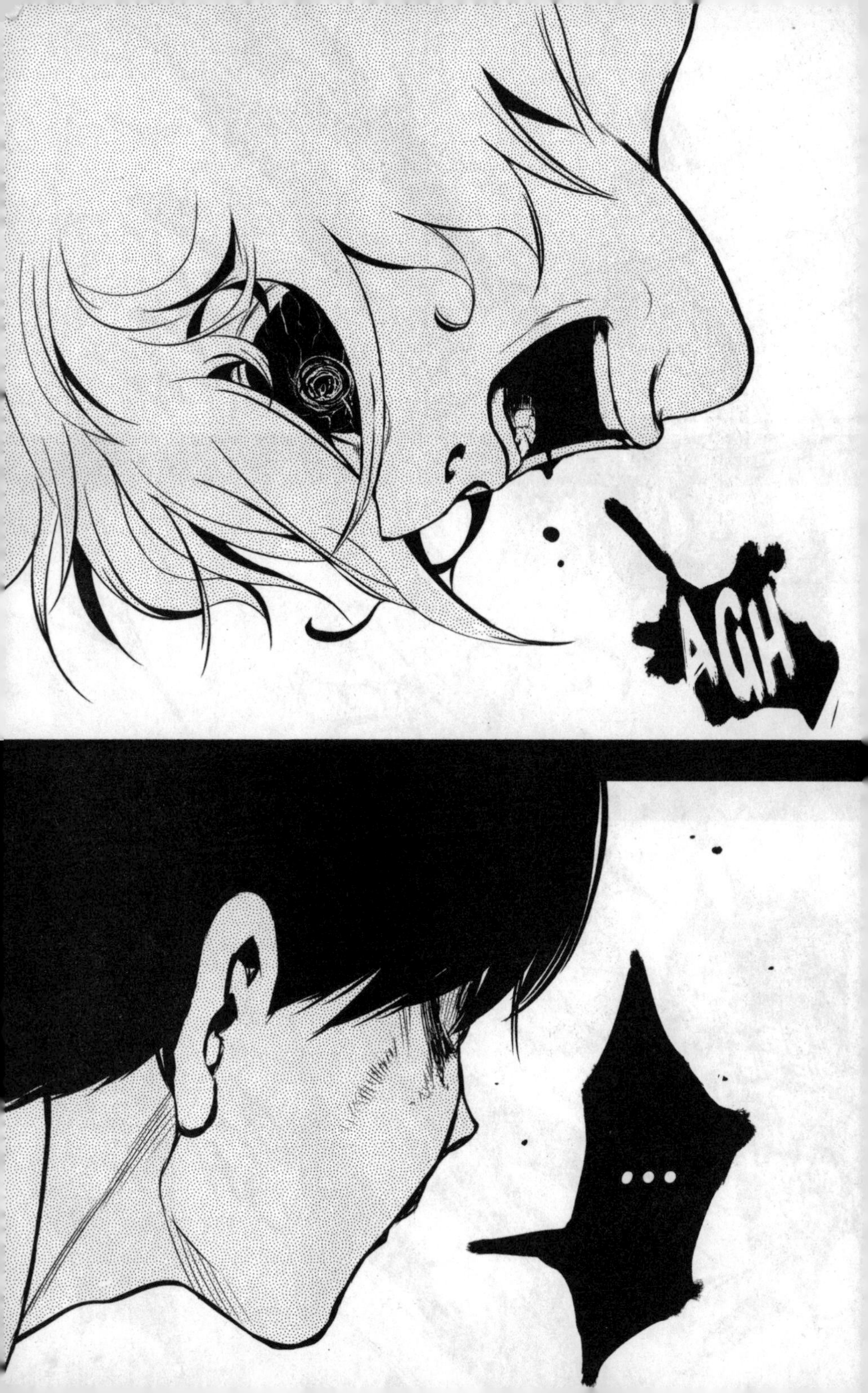
AGH
...

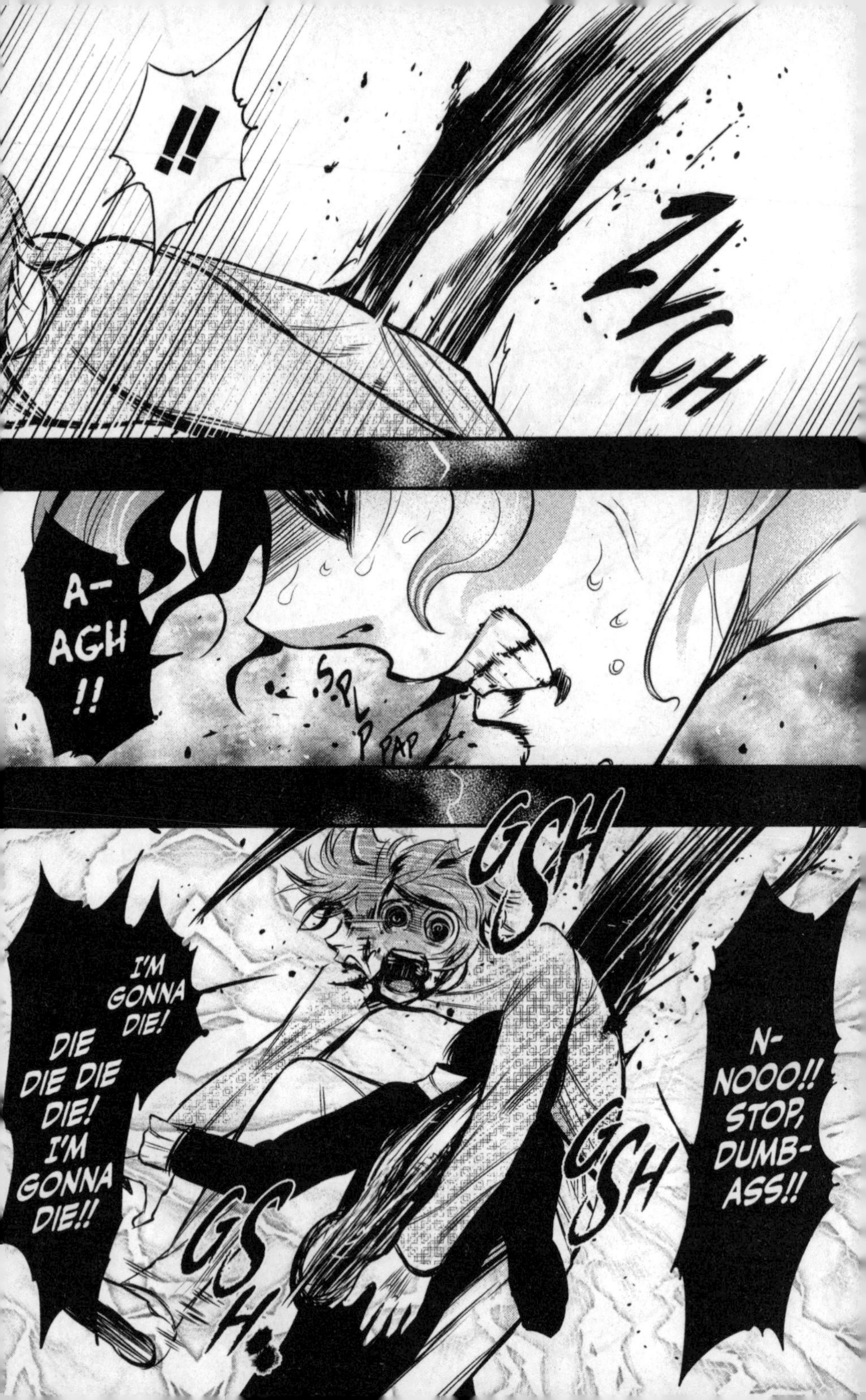
!!
ZUCH
A-AGH!!
SPLP
PAP
GSH
N-NOOO!! STOP, DUMB-ASS!!
GSH
I'M GONNA DIE!
DIE DIE DIE DIE! I'M GONNA DIE!!
GSH

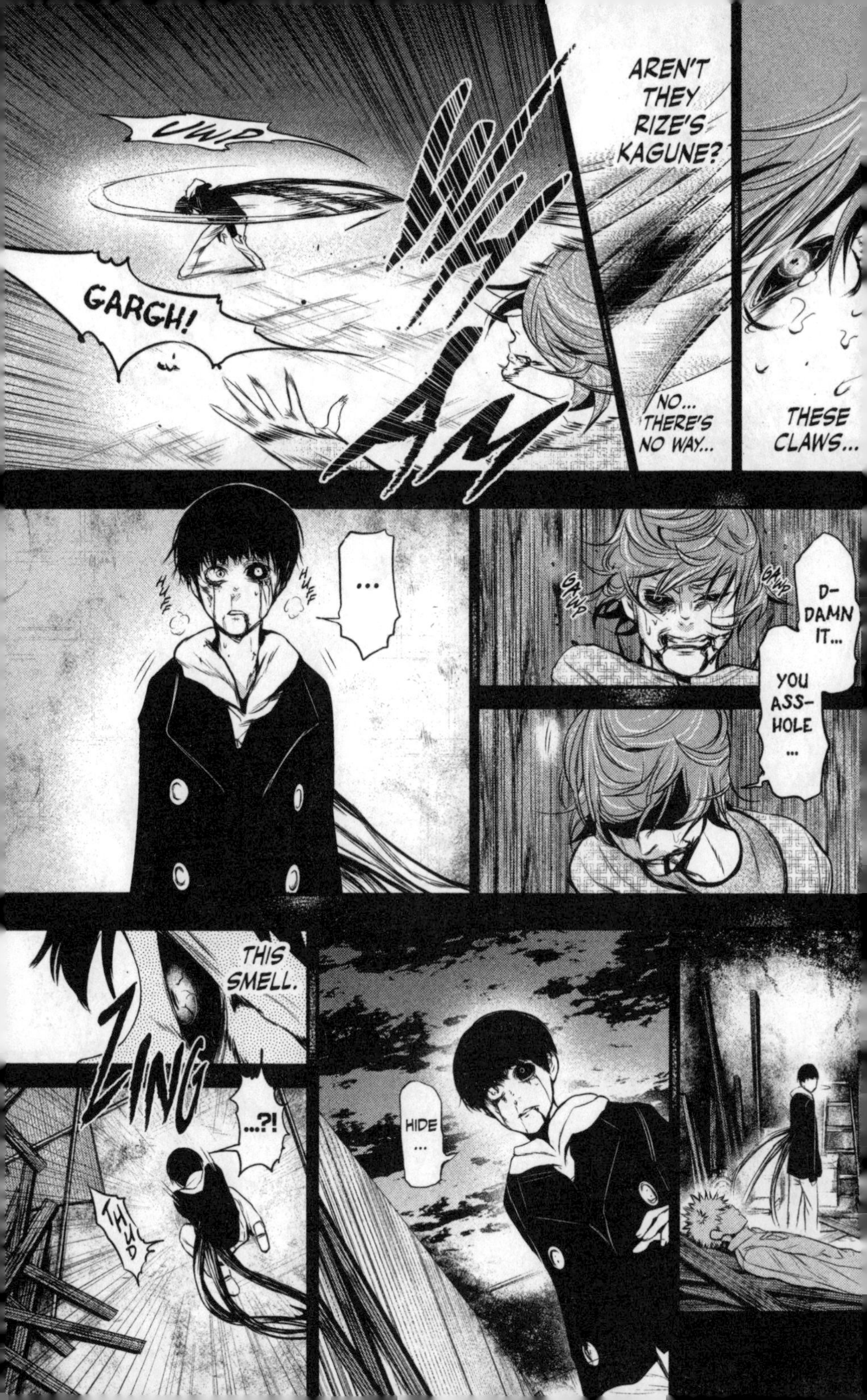
THESE CLAWS...
AREN'T THEY RIZE'S KAGUNE?
NO... THERE'S NO WAY...
UWIP
GARGH!
GAWP
GAWP
D-DAMN IT...
YOU ASS-HOLE ...
HUFF
HUFF
...
HIDE ...
THIS SMELL.
ZING
...?!
THUD

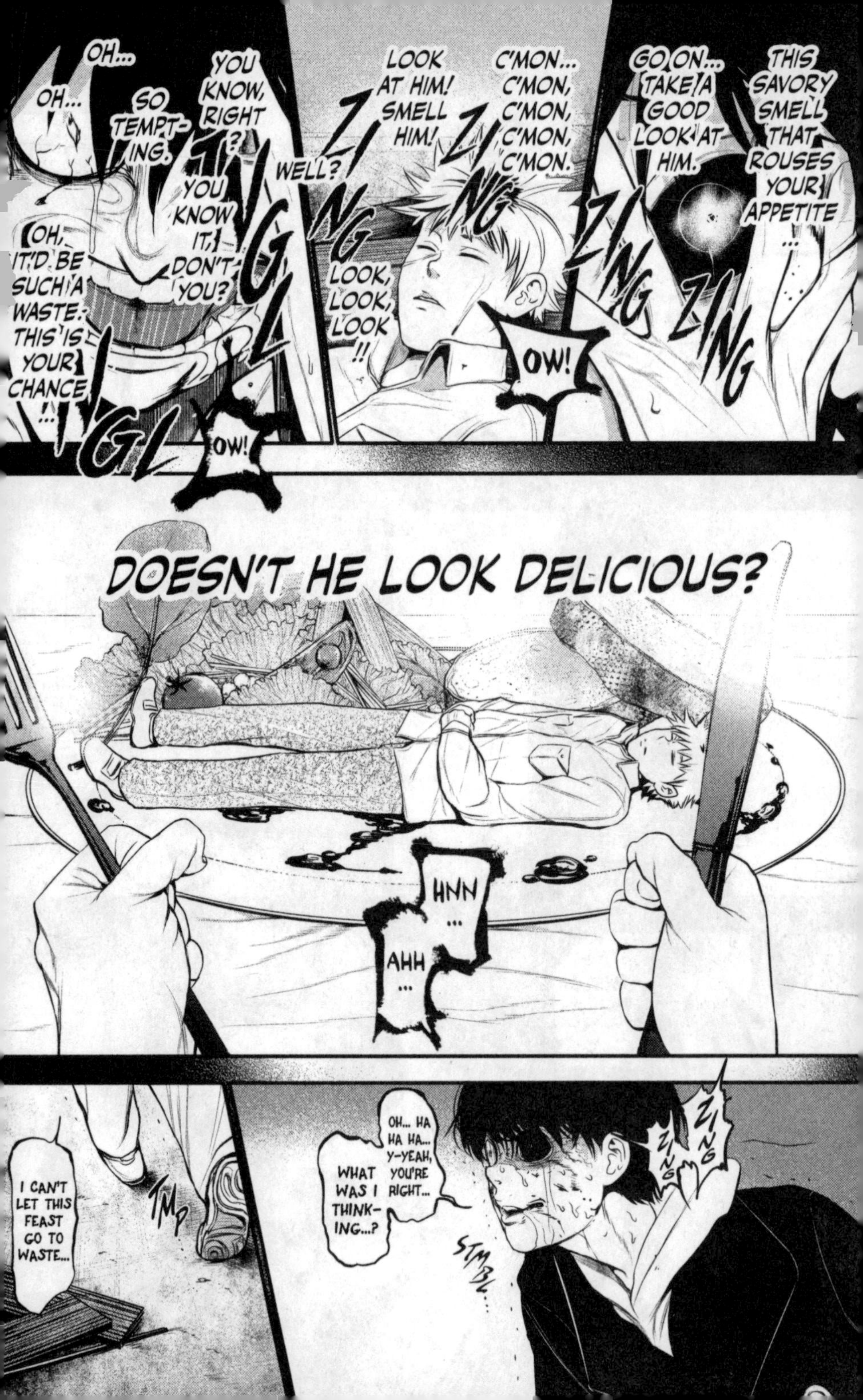
THIS SAVORY SMELL THAT ROUSES YOUR APPETITE...
GO ON... TAKE A GOOD LOOK AT HIM.
ZING ZING
ZING ZING
OW!
C'MON... C'MON, C'MON, C'MON.
LOOK AT HIM! SMELL HIM!
ZING
ZING
WELL?
LOOK, LOOK, LOOK!!
YOU KNOW, RIGHT?
YOU KNOW IT, DON'T YOU?
SO TEMPTING.
OH...
OH...
OH, IT'D BE SUCH A WASTE. THIS IS YOUR CHANCE...!
TINGL
GL
OW!
DOESN'T HE LOOK DELICIOUS?
HNN... AHH...
ZING ZING
OH... HA HA HA... Y-YEAH, YOU'RE RIGHT... WHAT WAS I THINKING...?
STMBL
TMP
I CAN'T LET THIS FEAST GO TO WASTE...

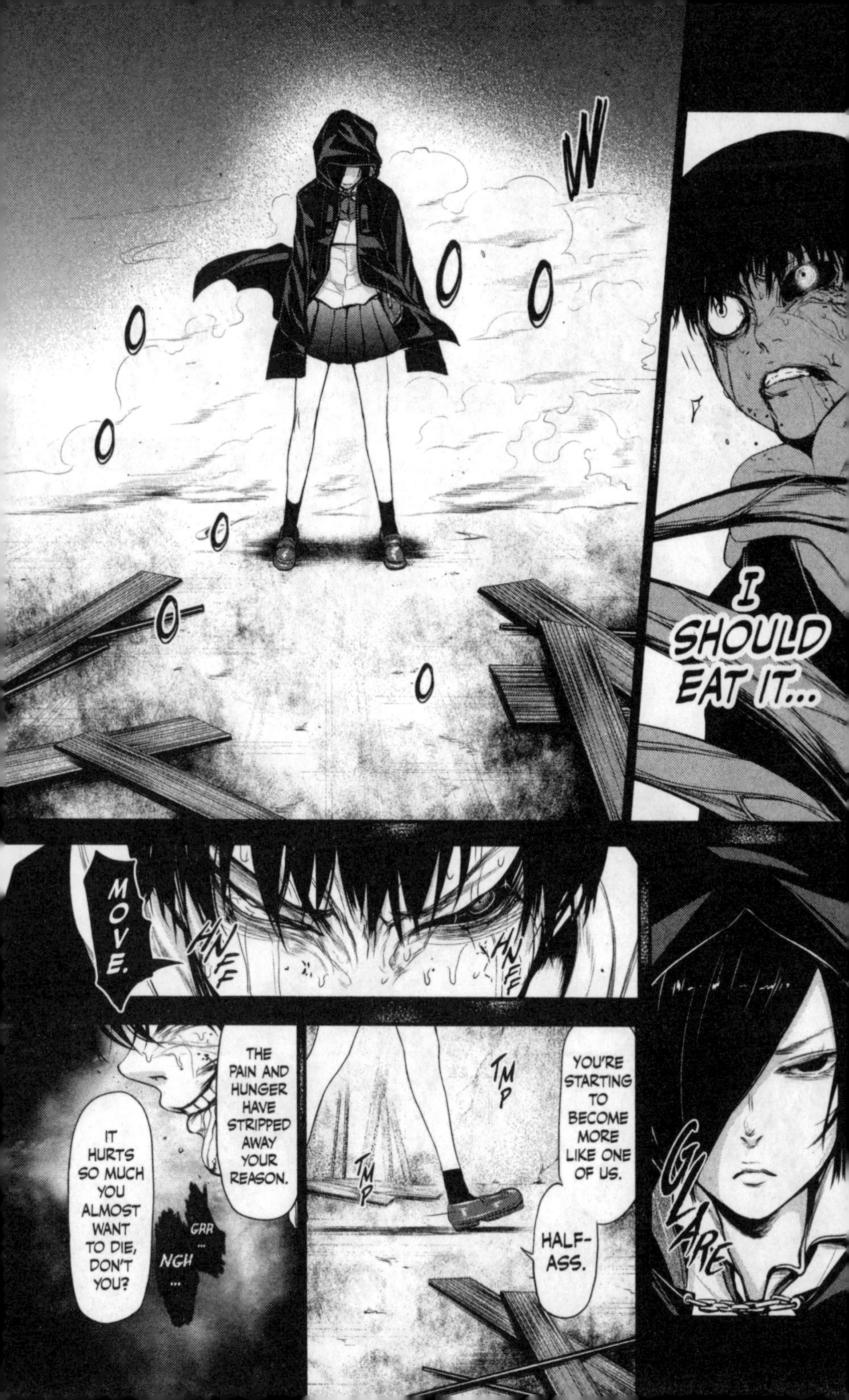
I SHOULD EAT IT...
WOOOOOOO
GLARE
MOVE.
HNFF
HNFF
TMP
TMP
YOU'RE STARTING TO BECOME MORE LIKE ONE OF US.
HALF-ASS.
THE PAIN AND HUNGER HAVE STRIPPED AWAY YOUR REASON.
IT HURTS SO MUCH YOU ALMOST WANT TO DIE, DON'T YOU?
GRR...
NGH...

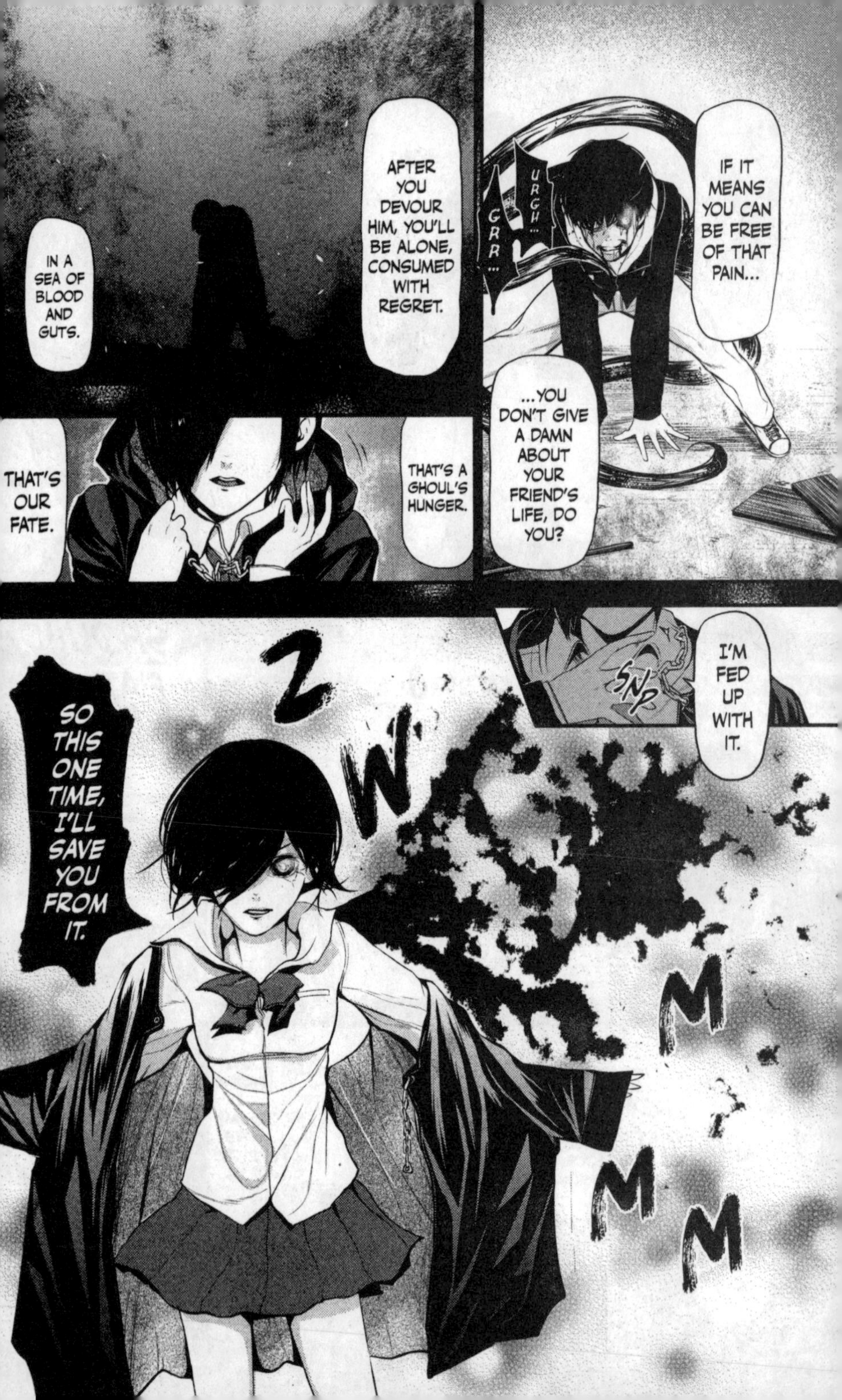
IF IT MEANS YOU CAN BE FREE OF THAT PAIN...
URGH...
GRR...
...YOU DON'T GIVE A DAMN ABOUT YOUR FRIEND'S LIFE, DO YOU?
AFTER YOU DEVOUR HIM, YOU'LL BE ALONE, CONSUMED WITH REGRET.
IN A SEA OF BLOOD AND GUTS.
THAT'S A GHOUL'S HUNGER.
THAT'S OUR FATE.
I'M FED UP WITH IT.
SNP
ZWMMMM
SO THIS ONE TIME, I'LL SAVE YOU FROM IT.

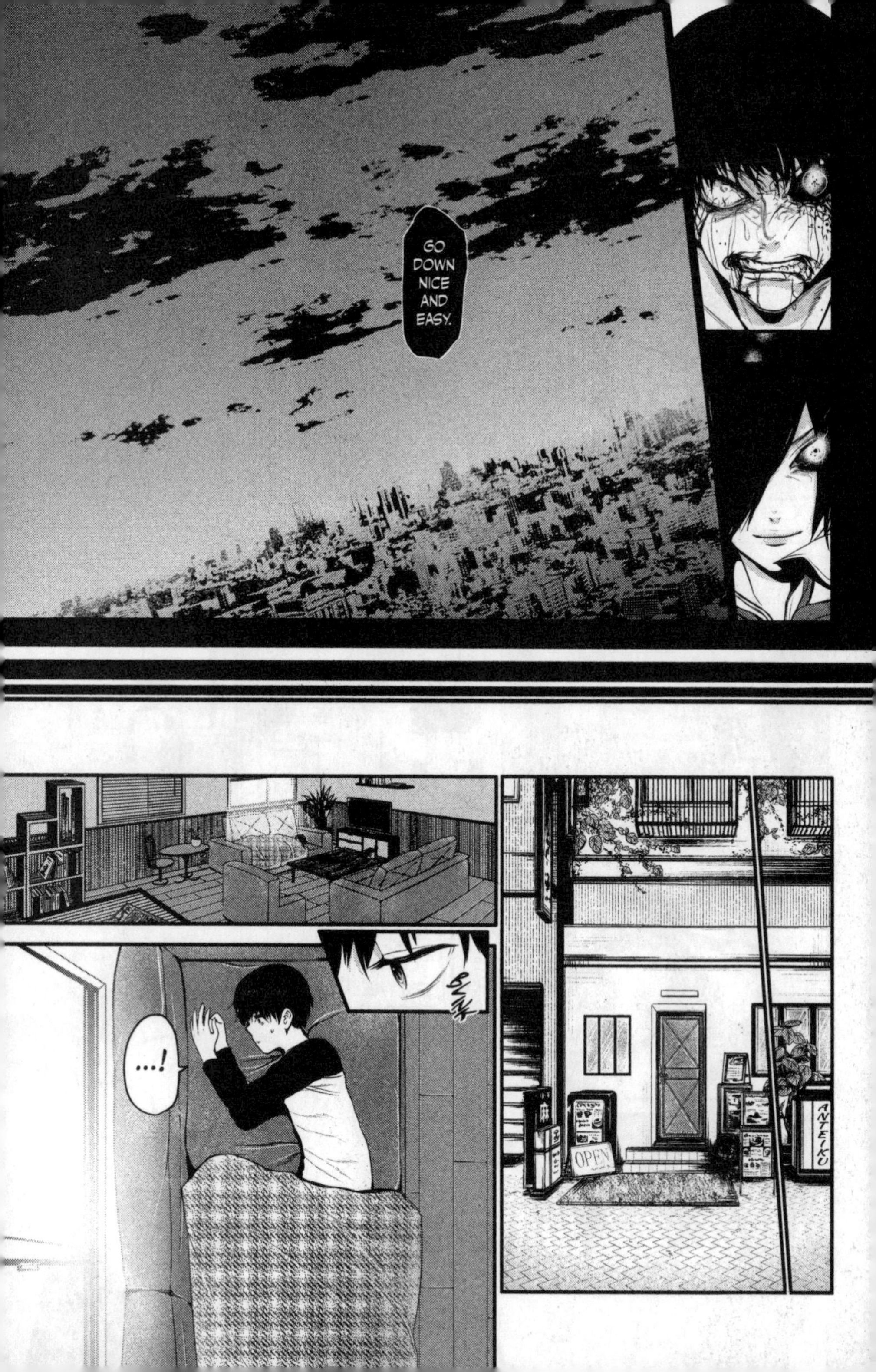
GO DOWN NICE AND EASY.
OPEN
ANTEIKU
BLINK
...!

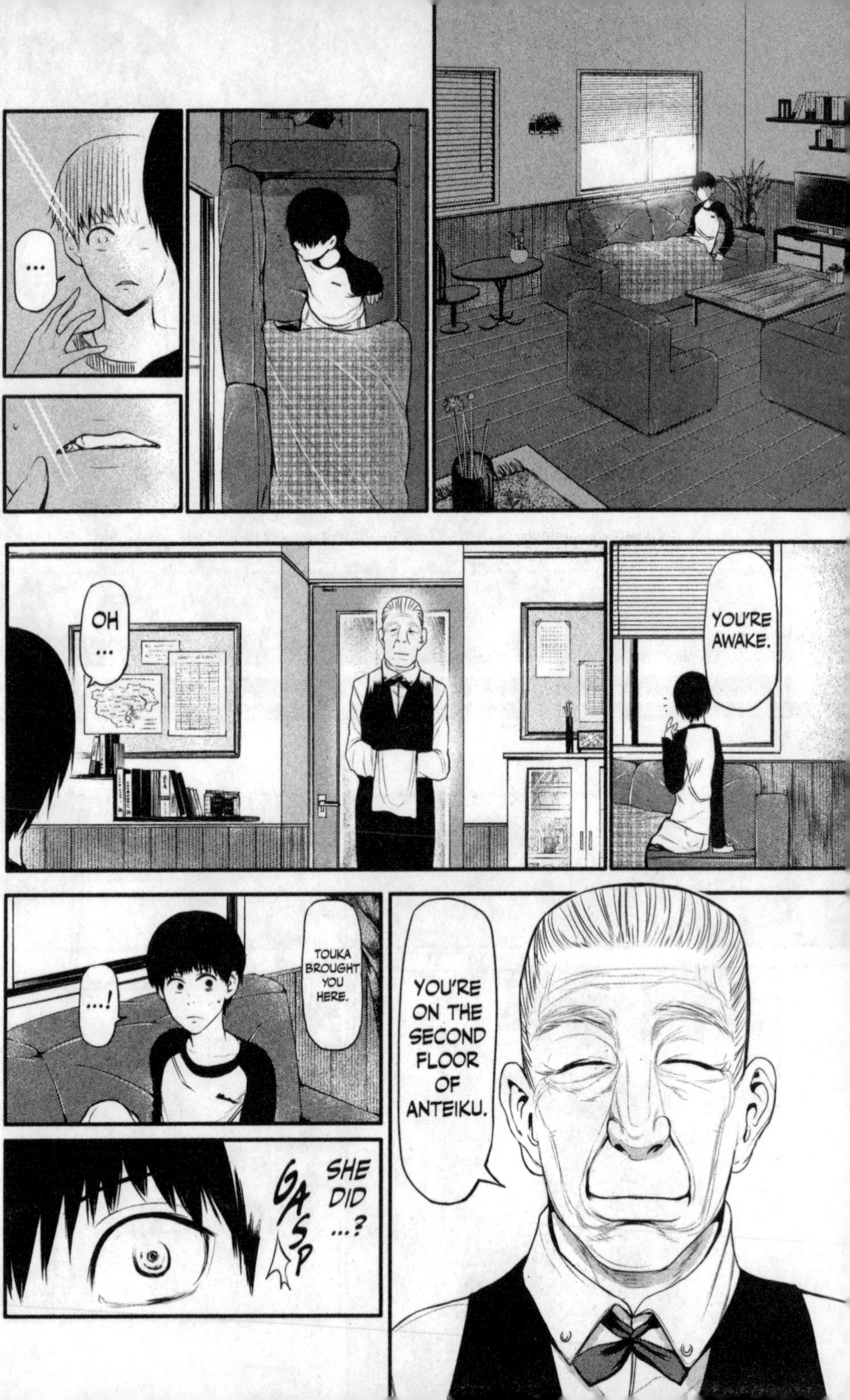
...
YOU'RE AWAKE.
OH ...
YOU'RE ON THE SECOND FLOOR OF ANTEIKU.
TOUKA BROUGHT YOU HERE.
...!
SHE DID ...?
GASP

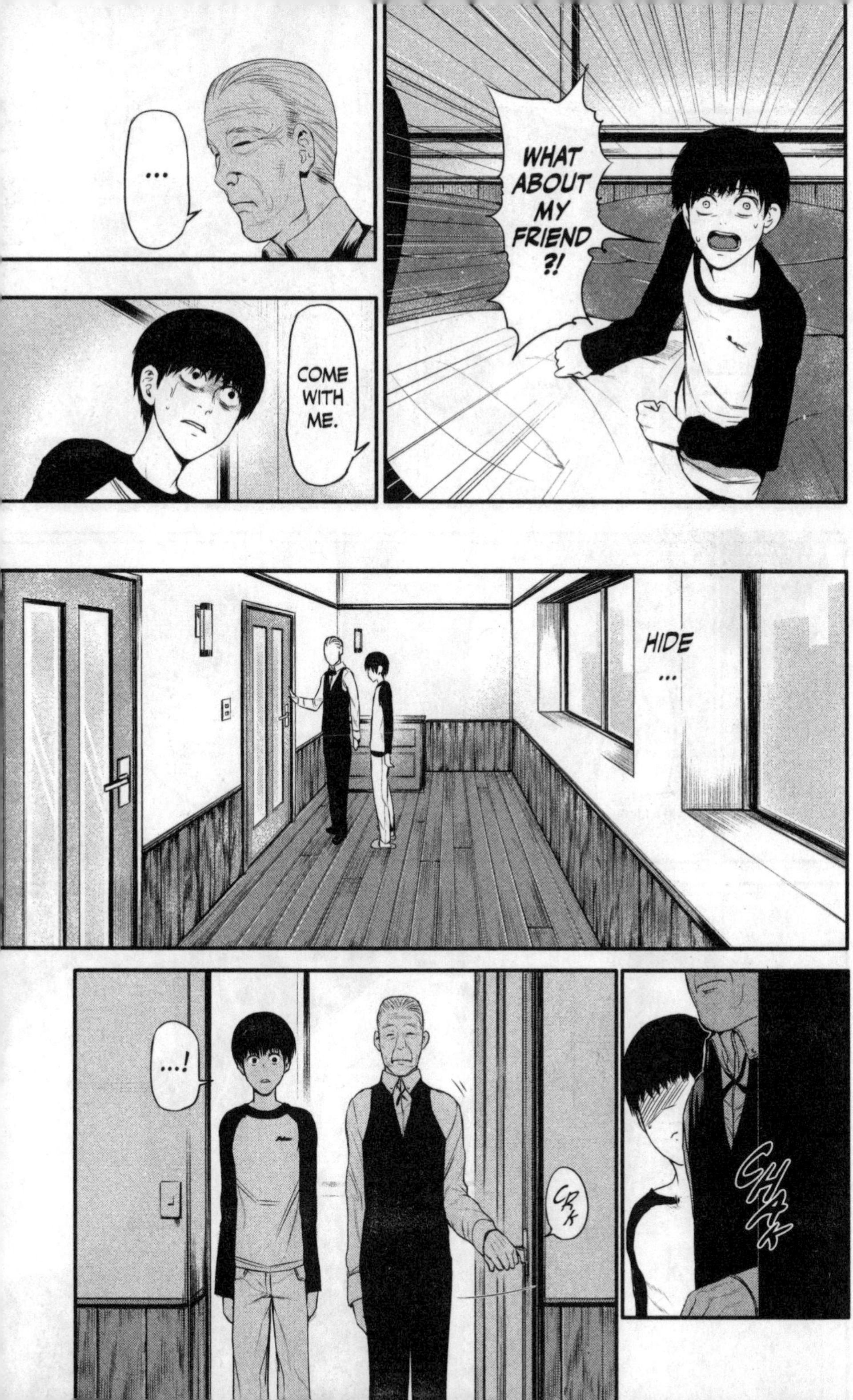
WHAT ABOUT MY FRIEND?!
...
COME WITH ME.
HIDE ...
CHAK
...!
CRK

ZZZ
...
HIDE...
TMP...
FREEZE
ZW RL
...

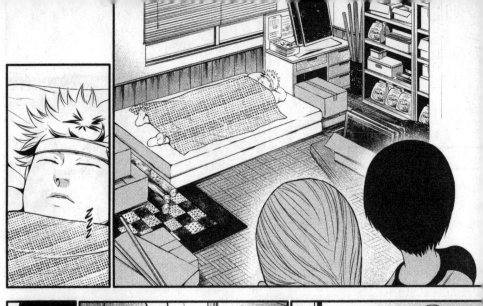

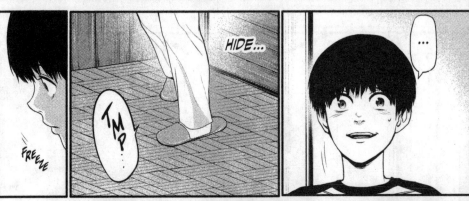

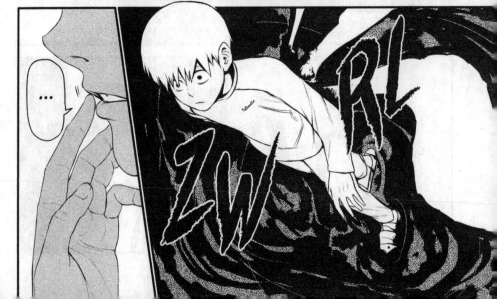

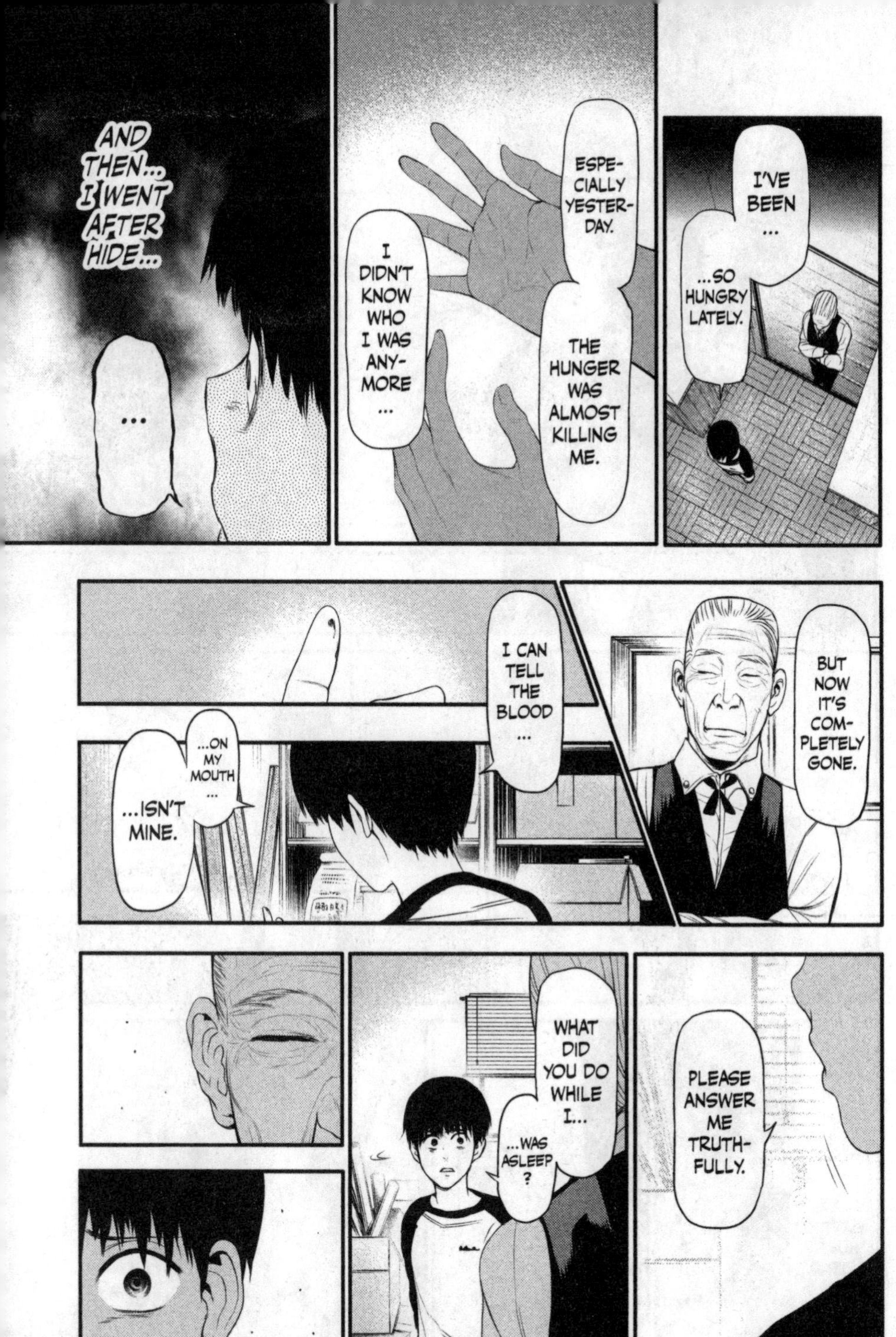
I'VE BEEN ...
...SO HUNGRY LATELY.
ESPE-CIALLY YESTER-DAY.
THE HUNGER WAS ALMOST KILLING ME.
I DIDN'T KNOW WHO I WAS ANY-MORE ...
AND THEN... I WENT AFTER HIDE...
...
BUT NOW IT'S COM-PLETELY GONE.
I CAN TELL THE BLOOD ...
...ON MY MOUTH ...
...ISN'T MINE.
PLEASE ANSWER ME TRUTH-FULLY.
WHAT DID YOU DO WHILE I...
...WAS ASLEEP?

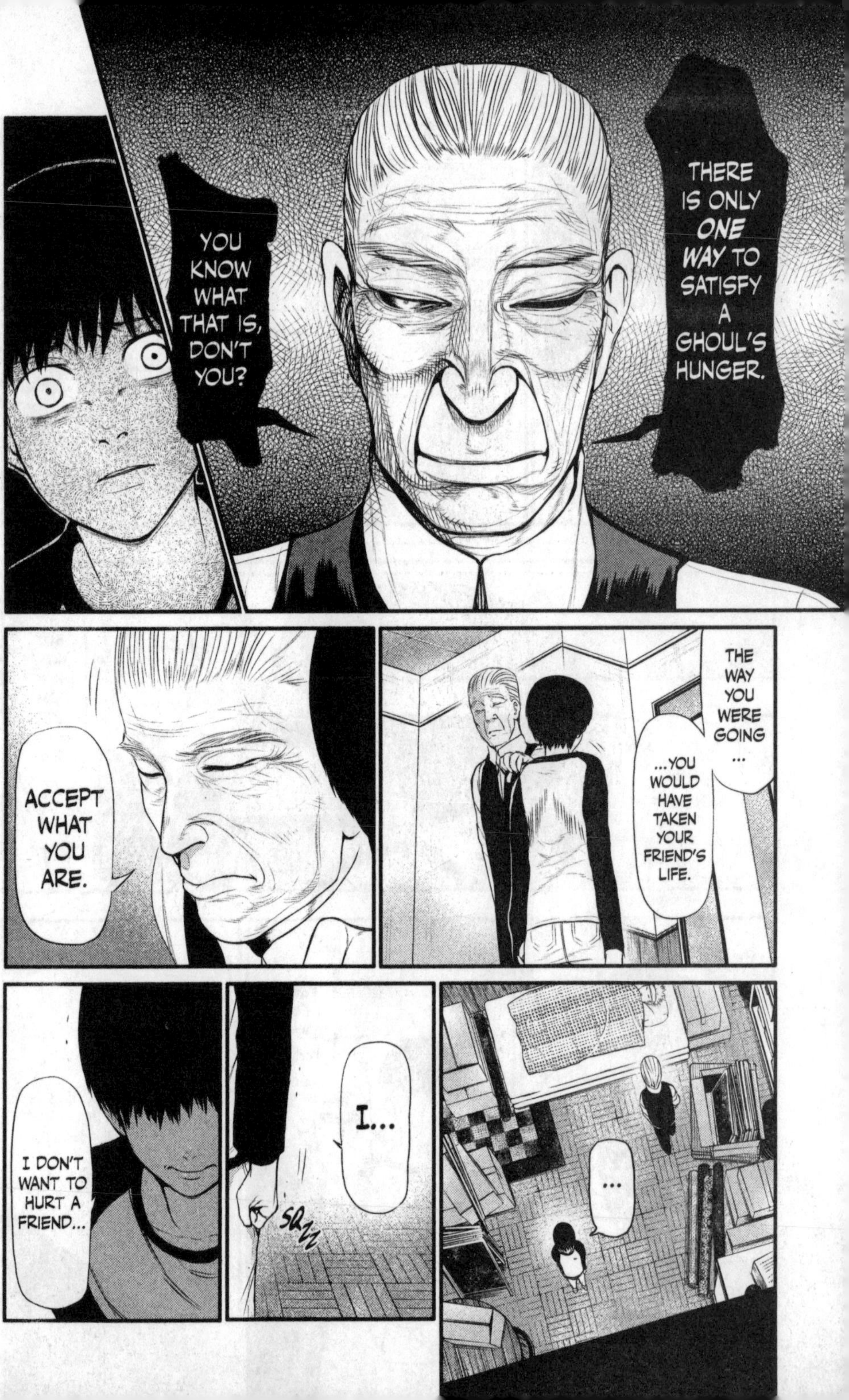
THERE IS ONLY ONE WAY TO SATISFY A GHOUL'S HUNGER.
YOU KNOW WHAT THAT IS, DON'T YOU?
THE WAY YOU WERE GOING ...
...YOU WOULD HAVE TAKEN YOUR FRIEND'S LIFE.
ACCEPT WHAT YOU ARE.
...
I...
SQZZ
I DON'T WANT TO HURT A FRIEND...

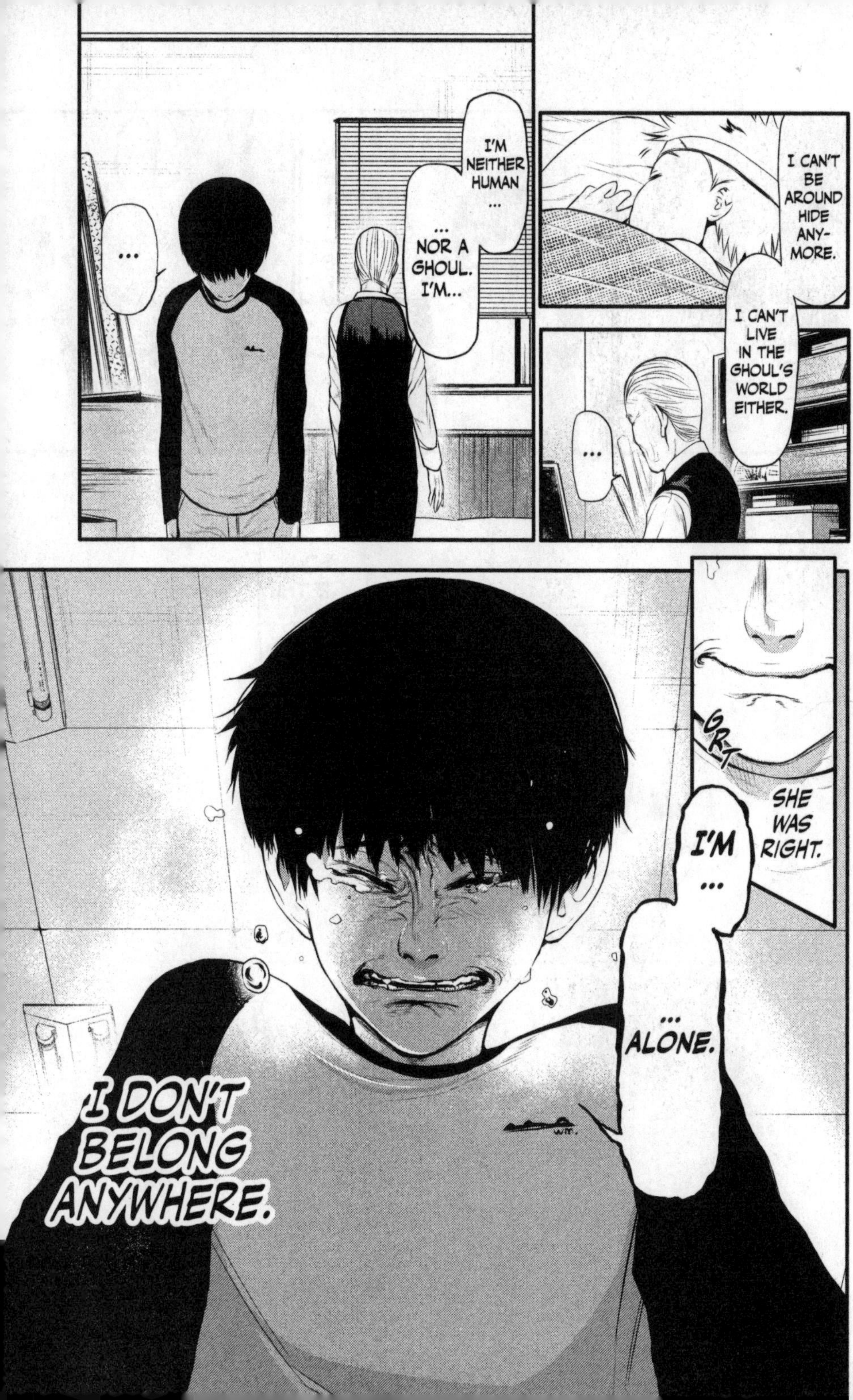
I CAN'T BE AROUND HIDE ANYMORE.
I CAN'T LIVE IN THE GHOUL'S WORLD EITHER.
...
I'M NEITHER HUMAN ...
... NOR A GHOUL. I'M...
...
GRT
SHE WAS RIGHT.
I'M ...
... ALONE.
I DON'T BELONG ANYWHERE.

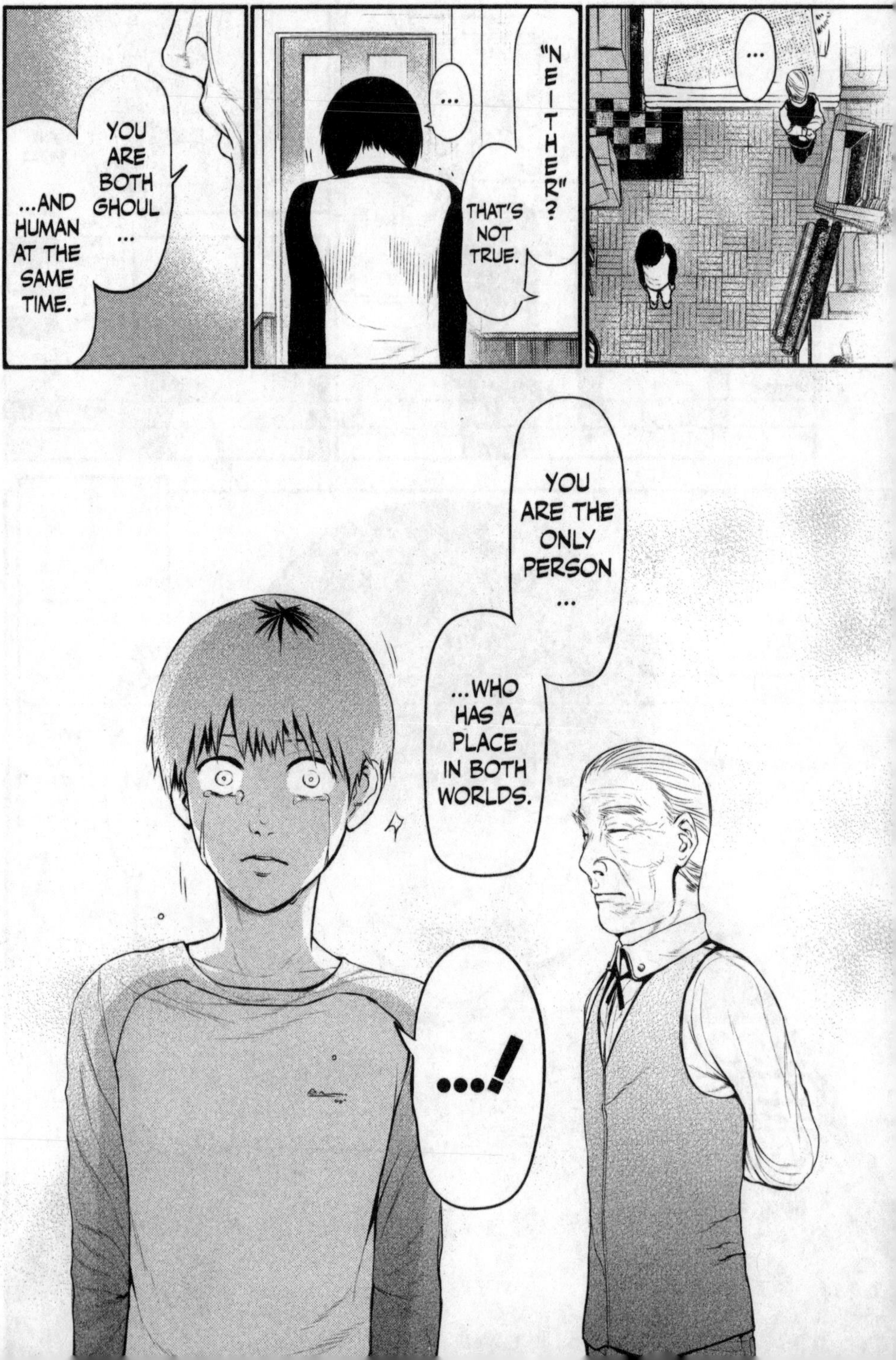
...
"NEITHER"?
THAT'S NOT TRUE.
...
YOU ARE BOTH GHOUL...
...AND HUMAN AT THE SAME TIME.
YOU ARE THE ONLY PERSON...
...WHO HAS A PLACE IN BOTH WORLDS.
...!

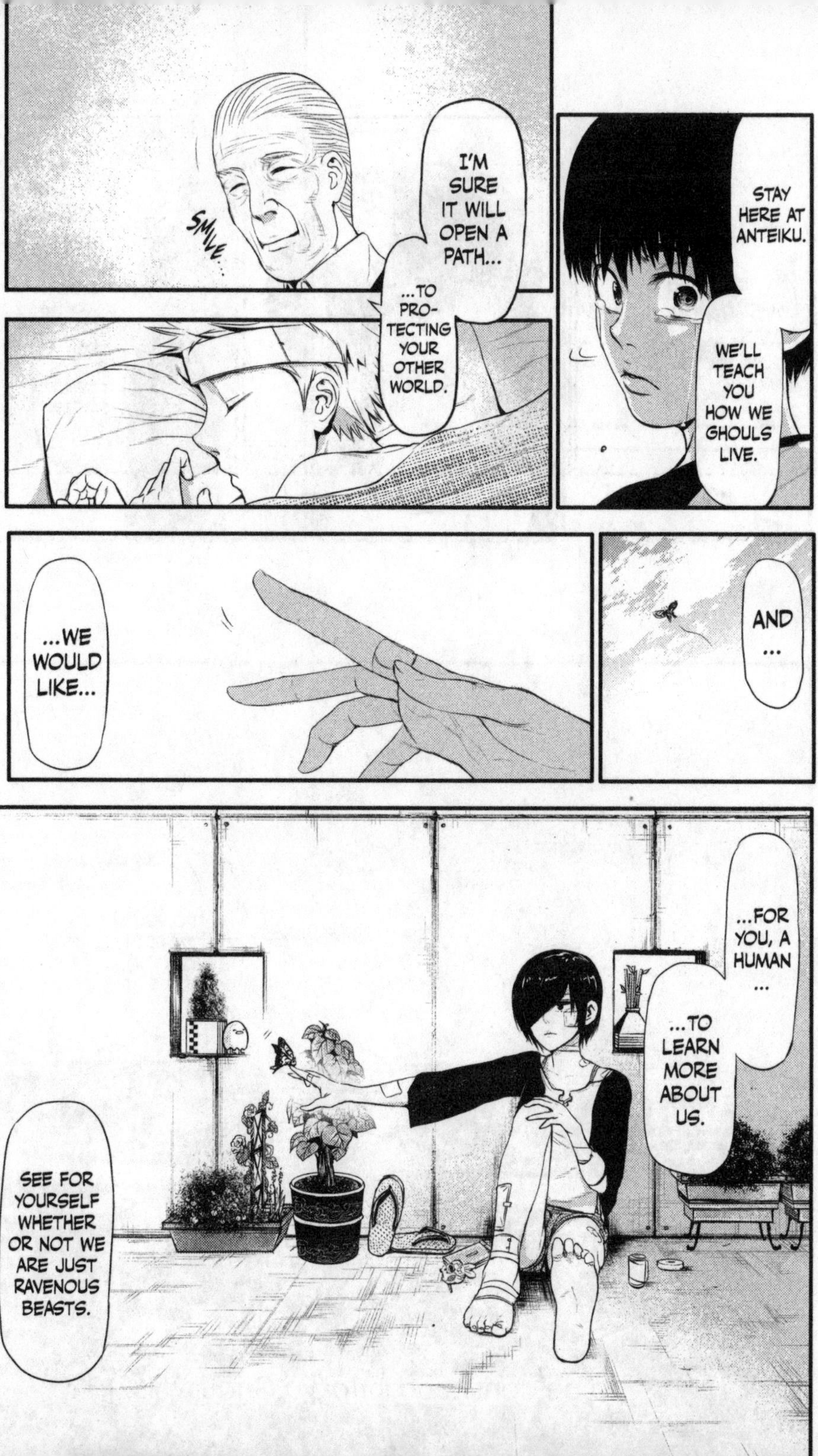
STAY HERE AT ANTEIKU.
WE'LL TEACH YOU HOW WE GHOULS LIVE.
I'M SURE IT WILL OPEN A PATH...
SMILE...
...TO PROTECTING YOUR OTHER WORLD.
AND ...
...WE WOULD LIKE...
...FOR YOU, A HUMAN ...
...TO LEARN MORE ABOUT US.
SEE FOR YOURSELF WHETHER OR NOT WE ARE JUST RAVENOUS BEASTS.

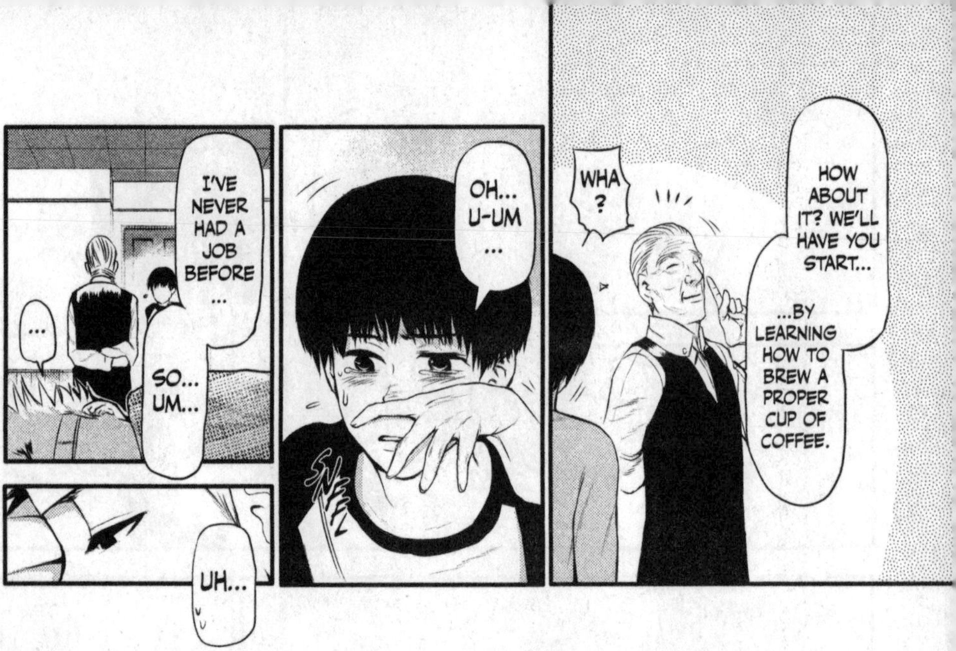
HOW ABOUT IT? WE'LL HAVE YOU START...
...BY LEARNING HOW TO BREW A PROPER CUP OF COFFEE.
WHA?
OH... U-UM ...
SNIFF
I'VE NEVER HAD A JOB BEFORE ...
SO... UM...
...
UH...
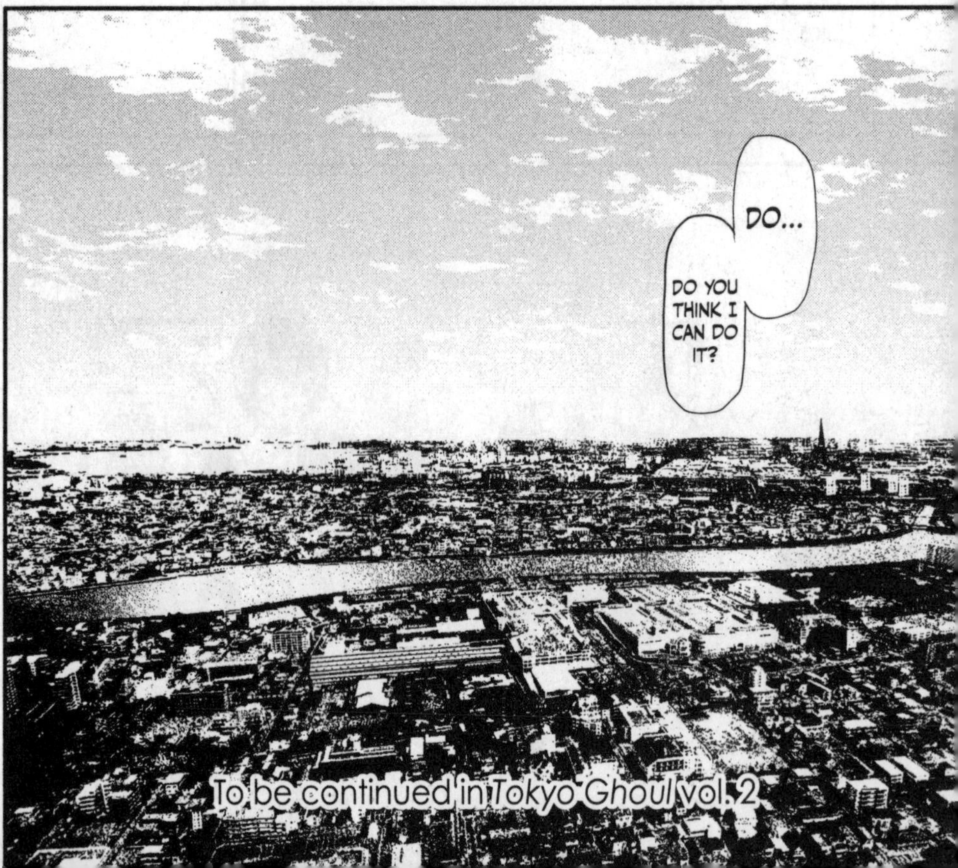
DO...
DO YOU THINK I CAN DO IT?
To be continued in Tokyo Ghoul vol. 2

Tokyo Ghoul
Sui Ishida

Assistant   eda
Thanks   Yu Muraoka Sensei
             My sisters
Editor   Jumpei Matsuo

Bonus Manga
Tokyo's Ghouls

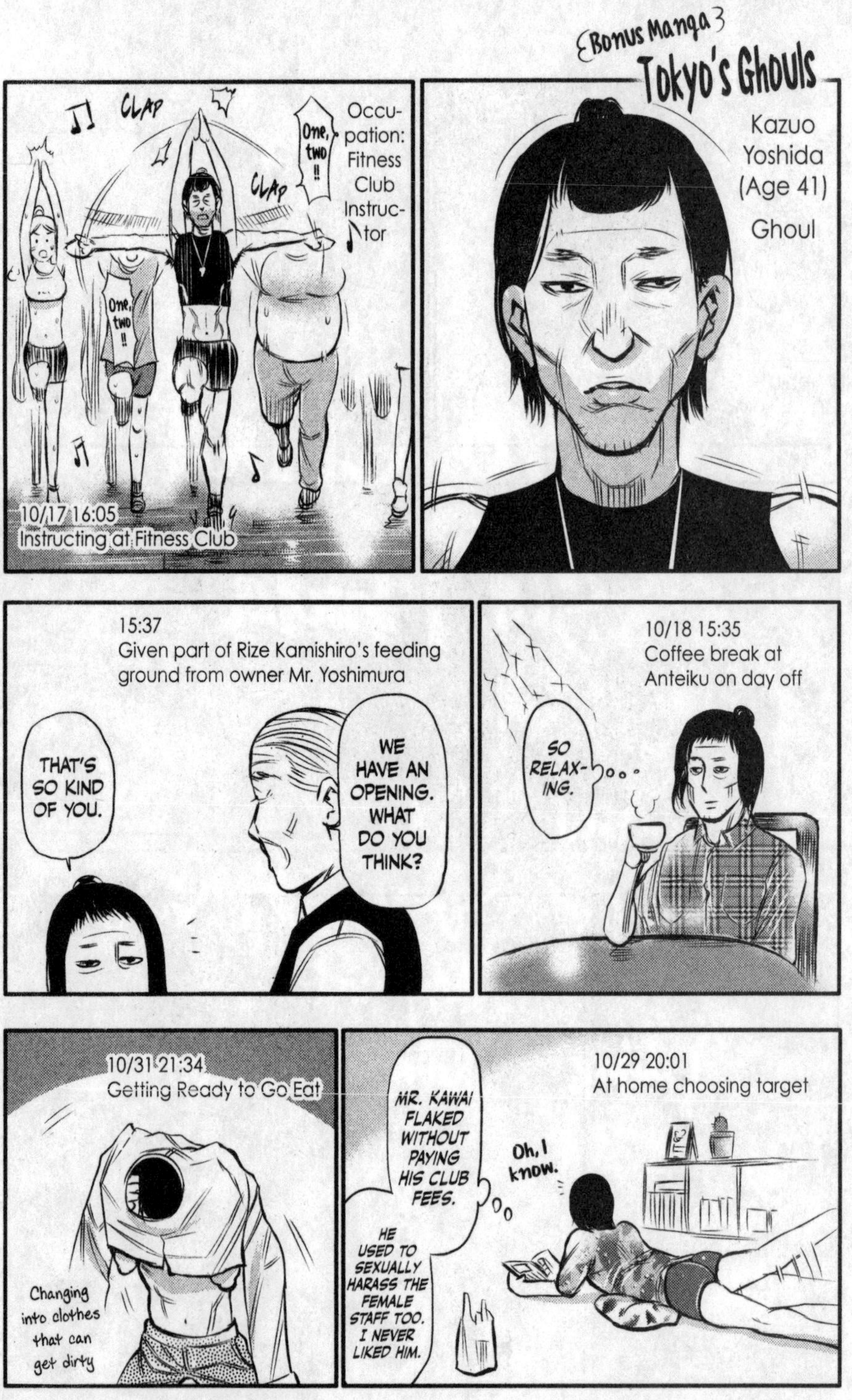
Kazuo Yoshida (Age 41)
Ghoul
Occupation: Fitness Club Instructor
One, two!!
CLAP
CLAP
One, two!!
10/17 16:05
Instructing at Fitness Club
10/18 15:35
Coffee break at Anteiku on day off
SO RELAXING.
15:37
Given part of Rize Kamishiro's feeding ground from owner Mr. Yoshimura
WE HAVE AN OPENING. WHAT DO YOU THINK?
THAT'S SO KIND OF YOU.
10/29 20:01
At home choosing target
Oh, I know.
MR. KAWAI FLAKED WITHOUT PAYING HIS CLUB FEES.
HE USED TO SEXUALLY HARASS THE FEMALE STAFF TOO. I NEVER LIKED HIM.
10/31 21:34
Getting Ready to Go Eat
Changing into clothes that can get dirty

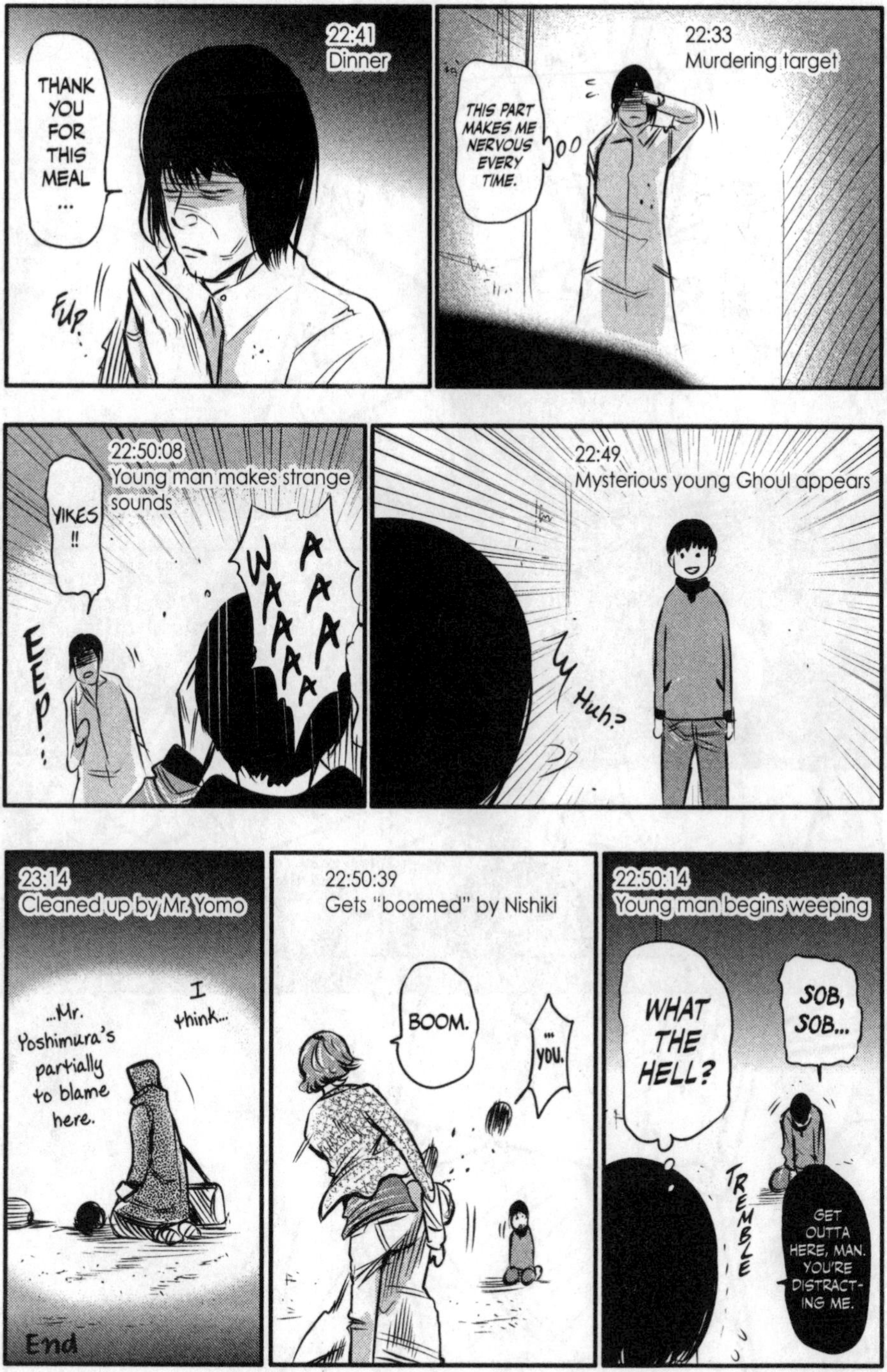
22:33
Murdering target
THIS PART MAKES ME NERVOUS EVERY TIME.
22:41
Dinner
THANK YOU FOR THIS MEAL ...
FUP...
22:49
Mysterious young Ghoul appears
Huh?
22:50:08
Young man makes strange sounds
YIKES!!
WAAAAAAAAA
EEP...
22:50:14
Young man begins weeping
SOB, SOB...
WHAT THE HELL?
TREMBLE
GET OUTTA HERE, MAN. YOU'RE DISTRACTING ME.
22:50:39
Gets "boomed" by Nishiki
BOOM.
... YOU.
23:14
Cleaned up by Mr. Yomo
I think...
...Mr. Yoshimura's partially to blame here.
End

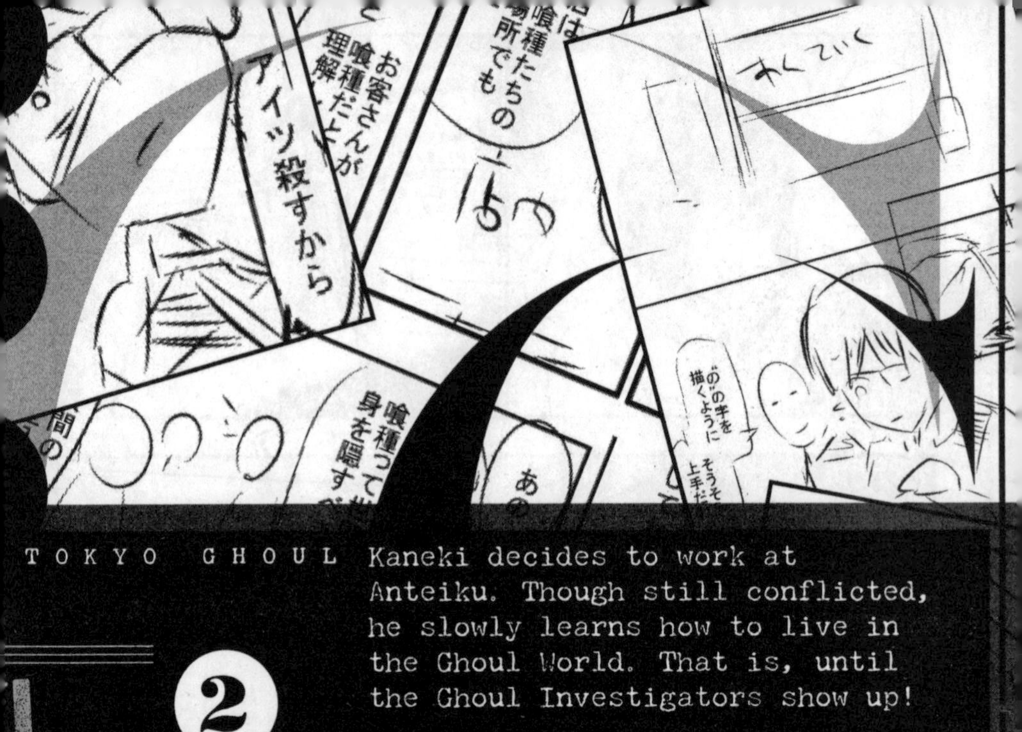

T O K Y O G H O U L

2

Kaneki decides to work at Anteiku. Though still conflicted, he slowly learns how to live in the Ghoul World. That is, until the Ghoul Investigators show up!

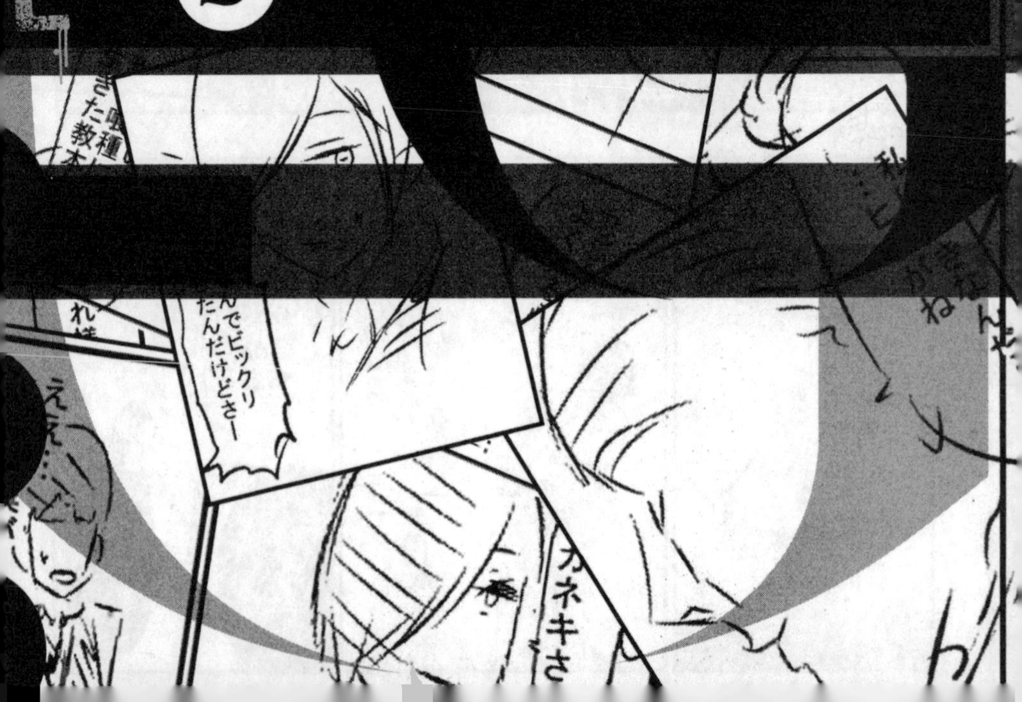